The Impact of the Environment on Psychiatric Disorder

The Impact of the Environment on Psychiatric Disorder explores the relationship between the environment and mental health, and suggests that environmental factors can play a role in the causation of psychiatric illness.

Hugh Freeman and Stephen Stansfeld bring together experts from the field to discuss a range of physical and social environmental settings that are linked to psychiatric disorders. International contributors discuss topics including:

- psychosocial processes linking the environment and mental health
- gene–environment interactions
- urban–rural differences
- social support
- migration
- how noise affects psychiatric disorders.

The book closes with a discussion of how disasters such as global warming and terrorism can affect mental health, and highlights the risks and protective factors for psychiatric disorders following such events.

The Impact of the Environment on Psychiatric Disorder illuminates the wide range of ways in which it is possible for the environment to influence mental health. It will appeal to both academics and professionals, and will interest anyone concerned with connections between the environment and mental health.

Hugh Freeman is Honorary Visiting Fellow, Green College, Oxford. He is also Honorary Professor at the University of Salford, and was formerly Editor of the *British Journal of Psychiatry*.

Stephen Stansfeld is Professor of Psychiatry at Barts and the London School of Medicine and Dentistry, University of London.

The Impact of the Environment on Psychiatric Disorder

Edited by
Hugh Freeman and Stephen Stansfeld

Routledge
Taylor & Francis Group
LONDON AND NEW YORK

First published 2008
by Routledge
27 Church Road, Hove, East Sussex BN3 2FA

Simultaneously published in the USA and Canada
by Routledge
711 Third Avenue, New York, NY 10017

First issued in paperback 2015

Routledge is an imprint of the Taylor & Francis Group, an informa business

Typeset in Bembo by RefineCatch Limited, Bungay, Suffolk

Cover design by Jim Wilkie

Cover image: City High Rises, Denis Thorpe, 12 May 2006.
Copyright © Guardian News & Media Ltd 2006.

This publication has been produced with paper manufactured to strict environmental standards and with pulp derived from sustainable forests.

British Library Cataloguing in Publication Data
A catalogue record for this book is available from the British Library

Library of Congress Cataloging-in-Publication Data
The impact of the environment on psychiatric disorder / edited by Hugh Lionel Freeman and Stephen Stansfeld.
p. cm.
Includes bibliographical references and index.
ISBN: 978–0–415–11618–3 (hardback)
1. Mental health—Environmental aspects. 2. Mental illness—Environmental aspects. I. Freeman, Hugh L. (Hugh Lionel). II. Stansfeld, Stephen A.
[DNLM: 1. Environment. 2. Mental Disorders—etiology. 3. Risk Factors. 4. Social Environment. 5. Socioeconomic Factors. WM 31 134 2008]
RC455.4.E58147 2008
616.89—dc22 2007036664

ISBN 13: 978-1-138-88446-5 (pbk)
ISBN 13: 978-0-415-11618-3 (hbk)

Contents

Acknowledgements

First we would like to thank our contributors who have provided most of the content of this book and who have been very patient during its long gestation period. Second, we appreciate the support of the publishers who have steadfastly supported us throughout the development of the book. We are very grateful for the tireless and dedicated secretarial assistance provided particularly by Lisa Kass and Louise Price. We are grateful to the World Psychiatric Association for allowing us to use the paper 'Gene–environment interactions in mental disorders', previously published in *World Psychiatry*, as the basis from which Chapter 2 was developed, thanking especially Jessica L. Bar and Stephen V. Faraone.

Finally, we owe an enormous debt of gratitude to our wives, Joan Freeman and Jenny Stansfeld, who gave us immense support through the development and writing of the book.

Contributors

Kamaldeep Bhui is Professor of Cultural Psychiatry and Epidemiology at The Centre for Psychiatry, Barts and The London School of Medicine and Dentistry, London, a consultant psychiatrist in East London, and a psychoanalytic psychotherapist. His research and practice interests include social exclusion, religion and mental health, organizational and environmental effects on health, cultural competence and transcultural health care.

Jane Boydell is a Clinical Lecturer at the Institute of Psychiatry part of King's College London. She is particularly interested in the role of social factors in the aetiology of psychosis. She is currently investigating whether the social cohesion of a community influences the incidence rate of schizophrenia within that community.

Traolach Brugha is Professor of Psychiatry and Director of Research at the Department of Health Sciences, University of Leicester. Throughout his career, studies of social support networks in longitudinal, experimental, community and clinical population samples have been at the centre of his interests. He has also made an impact on the development and evaluation of instruments in social and epidemiological psychiatry.

Charlotte Clark is a Lecturer in Environmental and Mental Health Epidemiology at The Centre for Psychiatry, Barts and The London School of Medicine and Dentistry, London. Her research focuses on how the environment can affect mental health. Recent research includes the effect of noise exposure on health and cognition, and lifecourse predictors of mental health in the National Child Development Study.

Sarah Curtis is Professor of Health and Risk at the University of Durham, UK. She has extensive international research experience in geography of health and health care. Her books include *Health and Inequality: Geographical Perspectives* (Sage, 2004). Other experience includes advice and consultancy to public agencies concerned with public health in the UK, Canada, France and the World Health Organization.

Gary W. Evans is the Elizabeth Lee Vincent Professor of Human Ecology at

Cornell University. He is an environmental and developmental psychologist interested in the physical environment and children's development. His research and teaching focus on environmental stressors, the environment of poverty, and children's development.

Hugh Freeman is Honorary Visiting Fellow, Green College, Oxford, and Honorary Professor at the University of Salford and was formerly Editor of the *British Journal of Psychiatry* and of *Current Opinion in Psychiatry*. He is an Honorary Fellow of the Royal College of Psychiatrists. He was awarded the Anniversary Medal of Merit from Charles University, Prague.

Jennifer M. Johnston is Director of Yoga Programs and a researcher at the Benson Henry Institute, as well as a licensed clinical mental health counsellor and yoga instructor. She has been studying the impact of mind/body practices on stress-related symptoms, works clinically with adolescents and adults with a wide range of mental health concerns, and teaches yoga in the Boston area.

Stephen J. Lepore is Professor of Public Health and PhD Director in the Department of Public Health, Temple University, Philadelphia. His research focuses on the interpersonal context of stress and its influence on physical and mental health. He has published an extensive series of empirical and theoretical papers on crowding and health with long-time colleague and friend, Gary Evans.

Alexander C. McFarlane is Professor of Psychiatry and Head of the University of Adelaide node of the Centre of Military and Veterans Health and Past President of the International Society for Traumatic Stress Studies. For 25 years his research and clinical work have focused on the epidemiology, neurobiology and effects of traumatic stress such as disasters, accidents, and war.

John McGrath is a psychiatrist based at the Queensland Centre for Mental Health Research. His research aims to generate and evaluate nongenetic risk factors for schizophrenia. He has forged productive cross-disciplinary collaborations linking risk factor epidemiology with developmental neurobiology. In addition, he has supervised major systematic reviews of the incidence and prevalence of schizophrenia.

Gordon Parker is Scientia Professor, University of New South Wales and Executive Director of the Black Dog Institute, Sydney. He was Editor of the *Australian & New Zealand Journal of Psychiatry*. He is an active researcher, focusing on mood disorders, and received a Citation Laureate as the most highly cited Australian in the field of 'Psychiatry/Psychology'.

Stephen Stansfeld is Professor of Psychiatry, Centre for Psychiatry, Barts and The London School of Medicine and Dentistry, London. He has a longstanding interest in the effects of the environment on mental health, and led a recent European-funded project on noise and children's cognition and health. He was previously Co-director of the Whitehall II study.

William S. Stone is Assistant Professor of Psychology, Massachusetts Mental Health Center (MMHC) Division of Public Sector Psychiatry in the Beth Israel Deaconess Medical Center Department of Psychiatry, Harvard Medical School and Director of Neuropsychology Training and Clinical Services at MMHC. His research focuses on genetic and environmental vulnerability in mental disorders, and psychopharmacological strategies for cognitive enhancement in schizophrenia.

Ming T. Tsuang is the Behavioral Genomics Endowed Chair and University Professor at the University of California and Distinguished University Professor of Psychiatry and Director of the Center for Behavioral Genomics at the University of California, San Diego. His research focuses on the interaction between genetic and environmental factors in psychiatric disorders.

Scott Weich is Foundation Professor of Psychiatry at Warwick Medical School. His research interests include socio-economic, gender, ethnic, and geographical inequalities in the occurrence, treatment and outcome of mental disorder. He currently leads a Department of Health-funded study to evaluate the effects of government policies to reduce ethnic inequalities in the experience of mental health care.

1 Introduction

Hugh Freeman and Stephen Stansfeld

In 1668, the German physician Johannes Hofer coined the word 'nostalgia' to indicate the sad mood that results from a desire to return to one's native land and home. Somewhat later, Cheyne (1733) considered 'the Humour of living in great, popular and consequently unhealthy Towns' to be one of the main causes of 'Distempers, with atrocious and frightful symptoms, scarce known to our Ancestors, and never rising to such fatal heights, nor afflicting such Numbers in any other known Nation'. Yet scientific interest in this subject is surprisingly recent. Both the clinical–phenomenological tradition and psychoanalysis, the twin foundations of present-day psychiatry, have been overwhelmingly concerned with the individual and their immediate family. More recently, social psychiatry has dealt with relevant human interactions – between individuals and between groups, both within the family and outside – but has not yet fully worked out its theories of causation. It emphasizes, though, that the social and biological aspects of mental disorder are complementary, not mutually exclusive. A psychiatry of the environment should be one of its constituents.

To start on a note of caution, it is very unlikely that direct cause-and-effect relationships will be found between specific features of the environment and abnormal mental states. The intervening processes must be extremely complex. Kasl (1977) has pointed out that three factors must be included in this equation of person–environment fit: the objective social environment; the individual's perceptions of it, related to his personal characteristics; and finally the physiological, affective, and behavioural reactions that act as mediators.

At any time, interactions are continuously occurring between social, cultural, and physical aspects of the environment on one hand and the human nervous system on the other. If a neurotic illness or psychosomatic condition should develop, this would only be after many variables had played their part in the intermediate processes. Furthermore, one feature of the environment will have widely varying effects on the different people who may be exposed to it, and these different effects result both from the variations between individuals' genetic constitutions (epigenetic effects) and from the influence on them of their life experiences. Two individuals exposed to the same environmental stress might show respectively a psychiatric disorder or a physical disorder (Figure 1.1).

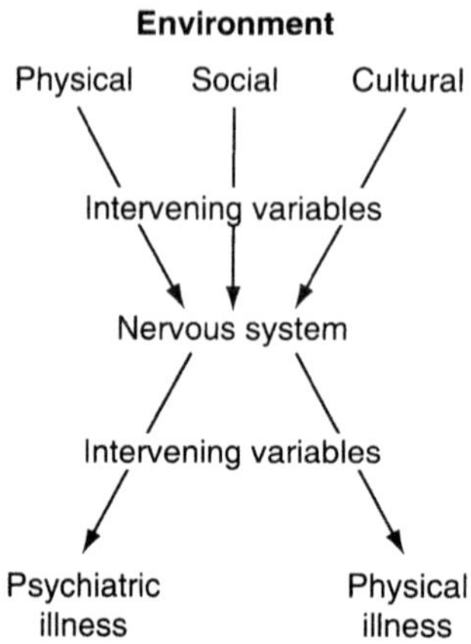

Figure 1.1 Pathways between environmental factors and psychiatric and physical illness.

In other individuals, it is possible for the same environmental influences to have no ill-effect at all, or even a beneficial effect, as when moderate anxiety improves performance.

Though certain social situations may be coincident with a high rate of a particular psychiatric disorder, this in itself allows us to say no more scientifically than that a connection between the two *could* exist, and the connection might be a very indirect one. Environmental input consists of a series of signals that are received by the body's sense organs and transmitted through psychological and physiological processes of enormous complexity. Eventually, some of the environmental signals will be experienced as emotion, but the biological significance of these emotions depends on factors such as the individual's culture and the way he or she has come to terms with their past environment.

Where a climate of danger has been established – as in many cities – otherwise trivial environmental stimuli such as a shadow will take on sinister significance. Trichopoulos *et al.* (1983) conclude that 'because of pre-existing conditioned reflex pathways, symbolic danger can generate stress as effectively as real danger', though the extent to which this diminishes by adaptation seems to be uncertain.

The role of the environment in the causation of psychiatric disorder is acknowledged to be complex, since the environment itself is multifaceted, continually changing, and difficult to measure. Humans are not passive recipients of these influences but have highly developed methods of coping with, and taking advantage of, environmental conditions. Moreover, populations have become more mobile, for example through wars and natural disasters, and the effects of change of environment have to be considered as well as the effects of migration itself on mental health (see Chapter 7).

The title of this book uses the term 'psychiatric disorder' to indicate primarily mental health problems which may be the concern of both psychiatrists and general practitioners, with their associated workers. This implies an emphasis on conditions of a severity sufficient to warrant clinical attention, usually accompanied by impairment of everyday functioning. Although this is the main focus, we acknowledge that environmental factors may be responsible for less severe morbidity, including impairment of well-being and individual symptoms. Although such responses seem trivial in relation to clinical illness, they nevertheless indicate impairment of quality of life, and are likely to affect very large numbers of people.

Psychiatrists today acknowledge that the disorders that concern them have in general a multifactorial origin, resulting from interaction between the organism's genotype and outside influences experienced from the time of conception, even including parents' exposures before conception. All such factors up to death could, strictly speaking, be described as 'environmental', but to consider them all would be to encompass the whole of psychiatry except for its strictly genetic aspects. Such scientific imperialism is to be avoided, and the present volume is concerned with those characteristics of people's physical and social surroundings for which there is evidence to suggest that they may be significant in relation to mental health and illness. The interactions between genetic and environmental influences are now recognized to be infinitely more complex than was envisaged earlier, primarily through the explosive growth of the science of genetics (Rutter, 2002).

Some authors confine their definitions of 'the environment' to the built or physical aspects. However, this is a restrictive approach, since neglecting the natural environment means ignoring important influences on health such as climate and natural disasters (Chapters 10, 11) that are likely to become even more influential as global warming proceeds. Natural disasters and the consequences of war and terrorism have come to dominate the public debate on environment and health and may be the dominant concern in the future. The long-term impact of such disasters on communities and individuals is only beginning to be understood, and the consequences for mental health could be immense (Alexander & Klein, 2003; Polatin *et al.*, 2005; Weisler *et al.*, 2006).

Yet to try to define either 'mental health' or 'environment' in a restrictive way can be to enter a semantic Slough of Despond. Any individual study tends to use definitions and classifications that are appropriate to its specific requirements and the particular population being studied. A classification of mental health criteria was made by Kasl and Rosenfield (1980): (a) indices based on treatment data; (b) psychiatric signs and symptoms; (c) indicators of mood, well-being, etc.; (d) indices of functional effectiveness and role performance; and (e) notions of 'positive mental health', e.g. adequacy of coping. All these have been used at different times as the basis for theoretical or empirical studies, so that there are obvious problems in comparing the results of different authors (Vaillant, 2003). Better then for our present purpose, perhaps, to use 'mental health' in common-sense and pragmatic terms as the absence of identifiable psychiatric disorder, according to current norms.

Sir Aubrey Lewis (1967) characteristically stated that:

> Sociological attempts to state the denotative characteristics of mental illness . . . do not stand on their social legs, but are propped up by medical struts and stays, which have three criteria – the patient feels ill; he has disordered functions of some part; and he has symptoms which conform to a recognisable clinical pattern.

Lewis' conclusion was that 'though the social effects of disease, like the social causes, are extremely important, it is impossible to tell from them whether a condition is healthy or morbid'. That decision needs to be based on the assessment of its physiological and psychological components, which requires medical skills. Though the scientific coverage of this book aims to be broad, it is founded on psychiatry as a medical discipline.

'Environment' also suffers from a surfeit of definitions, but is seen here primarily in structural and social terms. It therefore refers to people's surroundings as expressed in their homes, districts, regions, and sometimes countries. It also includes the social groupings outside their immediate family, beginning at the level of a residential community or ethnic or occupational group. Since it seems reasonable to assume that different kinds of social action will occur in varying residential areas, much of the behaviour related to residence may well be understood in terms, respectively, of household, immediate neighbourhood, district, and town (or rural authority). Based on data from north-west London, Whitley *et al.* (2005) proposed that the middle-level residential 'bubble' should be considered meaningful in relation to socio-environmental influences on mental health. This consists of the homes of immediate neighbours and the shared public space around them.

It is not proposed to deal here with the immediate family environment, which is undoubtedly important in the aetiology of mental ill-health (Repetti *et al.*, 2002), except in so far as it is involved in wider issues, as this could move the focus of discussion into another large scientific field. The question of social support is discussed in Chapter 6. Another approach that will be excluded is the toxicological aspect of environmental sciences; substances such as lead that are environmental pollutants can certainly have effects on psychological and emotional functioning, but the subject is a controversial one, with its own literature. For example, certain genetic and environmental factors can increase the damaging effects of lead on neural development, rendering some children more vulnerable to lead neurotoxicity (Järup, 2003; Lidsky & Schneider, 2003). Learning difficulties have also been excluded from this book, on the mainly practical grounds that this is now a substantial discipline of its own, which could not be covered adequately. Nor does this work cover the micro-environment of psychiatric hospitals, for instance, which comes more into the province of environmental psychology – another largely independent discipline.

Woman at a window, Mexico City (Image: City High Rises, Denis Thorpe, 12 May 2006. Copyright © Guardian News & Media Ltd 2006).

Methodological issues

Part of the difficulty in investigating the effects of the environment on psychiatric disorder is methodological. For instance, the way that people report environmental conditions is necessarily subjective, and the same applies to reports of their own mental health. This may lead to response bias, which could particularly be the case in those who respond with 'plaintive set', i.e. a tendency to report things more negatively, especially on self-report questionnaires. Underlying plaintive set may be negative affectivity – 'a mood dispositional dimension of emotionality including nervousness, anger and dissatisfaction, which may be seen as largely independent of any specific provoking agent' (Watson & Clark, 1984). In this context, any association between adverse reports of the environment and mental health might be explained by a generally negative view of the world, and may be independent of the real external environment. Such associations may be *caused* by mental ill-health, rather than being the stimulus for it.

To a certain extent, response bias can be overcome by restricting assessment of exposure to objective measures of the external environment. The disadvantage of this approach is that it excludes the influence of environmental perceptions that may be an important intervening factor between the external world and health. Another solution is to carry out longitudinal studies in which the examination of exposure precedes the measurement of outcome. In this way, response bias is lessened, while longitudinal associations provide greater support for causality than cross-sectional ones.

Though the contextual approach involves a risk of contamination by the 'ecological fallacy', focusing exclusively on individual-level risk factors can introduce the 'atomistic fallacy' of ignoring lessons to be learned from aggregated data (Diez-Roux, 1998). One theme that will be found to recur in subsequent chapters is the relative importance of 'compositional' versus 'contextual' factors. The former refers to attributes of the individuals making up the population of a particular area, while the latter factors belong to features of the area itself (physical structures and social relationships within it). From a review of the literature on health and place, Smith and Easterlaw (2005) concluded that composition explains much more than context. In their view, the more fundamental question is: 'How, why, and to what extent are people with different health experiences, whose health is at risk in different ways, differently and unequally positioned in society and in space?'

A further methodological challenge is the measurement of environmental contact. Studies that find environmental effects on physical health usually involve long-term exposure to physical agents, and for most exposures it is also likely that chronic effects would be needed to produce an influence on mental health, though natural disasters are an exception (see Chapter 11). Few studies have adequate long-term measures of environmental exposure. A further complication is that people tend to move around, so that their exposure to environmental agents varies; this will clearly tend to weaken the strength of any association between environmental factors and health.

Since environmental influences rarely affect health in isolation, in addition to the difficulties in measuring exposure, there are likely to be many potential confounding factors that could give rise to spurious associations. Social disadvantage is an example of this (see Chapter 4). For instance, in the case of the association between noise and health (see Chapter 9), areas that are exposed to high levels of noise are often those with high levels of social disadvantage.

Another important methodological issue is that of social selection. People, if they are able, will tend to leave adverse environments and move elsewhere. So far as possible, this will be to a better environment. Many factors may influence people's choice of environments and thus their exposure to risk. Clearly, the healthier, the wealthier, and those with more resources are more likely to move from adverse environments to good ones. This can be seen in the differential form of migration that occurs from inner-city areas (see Chapter 4).

However, the problem of measuring morbidity remains, since most data have been of treatment or service contacts, rather than of the distribution of illness, and these professional interventions must depend primarily on a community's level of economic and social development. If the activities of specialist psychiatric services can be recorded in relation to defined communities, it can reasonably be assumed that most cases of severe disorders will be included, at least in industrialized countries. But in the case of milder disorders, little more than 5 per cent of affected individuals receive specialist treatment in the UK (Goldberg & Huxley, 1980), and the proportion in most other countries is probably less. Therefore, the alternative method of measurement is by investigating a random sample of the general population; here, the choice of measurement instruments becomes particularly important.

While cross-cultural comparisons of morbidity have great potential for determining the relative significance of environmental factors, there are two major problems. These are the need to establish comparable definitions of psychiatric symptoms across cultures, and the lack of suitable techniques for measuring the relevant socio-cultural parameters.

However, definition becomes rather more complicated by the question of 'social pathology', which is generally understood as significant deviation from prevailing norms of behaviour, expressed in such forms as delinquency and crime, disordered or broken family relationships, sexual deviation, and addictions. Clearly, most of those who behave badly are not psychiatrically disordered (though the exact proportion that are so disordered is unknown), but the relative aetiological importance of individual disturbance and external social forces may as yet be unresolvable. In the case of children and adolescents, disturbed behaviour is often the leading feature of recorded psychiatric abnormality. Just as morality is 'in the nature of things', so appears to be the fact that communities with high rates of mental illness also tend to show high levels of behavioural deviance and of psychiatric sequelae to crime and social disturbance. The association of these problems was synthesised by Rutter (1981), who pointed out that 'city living is associated with an increased susceptibility to a quite wide range of problems' – not only crime and delinquency, but repression, emotional disturbance, educational problems, and family breakdown.

Aetiology

The magnitude of the effect of many environmental factors on health is often quite small. This may be the result of difficulties in measurement of exposure or through confounding factors. Additionally, it may be because the researcher is in fact measuring a proxy for the true exposure. Rutter (2005a) has pointed out the need to differentiate between risk indicators, i.e. factors that are associated with risk but are not on the causal pathway, and risk mediators, which are directly on that pathway (see Chapter 5).

A recurrent theme through the following chapters is the importance of social position and accompanying social disadvantage in relation to mental health (see Chapter 4). Both physical and mental health are strongly related to social disadvantage (Dohrenwend, 1992; Marmot, 2005), while material deprivation is a risk factor for depression, personality disorder, substance abuse, and suicide (Dohrenwend, 1992; Melzer *et al.*, 2004). Thus, the risks associated with mental health from some environmental factors may be explained by the confounding effect of experiencing social disadvantage. However, as mentioned above, people of lower social position, with high levels of material disadvantage, are also often exposed to many more adverse environmental factors. It may be, therefore, that the effects of social disadvantage are partially mediated through exposure to hazardous environmental conditions, especially where these conditions cluster together: e.g. poor housing, overcrowding, polluted environments, and fear of violence.

Rehkopf and Buka (2006) point out that suicide shows a markedly uneven geographical distribution that has persisted over time, both between and within countries. However, studies of the relationship between the socio-economic characteristics of areas and their suicide rates have produced divergent results. These authors found that the association depends on the size of the region examined; where areas are smaller, there are more inverse associations, which is consistent with most individual-level studies. If there are relevant 'contextual' processes (i.e. operating at an area level), these are most likely to be seen at the neighbourhood level. These authors concluded that area suicide rates are most strongly associated with the proportion of residents living below the poverty level. This was consistent with a contextual explanation, whereby these rates are driven by the social and economic isolation of neighbourhoods with higher levels of deprivation.

However, another aspect of this question is the possible relationship of suicide to 'social fragmentation', for which Congdon (1996) devised a census-derived index based on levels of private renting, single-person households, relationship breakdown, and turnover of population. This index predicted suicide rates in different districts of London more strongly than did measures of socio-economic deprivation.

To throw further light on this, Evans *et al.* (2004) examined data on psychiatric inpatient admissions and suicide for adults aged under 64 in Bristol, and matched them to the city's electoral wards. In this study the association between social fragmentation and suicide was not explained by socio-economic deprivation or the prevalence of severe mental illness within the relevant areas. This left the possibility that high levels of social fragmentation within a local area could have a direct causal role in provoking individual suicide.

Is it possible to separate physical and material environmental stressors such as poor housing from psychosocial stressors such as crowding? Poor housing includes such things as damp, cold, broken fittings, inadequate lighting, and badly placed rooms (see Chapter 8). Overcrowding implies an excessive number of persons per room in a dwelling – which seems a purely physical measure. But at the same time, the implications of overcrowding for health involve effects such as lack of privacy, increased arguments, lack of personal space or quiet time, and an inability to escape from others' activities. In this way, social risk factors and physical environmental conditions interact with each other, and these interactions may strengthen or weaken effects on health. Though the review by Clark *et al.* (2006) found little association between household density and mental health, either cross-sectionally or longitudinally, most studies had not made adequate adjustment for socio-economic factors, so that human density may have been confounded by social disadvantage.

Rutter (2005a) has also highlighted several important features of the research findings on environmental influences on mental health. First, these influences can act within the normal range of environmental exposures, although obviously, there are greater effects when these are excessive. Second, environmental effects in children may persist into adult life. Third, one needs to include the pre-conceptual and pre-natal as well as the post-natal environment. Fourth, there is huge individual variation in response to environmental stressors: some people are extremely resistant to them and described as 'resilient'. Others are less so or, at the other extreme, may be particularly vulnerable to such stressors. This may be a further reason for the weakness of overall environmental effects, i.e. disguising differing degrees of vulnerability in the population studied. Clearly, a key influence in an individual's resilience is that of genetic make-up (Rutter, 2005b), but in addition there are exposure-related factors that may be influential. These include strengthening or weakening experiences prior to exposure, protective influences at the time of exposure, and positive turning-point experiences subsequently. Leon Eisenberg (2005) has pointed out that 'clinical phenotypes reflect environments as well as genotypes' and that success in specifying genotypes will make it easier for clinicians to identify the relevant features of the familial and non-familial environment that influence the likelihood of disease.

Gene–environment interactions

One consequence of the enormous advances in the study of genetic influences on disease has been to throw into sharp contrast the contribution of environmental factors. Delineating the size of the genetic contribution allows some idea of the relative contribution of the environmental component to be gauged (see Chapter 2). Moreover, genetic studies can also establish whether there is vulnerability to environmental agents associated with disease. Since environmental risk factors vary in their aetiological importance according to the genetic makeup of the host, studies of gene–environment interactions offer an opportunity to measure more precisely how such external factors relate to mental disorder. For instance, the gene for the chemical transporter 5-HTT, which fine-tunes transmission of serotonin, has been identified as a moderating factor of the risk for depression in the Dunedin adolescent cohort study (Caspi *et al.*, 2003). Being homozygous on this gene increases the risk of developing depression when one is exposed to a life event. This raises the possibility of further refining the contribution of external factors to the aetiology of disorder following exposure to family disruption (see Chapter 2). A further such interaction is the increased risk of psychosis associated with cannabis use in young people. There is evidence (Caspi *et al.*, 2005) that a functional polymorphism in the catechol-o-methyltransferase gene moderates the influence of cannabis use in young people on the risk of developing psychotic symptoms in adulthood.

Family studies are a frequently used tool of genetic epidemiological analysis. Common exposure to parental influences and shared home environments seems to provide a way of ensuring a common environmental exposure for children in the same family. However, in studies of children and families, it is sometimes difficult to separate out genetic from environmental influences (Rutter, 2005a). Experiences within the family that are apparently 'child-specific', such as abuse, may also have a largely shared effect if the experience of siblings is sufficiently similar. Conversely, 'family-wide influences (such as poverty, conflict, or neglect) might have a largely non-shared effect if the key features impinge on the children to differing degrees . . . or if children vary in their vulnerability to risk environments' (Rutter, 2005a). One further problem with parentally related variables such as family conflict is that although they seem entirely environmental, they may be influenced by the parents' genes, which in turn will be related to those of the children.

Rutter (2005a) identifies three new challenges for environmental research. First, that there is a need for better understanding of the effects of 'restrictions on the possibility of a developing intense selective social relationships (as with institutional rearing), severe disruptions in the security of such relationships (as with neglect, rejection and scapegoating), life events that carry long-term threat to such relationships, and social ethos or group influences of a maladaptive kind (as with antisocial peer groups)'. His second challenge is to identify the origins of environmental risk factors where genes may have an impact on behaviour that shapes or selects environments and influences the likelihood of experiencing stress or adversity, or on societal elements such as racial discrimination and poverty. The third challenge is to determine the changes in the organism that provide the basis for the persistence of environmental effects on psychological functioning or psychopathology. This may be through environmental influences on gene expression, as well as through the effects of environments on programming of brain development and how these may influence neuroendocrine structure and functioning.

Mechanisms of environmental effects

Halpern (1995) suggested four possible ways in which the built environment can influence mental health: (i) as a source of stress; (ii) as an influence over social networks and support; (iii) through symbolic effects and social labelling; and (iv) through the action of the planning process. He provided examples of all these in his study of the effects of a programme of environmental changes carried out in a local authority housing estate. An alternative listing by Chu *et al.* (2004) consisted of: control over the internal environment; design and maintenance of housing; escape facilities; crime and fear of crime; and social participation.

But what are the mechanisms that underlie the association of environmental factors and mental ill-health? One obvious candidate is the stress hypothesis, in which ill-health arises from an excess of demands over personal resources. A wide range of stressors, both psychosocial and environmental, may lead to increased physiological arousal. In the acute situation, this may be manifest as the 'fight or flight response', with raised heart rate and blood pressure, increased muscle tension, and increased arousal, leading to elevated levels of catecholamines including adrenaline and noradrenaline (Brunner, 1997). This response to an acute exposure is easy to observe in the laboratory; what is more problematic is to discern how chronic exposure might lead to long-term changes in mental ill-health.

It has long been maintained that ill-health resulting from prolonged exposure to environmental stressors is the result of chronically elevated physiological arousal, leading to elevated cortisol and its consequent effects. Prolonged elevated cortisol response is associated with depression, while an 'exhausted' hypothalamic–pituitary axis resulting in low cortisol levels has been associated with post-traumatic stress disorder (Checkley, 1996).

It is important to consider the issue of adaptation and habituation. Humans are extraordinarily good at adapting to adverse environments and will alter their behaviour so as to minimize the negative consequences. In acute exposure, novel or threatening stimuli will elicit either an orienting response or, for more severe stimuli, a defence–startle response (Turpin & Siddle, 1983). These responses have obvious survival value in alerting the organism to novel environmental threats that might require a behavioural response. However, if the stimuli turn out not to require a change in behaviour, the organism will then habituate to repeated exposure to the stimulus. This habituation may benefit people by reducing arousal levels in highly stimulating environments, but it is possible that the adjustment is only achieved at some physiological cost (McEwen, 1998). Thus, in the longer term, there is a cost to the unending struggle to maintain equilibrium in bodily processes, and this may result in illness – somatic, psychiatric, or both.

Lifecourse influences

A continuing theme in psychiatric research and practice is the importance of early life influences on illness in adulthood. With the recent scientific interest in lifecourse factors in disease, there has been greater concern about understanding the mechanisms for these effects. The 'critical period' model implies an exposure during a specific developmental stage that has lasting or lifelong consequences for the risk of disease (Kuh & Ben-Shlomo, 2004). This model, also called 'biological programming', is the theoretical underpinning for the 'foetal origin of adult disease hypothesis' (Barker, 1988). Alternatively, the 'accumulation of risk' model assumes that exposures to health risks accumulate across the lifecourse, possibly with exposures at certain times having more impact than at others. Adverse exposures across the lifecourse may be independent of each other, but it is more likely that they are correlated, providing a special version of the accumulation model known as the 'accumulation model with risk clustering'. Clustering may very likely occur in relation to socio-economic position;

less advantaged social position in childhood tends to be related to poor nutrition, fewer educational opportunities, more financial problems, and more family disruption (Hobbs *et al.*, 1985). The 'chain of risk' or 'pathway' model, where one bad experience leads to another, has relevance for mental health. In this situation, each exposure can increase the risk of subsequent ones, but each may also add to the risk of ill-health. Of course, these models are not mutually exclusive. The 'critical period model' has relevance to resistance to stress across the lifecourse. Meaney's work (Meaney & Szyf, 2005) on the lack of maternal grooming in rat pups setting the lifelong receptivity of rats to stress, by resetting cortisol receptors, has obvious resonance with Bowlby's theories on early childhood attachment and its association with adult risk of depression and anxiety disorders.

However, the contribution of lifecourse factors to adult illness should not underestimate the effects of contemporaneous exposures. For common mental disorders at least, it is likely that both early life factors (e.g. living in low-quality public housing as a child) and adult factors (e.g. unemployment) may be important (Power *et al.*, 2002).

In a study of social causation of psychiatric disorders, Dohrenwend (2000) suggested that, using the evidence from epidemiological studies, the likelihood of the onset of these disorders is increased by two factors: '(1) the proportion of the individual's usual activities in which uncontrollable negative changes take place following a major negative event; and (2) how central the uncontrollable changes are to the individual's important goals and values'.

Life events have been studied as the classical social risk factor for depression in an important body of sociological research led by George Brown and Tirril Harris (e.g. Brown & Harris, 1978). Most early studies of life events were cross-sectional and the question arose as to the direction of causation. Concern about this issue led to the development of the elaborate Life Events & Difficulties Schedule by Brown and Harris that gathered contextual details of a person's life around the life event and assessed these objectively for the presence of severe threat. In order to avoid contamination of life events by existing illness, independent life events were conceptualized as 'apparently imposed upon the subject and . . . for all practical purposes, outside his or her control'.

Severe events with marked or moderate long-term threat were four times more common among depressed patients than among controls (Brown & Harris, 1978). Most events involved in depression included loss and disappointment: for example, death of a parent or life-threatening illness of someone close. In a study of women in Islington, most of the severe events that provoked depressive onset (41/58) involved feeling humiliated or trapped (Brown *et al.*, 1995). 'Trapped' referred to being confined in a punishing situation or feeling that any escape from an unrewarding setting was blocked. 'Humiliation' meant being devalued in relation to others or self. Chronic strains – described by Brown as 'major difficulties' – are important in both the aetiology and maintenance of depression. Chronic marital problems, poor housing, or continued financial difficulties may both initiate and maintain depression. Life events are not always negative in their impact: for instance, 'resolution events' that remove prolonged negative circumstances, such as re-employment after prolonged unemployment, may lead to the resolution of depression (Brown *et al.*, 1992). In the Islington study, the risk of depressive onset among single mothers was double that of married mothers (16% vs 7.9%) (Brown & Moran, 1997), related to financial hardship.

Differential vulnerability might explain why life events lead to depression in less than a quarter of the people exposed. Brown and Harris (1978) identified four vulnerability factors in their original study of working-class women. These were: the absence of a close confiding relationship, unemployment, looking after three or more children at home, and death of the subject's mother before the age of 11 years. In the Islington study, vulnerability factors were slightly different: low self-esteem and complex aspects of social support (Brown *et al.*, 1986). It seems that vulnerability factors are not fixed, but vary according to social circumstances. Low self-esteem has also been related to other psycho-social risk factors such as the quality of close relationships and early adverse experience (Andrews & Brown, 1993).

Research on the effects of loss of the mother during childhood on risk of adulthood depression has suggested that it is not the loss itself that is critical for increased risk, but the quality of the care of the child subsequent to the loss (Parker, 1983). By contrast, loss of father was unrelated to depression, once loss of mother had been taken into account. Both parental indifference and physical and sexual abuse also predict adult depression (Brown *et al.*, 1993; Bifulco *et al.*, 1994). The loss of mother is an important risk factor for adult disorder because it increases the chance of these negative experiences in childhood.

Spatial factors

The theme of personal space is one that recurs throughout this book, particularly in relation to topics such as crowding, density, and privacy, which are interrelated and often confused with each other. The concept of territory and of the need for personal space is of uncertain significance for humans, but can be seen in terms of the structuring of that part of static space for which a person feels possessiveness. Since some space has to be shared in most environments, elaborate social systems are contrived to allow this. Freedman (1975) argued against the existence of an independent territorial instinct, even in animals, since lack of space *per se* does not seem to trigger aggressive or defensive responses, nor other negative effects. Therefore, 'territoriality' represents little more than a description of behaviour, while any expression in humans would be likely to be merely symbolic. In other words, its functions are cognitive and social-organisational, rather than biological. Altman (1975) considered that privacy is the key to an understanding of crowding.

Whether or not this view is accepted, it would clearly be wrong to underestimate the significance of spatial factors, for which Hall (1968) constructed a body of theory (proxemics). He maintained that mental processes and behaviour take place within a cultural context, transmitted through both language and codes of spatial use; these codes vary from culture to culture, and may also be subject to individual differences.

Whereas *density* is a physical state, which can usually be represented by a mathematical ratio, *crowding* is predominantly a psychological experience. At the same time, area density is complex, including factors ranging from residential acreage per square mile to number of persons per room (Kirmeyer, 1978). Crowding was examined experimentally by Freedman (1975), who found that the sensation is certainly related to having little space, but distinct from it. When such factors as smell, heat, fear, or discomfort – usually associated with crowding – were excluded, no negative effects were found in physical, psychiatric or social terms. Freedman's findings led to the *density–intensity* theory, i.e. that crowding merely intensifies an individual's characteristic reaction to any situation, but this will not apply if the presence of others is irrelevant to a particular form of behaviour. Urban sociology has also been much influenced by the *density–pathology* hypothesis – that high density is responsible for numerous forms of social pathology, including an excess of psychiatric morbidity. In the study of these phenomena, a distinction has been made between high density and very large numbers; the latter situation may have generally negative effects at times, influencing people to withdraw socially and be more defensive, in a way that would not be caused by high density alone.

In some societies at least, an association between crowding and physical disease may derive from the particular kind of stress that arises from accompanying disordered social relationships (Cassel, 1971). Adverse effects of living at high density might be confined to periods following migration, and once settled, people may generally adapt to these conditions. Levy and Herzog (1974) concluded that crowding is unlikely to be a serious problem for mental or physical health in the absence of abject poverty, lack of sanitation, or poor nutrition. It is probably more the case that suffering people come to live densely than that density causes suffering (Fischer, 1976). This contrast between 'contextual' and 'compositional' factors is discussed in subsequent chapters.

It is hard, in fact, to separate density from other social, economic, and political factors, while a number of social–ecological aspects of the community either buffer or accentuate its effects on individuals' psychology, e.g. the visual and architectural qualities of the environment, conditions such as noise and light, and the number of interpersonal contacts per unit of space and time.

Rapaport (1975) regarded density as a perceived experience, rather than merely a mathematical ratio. Thus, depending on the individual's previous experience, the social organization of the setting, and the relationship between people and objects involved, places that contain identical numbers per unit area can have quite different perceived densities. For instance, when a population is homogeneous, it is easier to disregard other people, and the area is seen as having a relatively lower density, whereas people who are different cause uncertainty, a high rate of stimuli, and thus a 'reading' of high density. Judgement of density is made from the amount of information that needs to be processed; should this be evaluated as unwanted or uncontrollable, then a feeling of crowding will be experienced. Just as sensory overload and sensory deprivation are extreme ends of a continuum, so there is assumed to be a limited range of acceptable and perceived densities for any given group and context, with extremely low densities having undesirable effects as much as extremely high ones.

When social structural differences between urban neighbourhoods are held constant, population density appears to make a relatively trivial difference in the prediction of rates of social pathology in their populations (Choldin, 1978). Earlier ecological studies, for example in Chicago, made the fundamental mistake of not appreciating that factors usually associated with density (particularly poverty, minority status, and prevalence of migrants) had not been separated from any effects of density itself. Even though high density may not contribute importantly to medical or social pathologies, it may still have significant effects on the quality of life – for instance, the amount of socializing that takes place in the home, or degree of neighbourly contacts. Since these pathologies are usually of complex origin and develop over long periods, it should not be surprising that measures of density for large urban populations are not important causes of them (e.g. schizophrenia) (see Chapter 4).

The urban environment: the sociological contribution

Interest in the urban dimension of psychiatric disorder may derive in the first place from the sheer aggregation of human beings, and so from the multiplicity of interactions between them. Urbanization is mainly a feature of the modern era when, as Tuan (1979) pointed out, the built world effectively withstands the normal fluctuations of nature, but paradoxically:

> It is in the large city – the most visible symbol of human rationality and triumph over nature – that some of the old fear remains. The urban sprawl . . . is seen as a jungle, a chaos of buildings, streets and fast moving vehicles that disorient and alarm new comers. But the greatest single threat in the city is other people. Malevolence, no longer ascribed to nature, remains an attribute of human nature.

As a sociologist, Simmel (1950) referred to the 'intensification of emotional life due to the swift and continuous shift of external and internal stimuli'. The Chicago School of Sociology saw the difference between urban and rural life as involving different qualities of interpersonal relationships, and concluded that the type to be found in cities was generally harmful to the functioning of human personality. This was explained in terms of a particular type of stress – social alienation – which involves the demoralization of those who were no longer part of a meaningful group process.

A different conclusion about urban life, though, was reached by Fischer (1973); the published literature failed to support the view that malaise increases along with urban size, or that urban residence *per se* is independently related to malaise. In fact, there was more evidence of this phenomenon in rural than in urban areas, though the difference is small when social class is controlled, since greater economic opportunities represent one of the most positive qualities of cities. In many cities, evidence of malaise (particularly in central areas) might have been an effect of migration, because those with the ability to do so may move away to smaller communities (see Chapter 7). Such moves are likely to be influenced by idealized images of non-city life, and by possibly unreal hopes of maintaining urban opportunities in the small community. Nevertheless, when all covariates are controlled, there was evidence of a small trend for the largest cities to show malaise in their populations, and for this to be greater in city centres than in more peripheral areas.

Both sociological and psychological approaches today remain influenced by Georg Simmel's prediction (1908) of the possible effects of continuous contacts with innumerable people in cities: 'one would be completely atomised internally and come to an unimaginable psychic state'. Later, however, Louis Wirth showed that the impersonality and arbitrariness of the city was reduced through the creation of sub-communities, within which each person could establish some control over their immediate environment. As a sociologist, Elias (1969) criticized psychiatrists for vaguely conglomerating family, neighbourhood, community, and other social configurators into a single factor of 'environment' or 'social background', whereas for sociology, each of these represents a separate, highly structured element with dynamics of its own.

The sociology most directly relevant to this book is probably the urban, which, as mentioned above, evolved from the European classic tradition of Max Weber and Georg Simmel to the Chicago School of Park, Burgess, and Wirth, though the types of social organization that the latter described may have been more characteristic of twentieth-century industrial society in general than of cities as such. On the other hand, Gans (1962) suggested that contrasts between urban and suburban societies were explained more by the personal characteristics (e.g. social class) of the people who lived in each setting than by the size, density or heterogeneity of each type of community. This leads to the question of urban–rural differences, discussed in Chapter 4, and again raises the issue of 'contextual' versus 'compositional' effects.

On the borderland between sociology and psychology are the important writings of Kevin Lynch and Jane Jacobs. In *The Image of the City*, Lynch (1960) argued that those who made decisions on changes to the environment often based their choices on personal images that were implicit and not tested against others. The individual in the city, however, would be able to feel delight in 'ambiguity, mystery, and surprise, so long as they are contained within a basic order and as long as we can be confident of weaving the puzzle into some new, more intricate pattern'. The obvious pleasure with which visitors explore the old, winding, and now pedestrianized streets of a city like York is witness to the truth of Lynch's view. One of the tragedies of large-scale redevelopment and of present-day architectural doctrines is that they destroy all possibility of experiencing these environmental pleasures; the central city tends to be no more than a collection of huge, inhuman structures, surrounded by dereliction.

In *Death and Life of Great American Cities* (1961), Jane Jacobs argued that it was not enough to observe what was bad about cities; the good that existed should also be examined, and not just be equated with aesthetic appearance. It should focus on what actually worked to promote a stable social structure. In her view, successful city neighbourhoods had a close texture, high density, mixed land use, and many destinations within people's walking distance. Thus, there would be constant comings and goings of people on foot along a dense network of streets. As people come to be known by sight, their roles and talents can be called on by the community, without invading people's private lives. The informal monitoring of 'eyes in the street' is a strong deterrent to casual crime and disorder. Friendships can then mature naturally, without any need to force the pace, whereas people who pass each other in cars have no natural opportunities to build up a web of public acquaintanceship. Yet if few destinations are within walking distance, the circle of personal contacts is likely to remain small and the prevailing atmosphere one of anonymity. This can be particularly disadvantageous to children. On the other hand, where streets – and perhaps other public areas – are peopled with those who are known and familiar, children can be allowed out after the toddler stage. Having people of all ages around as models, they can find examples of acceptable behaviour and be helped to become successfully integrated into the adult community. Like those of Kevin Lynch, though, it has to be said that Jacobs' persuasive views have been more honoured in the breach than in the observance.

The geographical contribution

In addition to sociology and psychology, geography may be the scientific discipline most closely involved in this subject (see Chapter 3). Philo (2005) suggests that 'the spatio-environmental conditions for sustained good mental health' dovetail with 'broader concerns for geographical variations in human welfare or quality of life'. Both these concepts are, of course, strongly influenced by cultural and ideological factors. In Philo's view, earlier work was highly quantitative, correlating psychiatric data – such as admissions to hospital – with population densities, housing conditions, ethnic composition, etc. There was a fairly general consensus that the more 'stressful' a socio-economic environment was, the more likely it was that more psychiatric morbidity would be identified there. In terms of analysing the intermediate processes between the environment and emerging mental ill-health, greater difficulties emerged.

In this connection, Philo mentions the problem of identifying the precise differences between settlements and regions, even down to the distinction between 'urban' and 'rural' areas (see Chapter 4). Within particular settlements 'the patterns revealed are so complicated' that straightforward conclusions are difficult to make. But the addition of more subjective or 'qualitative' data – a demand being made in several aspects of psychiatric studies – needs to be approached with very great caution. Philo states that academic geographers offer 'a theorized sensitivity to the entangled relations of mental health, society, space and environment' and that as social constructions, these are 'unavoidably structured by power inequalities and infused with emotional resonances'. Yet the operationalizing into scientific terms of all these concepts is enormously difficult. Unless that can be done, though, their entry into broader data sets that can be analysed may have to be still postponed – a cautious, but disappointing view.

It has already been emphasized that both social and physical environmental factors have an impact on mental health and may interact. For instance, the design of housing estates can influence opportunities for social interaction. Willmott, in his study of a planned suburban housing project, Dagenham, found that cul-de-sacs were friendlier places to live, where more people described their neighbours as helpful than those living on 'through' roads (Willmott, 1963). If there is no semi-private space for neighbours to meet, or if that common space feels unsafe, social interaction is likely to be inhibited. At the same time, some control over the amount of interaction with neighbours and its setting is important for successful relationships. The physical environment can both enhance and inhibit opportunities for social interaction (see also Chapters 6 and 8). Conversely, social support, social networks, and community cohesion may provide the common resources needed for people to function in adverse physical environments with relatively few adverse health consequences. Clark *et al.* (2006) report 'Consistent . . . evidence that perceived neighbourhood disorder, such as vandalism, lack of facilities, vacant housing and litter, was associated with poor mental health'. Though this illustrates one way in which the environment may mediate the effect of exposure to crime, 'it is difficult to disentangle these associations, as individuals with poorer mental health are likely to be selected into poorer neighbourhoods'. In other words, 'composition' versus 'context' again.

The wider context

If psychiatrists have not been as involved as they should have been with the surroundings of patients' lives, what of those whose professional concern is the surroundings themselves – architects, planners, engineers, politicians, administrators? In general, the story is a melancholy one of inadequate interest in the human consequences of new structures, transport developments, or changes in the patterns of industry and commerce. Economic considerations have been overwhelming, irrespective of the political ideology on which any society operates. Environmental psychiatry may be at an early stage, but so far as architecture is concerned, the failure seems to be equally great. In 2006 a book was published called *The Architecture of Happiness* (de Botton, 2006), but in the view of one critic 'If architecture's capacity to generate happiness is inconsistent, this might be because happiness has rarely been the foundation of architecture' (Glancey, 2006). He added that in the current global machine for building, 'beauty . . . is increasingly irrelevant'.

Environmental psychiatry, therefore, might perhaps teach other professions many things that should really have emerged within these disciplines themselves. The human–environment science, then, can be divided into two aspects: for architects and planners, it is the systematic analysis of human behaviour related to the settings they create; for human scientists, it is the environmental contexts of that behaviour (Craik, 1973). These two aspects have been seen as contrary, but environmental psychiatry should be equally concerned with both.

Early nineteenth-century psychiatry, like the rest of medicine at that time, was based on the view that all parts of the body were interdependent, and that both health and disease resulted from the interaction of individuals with their environment. The concept of 'moral treatment', developed in the 1780s at The Retreat in York, was largely equivalent to the construction of a specific environment that would have a therapeutic effect. Like almost every other form of psychiatric intervention, before and since, this one had more success with acute disorders than with the chronic; it tended to fall into disrepute, though, with the advance of scientific medicine later in the century, until its rediscovery in the 1940s as the 'therapeutic community'. Leon Eisenberg has pointed out that every use of a therapeutic milieu is in fact a rediscovery of moral treatment.

Limits of environmental psychiatry

It should be made clear that there is no objective here to construct some psychiatric blueprint for the future of society – of whatever political complexion. If societies could be changed so that frustration, conflict, and aggression were reduced, much psychiatric disorder could no doubt be prevented. However:

> the psychiatrist functions solely in the realm of behavioural dysfunction. He is not an expert in dealing with poverty, overpopulation, urban renewal, automation or war . . . he should be capable of [helping] the behavioural difficulties that might arise in people who suffer from deprivation, crowding, slums, unemployment or massive stress [but] lacks the power to implement social action outside the mental health field.
>
> (Grinker, 1982)

In the same vein, Jablensky (1982) pointed out that attempts to apply psychiatric knowledge to the social field, for example in advice to urban planners and industrial managers, have so far rarely produced more than trivial recommendations. The present limits of knowledge and pitifully small resources devoted to such applied research make psychiatry's contribution to social development so far very unimpressive.

One of the reasons for this relative failure is that efforts tend to be focused at the wrong level, usually one that is far too ambitious. For instance, Rutter (1981) emphasized that when preventive policies are considered, there is a tendency to assume that these must in some way deal with 'basic' causes, but that 'this model involves a most naive and simplistic notion of "causation" '. There are, as he points out, many practical ways in which society could reduce psychiatric and social pathology, on the basis of established knowledge and within the limits of its resources. In fact, progress can only come through scrupulous, painstaking research, based on clear concepts, and through action that is directly related to what has been scientifically demonstrated. Society has not needed psychiatrists to tell it such truisms as that good housing is better than bad, but there continue to be political pressures on issues that should remain scientific. Callard (2005) warns that public mental health debates 'must ensure their gaze does not slip from questions of access and social justice in the rush to endorse the worthiness of creating better quality houses and public spaces'. In a democratic society, though, mental health specialists have no greater authority than any other citizens on matters such as social justice.

There are now too many worldwide interdependencies of countries and continents to focus on local solutions for conditions whose origins are international. Economic depression spreads throughout industrialized nations, drugs are trafficked from Asia to Europe and America, and people migrate in huge numbers from less to better developed societies with very different cultures. The search for pragmatic solutions to problems of mental health in different environments is not helped by constant changes in the scenario, but this does not mean that it is a fruitless one.

Before drawing conclusions about the relationship of any individual's mental health to current environmental conditions, though, it would be as well to be reminded of the anthropological and biological context of this discussion:

> Our evolved repertoire was not intended for this environment. We are certainly evolved to be gregarious, but not in nations of 600 million, or in cities of 15 million . . . we were formed slowly over several million years, and at least 99 per cent of our existence . . . was the existence of a small-scale hunter. The agricultural sedentary world is a mere 10,000 years old; and the industrial world with its even more alarming transformations is only 200 years old . . . We are an old animal coping with a startling new world of its own creation that has got out of hand.
>
> (Fox, 1982)

With that background, the subject of mental health and environment in its scientific aspects needs to be approached with a due sense of humility.

Certainly, cities do tend to house concentrations of multiply disadvantaged people, who may show poor mental health along with other unfavourable attributes, but it would be quite wrong to extrapolate this picture to whole city populations (Freeman, 1984). There may, however, be an optimum size beyond which the costs of cities start to outweigh their benefits, resulting in an escalation of levels of social pathology. Currently, urban settlements are growing to sizes never previously known in human history, and this is happening mainly in the less industrialized parts of the world, where up to now, no way has been found of limiting those explosive developments.

Psychological conservation

On the basis of the evidence presented in this book, there would seem to be an urgent need to pay attention to the psychological conservation of the environment – retaining familiar landmarks and forms of housing – in the same way that physical Conservation Areas have been established in Britain.

Thus, the social matrix that forms the identity of place, and that is almost certainly related to the identity of person and group (Canter, 1977), may be preserved or restored. By contemporary standards, the great cities of the nineteenth century were mostly quite small, and a few, such as Vienna, still are; they had comprehensible boundaries and remained in touch with the surrounding countryside. But the sheer size of today's urban settlements may involve what Cappon (1975) has called 'the destruction of whatever natural order of territoriality was established by historical and social usage'.

But psychological conservation applies even more urgently to rural areas: the Campaign for the Protection of Rural England (2006) has developed a map of tranquil areas in England that can used 'to identify, protect, enhance and reclaim places where we can experience tranquillity' in England. Such an exercise helps raise consciousness about the importance and value of rapidly disappearing tranquil rural areas for well-being and mental health.

We believe there is a need to restore to human settlements the benefits of urbanity – of a social matrix in which a worthwhile quality of life and work can be sustained. This objective is not mere whimsical folksiness, but would regain a milieu that can be a very efficient one for conducting business and other essential activities. In particular, one contribution that social psychiatry might make, in collaboration with other disciplines, is to oppose the overwhelming preoccupation that planners, architects, and local governments have had for many years with reduction of high urban density. It is even more important, in fact, to recognize – as the pioneering sociologist Durkheim did originally – that high density is actually essential for the positive qualities of towns and cities, such as cultural life and specialised professional services; the low densities of suburbs make these facilities difficult to provide without imposing a degree of car travel, which is both environmentally damaging and unjust to the more disadvantaged sections of society.

Sampson (1982) suggested that the British, 'with their long tradition of close communities, privacy, leisure, houses, and gardens, could be better equipped to manage the process of deindustrialization than most Europeans, with their competitiveness, and cooped-up apartments'. Another contribution to social policy of social psychiatry and sociology, as Carstairs (1969) pointed out, is to show that the clustering of such forms of social pathology as alcoholism, parasuicide, and violent crime in the overcrowded, underprivileged areas of large cities cannot be explained simply on grounds of material circumstances. Equally important seems to be the alienation from participation in the general life of society that is felt by many people living in such situations. Carstairs summarized such circumstances as: long-settled means of production and traditional occupations being rapidly superseded by new techniques, throwing many people out of work; different sectors of a population experiencing widely contrasting standards of living; weakening of traditional values, with protective functions no longer being fulfilled by customary authorities; and an all-pervading sense of uncertainty about the future. This fits the situation of our own times in many parts of the world too closely for comfort.

The result of these processes was described in the case of Chicago by Saul Bellow (1982) as: 'huge rectangles, endless regions of the stunned city – many, many square miles of civil Passchendaele or Somme. Only at the centre of the city, visible from all points over fields of demolition, the tall glamour of the skyscrapers'. As for the human consequences of such environmental changes, they are likely to produce 'that underclass . . . which is economically "redundant", a culture of despair and crime'. Thus, those who are multiply disadvantaged become ecologically trapped, unable to work because employment has moved to far suburbs or become strung along motorways, and there is no accessible public transport to take them there. Economic activity now tends to occur increasingly in inter-urban clusters, focused on road and air travel, and linked more by telephone and computer than by the meeting of people; it is a capital-intensive, high-technology environment, needing fairly small numbers of personnel, who will mostly have to be young, intelligent, and mentally and physically healthy to measure up to its demands.

There is much that is still unknown about the relationship of the environment to mental health. More needs to be understood about these relationships and the effects need to be more precisely quantified before policy-makers can be confidently advised about the risks and benefits of particular environmental conditions. The progress of genetic research should ideally be counterbalanced by an equal development in the investigation of environmental factors. As Owen (2006) put it, 'genes are not deterministic and they do not "cause" behaviours or psychiatric disorders such as autism or schizophrenia in any direct way. Rather their effects on behaviour are indirect and mediated to a considerable extent via the environment'. It is to be hoped that in the long run, increasing sophistication in data collection and analysis, together with better integration of the work of different disciplines, will help to achieve this aim.

References

Alexander, D. A. and Klein, S. (2003) 'Biochemical terrorism: too awful to contemplate, too serious to ignore: subjective literature review'. *British Journal of Psychiatry*, *183*, 491–497.

Altman, I. (1975) *The environment and social behaviour.* Monterey, CA: Brooks Cole.

Andrews, B. and Brown, G. W. (1993) 'Self-esteem and vulnerability to depression: the concurrent validity of interview and questionnaire measures'. *Journal of Abnormal Psychology, 102*, 565–572.

Barker, D. J. (1988) 'In utero programming of chronic disease'. *Clinical Science, 95*, 115–128.

Bellow, S. (1982) *The dean's December*. New York: Harper & Row.

Bifulco, A., Brown, G. W. and Harris, T. O. (1994) 'Childhood Experience of Care and Abuse (CECA): a retrospective interview measure'. *Journal of Child Psychology and Psychiatry, 35*, 1419–1435.

Brown, G. W. and Harris, T. O. (1978) *Social origins of depression: A study of psychiatric disorder in women*. London: Tavistock.

Brown, G. W. and Moran, P. M. (1997) 'Single mothers, poverty and depression'. *Psychological Medicine, 27*, 21–33.

Brown, G. W., Harris, T. O. and Eales, M. J. (1993) 'Aetiology of anxiety and depressive disorders in an inner-city population. 2. Comorbidity and adversity'. *Psychological Medicine, 23*, 155–165.

Brown, G. W., Harris, T. O. and Hepworth, C. (1995) 'Loss, humiliation and entrapment among women developing depression: a patient and non-patient comparison'. *Psychological Medicine, 25*, 7–21.

Brown, G. W., Lemyre, L. and Bifulco, A. (1992) 'Social factors and recovery from anxiety and depressive disorders: a test of specificity'. *British Journal of Psychiatry, 161*, 44–54.

Brown, G. W., Andrews, B., Harris, T., Adler, Z. and Bridge, L. (1986) 'Social support, self-esteem and depression'. *Psychological Medicine, 16*, 813–831.

Brunner, E. (1997) 'Stress and the biology of inequality'. *British Medical Journal, 314*, 1472–1476.

Callard, F. (2005) 'Editorial'. *Journal of Public Mental Health, 4*, no. 4, 2–5.

Campaign for the Protection of Rural England (2006) *Saving tranquil places: How to protect and promote a vital asset*. London: CPRE.

Canter, D. (1977) *The psychology of place*. New York: St Martin's Press.

Cappon, D. (1975) 'Designs for improvements in the quality of life in downtown cores'. *International Journal of Mental Health, 4*, 31–47.

Carstairs, G. M. (1969) 'Overcrowding and human aggression', in *The history of violence in America*. New York: Praeger.

Caspi, A., Moffitt, T. E., Cannon, M., McClay, J., Murray, R., Harrington, H. *et al.* (2005) 'Moderation of the effect of adolescent-onset cannabis use on adult psychosis by a functional polymorphism in the catechol-O-methyltransferase gene: longitudinal evidence of a gene X environment interaction'. *Biological Psychiatry, 57*, 1117–1127.

Caspi, A., Sugden, K., Moffitt, T. E., Taylor, A., Craig, I. W., Harrington, H., *et al.* (2003) 'Influence of life stress on depression: moderation by a polymorphism in the 5-HTT gene'. *Science, 301*, 386–389.

Cassel, J. C. (1971) 'Health consequences of population density and crowding', in National Academy of Science (ed.), *Rapid population growth: Consequences and policy implications: Volume 1*. Baltimore, MD: Johns Hopkins University Press.

Checkley, S. (1996) 'The neuroendocrinology of depression and chronic stress'. *British Medical Bulletin, 52*, 597–617.

Cheyne, G. (1733) *The English malady: Or a treatise on nervous diseases of all kinds*: Bath and London: G. Strahan & J. Leake.

Choldin, H. M. (1978) 'Urban density and pathology'. *Annual Review of Sociology, 4*, 91–113.

Chu, A., Thorne, A. and Guite, H. (2004) 'The impact on mental well-being of the urban and physical environment'. *Journal of Mental Health Promotion, 3*, 17–32.

Clark, C., Candy, B. and Stansfeld, S. A. (2006) *A systematic review on the effect of the built and physical environment on mental health*. London: Mental Health Foundation.

Congdon, P. (1996) 'Suicide and parasuicide in London: a small-area study'. *Urban Studies, 33*, 137–158.

Craik, K. H. (1973) 'Environmental psychology'. *Annual Review of Psychology, 24*, 403–422.

de Botton, A. (2006) *The architecture of happiness*. London: Hamish Hamilton.

Diez-Roux, A. V. (1998) 'Bringing context back into epidemiology: variables and fallacies in multilevel analysis'. *American Journal of Public Health, 88*, 216–222.

Dohrenwend, B. P. (2000) 'The role of adversity and stress in psychopathology: some evidence and its implications for theory and research'. *Journal of Health and Social Behaviour, 41*, 1–19.

Dohrenwend, B. P., Levav, I., Shrout, P. E., Schwartz, S., Naveh, G., Link, B. G. *et al.* (1992) 'Socioeconomic status and psychiatric disorders: the causation–selection issue'. *Science, 255*, 946–52.

Durkheim, E. (1952) *Suicide: A study in sociology* (trans. by J. A. Spaulding and G. Simpson). London: Routledge and Kegan Paul.

Eisenberg, L. (2005) 'Are genes destiny? Have adenine, cytosine, guanine and thymine replaced Lachesis, Clotho and Atropos as the weavers of our fate?'. *World Psychiatry, 4*, 3–8.

Elias, N. (1969) 'Sociology and psychiatry', in S. H. Foulkes and G. S. Prince (eds), *Psychiatry in a changing society*. London: Tavistock.

Evans, J., Middleton, N. and Gunnell, D. (2004) 'Social fragmentation, severe mental illness and suicide'. *Social Psychiatry and Psychiatric Epidemiology, 39*, 165–170.

Fischer, C. S. (1973) 'Urban malaise'. *Social Forces, 52*, 221–235.

Fischer, C. S. (1976) *The urban experience*. New York: Harcourt, Brace, Jovanovich.

Fox, R. (1982) 'Of inhuman native and unnatural rights'. *Encounter, 58*, 47–53.

Freedman, J. L. (1975) *Crowding and behaviour*. San Francisco: W. H. Freeman.

Freeman, H. L. (1984) *Mental health and the environment*. London: Churchill Livingstone.

Gans, H. (1962). 'Urbanism and suburbanism as ways of life: a re-evaluation of definitions', in A. Rose (ed.), *Human behavior and social processes*, pp. 625–648. Boston: Houghton Mifflin.

Glancey, J. (2006) Review of the *The architecture of happiness*. *The Guardian*, 29 April.

Goldberg, D. and Huxley, P. (1980) *Mental illness in the community: The pathway to psychiatric care*. London: Tavistock.

Grinker, R. (1982) In M. Shepherd (ed), *Psychiatrists on psychiatry*. Cambridge: Cambridge University Press.

Hall, E. T. (1968) 'Proxemics'. *Current Anthropology, 9*, 83–95.

Halpern, D. (1995) *Mental health and the built environment: More than bricks and mortar*. London: Taylor & Francis.

Hobbs, P. R., Ballinger, C. B., McClure, A., Martin, B. and Greenwood, C. (1985) 'Factors associated with psychiatric morbidity in men – a general practice survey'. *Acta Psychiatrica Scandinavica, 71*, 281–286.

Jablensky, A. (1982) In M. Shepherd (ed.), *Psychiatrists on psychiatry*. Cambridge: Cambridge University Press.

Jacobs, J. (1961) *Death and life of great American cities*. New York: Random House.

Järup, L. (2003) 'Hazards of heavy metal contamination', in D. J. Briggs, M. Joffe and

P. Elliott (eds), *Impact of environmental pollution on health.* Oxford: Oxford University Press.

Kasl, S. V. (1977) *The effect of the man-made environment on health and behavior.* Atlanta, GA: Center for Disease Control.

Kasl, S. V. and Rosenfield, S. (1980) 'The residential environment and its impact on the mental health of the aged', in J. E. Birren and R. B. Sloane (eds), *Handbook of mental health and aging.* Englewood Cliffs, NJ: Prentice Hall.

Kirmeyer, S. L. (1978) 'Urban density and pathology: a review of research'. *Environment and Behavior, 10,* 247–269.

Kuh, D. and Ben-Shlomo, Y. (2004). *A life course approach to chronic disease epidemiology,* 2nd Ed. Oxford: Oxford University Press.

Levy, L. and Herzog, A. N. (1974) 'Effects of population density and crowding on health and social adaptation in the Netherlands'. *Journal of Health and Social Behaviour, 15,* 228–240.

Lewis, A. (1967) *The state of psychiatry: Essays and addresses.* London: Routledge & Kegan Paul.

Lidsky, T. I. and Schneider, J. S. (2003) 'Lead neurotoxicity in children: basic mechanisms and clinical correlates'. *Brain, 126,* 5–19.

Lynch, K. (1960) *The image of the city.* Cambridge, MA: MIT Press.

Marmot, M. (2005) 'Social determinants of health inequalities', *Lancet, 365,* 1099–1104.

McEwen, B. S. (1998) 'Stress, adaptation and disease: allostasis and allostatic load'. *Annals of the New York Academy of Sciences, 840,* 33–44.

Meaney, M. J. and Szyf, M. (2005) 'Environmental programming of stress responses through DNA methylation: life at the interface between a dynamic environment and a fixed genome'. *Dialogues in Clinical Neuroscience,* 7, 103–123.

Melzer, D., Fryers, T. and Jenkins, R. (2004) *Social inequalities and the distribution of the common mental disorders.* Maudsley Monographs 44. Hove, UK: Psychology Press.

Owen, M. J. (2006) 'Review of genes of behaviour'. *British Journal of Psychiatry, 189,* 192–193.

Parker, G. (1983) 'Parental "affectionless control" as an antecedent to adult depression, a risk factor delineated'. *Archives of General Psychiatry, 40,* 956–960.

Philo, C. (2005) 'The geography of mental health: an established field?'. *Current Opinion in Psychiatry, 18,* 585–91.

Polatin, P. B., Young, M., Mayer, M. and Gatchel, R. (2005) 'Bioterrorism, stress, and pain: the importance of an anticipatory community preparedness intervention'. *Journal of Psychosomatic Research, 58,* 311–316.

Power, C., Stansfeld, S. A., Matthews, S., Manor, O. and Hope, S. (2002) 'Childhood and adulthood risk factors for socio-economic differentials in psychological distress: evidence from the 1958 British birth cohort'. *Social Science and Medicine, 55,* 1989–2004.

Rapaport, A. (1975) 'Toward a redefinition of density'. *Environment and Behavior,* 7, 133–158.

Rehkopf, D. H. and Buka, S. L. (2006) 'The association between suicide and the socio-economic characteristics of geographical areas: a systematic review'. *Psychological Medicine, 36,* 145–157.

Repetti, R. L., Taylor, S. E. and Seeman, T. E. (2002) 'Risky families: family social environments and the mental and physical health of offspring'. *Psychological Bulletin, 128,* 330–366.

Rutter, M. (1981) 'The city and the child'. *American Journal of Orthopsychiatry, 51,* 610–625.

Rutter, M. (2002) 'The interplay of nature, nurture, and developmental influences: the challenge ahead for mental health'. *Archives of General Psychiatry, 59*, 996–1000.

Rutter, M. (2005a) 'How the environment affects mental health'. *British Journal of Psychiatry, 186*, 4–6.

Rutter, M. (2005b) 'Environmentally mediated risks for psychopathology: research strategies and findings'. *Journal of the American Academy of Child and Adolescent Psychiatry, 44*, 3–18.

Sampson, A. (1982) *Changing anatomy of Britain*. London: Hodder & Stoughton.

Simmel, G. (1908). *Conflict in sociology*. Glencoe, NY: Free Press.

Simmel, G. (1950) 'The metropolis and mental life', in K. Wolf (ed.), *The sociology of George Simmel*. Glencoe, NY: Free Press.

Smith, B. J. and Easterlaw, D. (2005) 'The strange geography of health inequalities'. *Transactions of the Institute of British Geographers, 30*, 173–190.

Trichopoulos, D., Katsouyanni, K., Zavitsanos, X., Tzonou, A. and Dalla-Vorgia, P. (1983) 'Psychological stress and fatal heart attack: the Athens (1981) earthquake natural experiment'. *Lancet, 1*, 441–444.

Tuan, Y. (1979) *Landscapes of fear*. Oxford: Blackwell.

Turpin, G. and Siddle, D. A. T. (1983) 'Effects of stimulus intensity on cardiac activity'. *Psychophysiology, 20*, 611–624.

Vaillant, G. E. (2003) 'Mental health'. *American Journal of Psychiatry, 160*, 1373–1384.

Watson, D. and Clark, L. A. (1984) 'Negative affectivity: the disposition to experience aversive emotional states'. *Psychological Bulletin, 96*, 465–490.

Weisler, R. H., Barbee, J. G. and Townsend, M. H. (2006) 'Mental health and recovery in the Gulf Coast after Hurricanes Katrina and Rita'. *Journal of the American Medical Association, 296*, 585–588.

Whitley, E., Gunnell, D., Dorling, D. and Smith, G. D. (1999) 'Ecological study of social fragmentation, poverty, and suicide'. *British Medical Journal, 319*, 1034–1037.

Whitley, R., Prince, M. and Cargo, M. (2005) 'Thinking inside the bubble: evidence for a new contextual unit in urban mental health'. *Journal of Epidemiology and Community Health, 59*, 893–897.

Willmott, P. (1963) *The evolution of a community*. London: Routledge & Kegan Paul.

2 Gene–environment interactions in mental disorders

A current view

Ming T. Tsuang, William S. Stone and Jennifer M. Johnston

Family, twin, and adoption studies firmly establish the roles of both genes and environment in mental disorders. It remains difficult, however, to find genes for these disorders, and to characterize the environmental circumstances under which psychopathology emerges (although putative genes for some disorders, including schizophrenia, have been proposed (e.g. Harrison & Weinberger, 2005). The reason for this difficulty lies in the complex nature of mental disorders. Many disorders – like many normal physiological conditions (e.g. blood pressure) and cognitive abilities (e.g. intelligence) – almost certainly result from the combined action of multiple genes of small effect together with a variety of environmental factors. In addition, genetic and environmental factors interact with each other in complex ways to influence gene expression and subsequent phenotype (Faraone *et al.*, 1999; Kramer, 2005; Moffitt *et al.*, 2005). In other words, genes and environmental factors exert their effects only via interaction with other genes and other environmental factors. The issue is not one of nature *versus* nurture; rather, we must ask: how do genes and environment *interact* to produce a behavioural phenotype?

The study of genetic and environmental interactions has long been a subject of speculation, but such interactions were considered rare until recently (Moffitt *et al.*, 2005). Instead, the notion that most genetic influences on mental disorders reflected additive and direct effects formed the underlying rationale for most genetic studies. This view has changed in recent years as both conceptual and technical advances now point to the importance of gene–environment interactions, and to ways of measuring them.

In this chapter, we will focus on 'gene–environment interaction' in mental disorders, using genetic control of sensitivity to the environment as our definition of that term (Kendler & Eaves, 1986). Gene–environment interactions occur when environmental influences on a trait differ according to a person's genetic predisposition, or when a person's genetic predisposition is expressed differently in different environments. Interaction phenomena are important, and the products of interactions are becoming more measurable (Mirnics & Pevsner, 2004; Moffitt *et al.*, 2005). By ignoring interactions, true genetic and environmental effects can be obscured, which leads to false negative results and, more generally, to inconsistent findings in the literature. Fortunately, these interactions are receiving increased attention as molecular biological technology is making interaction effects more measurable (e.g. gene expression), and as the concept of interaction effects becomes more accepted.

The subsequent discussion begins with a consideration of methodological and measurement issues involving gene–environment interactions, with examples involving psychiatric and neurological conditions. This will be followed by a representative review of interactions in psychiatric disorders using twin, adoption and association designs. Finally, gene–environment interactions will be considered in selected neurodevelopmental disorders (autism and schizophrenia) to highlight their potential to shed light on underlying aetiological mechanisms in this class of psychiatric conditions.

Methodology and measurement issues

Several excellent reviews discuss some of the methodological issues and problems involved in assessing gene–environment interaction, and the reader is referred to these for a more detailed discussion (Khoury & Beaty, 1987; Khoury *et al.*, 1988, 1993; Kramer, 2005; Moffitt *et al.*, 2005; Ottman, 1996; Rutter & Silberg, 2002; Yang & Khoury, 1997). Some of these problems involve definition and assessment, i.e. in order to test for gene–environment interaction, individuals must be classified according to presence or absence of genetic and environmental risk, and the specification of both can be difficult. Environmental exposures are difficult to define and measure precisely, and are under-studied in the context of genetic research designs (Cooper, 2001). Moreover, putative environmental risk factors may not be truly environmental. This phenomenon is known as gene–environment correlation, in which an individual's genotype influences his exposure to the environment. In other words, 'environmental' factors are themselves attributable to genetic influences (Scarr & McCartney, 1983). Gene–environment interaction is difficult to measure in the presence of gene–environment correlation (Rutter & Silberg, 2002).

On the other hand, there are several different ways of measuring genotype (Ottman, 1996). Unfortunately, because of the lack of well-established candidate genes for mental disorders (and relatively little knowledge of the biological processes that give rise to mental disorders), researchers have to rely on less direct ways of classifying a person according to genetic risk. This point underscores the potential impact of developments in both intermediate biobehavioural expressions of disease (i.e. 'endophenotypes'; Gottesman & Gould, 2003), and in molecular genetics (Harrison & Weinberger, 2005; Moffitt *et al.*, 2005), which will make it easier to identify genes and genetic markers associated with mental disorders. These ongoing advances will eventually allow the assessment of specific genotypes in specific environments, which will facilitate direct and systematic investigations of gene–environment interactions.

The impact of advances in molecular genetics (i.e. identifying genetic variants associated with mental disorders) can be illustrated using the example of Alzheimer's disease (AD). An allelic association exists between AD and the ε4 allele of the apolipoprotein E (APOE) gene (Corder *et al.*, 1993), which results in a six-fold risk for AD in individuals with one or two copies of this allele (Nalbantoglu *et al.*, 1994; Reynolds *et al.*, 2006). APOE is considered a 'susceptibility gene', because it is neither necessary nor sufficient for the development of AD. Other genes or environmental agents must be present for the ε4 allele to increase risk for AD. One of the earliest environmental risk factors associated with AD was a history of head injury (Mortimer *et al.*, 1985; Whalley, 1991). Because a positive family history was also a risk factor for the disease (van Duijn *et al.*, 1991), attempts were made to find evidence for gene–environment interaction, using family history as an indicator of genetic risk. However, results of early studies failed to demonstrate convincing evidence of interaction (Mayeux *et al.*, 1993; Van Duijn *et al.*, 1994). Mayeux *et al.* (1995) then studied the combined effects of head injury and genetic susceptibility on risk for AD, and found no increase in risk associated with head injury in the absence of the ε4 allele, a two-fold increase in risk with ε4 alone, and a 10-fold increase in risk with both ε4 and a history of head injury. These findings and those from subsequent studies examining frequency of the APOE-ε4 allele in patients with head injury have led to hypotheses regarding a biological mechanism whereby head injury contributes to the pathogenesis of AD by increasing beta-amyloid precursor protein (APP) deposition in the cerebral cortex, which exacerbates the effect of the APOE-ε4 allele (which is thought to be related to cerebral beta-APP deposition).

Malaspina *et al.* (2001) found similar evidence for gene–environment interaction in schizophrenia, another mental disorder that has been associated with head injury. Using membership in multiplex schizophrenia and bipolar pedigrees as proxies for, respectively, greater and lesser genetic loading, they found that schizophrenic subjects from schizophrenic pedigrees were more likely to have experienced a traumatic brain injury (19.6%) than schizophrenic subjects from bipolar pedigrees (4.5%). Within the schizophrenia pedigrees, head injury was associated with a greater risk of schizophrenia (odds ratio (OR) = 2.06), consistent with a synergistic effect between genes and environment. While these results are provocative, their implications are limited by the lack of information about schizophrenia susceptibility genes. As was the case with AD, once these have been identified with the aid of advances in molecular genetics, it will be relatively easy to incorporate this information into epidemiological studies, resulting in a rapid increase in knowledge about disease pathogenesis.

Currently, alcohol use provides a paradigm for studying gene–environment interaction similar to AD. Two polymorphisms – in the aldehyde dehydrogenase (ALDH) and alcohol dehydrogenase (ADH) genes – are associated with risk for alcohol dependence in Asian populations (Higuchi, 1994; Higuchi *et al.*, 1994), providing the basis for studies examining the relationship between these genetic risk factors and the effects of known environmental risk/protective factors for alcohol abuse and dependence, such as early family rearing environment.

Until now, however, most knowledge about gene–environment interaction has come from traditional quantitative genetic studies, in which family history and monozygotic/dizygotic (MZ/DZ) concordance are used as indices of genetic risk. While there are methodological limitations to these studies (for example, the possibility of genetic misclassification), twin and adoption studies have been influential in demonstrating gene–environment interaction effects (Ottman, 1996).

Twin studies

Twins can be a useful tool in the investigation of gene–environment interaction (MacGregor *et al.*, 2000). For example, MZ discordant twins can provide evidence for the influence of non-inherited characteristics on a disorder. A greater incidence of obstetric complications (OCs; McNeil *et al.*, 1994) and of dysmorphological handprint signs suggestive of abnormal foetal development (Bracha *et al.*, 1991) has been observed in MZ twins with schizophrenia than in their unaffected co-twins. A different approach involves comparing heritabilities (i.e. the proportion of phenotypic variance due to genetic variance) according to the presence or absence of identified specific environmental risk factors. In addition to having main effects on rates and/or symptom levels of a disorder, environmental variables may also have moderating effects on the relative magnitude of genetic and environmental influences on the disorder. This is a form of gene–environment interaction: changes in the environment may render genes or environment more or less salient as influences on behaviour. In other words, the amount of variability in a disorder due to genetic or environmental influences may differ at different levels of an environmental variable, distinct from any main effect of that variable (i.e. in the absence of phenotypic change).

Several twin studies examined the impact of broad personal variables on symptoms of mental disorders. Among these, the effects of socioregional variables on adolescent alcohol use were examined in a population-based sample of Finnish twins (Dick *et al.*, 2001; Rose *et al.*, 2001). In the first study, Rose *et al.* (2001) found that although drinking frequencies were similar for adolescents in urban and rural environments, genetic factors played a larger role in urban areas, whereas shared environment had a greater influence in rural settings. In an effort to elucidate the nature of this urban/rural effect, this same group then examined more specific, continuous measures of the environment, and found that the magnitude of genetic influences on drinking frequency was nearly five times greater in environments characterized by a greater percentage of young adults, higher migration rates, and proportionately greater alcohol sales (Dick *et al.*, 2001).

Marital status has been found to exert moderating effects on the expression of genetic and environmental influences on alcohol consumption (Heath *et al.*, 1989) and on symptoms of depression (Heath *et al.*, 1998) in a sample of female adult Australian twin pairs. Genetic influences accounted for a greater proportion of the variance in both alcohol consumption and symptoms of depression in unmarried twins than in twins involved in a marriage-like relationship. In other words, having a marriage-like relationship reduced the impact of genetic influences on psychiatric symptoms. Religiosity has also been found to have a moderating effect on alcohol use initiation (Koopmans *et al.*, 1999) and disinhibition, as measured by the Sensation Seeking Scale (Boomsma *et al.*, 1999) in a Dutch twin sample. In both of these studies, while there was no association between religious upbringing and either alcohol use initiation or disinhibition, the influence of genetic factors on these variables was much greater in subjects without a religious background. These results suggest that receiving a religious upbringing, like being involved in a marriage-like relationship, may act as a protective factor in reducing the influence of genetic liability to psychiatric symptoms (Heath *et al.*, 1998). Consistent with this possibility, a recent twin study provided suggestive evidence (the sample was small) that African-American twin pairs did not show expected MZ–DZ differences, but did show greater religious affiliations and later onsets of drinking than Caucasian twin pairs (Prescott *et al.*, 2005).

These studies are consistent with a sociological perspective that regards heritability as representing an individual's proportion of actualized genetic potential (Bronfenbrenner & Ceci, 1994). According to this definition, the reason that heritability varies across environmental contexts is that different environments provide different opportunities for genetic potentials to be actualized. Structured situations are those that provide relatively unambiguous cues to guide behaviour. Conversely, less structured situations are more ambiguous (Monson & Snyder, 1977; Snyder & Ickes, 1985). Because there are few salient cues in the environment, individuals must rely to a greater extent on their own disposition to guide behaviour. It follows that the causes of behaviour in structured situations should be more situational than dispositional, whereas individual differences are more likely to be the causes of behaviour in less structured situations. Consistent with this prediction, in the above studies, heritabilities for various clinical problems increased in environments that were less controlling, i.e. in subjects living in urban areas, in subjects who were unmarried, and in subjects without a religious upbringing, and the impact of shared environmental influences was greater in environments that theoretically provided a narrower range of opportunities to express individual differences in behaviour. Results such as these, demonstrating differences in genetic and environmental influences in differing environmental circumstances, provide one explanation for the heterogeneity among heritability estimates for the same disorder, and point to the need to incorporate measures of the environment into genetically informative designs.

Kendler and colleagues have also used large population-based twin samples to study the impact of life events on depression and anxiety in women. Studies investigating the comorbidity of generalized anxiety disorder (GAD) and major depression (MD) in female twins found that all the genes that influenced lifetime risk for MD and GAD appeared to be completely shared between the two disorders (Kendler, 1996; Kendler *et al.*, 1987; Kendler *et al.*, 1992).

Common or familial environment was not a factor in the aetiology of either disorder. Some non-shared or unique environmental factors, however, may be relatively specific to either GAD or MD (e.g. stressful life events), while others may be both depressogenic and anxiogenic. These results suggest that it is likely that environmental factors are largely responsible for whether a female expresses genetic vulnerability as anxiety or depression. Roy *et al.* (1995) replicated these results in a clinical twin sample that included both male and female subjects and suggested that MD may be associated with stressful life events that involve loss, while GAD may be primarily related to life events that involve danger, consistent with the fact that MD and GAD have been associated with different sociodemographic predictors (Finlay-Jones & Brown, 1981).

Following these results, Kendler *et al.* (1995) set out to investigate the relationship between stressful life events and the onset of depression in this sample. They found that the risk of onset of a major depressive episode in the month following the occurrence of any of four types of severe life events (death of a close relative, assault, divorce or marriage breakup, serious marital conflict) was highest in those at greatest genetic risk (as gauged by twin concordance). The one-month probability of onset of MD in individuals at lower genetic risk (i.e. with an unaffected co-twin) was 0.5% and 6.2%, respectively, depending on the absence or presence within that month of a severe life event. For individuals at high genetic risk (i.e. with an affected co-twin), the probabilities were 1.1% and 14.6%, respectively. These results are indicative of a gene–environment effect, in which genetic susceptibility increases an individual's sensitivity to the psychological impact of stressful life events. Similarly, Kendler *et al.* (2005) studied interactions between effects of stressful life events and polymorphisms in a serotonin transporter. Individuals with two 'short' alleles showed an elevated vulnerability to depression, but only if they were exposed to stressful life events. Individals with one or two 'long' alleles did not show these depressogenic effects. These findings have also been reported by other (e.g. Eley *et al.*, 2004), though not all (Gillespie *et al.*, 2004) researchers.

Genetic factors, however, play a role in individual exposure to life events (Kendler *et al.*, 1995) and, moreover, the genetic liability to experience stressful life events overlaps with the genetic liability for depression (i.e. gene–environment correlation (Silberg *et al.*, 1999)). Thus, Silberg (2001) conducted a more rigorous test of this gene–environment interaction effect by examining the relationship between risk for anxiety and depression and independent life events, i.e. those life events involving no genetic mediation, in a sample of adolescent female twins. They found a gene–environment effect similar to that of Kendler *et al.*, (1995), in which the occurrence of an independent stressful life event in the past year (a new stepbrother/stepsister, brother/sister leaving home, father losing his job) had no effect on the depression scores of girls at low genetic risk (as indexed by the absence of parental emotional disorder), but significantly increased the scores of girls who had a parent with a history of depression or anxiety. In addition, life events exerted a moderating effect on the genetic and environmental influences on depression and anxiety, such that genetic variance increased with increasing exposure to stressful life events, a result in accord with the hypotheses regarding protective environments advanced in the studies discussed above (Dick *et al.*, 2001; Heath *et al.*, 1998). This study illustrates just one of the difficulties in finding evidence for gene–environment interaction in complex disorders: genes influence both exposure and susceptibility to environmental risk factors. Gene–environment correlation and gene–environment interaction both operate to influence phenotype, and disentangling the two will require conceptual advances such as that illustrated by this study. Genetic and environmental effects shown by behavioural genetic twin studies reflect a significant point that is also being made in molecular genetic studies, which is that genetic effects are not static, but are often flexible and responsive to environmental contingencies. Moreover, the range of available genetic expressions allows, or will allow eventually for the identification of protective as well as vulnerability factors.

Adoption studies

More than twin and and family studies, adoption studies allow for the separation of genetic and environmental effects, because children do not share home environments with their biological parents. The major drawback to this type of design is that adoptive homes underrepresent high-risk environments, i.e. those at the extremes of poverty and deprivation (see Rutter & Silberg, 2002, for additional limitations). This is especially important because it has been suggested that gene–environment interactions may only exist at the extremes of genetic and environmental variation, hence adoption studies may underestimate the effects of environmental risk and protective factors and may not always detect true gene–environment interactions (McGue & Bouchard, 1998).

For the most part, adoption study investigations of gene–environment interaction have used biological family history of mental disorder as an indicator of genetic risk, and examined its relationship to psychosocial risk and protective factors in the adoptive family. Results from studies investigating the effects of family variables such as family conflict, poor cohesion, and deviant communication indicate that a wide range of mental disorders, including alcoholism, antisocial behaviour (ASB), depression, and schizophrenia have these risk factors in common and that, for each disorder, these environmental influences interact with genetic risk to exacerbate psychiatric symptoms.

An early adoption study found that male (but not female) adoptees with an alcoholic biological parent were more likely to develop certain types of alcoholism if they were also at environmental risk, based on adoptive family characteristics, pre-placement conditions, and age at adoptive placement (Cloninger *et al.*, 1981). Cutrona *et al.* (1994) found evidence for gene–environment interactions in alcoholism in a US sample of adoptees. Neither a biological background of alcoholism nor any family environmental variables increased risk for alcohol abuse or dependence in female adoptees. However, women (but not men) with at least one alcoholic biological parent who also experienced early-life family conflict and/or adoptive family psychopathology were more likely to become alcoholic than those with low levels of family conflict. In other words, neither a biological background of alcoholism nor environmental stress alone was sufficient to lead to alcoholism in the adoptees, but a combination of the two increased the risk.

Adoption studies have also found evidence for a gene–environment effect on ASB, such that individuals at high genetic risk are more sensitive to adoptive family conflict. Cloninger *et al.* (1982) found a synergistic effect for genetic and environmental risk factors in the Swedish sample, such that adoptees at both genetic risk (i.e. criminal biological parents) and environmental risk (i.e. adverse rearing experiences and poor-quality adoptive placements) had significantly higher rates of petty criminality than adoptees at either biological or environmental risk alone. In other words, adoptees with genetic predispositions towards criminality were also more likely to be affected by negative environmental experiences. Rutter (1997) noted that a problem with this type of study involved the use of parental criminality as a measure of genetic risk, both because it was crude and also because it did not provide information on the mechanism of the genetic effect. Parental criminality could be an index of any of a number of psychopathological, physiological, or cognitive risk factors in the child.

Cadoret and colleagues conducted a series of adoption studies investigating ASB and consistently found evidence for an interaction between a genetic background of ASB and an adverse adoptive home enviroment (Cadoret, 1985; Cadoret & Cain, 1981; Cadoret *et al.*, 1983; Cadoret *et al.*, 1995). In a more recent study, antisocial personality disorder (ASPD) and substance abuse/dependence in the biological parent were used as indicators of genetic risk; environmental risk was indexed by a composite measure of marital, legal, and psychological problems in the adoptive parents (Cadoret *et al.*, 1995). These family environmental factors increased the risk for childhood aggression, adolescent aggression, and conduct disorder (but not adult ASB), but only in the presence of a biological background of ASPD. There was virtually no effect of the environment on those adoptees not at genetic risk. Unlike the earlier studies which combined ASB and substance abuse as an index of genetic risk (Cadoret *et al.*, 1983), this study was able to separate the genetic influences associated with each. The results showed that a biological background of alcohol abuse did not interact with adverse adoptive home environment to increase risk for ASB, which demonstrates the specificity of the genetic diathesis for ASB.

Not all adoption studies, however, replicated the observed gene–environment interaction between a biological background of antisocial behaviour/traits and environmental risk, in the form of adoptive parent antisocial behaviour/traits (Mednick *et al.*, 1984; Willerman *et al.*, 1992). Moreover, evidence for gene–environment correlation in adoptee ASB demonstrates that additional factors may be operating to influence child ASB, and that care must be taken when conducting studies investigating gene–environment interaction. Both Ge *et al.* (1996) and O'Connor *et al.* (1998) found an association between a biological background of antisociality and adoptive parenting behaviour that was mediated by the child's behaviour, such that adoptee antisociality led to harsh and inconsistent behaviour on the part of the adoptive parents, which increased the child's own antisocial behaviour.

The same disturbed adoptive parent variable examined in Cadoret *et al.* (1995) also interacts with genetic risk factors to influence MD in women. In another study, for instance, Cadoret *et al.* (1996) showed that females (but not males) with a genetic background of alcoholism are at increased risk for MD if they live in an adoptive family with a high level of disturbed behaviour. There was no effect of environmental stress in the absence of an alcoholic background. This finding is in accord with theories suggesting that alcoholism is a marker for genetic risk that leads to depression and alcoholism in females, but only alcoholism in males (Winokur *et al.*, 1971).

An adverse adoptive home environment has also been implicated as a source of potential risk for schizophrenia. Findings from the Finnish adoption studies show an increased risk for schizophrenia in the biological offspring of schizophrenic versus non-schizophrenic parents, but only for those high-risk adoptees who were also exposed to a dysfunctional family rearing environment (Tienari, 1991; Tienari *et al.*, 1994). Wahlberg *et al.* (1997), also using the Finnish sample, demonstrated that symptoms of thought disorder (i.e. an indicator of schizophrenia vulnerability) in offspring of schizophrenic mothers were more probable when they were raised by adoptive mothers who themselves showed elevated levels of 'communication deviance'. In contrast, offspring of schizophrenic mothers, raised by adoptive parents with low communication deviance, were less likely to show thought disorder. There was no relationship between thought disorder in control adoptees and communication deviance in the adoptive parents. In other words, this gene–environment interaction effect suggests that adoptees without a pre-existing genetic liability were not vulnerable to the effects of a disturbed family environment (at least with respect to thought disorder), and individuals with a pre-existing genetic liability expressed this liability only in the presence of additional adverse environmental factors. More recently, Tienari *et al.* (2004) also showed that high-risk adoptees (i.e. offspring of a schizophrenic mother) were more sensitive to problems in their adoptive environments than were adoptees at low genetic risk. Moreover, problems in the adoptive families were more predictive of clinical outcomes in the schizophrenia spectrum for high-risk than for low-risk adoptees.

Rutter and Silberg (2002) suggested that results such as these from twin and adoption genetic studies, i.e. demonstrating gene–environment interaction, have so far been supportive of the hypothesis that the impact of environmental risk factors on psychopathology is slight in the absence of genetic risk. They are also consistent with studies showing, for example, higher rates of psychotic symptoms or schizophrenia-related disorders in high-risk (versus low-risk) individuals who were exposed to other environmental events such as childhood abuse or neglect (Read *et al.*, 2005), or even to otherwise neutral conditions, such as an urban environment (Spauwen *et al.*, 2006).

It is likely that research into gene–environment interaction will progress further once genetic marker information can be incorporated into quantitative genetic studies, so that subjects with known genotypes can be exposed to environmental manipulations, allowing for a more experimental approach to the investigation of nature–nurture interplay in human beings. One method of incorporating genotypes into studies of gene–environment interaction is considered in the following section.

Association studies

Association studies provide a potentially useful approach to the detection of gene–environment interactions in mental disorders (i.e. controlling and manipulating both genes and environment). They provide clues about the interaction in various (non-human) animal protocols (Crabbe, 2003; Phillips *et al.*, 2002). The risk and protective effects of perinatal rearing experiences (for example, maternal separation or loss, abuse or neglect, social deprivation) on anxiety- and depression-like behaviour have been demonstrated in both rodents and non-human primates (Anisman *et al.*, 1998; Sanchez *et al.*, 2001). For example, genetically different strains of rodents that vary in their response to stress show additional differences in gene expression and in behaviour, when exposed to adverse rearing experiences.

Gene–environment interaction effects might thus provide one explanation for inconsistent findings among association studies between genetic markers and mental disorders, just as they may explain the variability in heritability estimates for the same disorder. For example, the role of the serotonin transporter gene (5-HTT) in anxiety in humans is controversial, while some studies have reported an association between a functional polymorphism in the regulatory region of this gene (5-HTTLPR) and anxiety-related behaviour (Lesch *et al.*, 1996; Ohara *et al.*, 1998), others did not replicate the finding (Lesch, 2003). Similar contradictory findings have been reported between this polymorphism and both major depression and bipolar disorder (Lesch, 2003). Studies in rhesus monkeys, however, have demonstrated the role of gene–environment interaction in the association between this polymorphism and anxiety-related behaviour (Bennett *et al.*, 2002; Champoux *et al.*, 2002). Monkeys at greater genetic risk (i.e. with a greater number of the high-risk, low-activity allele) show differences in measures of 5-HTT expression that are associated with various adverse behavioural outcomes (for example, lower rank within a social group, less competent social behaviour, and greater impulsive aggression), as well as greater anxiety- and depression-related behaviour (for example, diminished orientation, lower attentional capabilities, and increased affective responding). These genotype effects are more pronounced for peer-raised (i.e. separated at birth from mothers) than for mother-raised monkeys. Moreover, as noted above, people with two copies of the short allele polymorphism of the 5-HTT gene are more susceptible to depression following stressful life events than are people with one or two copies of the long allele (Eley *et al.*, 2004; Kendler *et al.*, 2005).

Another gene whose association with human behaviour is controversial is the dopamine D2 receptor gene (DRD2). Associations have been reported between DRD2 variants and several psychological disorders and traits, including alcoholism and other substance use disorders, schizophrenia, post-traumatic stress disorder, and certain personality traits, although, with the exception of schizophrenia (Glatt *et al.*, 2003), none of these associations has been replicated with enough consistency (Noble, 2003). However, some recent studies using human subjects have demonstrated evidence for association, and for gene–environment interaction, by taking account of environmental measures.

An association between the DRD2 Taq1 polymorphism on chromosome 11 and alcoholism was first reported in 1990 (Blum *et al.*, 1990). Since that time, many attempts at replication have taken place, with variable results (Stone & Gottesman, 1993). Meta-analyses of DRD2/alcoholism studies found that, overall, alcoholics had a higher prevalence of the high-risk allele than controls, and that the prevalence was higher in more severe than in less severe alcoholism (Noble, 1998; Pato *et al.*, 1993). Recently, Connor *et al.* (2005) demonstrated that adolescent boys with the DRDR A1 (+) allele showed higher rates of intoxication with alcohol, use of other substances, and development of a tobacco-related habit than did boys with the A1 (–) allele. Still, the association remains controversial (Gorwood *et al.*, 2000; Vanyukov & Tarter, 2000).

Madrid *et al.* (2001) measured alcoholism and stress exposure in a sample of Honduran males, and found that neither was related to DRD2 genotypes. They did find, however, a significant interaction between genotype and stress score, such that individuals homozygous for the low-risk allele had similar alcoholism scores, regardless of level of stress exposure. Alcoholism scores for heterozygous individuals increased modestly with increasing stress, while alcoholism scores for individuals homozygous for the high-risk allele increased greatly. These results suggest that: (a) individuals at genetic risk have a greater sensitivity to stress than those not at genetic risk; and (b) the presence of environmental stress may be necessary for the development of alcoholism in this population.

Similar relationships between DRD2 genotype and environmental stress occur with regard to both cognitive markers and the personality trait of extraversion. Berman and Noble (1997) found no relationship between family stress and cognitive markers (including visuospatial ability and event-related potentials, both of which have been linked to alcoholism (Berman & Noble, 1995; Hill *et al.*, 2000)) in preadolescent boys lacking the Taq1 high-risk allele. However, in boys with one or two copies of this allele, cognitive scores were negatively correlated with family stress scores. There were no differences in performance scores between boys from low-risk and high-risk family environments, regardless of genotype. Ozkaragoz and Noble (2000) measured extraversion in a sample of children of alcoholic or control parents, under the hypothesis that children growing up in an alcoholic home would experience more environmental stress than those growing up in a non-alcoholic home. While there were no significant main effects of DRD2 genotype or family environment on extraversion, there was a significant gene–environment interaction such that children with the high-risk allele displayed greater levels of extraversion when living in an alcoholic than in a non-alcoholic home, again suggesting an increased sensitivity to stress in those indidivuals at high genetic risk.

Interestingly, among Honduran males living in a less stressful environment, subjects at low genetic risk (i.e. with no copies of the high-risk allele) received higher alcoholism scores than subjects at high genetic risk (Madrid *et al.*, 2001), and the adolescent boys at low genetic risk received higher extraversion scores when living in a non-alcoholic family than an alcoholic family (Ozkaragoz & Noble, 2000). In other words, results from these studies suggest that greater psychopathology is associated with a less stressful environment in subjects who do not possess the high-risk DRD2 Taq 1 allele. One potential explanation for this phenomenon is that individuals with different DRD2 genotypes might respond to stressors in different ways. For example, Ozkaragoz and Noble (2000) suggest that boys possessing the high-risk allele might cope with stress by increasing their level of activity, whereas boys with the low-risk allele might cope with stress by decreasing their activity. Thus it would be that in a less stressful environment, boys at low genetic risk would appear to be more active than boys at high genetic risk.

Gene–environment interaction in neurodevelopmental disorders

Neurodevelopmental disorders are particularly likely to express gene–environment interactions, because development itself is a dynamic process that results from a constant interplay between genetic and environmental determinants. The combination of these aetiological factors begins early in development, with a greater liability for psychopathology arising when genetic susceptibility interacts with adverse biological consequences of untoward environmental events in the prenatal or perinatal period. This aetiology may result in a variety of outcomes, based on the severity of both genetic and environmental 'loadings' for a particular disorder, and also on the presence or absence of other genetic and environmental 'protective factors', which may lower the risk for subsequent psychopathology. Two examples of neurodevelopmental disorders, autism and schizophrenia, will be reviewed for evidence of gene–environmental interactions.

While twin studies provide clear evidence of a genetic basis for autism (Bailey *et al.*, 1995; Folstein & Rutter, 1977; Gottesman & Hanson, 2005; Muhle *et al.*, 2004) (but see also Hallmayer *et al.*, 2002), environmental factors also play a major role, although convincing evidence for any particular environmental factor is lacking (London, 2000). For example, twin studies show evidence of increased obstetrical complications (OCs) among autistic members of discordant MZ twin pairs (Folstein & Rutter, 1977; Steffenburg *et al.*, 1989), but perinatal adversity may be a consequence, rather than cause, of autism (Bailey, 1993). The work of Pletnikov *et al.* (2002a) provides an example of how animal models may be used to test hypotheses about gene–environment interactions. Viral infections have been hypothesized to play a role in autistic disorders (Chess, 1977; Johnson, 1998), and neonatal Borna disease virus (BDV) infection has been used as an experimental teratogen in animal studies to induce neurodevelopmental damage and behavioural deficits similar to those found in autistic spectrum disorders. Pletnikov *et al.* (2002b) exposed different strains of rats to BDV neonatally to study potential gene–environment interactions. Significant strain differences were evident in brain pathology, behaviour, neurochemistry (monoamine brain systems), and in the response to pharmacological treatments. For instance, one strain displayed a significantly greater thinning of the neocortex than the other, which was associated with greater novelty-induced hyperactivity and impaired habituation of the acoustic startle response in a prepulse inhibition paradigm. Results such as these provide support for an interaction between specific environmental risk factors (i.e. viral infection) and genetic liability (i.e. the strain of mouse) in the aetiology of a neurodevelopmental disorder, and suggest novel avenues for research into other putative disorders of neurodevelopment.

The importance of both genetic and environmental factors in schizophrenia is well established in behavioural genetic and, more recently, molecular genetic studies (Gottesman, 2001; Gottesman & Hanson, 2005). While the risk of developing schizophrenia is associated strongly with the number of shared genes between a family member and an individual with schizophrenia, no degree of shared genes results in a certainty of developing the illness. For example, having two parents or an MZ twin with schizophrenia results in a risk of approximately 50% for developing the disorder. If having the same genes were the only aetiological factor, then the risk should be close to 100% in these cases (Faraone *et al.*, 1999). Instead, the interaction between genetic liability and environmental factors plays an important role in determining outcome. Environmental factors implicated in the development of schizophrenia range from biological to psychosocial in nature and include, among others, pregnancy and birth complications, location of birth/residence, and family environment (Brown, 2006; Read *et al.*, 2005; Spauwen *et al.*, 2006; Tsuang *et al.*, 2001).

Recently, we modified Paul Meehl's use of the term 'schizotaxia' (Meehl, 1962) to describe the liability to schizophrenia or schizophrenia-like conditions based on the theoretical premise that the neurobiological basis for schizophrenia is formed by the integrated effect of genes and adverse environmental risk factors. Our reformulation (Faraone *et al.*, 2001; Stone *et al.*, 2005) describes genetically vulnerable individuals who are probably exposed to early adverse events (e.g. OCs) that result in abnormal development of certain brain structures. This liability presents from childhood as schizotaxia, which is expressed through a combination of cognitive, neurobiological, and social skill deficits that vary in severity. For most individuals, the condition remains stable throughout their lifespan, but for some, a combination of the liability with later adverse environmental events (e.g. substance abuse or stressful psychosocial circumstances) may predispose individuals to develop psychosis and chronic schizophrenia.

Consistent with the view of schizotaxia as resulting from a combination of genetic and environmental factors, several studies demonstrate evidence for an interaction between neonatal insults and genetic susceptibility to schizophrenia. For example, these insults likely include OCs and exposure to viral infections (including herpes simplex) (Tsuang & Faraone, 1995a). The times of greatest vulnerability to the developing brain may include the second and third trimesters of pregnancy. During this period, environmental factors may disrupt neuronal migration of cells to the cortex, which results in abnormal development of the prefrontal cortex, the entorhinal cortex, and the hippocampus (Arnold & Trojanowski, 1996).

Delivery complications associated with increased risk for schizophrenia include foetal hypoxia, ischaemia, extreme prematurity, low birth weight, and post-term birth. Overall, pre-eclampsia has the highest individual obstetric risk factor for schizophrenia (Jones & Cannon, 1998). Pre-eclampsia, leading to hypoxia during pregnancy, results in foetal malnutrition including lack of oxygen, iodine, glucose, and iron. Chronic hypoxia can result in restricted foetal growth and subtle damage to brain regions. Moreover, blood and oxygen deprivation due to pre-eclampsia during delivery can also result in injury to the hippocampus and cortex (Dalman *et al.*, 1999). Seidman *et al.* (2000), utilising the New England cohort of the US National Collaborative Perinatal Project, demonstrated a relationship between obstetrical complications and neuropsychological deficits in children at seven years of age. Low birth weight had the strongest association with neuropsychological impairments, followed by an index of inferred hypoxic insults, and then by maternal conditions suggesting chronic hypoxia.

Zornberg *et al.* (2000) reported results from a 19-year follow-up study of a large sample of individuals with a previously documented history of birth complications, and of matched controls. The individuals with a history of birth complications were classified according to whether or not the complications were hypoxic-ischaemia-related. A significant relationship occurred between hypoxic-ischaemia-related complications and increased risk for schizophrenia. These data thus suggested that pregnancy and birth complications interacted with genetic liability to increase the likelihood of subsequently developing schizophrenia. Consistent with these findings, Cannon (1996) reported a dose-dependent relationship between risk of schizophrenia and severity of perinatal hypoxia in offspring of schizophrenic parents. In contrast, birth complications were unrelated to the development of schizophrenia in a control, low-risk group whose parents did not have schizophrenia. Similarly, Parnas *et al.* (1982) followed-up offspring of mothers with severe schizophrenia and found the risk of developing the illness was highest for those who were exposed to perinatal complications. Pregnancy and birth complications themselves occur more frequently in schizophrenic mothers compared to normal controls (Geddes & Lawrie, 1995; Jablensky, 1995; Lewis & Murray, 1987; Tsuang & Faraone, 1995b), which raises the level of risk for their (already vulnerable) children further.

Other studies also examined relationships between OCs and structural brain abnormalities in individuals with schizophrenia and their relatives (Cannon *et al.*, 1993; Jones & Cannon, 1998). Among these relationships, increases in ventricular enlargement in individuals at increasing genetic risk for schizophrenia interacted with OCs, with the association between ventricular enlargement and OCs increasing with the degree of genetic risk. Suddath *et al.* (1990) reported larger ventricles and greater temporal lobe volumes in the affected co-twin of MZ pairs discordant for schizophrenia. These structural differences were associated with higher rates of OCs in the affected co-twins (McNeil *et al.*, 2000). Cannon *et al.* (2002) reported that foetal hypoxia was associated with reduced cortical grey matter and increased cerebrospinal fluid among patients with schizophrenia and their non-psychotic siblings, but not among controls. Effect sizes were greatest for low birthweight subjects, consistent with other findings showing higher rates of subsequent schizophrenia in individuals subjected to prenatal underdevelopment (Cannon *et al.*, 1997; Fish *et al.*, 1992; Rifkin *et al.*, 1994). The relationship between hypoxia and brain abnormalities was stronger among patients than siblings, and hypoxia was related to ventricular enlargement only among patients, both findings consistent with a gene–environment interaction model in which the liability to schizophrenia is increased in the presence of environmental risk factors. While hypoxia did not occur more frequently among patients than among their unaffected siblings in this study, Rosso *et al.* (2000), using the same sample, found a greater number of hypoxic-associated OCs among early-onset than among late-onset cases or siblings, as well as an almost three-fold increased risk of early-onset schizophrenia per hypoxic OC.

Seasonality of birth is another possible environmental risk factor for schizophrenia, with winter–spring births being associated with increased risk (Jones *et al.*, 1998). The increase could be due to a higher incidence of maternal infection (e.g. influenza), and the cumulative evidence from many studies suggests that maternal influenza infection in pregnancy, leading to foetal brain damage, is associated with an increased risk for schizophrenia (Munk-Jorgensen & Ewald, 2001). Support for a gene–environment interaction effect involving winter birth comes from a study by Pulver *et al.* (1992), in which winter birth was associated with a positive family history in schizophrenic probands, although associations in the absence of family history occur as well (O'Callaghan *et al.*, 1991; Shur, 1982; also see Chapter 10).

Conclusions

The nature–nurture controversy is far less germane than it once was for understanding psychiatric disorders. Research clearly shows that both nature and nuture play important roles in the genesis of psychopathology. As the preceding discussion showed, gene–environment interactions are evident both in a broad variety of mental disorders and also in a wide range of experimental methodologies used to assess the relative contributions of genes and environment in mental disorders.

The salience of this issue will only increase as advances in neuroscience and molecular biology identify new potential sources of gene–environment interaction. For example, while many studies have focused on relationships between specific alleles and clinical diagnoses, or between independent measures of clinical function and clinical diagnoses, there is a growing focus on 'endophenotypic' expressions of mental disorders. Endophenotypes are features that are somewhat intermediate between the genotype and phenotype for a particular disorder (Gottesman, 1991; Gottesman & Gould, 2003) and often involve cognitive or neurobiological functions. Because endophenotypes may be closer to their underlying aetiologies, they open windows on the mechanisms involved in both normal and abnormal mental functions. For example, in both patients with schizophrenia and normal controls, Egan *et al.* (2001) showed that a common polymorphism in the catechol-O-methyltransferase (COMT) gene produced a four-fold range in COMT activity and dopamine catabolism. The range of COMT activity in both groups was associated with a related range of performance on a neuropsychological test of executive function, and on the efficiency of prefrontal and cingulate cortical function during an information-processing test. Because many mental functions and mental disorders are complex, multifactorial, polygenetic conditions (Faraone *et al.*, 1999; Gottesman, 2001; Gottesman & Gould, 2003; Moldin & Gottesman, 1997), results from studies like that by Egan *et al.* clarify specific mechanisms that are likely to contribute to both efficient and inefficient biological function, and thus to mental function and dysfunction. This in turn provides increasing opportunities to specify environmental contingencies that interact with these mechanisms to increase or decrease the liability for mental disorders. At this point, multiple genes have been proposed to increase vulnerability to schizophrenia (Harrison & Weinberger, 2005), and these are also likely to interact with environmental contingencies.

As candidate genes are identified, their expression may be assessed under different environmental circumstances, and sources of modulation may be identified more directly than through broad environmental stimuli, such as an urban environment, or an obstetrical complication. Mechanisms of DNA methylation, for example, represent a promising direction for understanding how gene expression may be modulated in different environments (Abdolmaleky *et al.*, 2004). Similarly, the utilization of gene expression techniques in genomic analyses will allow more direct ways to assess gene–environment interactions in the near future (Mirnics & Pevsner, 2004; Tsuang *et al.*, 2005).

Ultimately, then, the study of gene–environment interactions will further our understanding of how to identify, diagnose, and treat mental disorders. As the pool of potential treatment targets increases, so will opportunities for the development of early intervention strategies for many common but difficult-to-treat mental disorders (Faraone *et al.*, 2002; Tsuang *et al.*, 2000, 2002). While the study of gene–environment interactions is but one of several promising ways to approach that goal, its potential warrants additional attention.

Acknowledgements

Preparation of this chapter was supported, in part, by the National Institute of Mental Health (NIMH) Grants 43518 and 065571 (COGS: Consortium on the Genetics of Schizophrenia). Portions of this chapter were originally published as Tsuang, M. T., Bar, J. L., Stone, W. S. and Faraone, S. V. (2004) 'Gene–environment interactions in mental disorders'. *World Psychiatry*, *3*, 73–83.

References

Abdolmaleky, H. M., Smith, C. L., Faraone, S. V., Shafa, R., Stone, W., Glatt, S. J. and Tsuang, M. T. (2004) 'Methylomics in psychiatry: modulation of gene–environment interactions may be through DNA methylation'. *American Journal of Medical Genetics (Neuropsychiatric Genetics)*, *127B*(1), 51–59.

Anisman, H., Zaharia, M. D., Meaney, M. J. and Merali, Z. (1998) 'Do early-life events permanently alter behavioral and hormonal responses to stressors?'. *International Journal of Developmental Neuroscience*, *16*, 149–164.

Arnold, S. E. and Trojanowski, J. Q. (1996) 'Recent advances in defining the neuropathology of schizophrenia'. *Acta Neuropathologica (Berl.)*, *92*, 217–231.

Bailey, A., Le Couteur, A., Gottesman, I., Bolton, P., Simonoff, E., Yuzda, E. and Rutter, M. (1995) 'Autism as a strongly genetic disorder: evidence from a British twin study'. *Psychological Medicine*, *25*, 63–77.

Bailey, A. J. (1993) 'The biology of autism'. *Psychological Medicine*, *23*, 7–11.

Bennett, A. J., Lesch, K. P., Heils, A., Long, J. C., Lorenz, J. G., Shoaf, S. E., Champoux, M., Suomi, S. J., Linnoila, M. V. and Higley, J. D. (2002) 'Early experience and serotonin transporter gene variation interact to influence primate CNS function'. *Molecular Psychiatry*, 7, 118–122.

Berman, S. M. and Noble, E. P. (1995) 'Reduced visuospatial performance in children with the D2 dopamine receptor A1 allele'. *Behaviour Genetics*, *25*, 45–58.

Berman, S. M. and Noble, E. P. (1997) 'The D2 dopamine receptor (DRD2) gene and family stress; interactive effects on cognitive functions in children'. *Behaviour Genetics*, *27*, 33–43.

Blum, K., Noble, E. P., Sheridan, P. J., Montgomery, A., Ritchie, T., Jagadeeswaran, P., Nogami, H., Briggs, A. H. and Cohn, J. B. (1990) 'Allelic association of human dopamine D2 receptor gene in alcoholism'. *Journal of the American Medical Association*, *263*, 2055–2060.

Boomsma, D. I., de Geus, E. J., van Baal, G. C. and Koopmans, J. R. (1999) 'A religious upbringing reduces the influence of genetic factors on disinhibition: evidence for interaction between genotype and environment on personality'. *Twin Research*, *2*, 115–125.

Bracha, H. S., Torrey, E. F., Bigelow, L. B., Lohr, J. B. and Linington, B. B. (1991) 'Subtle signs of prenatal maldevelopment of the hand ectoderm in schizophrenia: a preliminary monozygotic twin study'. *Biological Psychiatry*, *30*, 719–725.

Bronfenbrenner, U. and Ceci, S. J. (1994) 'Nature–nurture reconceptualized in developmental perspective: a bio-ecological model'. *Psychological Review*, *101*, 568–586.

Brown, A. S. (2006) 'Prenatal infection as a risk factor for schizophrenia'. *Schizophrenia Bulletin*, *32*, 200–202.

Cadoret, R. (1985) 'Environment and their interaction in the development of psychopathology', in Sakai, T. and Tsuboi, T. (eds), *Genetic aspects of human behavior*. Tokyo: Igaku Shoin.

Cadoret, R. and Cain, C. A. (1981) 'Environmental and genetic factors in predicting antisocial behavior in adoptees'. *Psychiatric Journal of the University of Ottawa, 6*, 225.

Cadoret, R. J., Cain, C. A. and Crowe, R. R. (1983) 'Evidence for gene–environment interaction in the development of adolescent antisocial behavior'. *Behaviour Genetics, 13*, 301–310.

Cadoret, R. J., Yates, W. R., Troughton, E., Woodworth, G. and Stewart, M. A. (1995) 'Genetic–environmental interaction in the genesis of aggressivity and conduct disorders'. *Archives of General Psychiatry, 52*, 916–924.

Cadoret, R. J., Winokur, G., Langbehn, D., Troughton, E., Yates, W. R. and Stewart, M. A. (1996) 'Depression spectrum disease, I: the role of gene–environment interaction'. *American Journal of Psychiatry, 153*, 892–899.

Cannon, M., Jones, P., Gilvarry, C., Rifkin, L., McKenzie, K., Foerster, A. and Murray, R. M. (1997) 'Premorbid social functioning in schizophrenia and bipolar disorder: similarities and differences'. *American Journal of Psychiatry, 154*, 1544–1550.

Cannon, T. D. (1996) 'Abnormalities of brain structure and function in schizophrenia: implications for aetiology and pathophysiology'. *Annals of Medicine, 28*, 533–539.

Cannon, T. D., Mednick, S. A., Parnas, J., Schulsinger, F., Praestholm, J. and Vestergaard, A. (1993) 'Developmental brain abnormalities in the offspring of schizophrenic mothers. I. Contributions of genetic and perinatal factors'. *Archives of General Psychiatry, 50*, 551–564.

Cannon, T. D., van Erp, T. G., Rosso, I. M., Huttunen, M., Lonnqvist, J., Pirkola, T., Salonen, O., Valanne, L., Poutanen, V. P. and Standertskjold-Nordenstam, C. G. (2002) 'Fetal hypoxia and structural brain abnormalities in schizophrenic patients, their siblings, and controls'. *Archives of General Psychiatry, 59*, 35–41.

Champoux, M., Bennett, A., Shannon, C., Higley, J. D., Lesch, K. P. and Suomi, S. J. (2002) 'Serotonin transporter gene polymorphism, differential early rearing, and behavior in rhesus monkey neonates'. *Molecular Psychiatry*, 7, 1058–1063.

Chess, S. (1977) 'Follow-up report on autism in congenital rubella'. *Journal of Autism and Childhood Schizophrenia*, 7, 69–81.

Cloninger, C. R., Bohman, M. and Sigvardsson, S. (1981) 'Inheritance of alcohol abuse: cross-fostering analysis of adopted men'. *Archives of General Psychiatry, 38*, 861–868.

Cloninger, C. R., Sigvardsson, S., Bohman, M. and von Knorring, A. L. (1982) 'Predisposition to petty criminality in Swedish adoptees. II. Cross-fostering analysis of gene–environment interaction'. *Archives of General Psychiatry, 39*, 1242–1247.

Connor, B. T., Noble, E. P., Berman, S. M., Ozkaragoz, T., Ritchie, T., Antolin, T. and Sheen, C. (2005) 'DRD2 genotypes and substance use in adolescent children of alcoholics'. *Drug and Alcohol Dependence, 79*, 379–387.

Cooper, B. (2001) 'Nature, nurture and mental disorder: old concepts in the new millennium'. *British Journal of Psychiatry, 178*, 91–101.

Corder, E. H., Saunders, A. M., Strittmatter, W. J., Schmechel, D. E., Gaskell, P. C., Small, G. W., Roses, A. D., Haines, J. L. and Pericak-Vance, M. A. (1993) 'Gene dose of apolipoprotein E type 4 allele and the risk of Alzheimer's disease in late onset families'. *Science, 261*, 921–923.

Crabbe, J. C. (2003) 'Finding genes for complex behaviors: progress in mouse models of the addictions', in Plomin, R., DeFries J. C., Craig I.W. and McGuffin, P. (eds), *Behavioral genetics in the postgenomic era*. Washington: APA Books.

Cutrona, C. E., Cadoret, R. J., Suhr, J. A., Richards, C. C., Troughton, E., Schutte, K. and

Woodworth, G. (1994) 'Interpersonal variables in the prediction of alcoholism among adoptees: evidence for gene–environment interactions'. *Comprehensive Psychiatry, 35*, 171–179.

Dalman, C., Allebeck, P., Cullberg, J., Grunewald, C. and Koster, M. (1999) 'Obstetric complications and the risk of schizophrenia: a longitudinal study of a national birth cohort'. *Archives of General Psychiatry, 56*, 234–240.

Dick, D. M., Rose, R. J., Viken, R. J., Kaprio, J. and Koskenvuo, M. (2001) 'Exploring gene–environment interactions: socioregional moderation of alcohol use'. *Journal of Abnormal Psychology, 110*, 625–632.

Egan, M. F., Goldberg, T. E., Kolachana, B. S., Callicott, J. H., Mazzanti, C. M., Straub, R. E., Goldman, D. and Weinberger, D. R. (2001) 'Effect of COMT Val108/158 Met genotype on frontal lobe function and risk for schizophrenia'. *Proceedings of the National Academy of Sciences of the United States of America, 98*, 6917–6922.

Eley, T. C., Sugden, K., Corsico, A., Gregory, A. M., Sham, P., McGuffin, P., Plomin, R. and Craig, I. W. (2004) 'Gene–environment interaction analysis of serotonin system markers with adolescent depression'. *Molecular Psychiatry, 9*, 908–915.

Faraone, S. V., Tsuang, D. and Tsuang, M. T. (1999) *Genetics of mental disorders: A guide for students, clinicians, and researchers*. New York: Guilford.

Faraone, S. V., Brown, C. H., Glatt, S. J. and Tsuang, M. T. (2002) 'Preventing schizophrenia and psychotic behaviour: definitions and methodological issues'. *Canadian Journal of Psychiatry, 47*, 527–537.

Faraone, S. V., Green, A. I., Seidman, L. J. and Tsuang, M. T. (2001) ' "Schizotaxia": clinical implications and new directions for research'. *Schizophrenia Bulletin, 27*, 1–18.

Finlay-Jones, R. and Brown, G. W. (1981) 'Types of stressful life event and the onset of anxiety and depressive disorders'. *Psychological Medicine, 11*, 803–815.

Fish, B., Marcus, J., Hans, S. L., Auerbach, J. G. and Perdue, S. (1992) 'Infants at risk for schizophrenia: sequelae of a genetic neurointegrative defect: a review and replication analysis of pandysmaturation in the Jerusalem Infant Development Study'. *Archives of General Psychiatry, 49*, 221–235.

Folstein, S. and Rutter, M. (1977) 'Infantile autism: a genetic study of 21 twin pairs'. *Journal of Child Psychology and Psychiatry, 18*, 297–321.

Ge, X. J., Confer, R. D. and Cadoret, R. J. (1996) 'The developmental interface between nature and nurture: a mutual influence model of child antisocial behavior and parent behaviors'. *Developmental Psychology, 32*, 574–589.

Geddes, J. R. and Lawrie, S. M. (1995) 'Obstetric complications and schizophrenia: a meta-analysis'. *British Journal of Psychiatry, 167*, 786–793.

Gillespie, N. A., Whitfield, J. B., Williams, D., Heath, A. C. and Martin, N. G. (2004) 'The relationship between stressful life events, the serotonin transporter (5-HTTLPR) genotype and major depression'. *Psychological Medicine, 35*, 101–111.

Glatt, S. J., Faraone, S. V. and Tsuang, M. T. (2003) 'Meta-analysis identifies an association between the dopamine D2 receptor gene and schizophrenia'. *Molecular Psychiatry, 8*, 911–915.

Gorwood, P., Batel, P., Gouya, L., Courtois, F. and Feingold, J. (2000) 'Reappraisal of the association between the DRD2 gene, alcoholism and addiction'. *European Psychiatry, 15*, 90–96.

Gottesman, I. I. (1991) *Schizophrenia genesis: The origin of madness*, New York: Freeman.

Gottesman, I. I. (2001) 'Psychopathology through a life-span genetic prism'. *American Psychologist, 56*, 864–878.

Gottesman, I. I. and Gould, T. D. (2003) 'The endophenotype concept in psychiatry: etymology and strategic intentions'. *American Journal of Psychiatry, 160*, 636–645.

Gottesman, I. I. and Hanson, D. R. (2005) 'Human development: biological and genetic processes'. *Annual Review of Psychology, 56*, 263–286.

Hallmayer, J., Glasson, E. J., Bower, C., Petterson, B., Croen, L., Grether, J. and Risch, N. (2002) 'On the twin risk in autism'. *American Journal of Human Genetics, 71*, 941–946.

Harrison, P. J., and Weinberger, D. R. (2005) 'Schizophrenia genes, gene expression, and neuropathology: on the matter of their convergence'. *Molecular Psychiatry, 10*, 40–68.

Heath, A. C., Eaves, L. J. and Martin, N. G. (1998) 'Interaction of marital status and genetic risk for symptoms of depression'. *Twin Research, 1*, 119–122.

Heath, A. C., Jardine, R. and Martin, N. G. (1989) 'Interactive effects of genotype and social environment on alcohol consumption in female twins'. *Journal of Studies on Alcohol, 50*, 38–48.

Higuchi, S. (1994) 'Polymorphisms of ethanol metabolizing enzyme genes and alcoholism'. *Alcohol and Alcoholism*, Supplement 2, 29–34.

Higuchi, S., Matsushita, S., Imazeki, H., Kinoshita, T., Takagi, S. and Kono, H. (1994) 'Aldehyde dehydrogenase genotypes in Japanese alcoholics'. *Lancet, 343*, 741–742.

Hill, S. Y., Shen, S., Lowers, L. and Locke, J. (2000) 'Factors predicting the onset of adolescent drinking in families at high risk for developing alcoholism'. *Biological Psychiatry, 48*, 265–275.

Jablensky, A. (1995) 'Schizophrenia: recent epidemiologic issues'. *Epidemiologic Reviews, 17*, 10–20.

Johnson, R. T. (1998) *Viral infections of the nervous system*. Philadelphia: Lippincott-Raven.

Jones, P. and Cannon, M. (1998) 'The new epidemiology of schizophrenia'. *Psychiatric Clinics of North America, 21*, 1–25.

Jones, P. B., Rantakallio, P., Hartikainen, A.-L., Isohanni, M. and Sipila, P. (1998) 'Schizophrenia as a long-term outcome of pregnancy, delivery, and perinatal complications: a 28-year follow-up of the 1966 North Finland general population birth cohort'. *American Journal of Psychiatry, 155*, 355–364.

Kendler, K. S. (1996) 'Major depression and generalised anxiety disorder: same genes, (partly) different environments – revisited'. *British Journal of Psychiatry*, Supplement 30, 68–75.

Kendler, K. S. and Eaves, L. J. (1986) 'Models for the joint effect of genotype and environment on liability to psychiatric illness'. *American Journal of Psychiatry, 143*, 279–289.

Kendler, K. S., Heath, A. C., Martin, N. G. and Eaves, L. J. (1987) 'Symptoms of anxiety and symptoms of depression: same genes, different environments?'. *Archives of General Psychiatry, 44*, 451–457.

Kendler, K. S., Kuhm, J. W., Vittum, J., Prescott, C. A. and Riley, B. (2005) 'The interaction of stressful life events and a serotonin transporter polymorphism in the prediction of episodes of major depression'. *Archives of General Psychiatry, 62*, 529–535.

Kendler, K. S., Neale, M. C., Kessler, R. C., Heath, A. C. and Eaves, L. J. (1992) 'Major depression and generalized anxiety disorder. Same genes, (partly) different environments?' *Archives of General Psychiatry, 49*, 716–722.

Kendler, K. S., Kessler, R. C., Walters, E. E., MacLean, C., Neale, M. C., Heath, A. C. and Eaves, L. J. (1995) 'Stressful life events, genetic liability, and onset of an episode of major depression in women'. *American Journal of Psychiatry, 152*, 833–842.

Khoury, M. J. and Beaty, T. H. (1987) 'Recurrence risks in the presence of single gene susceptibility to environmental agents'. *American Journal of Medical Genetics, 28*, 159–169.

Khoury, M. J., Adams, M. J., Jr and Flanders, W. D. (1988) 'An epidemiologic approach to ecogenetics'. *American Journal of Human Genetics, 42*, 89–95.

Khoury, M. J., Beaty, T. H. and Cohen, B. H. (1993) *Fundamentals of genetic epidemiology*. New York: Oxford University Press.

Koopmans, J. R., Slutske, W. S., van Baal, G. C. and Boomsma, D. I. (1999) 'The influence of religion on alcohol use initiation: evidence for genotype X environment interaction'. *Behavioural Genetics, 29*, 445–453.

Kramer, D. A. (2005) 'Commentary: gene–environment interplay in the context of genetics, epigenetics and gene expression'. *Journal of the Academy of Child and Adolescent Psychiatry, 44*, 19–27.

Lesch, K. P. (2003) 'Neuroticism and serotonin: a developmental genetic perspective', in Plomin, R., DeFries, J. C. and Craig, I. W. (eds), *Behavioral genetics in the postgenomic era*. Washington, DC: APA Books.

Lesch, K. P., Bengel, D., Heils, A., Sabol, S. Z., Greenberg, B. D., Petri, S., Benjamin, J., Muller, C. R., Hamer, D. H. and Murphy, D. L. (1996) 'Association of anxiety-related traits with a polymorphism in the serotonin transporter gene regulatory region'. *Science, 274*, 1527–1531.

Lewis, S. W. and Murray, R. M. (1987) 'Obstetric complications, neurodevelopmental deviance, and risk of schizophrenia'. *Journal of Psychiatric Research, 21*, 413–421.

London, E. A. (2000) 'The environment as an etiologic factor in autism: a new direction for research'. *Environmental Health Perspectives, 108*, Supplement 3, 401–404.

MacGregor, A. J., Snieder, H., Schork, N. J. and Spector, T. D. (2000) 'Twins: novel uses to study complex traits and genetic diseases'. *Trends in Genetics, 16*, 131–134.

Madrid, G. A., MacMurray, J., Lee, J. W., Anderson, B. A. and Comings, D. E. (2001) 'Stress as a mediating factor in the association between the DRD2 TaqI polymorphism and alcoholism'. *Alcohol, 23*, 117–122.

Malaspina, D., Goetz, R. R., Friedman, J. H., Kaufmann, C. A., Faraone, S. V., Tsuang, M., Cloninger, C. R., Nurnberger, J. I., Jr and Blehar, M. C. (2001) 'Traumatic brain injury and schizophrenia in members of schizophrenia and bipolar disorder pedigrees'. *American Journal of Psychiatry, 158*, 440–446.

Mayeux, R., Ottman, R., Tang, M. X., Noboa-Bauza, L., Marder, K., Gurland, B. and Stern, Y. (1993) 'Genetic susceptibility and head injury as risk factors for Alzheimer's disease among community-dwelling elderly persons and their first-degree relatives'. *Annals of Neurology, 33*, 494–501.

Mayeux, R., Ottman, R., Maestre, G., Ngai, C., Tang, M. X., Ginsberg, H., Chun, M., Tycko, B. and Shelanski, M. (1995) 'Synergistic effects of traumatic head injury and apolipoprotein-epsilon 4 in patients with Alzheimer's disease'. *Neurology, 45*, 555–557.

McGue, M. and Bouchard, T. J., Jr (1998) 'Genetic and environmental influences on human behavioral differences'. *Annual Review of Neuroscience, 21*, 1–24.

McNeil, T. F., Cantor-Graae, E. and Weinberger, D. R. (2000) 'Relationship of obstetric complications and differences in size of brain structures in monozygotic twin pairs discordant for schizophrenia'. *American Journal of Psychiatry, 157*, 203–212.

McNeil, T. F., Cantor-Graae, E., Torrey, E. F., Sjostrom, K., Bowler, A., Taylor, E., Rawlings, R. and Higgins, E. S. (1994) 'Obstetric complications in histories of monozygotic twins discordant and concordant for schizophrenia'. *Acta Psychiatrica Scandinavica, 89*, 196–204.

Mednick, S. A., Gabrielli, W. F., Jr. and Hutchings, B. (1984) 'Genetic influences in criminal convictions: evidence from an adoption cohort'. *Science*, *224*, 891–894.

Meehl, P. E. (1962) 'Schizotaxia, schizotypy, schizophrenia'. *American Psychologist, 17*, 827–838.

Mirnics, K. and Pevsner, J. (2004) 'Progress in the use of microarray technology to study the neurobiology of disease'. *Nature Neuroscience*, 7, 1–6.

Moffitt, T. E., Caspi, A., and Rutter, M. (2005) 'Strategies for investigating interactions between measured genes and measured environments'. *Archives of General Psychiatry, 62*, 473–481.

Moldin, S. O. and Gottesman, I. I. (1997) 'At issue: genes, experience, and chance in schizophrenia – positioning for the 21st century'. *Schizophrenia Bulletin, 23*, 547–561.

Monson, T. C. and Snyder, M. (1997) 'Actors, observers, and the attribution process: toward a reconceptualization'. *Journal of Experimental Social Psychology, 13*, 89–111.

Mortimer, J. A., French, L. R., Hutton, J. T. and Schuman, L. M. (1985) 'Head injury as a risk factor for Alzheimer's disease'. *Neurology, 35*, 264–267.

Muhle, R., Trentacoste, S. V. and Rapin, I. (2004) 'The genetics of autism'. *Pediatrics, 113*, 472–486.

Munk-Jorgensen, P. and Ewald, H. (2001) 'Epidemiology in neurobiological research: exemplified by the influenza–schizophrenia theory'. *British Journal of Psychiatry, 178*, 30–32.

Nalbantoglu, J., Gilfix, B. M., Bertrand, P., Robitaille, Y., Gauthier, S., Rosenblatt, D. S. and Poirier, J. (1994) 'Predictive value of apolipoprotein E genotyping in Alzheimer's disease: results of an autopsy series and an analysis of several combined studies'. *Annals of Neurology, 36*, 889–895.

Noble, E. P. (1998) 'The D2 dopamine receptor gene: a review of association studies in alcoholism and phenotypes'. *Alcohol, 16*, 33–45.

Noble, E. P. (2003) 'D2 dopamine receptor gene in psychiatric and neurologic disorders and its phenotypes'. *American Journal of Medical Genetics, Part B, Neuropsychiatric Genetics, 116*, 103–125.

O'Callaghan, E., Gibson, T., Colohan, H. A., Walshe, D., Buckley, P., Larkin, C. and Waddington, J. L. (1991) 'Season of birth in schizophrenia: evidence for confinement of an excess of winter births to patients without a family history of mental disorder'. *British Journal of Psychiatry, 158*, 764–769.

O'Connor, T. G., Deater-Deckard, K., Fulker, D., Rutter, M. and Plomin, R. (1998) 'Genotype–environment correlations in late childhood and early adolescence: antisocial behavioral problems and coercive parenting'. *Developmental Psychology, 34*, 970–981.

Ohara, K., Nagai, M., Suzuki, Y., Ochiai, M. and Ohara, K. (1998) 'Association between anxiety disorders and a functional polymorphism in the serotonin transporter gene'. *Psychiatry Research, 81*, 277–279.

Ottman, R. (1996) 'Gene–environment interaction: definitions and study designs'. *Preventive Medicine, 25*, 764–770.

Ozkaragoz, T. and Noble, E. P. (2000) 'Extraversion: interaction between D2 dopamine receptor polymorphisms and parental alcoholism'. *Alcohol, 22*, 139–146.

Parnas, J., Schulsinger, F., Teasdale, T. W., Schulsinger, H., Feldman, P. M. and Mednick, S. A. (1982) 'Perinatal complications and clinical outcome within the schizophrenia spectrum'. *British Journal of Psychiatry, 140*, 416–420.

Pato, C. N., Macciardi, F., Pato, M. T., Verga, M. and Kennedy, J. L. (1993) 'Review of the putative association of dopamine D2 receptor and alcoholism: a meta-analysis'. *American Journal of Medical Genetics (Neuropsychiatric Genetics)*, *48*, 78–82.

Phillips, T. J., Belknap, J. K., Hitzemann, R. J., Buck, K. J., Cunningham, C. L. and Crabbe, J. C. (2002) 'Harnessing the mouse to unravel the genetics of human disease'. *Genes Brain and Behaviour*, *1*, 14–26.

Pletnikov, M. V., Rubin, S. A., Vogel, M. W., Moran, T. H. and Carbone, K. M. (2002a) 'Effects of genetic background on neonatal Borna disease virus infection-induced neurodevelopmental damage. I. Brain pathology and behavioral deficits'. *Brain Research*, *944*, 97–107.

Pletnikov, M. V., Rubin, S. A., Vogel, M. W., Moran, T. H. and Carbone, K. M. (2002b) 'Effects of genetic background on neonatal Borna disease virus infection-induced neurodevelopmental damage. II. Neurochemical alterations and responses to pharmacological treatments'. *Brain Research*, *944*, 108–123.

Prescott, C. A., Caldwell, C. B., Carey, G., Vogler, G. P., Trumbetta, S. L. and Gottesman, I. I. (2005) 'The Washington University twin study of alcoholism'. *American Journal of Medical Genetics (Neuropsychiatric Genetics)*, *134B*, 48–55.

Pulver, A. E., Liang, K. Y., Brown, C. H., Wolyniec, P., McGrath, J., Adler, L., Tam, D., Carpenter, W. T. and Childs, B. (1992) 'Risk factors in schizophrenia: season of birth, gender, and familial risk'. *British Journal of Psychiatry*, *160*, 65–71.

Read, J., van Os, J., Morrison, A. P., and Ross, C. A. (2005) 'Childhood trauma, psychosis and schizophrenia: a literature review with theoretical and clinical implications.' *Acta Psychiatrica Scandinavica*, *112*, 330–350.

Reynolds, C. A., Prince, J. A., Feuk, L., Brookes, A. J., Gatz, M. and Pedersen, N. (2006) 'Longitudinal memory performance during normal aging: twin association models of APOE and other Alzheimer candidate genes'. *Behavioral Genetics*, *36*, 185–194.

Rifkin, L., Lewis, S., Jones, P., Toone, B. and Murray, R. (1994) 'Low birth weight and schizophrenia'. *British Journal of Psychiatry*, *165*, 357–362.

Rose, R. J., Dick, D. M., Viken, R. J. and Kaprio, J. (2001) 'Gene–environment interaction in patterns of adolescent drinking: regional residency moderates longitudinal influences on alcohol use'. *Alcoholism, Clinical and Experimental Research*, *25*, 637–643.

Rosso, I. M., Cannon, T. D., Huttunen, T., Huttunen, M. O., Lonnqvist, J. and Gasperoni, T. L. (2000) 'Obstetric risk factors for early-onset schizophrenia in a Finnish birth cohort'. *American Journal of Psychiatry*, *157*, 801–807.

Roy, M. A., Neale, M. C., Pedersen, N. L., Mathe, A. A. and Kendler, K. S. (1995) 'A twin study of generalized anxiety disorder and major depression'. *Psychological Medicine*, *25*, 1037–1049.

Rutter, M. and Silberg, J. (2002) 'Gene–environment interplay in relation to emotional and behavioral disturbance'. *Annual Review of Psychology*, *53*, 463–490.

Rutter, M. L. (1997) 'Nature–nurture integration – the example of antisocial behavior'. *American Psychology*, *52*, 390–398.

Sanchez, M. M., Ladd, C. O. and Plotsky, P. M. (2001) 'Early adverse experience as a developmental risk factor for later psychopathology: evidence from rodent and primate models'. *Development and Psychopathology*, *13*, 419–449.

Scarr, S. and McCartney, K. (1983) 'How people make their own environments: a theory of genotype → environment effects'. *Child Development*, *54*, 424–435.

Seidman, L. J., Buka, S. L., Goldstein, J. M., Horton, N. J., Rieder, R. O. and Tsuang, M. T. (2000) 'The relationship of prenatal and perinatal complications to cognitive functioning at age 7 in the New England Cohorts of the National Collaborative Perinatal Project'. *Schizophrenia Bulletin*, *26*, 309–321.

Shur, E. (1982) 'Season of birth in high and low genetic risk schizophrenics'. *British Journal of Psychiatry, 140*, 410–415.

Silberg, J., Rutter, M., Neale, M. and Eaves, L. (2001) 'Genetic moderation of environmental risk for depression and anxiety in adolescent girls'. *British Journal of Psychiatry, 179*, 116–121.

Silberg, J., Pickles, A., Rutter, M., Hewitt, J., Simonoff, E., Maes, H., Carbonneau, R., Murrelle, L., Foley, D. and Eaves, L. (1999) 'The influence of genetic factors and life stress on depression among adolescent girls'. *Archives of General Psychiatry, 56*, 225–232.

Snyder, M. and Ickes, W. (1985) 'Personality and social behavior', in Lindze, G. and Aronson, E. (eds), *Handbook of social psychology*. New York: Random House.

Spauwen, J., Krabbendam, L., Lieb, R., Wittchen, H. U. and van Os, J. (2006) 'Evidence that the outcome of developmental expression of psychosis is worse for adolescents growing up in an urban environment'. *Psychological Medicine, 36*, 407–415.

Steffenburg, S., Gillberg, C., Hellgren, L., Andersson, L., Gillberg, I. C., Jakobsson, G. and Bohman, M. (1989) 'A twin study of autism in Denmark, Finland, Iceland, Norway and Sweden'. *Journal of Child Psychology and Psychiatry, 30*, 405–416.

Stone, W. S. and Gottesman, I. I. (1993) 'A perspective on the search for the causes of alcoholism: slow down the rush to genetical judgements'. *Neurological Psychiatry and Brain Research, 1*, 123–132.

Stone, W. S., Faraone, S. V., Seidman, L. J., Olson, E. A. and Tsuang, M. T. (2005) Searching for the liability to schizophrenia: concepts and methods underlying genetic high-risk studies of adolescents. *Journal of Child and Adolescent Psychopharmacology, 15*, 403–417.

Suddath, R. L., Christison, G. W., Torrey, E. F., Casanova, M. F. and Weinberger, D. R. (1990) 'Anatomical abnormalities in the brains of monozygotic twins discordant for schizophrenia'. *New England Journal of Medicine, 322*, 789–794.

Tienari, P. (1991) 'Interaction between genetic vulnerability and family environment: the Finnish adoptive family study of schizophrenia'. *Acta Psychiatrica Scandinavica, 84*, 460–465.

Tienari, P., Wynne, L. C., Sorri, A., Lahti, I., Laksy, K., Moring, J., Naarala, M., Nieminen, P. and Wahlberg, K.-E. (2004) 'Gene–environment interaction in schizophrenia-spectrum disorder'. *British Journal of Psychiatry, 184*, 216–222.

Tienari, P., Wynne, L. C., Moring, J., Lahti, I., Naarala, M., Sorri, A., Wahlberg, K. E., Saarento, O., Seitamaa, M., Kaleva, M. and Laksy, K. (1994) 'The Finnish adoptive family study of schizophrenia: implications for family research'. *British Journal of Psychiatry, 23*, 20–26.

Tsuang, M. T. and Faraone, S. V. (1995a) 'The case for heterogeneity in the etiology of schizophrenia'. *Schizophrenia Research, 17*, 161–175.

Tsuang, M. T. and Faraone, S. V. (1995b) 'Genetic heterogeneity of schizophrenia'. *Psychiatria et Neurologia Japonica, 97*, 485–501.

Tsuang, M. T., Stone, W. S. and Faraone, S. V. (2000) 'Towards the prevention of schizophrenia'. *Biological Psychiatry, 48*, 349–356.

Tsuang, M. T., Stone, W. S. and Faraone, S. V. (2001) 'Genes, environment and schizophrenia'. *British Journal of Psychiatry*, Supplement 40, 18–24.

Tsuang, M. T., Stone, W. S. and Faraone, S. V. (2002) 'Understanding predisposition to schizophrenia: toward intervention and prevention'. *Canadian Journal of Psychiatry, 47*, 518–526.

Tsuang, M. T., Nossova, N., Yager, T., Tsuang, M.-M., Guo, S.-C., Shyu, K. G., Glatt, S. J., and Liew, C. C. (2005) 'Assessing the validity of blood-based gene expression profiles for the classification of schizophrenia and bipolar disorder: a preliminary report'. *American Journal of Medical Genetics (Neuropsychiatric Genetics), 133B*, 1–5.

Van Duijn, C. M., Stijnen, T. and Hofman, A. (1991) 'Risk factors for Alzheimer's disease: overview of the EURODEM collaborative re-analysis of case–control studies. EURODEM Risk Factors Research Group'. *International Journal of Epidemiology, 20*, s4–s12.

Van Duijn, C. M., Clayton, D. G., Chandra, V., Fratiglioni, L., Graves, A. B., Heyman, A., Jorm, A. F., Kokmen, E., Kondo, K., Mortimer, J. A., Rocca, W. A., Shalat, S. L., Soinenen, H. and Hofman, A. (1994) 'Interaction between genetic and environmental risk factors for Alzheimer's disease: a reanalysis of case–control studies. EURODEM Risk Factors Research Group'. *Genetic Epidemiology, 11*, 539–551.

Vanyukov, M. M. and Tarter, R. E. (2000) 'Genetic studies of substance abuse'. *Drug and Alcohol Dependence, 59*, 101–123.

Wahlberg, K. E., Wynne, L. C., Oja, H., Keskitalo, P., Pykalainen, L., Lahti, I., Moring, J., Naarala, M., Sorri, A., Seitamaa, M., Laksy, K., Kolassa, J. and Tienari, P. (1997) 'Gene–environment interaction in vulnerability to schizophrenia: findings from the Finnish Adoptive Family Study of Schizophrenia'. *American Journal of Psychiatry, 154*, 355–362.

Whalley, L. J. (1991) 'Risk factors in Alzheimer's disease'. *British Medical Journal, 303*, 1215–1216.

Willerman, L., Loehlin, J. C. and Horn, J. M. (1992) 'An adoption and a cross-fostering study of the Minnesota Multiphasic Personality Inventory (MMPI) Psychopathic Deviate Scale'. *Behavioural Genetics, 22*, 515–529.

Winokur, G., Cadoret, R., Dorzab, J. and Baker, M. (1971) 'Depressive disease: a genetic study'. *Archives of General Psychiatry, 24*, 135–144.

Yang, Q. and Khoury, M. J. (1997) 'Evolving methods in genetic epidemiology. III. Gene–environment interaction in epidemiologic research'. *Epidemiologic Reviews, 19*, 33–43.

Zornberg, G. L., Buka, S. L. and Tsuang, M. T. (2000) 'Hypoxic-ischemia-related fetal/neonatal complications and risk of schizophrenia and other non-affective psychoses: a 19-year longitudinal study'. *American Journal of Psychiatry, 157*, 196–202.

3 Geographical perspectives on psychiatric disorder

Sarah Curtis

This chapter concerns the significance of space and place factors in mental health and psychiatric disorder; it discusses some relatively recent additions to the large body of geographical literature concerning environmental factors in mental health (earlier reviews include Freeman, 1984a). Studies of variation in psychiatric and psychosocial health suggest that spatial relationships both reflect and affect social relations (for example, see discussion by Kearns and Joseph (1993)) so that spatial patterns may often relate to social relations in complex ways. Geographical perspectives on health distinguish between space and place (this is discussed, for example, by Curtis & Jones, 1998).

Studies that focus on space may assess spatial patterns of health in terms of conventionally measurable distances and relative positions or, more abstractly, in terms of degrees of separation or of intensity of communications and linkages. These spatial perspectives allow us, for example, to examine how the health of populations is spatially associated with other population attributes, including social and economic conditions, giving rise to the ecological studies considered below. Geographical distributions of populations and facilities are important in social relations partly because of the ways that human interactions tend to vary in space. The tendency for these interactions to vary in inverse proportion with the distance to be travelled and in direct proportion to the degree of concentration of population is summarized in the 'gravity model'. As discussed below, this helps us to understand patterns of health service use. The model predicts that there will be greater interactions between places with larger populations, and fewer interactions between places that are more distant from each other.

Spatial segregation in different residential areas housing different socio-economic and ethnic groups is another manifestation of socio-spatial inter-relationships. The spatial separation may be a reflection of the 'social distance' between groups, but this separation may also contribute to the maintenance of social distance by making social interaction between groups less possible. Conversely, close geographical proximity of groups that see their interests as different or conflicting may seem to exacerbate existing social tensions, because proximity may heighten the awareness of these differences. Regardless of distance, levels of interaction are greater between large concentrations of people (e.g. large cities) than between small concentrations (e.g. villages); this has implications for the degree of social isolation and connectivity of communities in both large and small settlements.

Health geographers are also concerned with the importance of places for health. The characteristics that make places distinctive and different from each other are significant here. Aspects of place include location (geographical position relative to other places) and also the nature of a locale, or locality, in which certain social, political, and economic processes interact, giving a place its particular character. Dimensions contributing to the unique characteristics of a place include the demographic and social composition of the population, the built environment, and the local economy. Geographers are also concerned with imagined attributes of places that are imbued with particular social and cultural meanings, leading to the idea of senses of place (Tuan, 1974). As shown below, this may be especially important for mental health because they can be closely associated with individual sense of identity and wellbeing. Senses of place derive from historical and cultural associations, emotional bonds, and the accumulated impressions of lived experience.

Three recurrent questions arise in discussion of the research outlined in this chapter. They are, in fact, more generally important for studies of variation in population health and represent interconnected problems in explanation of health differences. The first concerns the issue of the 'ecological fallacy', which is of special importance in geography because so much of the work involves analysis of information aggregated in terms of geographically defined populations (for example, see discussion in Curtis & Taket, 1996: 156–157). The second issue relates to different interpretations of causality, and particularly the 'breeder' and 'drift' hypotheses. The third question is a fundamentally geographical one – about the significance of context for individual experience.

The problem of the ecological fallacy as it relates to health geography has been discussed by several authors. For example, Jones and Moon (1987: 206–207) explain it in relation to mental health specifically, highlighting how this problem may arise if average attributes for a geographically defined population are erroneously assumed to apply to all individuals in the population. This fallacy might cause us to draw spurious conclusions about associations and causal relationships, which misrepresent individual risks for mental health. On the other hand, Schwartz (1994) also points out that the potential for the ecological fallacy needs to be balanced against the dangers of the atomistic fallacy. The latter occurs if the explanation for variations in mental health and health care is wrongly attributed to individual factors, when in fact the causal processes operate at the collective level of whole populations or communities. This could lead us to ignore some of the structural social and environmental factors that frame individual experience.

Discussion reported in this chapter often centres on two well-known, and potentially competing, hypotheses that can be put forward to explain the relatively high concentration of mental illness in poor areas. These explanations emphasize, respectively, 'breeder' and 'drift' processes. The 'breeder' thesis postulates that certain conditions (particularly those of community deprivation, social malaise, and social isolation) produce or exacerbate mental health and behavioural problems. The 'drift' hypothesis emphasizes processes by which people with mental health problems or antisocial behaviour tend to move towards poorer areas. As was proposed by Giggs (1975) and other authors since then, much of the research reviewed here suggests that in fact these are not so much competing hypotheses, but complementary explanations of a complex of processes that influence the geography of mental illness.

Particularly during the 1990s, there was a growth of interest in the role that context or environment may play in determining individual health differences. Contextual factors are often defined in terms of aspects of the place or geographically defined community in which individuals are living. Interpretations of the different aspects of space and place discussed above are often used in theories that postulate the causal pathways accounting for geographical and social variations in health. These discussions often focus on the extent to which health may be influenced both by the characteristics of individual people and by the context that surrounds them. It is often difficult, and not very useful, to make a rigid distinction between factors that operate solely at the individual level and those that are purely due to context or place. Nevertheless, the work in this area does provide interesting examples of how individuals interact with their environment. Examples of these discussions, which are often cited in the geographical literature, include Curtis and Jones (1998), Jones and Moon (1993), Kearns (1991), Kearns and Joseph (1993), Macintyre *et al.* (1993) and Popay *et al.* (1998). Macintyre *et al.* (1993) have suggested various attributes of places that can influence health. These include the risks and opportunities offered by the physical environment, the services and facilities afforded by the local infrastructure of a place, labour markets, and social and cultural characteristics of communities, as opposed to individual attributes. Curtis and Jones (1998) and Curtis (2004) focus on the linkages between these theoretical influences of place and broader theoretical frameworks. They discuss how our understanding of the significance of 'place effects' for health is informed by a number of different theories. Relevant to this are theories of production, reproduction and consumption that influence material living conditions and poverty, as well as consumption of goods and services that are important to psychosocial health. Also important for the geography of mental health variation are theories concerning the operation of social control and territoriality, as well as humanist and psychological theories that seek to explain how place relates to emotions and sense of identity.

Reviews of the literature in this field also illustrate the range of methods used by geographers and others to test for empirical evidence of 'place effects' or 'contextual effects'. These include statistical methods such as multilevel modelling (e.g. Congdon *et al.*, 1997; Duncan & Jones, 1995; Ecob, 1996; Mitchell *et al.*, 2000; Shouls *et al.*, 1996a; Sloggett & Joshi, 1998) and methods employing Bayesian approaches (e.g. Congdon, 1997, 2001; Congdon *et al.*, 1998). Several of the statistical studies incorporate data on the attributes of individuals together with attributes of the places where they live. These suggest that individual-level variables explain the greatest part of the variation in health observed, but that some variation is independently explained by attributes of areas. Furthermore, the impact of individual characteristics may be modified by conditions in the environment, in ways discussed in this chapter. Some studies have examined variation between small areas and also incorporated data on wider regions. These show that while the small area relationships (e.g. for electoral wards in England) account for the largest part of the variation, health differences also occur independently at a wide, regional scale.

Qualitative, intensive methods seek to provide rich descriptions and explanations of the experiences of individuals that reflect the importance of place and environment for their health. As mentioned above, these often show how 'sense of place' is important to health and how the local environment impacts on the individual. Writings edited by Kearns and Gesler (1998) and by Williams (1999) include numerous examples, some of which are discussed below. Geographical work also draws on anthropological and psychological theories concerning identity and understanding of the body and its significance (Cummins & Milligan, 2000). These illustrate a more abstract conceptualization of 'space' and 'place', including the social construction of place, and 'inner' spaces of the imagined body, as well as space external to the body. The present review illustrates some of these approaches as they have been applied to the study of mental health and illness from a geographical perspective.

Not all of the work cited here is by researchers who would consider themselves geographers, but all have contributed to what might be considered a geographical perspective. Since there is a bias in the following review towards research by geographers, it certainly cannot be wholly representative of work in other disciplines. For further background the reader may wish to consult, for example, reviews by Dear and Wolch (1987), Jones and Moon (1987: 190–216), Philo (1997), Smith (1977), Smith and Giggs (1988) and Wolch and Philo (2000).

To illustrate some of the pathways by which mental health may be linked to various dimensions of the geographical environment, attention will first be focused on work that examines the correlation between mental illness and material disadvantages associated with deprivation and poverty in both urban and rural settings. The discussion then considers the mental health impact of the presence or absence of supportive social settings and therapeutic landscapes. This leads to a consideration of research on therapeutic environments that promote better mental health. Finally, this chapter reviews research on mental health services that explores geographical aspects of the utilization of health care. The chapter concludes with some discussion of the implications of geographical perspectives for policy.

Geographies of mental illness and poverty

Much of the empirical work on the geography of mental health has involved mapping and analysing the pattern of mental illness as it varies between

Urban decay: Children playing in Edinburgh, Scotland, 1997 (used with permission of Dan Tuffs/Rex Features).

geographically defined populations. A good deal of attention focuses on how geographical indicators of mental illness are correlated with other attributes of the population such as socio-economic indicators of poverty and social disadvantage. These associations have been used both as the basis for hypothesizing about some of the causal pathways producing mental illness and also as measures of health service need that in the British case are relevant for National Health Service resource allocation formulae and local service planning.

Various indicators of levels of mental health have been used in these ecological analyses, including: data on diagnosed illness from health service registers; data on service activity such as psychiatric hospital admissions; and population survey measures of psychological state or psychosocial health status, which may be more indicative of the prevalence of milder as well as severe mental illness. It is difficult to make direct comparisons between studies or to generalize across the whole body of research, because of the diversity of measures and methods of analysis that have been employed. Nevertheless, some consistency emerges concerning the link between mental illness and poor socio-economic circumstances in deprived urban areas. There are also some interesting findings about the differences between urban and rural milieux. These differences are covered extensively in Chapter 4, while the discussion here is restricted to some studies that are particularly illustrative of geographical research in this field.

Studies of serious mental illness and of its outcome in terms of suicide have identified ecological associations with socio-economic deprivation at the scale of small geographical areas. Examples include early research by Giggs (1973) on the geographical distribution of hospital patients from the city of Nottingham suffering from schizophrenia, which used factor analysis to examine the relationship between 'standardized schizophrenia attack rates' for small areas of the city and a range of socio-economic indicators derived from small-area census data. This demonstrated a positive association between urban social deprivation and a concentration in the population of people with severe mental illness. Dean and James (1981) examined the correlations at small-area level between rates of hospital admissions due to schizophrenia and a number of socio-economic variables. Indicators of low social class and of rented accommodation which is of poor quality and lacking amenities showed a positive association with the rates of 'first time' hospital admissions of males due to schizophrenia. More recently, Harvey *et al.* (1996) showed that in the London Borough of Camden, the distribution of patients with schizophrenia showed a significant association with socio-demographic measures of urban deprivation. (See further discussion of urban–rural differences in schizophrenia prevalence and incidence in Chapter 4.)

Studies of the prevalence of depression also show links with poverty in residential neighbourhoods. For example, Wilson *et al.* (1999), in a survey sample of elderly people in Liverpool, showed that depression was associated with deprivation, as measured by indicators suggested by Townsend *et al.* (1988) (unemployment, lack of a car, crowded housing and housing that is not owner-occupied). This work reinforces findings from earlier research concerning the positive association between social deprivation and depression (e.g. Brown & Harris, 1978) and the direct correlation between suicide rates in London and indices of social isolation (Sainsbury, 1955).

Congdon (1996b) examined suicide rates in London as an outcome indicator of serious mental illness, first for boroughs and then at the more local scale of electoral wards. The associations were analysed with census variables, applying Bayesian smoothing methods for the small-area suicide data. This analysis examined the associations with a set of socio-economic variables associated with suicide, which he interpreted as reflecting aspects of 'anomie' (discussed in the next section) as well as social class and material deprivation (using Townsend *et al.*'s, 1988, indicator). Particularly for males, deprivation factors showed a positive association with suicide levels at borough level, and also for wards. There was also some evidence that in areas of less extreme deprivation, outside the typically intensely deprived inner city, local levels of deprivation might have particularly strong effects on variation in suicide. This finding reflects the growing body of findings in recent geographical research (not restricted to mental health), that associations between deprivation and health for individual people are not always manifested in the same way in all areas (Duncan & Jones, 1995; Ecob, 1996; Mitchell *et al.*, 2000; Shouls *et al.*, 1996a; Sloggett & Joshi, 1998). Similar arguments have been put forward by Congdon *et al.* (1997), who reported a multilevel analysis of data on long-term impairing illness reported in the 1991 census. This reflects both physical and mental morbidity for small areas within larger districts and regions. Their results show that small-area associations between morbidity and deprivation are not consistent in all parts of the country, but are variable at the broader scales of districts or regions. Possible health determinants that might explain this include regional economic conditions, physical environmental factors operating at a broad scale, and regional cultural factors.

Several studies have examined the ecological relationship between general psychiatric health service use and socio-economic attributes of the population. Many of these have aimed to provide information about the factors affecting demand for psychiatric care, and to make geographical distribution of resources more equitable in relation to varying pressures on mental health services. The resulting 'need indicators' often reflect the associations between deprivation and higher levels of psychiatric service use in cities. For example, Jarman and Hirsch (1992) reported a multivariate regression analysis of acute psychiatric hospital admissions in 185 English health districts in the mid-1980s, which they tested for correlation with a large number of other variables. Admission rates were positively associated with measures of population density (indicating higher admission rates in urban areas) and with social deprivation and poverty, notification of drug misuse, and health disadvantage reflected in general levels of mortality and morbidity (measured as percentage permanently sick). At a finer geographical scale, a later study by Glover *et al.* (1998) generated ecological data using information on the areas of residence of patients admitted for acute psychiatric hospital care in parts of London and of the outer metropolitan region. The data were used to calculate admission rates for small areas, which were found to be associated with characteristics of the ward populations. This ecological association was used to develop a Mental Illness Needs Index (MINI) – a composite measure comprising information on social isolation, poverty, unemployment, permanent sickness, and temporary and insecure housing, which effectively predicted rates of psychiatric hospital admission. In a study in New York City, Siegel *et al.* (2000) used a conceptual model that linked mental health outcome to domains of influence of socio-economic conditions, needs, and supports; an index was developed to measure these domains. Driessen *et al.* (1998) analysed individual records and residential area statistics for patients with non-psychotic, non-organic mental disorder in the city of Maastricht. After individual deprivation was adjusted for, people from deprived areas had greater levels of service use. They argue that 'elements in the shared social environment influence both incidence and severity of non-psychotic, non-organic disorders, over and above any individual-level effect'. Their study demonstrates that contextual as well as individual aspects of poverty may be important for variation in mental health.

The studies cited so far have mainly focused on associations between mental illness and urban deprivation. However, impoverished conditions also show a link with psychiatric illness in rural areas. The point is often made in geographical research that ecological studies of deprivation in rural areas may underestimate levels of poverty because there are not the same large concentrations of poor people as in deprived urban areas. Within the populations of small rural areas, there is a greater heterogeneity of levels of wealth and poverty (e.g.

Haynes & Gale, 1999; Pacione, 1995; Sim, 1984). In counterpoint to research showing that mental health tends to be worse in poor urban areas, Higgs (1999) summarizes findings from several studies in high-income countries that point to high risks of psychiatric morbidity and mortality in some rural areas, as well as in cities. Other studies which suggest that especially more deprived and backward rural settings are associated with poorer mental health include that by Hoyt *et al.* (1997), which showed some variability in patterns of rural mental health risks in America. For men, but not for women, those living in rural villages and small towns had a higher risk of depressive symptoms than those in larger towns and cities. Those in the most rural environments were also more likely to hold stigmatized views of mental health care and to be unlikely to use mental health services. An example of related research in a low-income country is reported by Hays and Zouari (1995) on mental health among women in Tunisian urban and village settings and among rural Bedouin communities. Stressors were greater in the rural environment, especially among Bedouins, largely due to extreme poverty. Hays and Zouari suggest that social improvements have been beneficial to middle-class women in villages and cities, but not to poor rural women. Vorster *et al.* (2000) studied the impact of urbanization and demographic transition on physical and mental health of Africans in 37 urban and rural areas of the North West Province of South Africa. Better socio-economic circumstances in the wealthier urban areas were associated both with higher scores of psychological well-being and lower levels of psychological pathology, while health was worse in both poor rural and poor urban areas. This is further discussed in Chapter 4.

In addition to these studies of morbidity, Kelly *et al.* (1995) identified high suicide rates for those employed in the agricultural (predominantly rural) economic sector. Sanderson and Langford (1996) used Bayesian analysis to overcome problems associated with small numbers of deaths in district populations. They showed relatively high rates of suicide in parts of rural England, as well as in urban areas. However, their analysis compared maps of suicide rates using Standardized Mortality Ratios (SMRs) calculated by both conventional and Bayesian methods, showing that the SMR method generated apparently high suicide rates in more of the rural districts than the statistically smoothed Bayesian estimates. This suggests that some of the rural excess reported in other research might be due to problems of statistical variability in small populations.

These studies show some urban and rural differences, but the patterns cannot be explained simply in terms of an urban–rural divide. This is not surprising, in view of the fact that urban and rural conditions are extremes of a continuum rather than clearly differentiated. Furthermore, studies of general mortality and morbidity do not indicate simple linear gradients in health disadvantage from the most urban to the most rural areas (Bentham, 1984; Shouls *et al.*, 1996b). A review by Verheij (1996) does not support the idea that mental health is consistently worse in urban areas. It seems likely that urban and rural effects, where they are important, interact variably with other characteristics of the population such as socio-economic status, race, age, and gender.

The studies from more developed countries discussed here enhance the impression that there is an association between mental health and poverty, material deprivation, and high-density living in urban areas. The strengths of these associations are such that, in the absence of direct information on mental health status, poverty and deprivation are often among the indicators used as surrogate measures of local need for mental health care (e.g. Glover *et al.*, 1998).

However, these associations between deprivation and poor mental health do not automatically imply that we should adopt the 'breeder' hypothesis that material deprivation due to poverty causes poor mental health. In ecological studies using aggregated data on poverty and mental illness, we cannot be certain that deprived individuals are those with the worst mental health in the population, as pointed out in the discussion above of the 'ecological fallacy'. Also, there is the possibility that mental illness leads to poverty, rather than being caused by poverty. For further discussion of this issue see Chapter 4. On the other hand, some empirical evidence at the level of individuals does tend to support the argument that material deprivation can cause mental illness in individuals. Furthermore, theories do exist that propose pathways by which poverty might cause mental illness. Notably, two particular aspects of material deprivation – poor conditions of housing and of work – have been argued to show close relationships with mental illness at the individual level and are both more likely to be problematic in deprived urban areas than elsewhere.

Several reviews have pointed to evidence of links between poor housing and health (e.g. Bardsley & Jones, 1998; Best, 1995, 1999; British Medical Association, 1987; Burridge & Ormandy, 1993; Freeman, 1984b; Lowry, 1991; Victor, 1997). Several different theories have been proposed to account for the causal pathways that may explain these associations at the individual level. In Britain, a large proportion of low-cost housing in urban areas is in flats, often in high-rise buildings. Lowry (1991) discussed evidence that the mental health of mothers and children living in flats may be worse, perhaps due to the isolating and restricting effects of difficulties of getting out of the home. Evidence for women in Britain suggests that high-density, overcrowded housing may be damaging to mental health (Gabe & Williams, 1993). Furthermore, Fuller *et al.* (1996) tested the association between mental health and household crowding in Bangkok, Thailand, where housing shows more extreme levels of crowding than those typically found in western countries. They found that both objective and subjective measures of crowding were associated with higher levels of mental illness or distress. Macintyre *et al.* (1998) have explored the reasons why housing conditions and tenure are associated with psychosocial health. In Britain, much of the stock of rented social housing is of poor quality. Mental health may be affected by real or perceived exposure to material risks, such as damp or cold, or safety hazards in the wider neighbourhood from crime or traffic, or poor maintenance and cleansing of public spaces. Housing tenure may also have an impact on sense of ontological security such as an individual's perception of the protection, prestige, and personalization afforded by the home. Residents in run-down, rented social housing are thought to be most likely to suffer negative psychosocial health effects from such processes. In general, the health effects of poor housing are determined partly by individual or family factors, but also by wider contextual variables, especially the local housing market, the social environment of the neighbourhood, and the operation of local policies with respect to social housing in these populations.

Homelessness shows especially strong links with mental illness. Ducq *et al.* (1997) reviewed studies of mental health among the homeless. They comment on the diverse nature of these English-language studies, which make macro-level assessment more difficult, but conclude that a third of homeless adults have a prior history of psychiatric hospitalization, and rates of psychosis range up to a maximum of 70%. High prevalence rates of alcoholism and substance abuse have also been reported.

Similarly, poor working conditions and unemployment have often been found in studies of individuals to be associated with psychiatric disorder and distress. Reviews of these associations include: Barnett (1995), Bartley (1994) and Schwefel (1996). Longitudinal studies of individuals which have illustrated mental illness and distress associated with unemployment or the threat of unemployment include: Bolton and Oatley (1987), Joelson and Wahlquist (1987), Mattiasson *et al.* (1990) and Morrell *et al.* (1994). Mental health effects of stressful working conditions, including lack of job control and imbalance between demands and control, have also been reported by Bosma *et al.* (1997, 1998), Stansfeld *et al.* (1999) and Theorell and Karasek (1996). Bourbonnais *et al.* (1996) also reported an association between psychological distress and job strain (defined as a combination of high psychological demand and low decision latitude). This association was found to persist after controlling for a range of other aspects of individuals' characteristics, their work, and home circumstances that might also be associated with distress. The likelihood of exposure to these types of individual work-related risks depends partly on conditions that operate at the level of firms (which determine human resource strategies) and also labour markets (operating on the scale of geographical areas). Haynes *et al.* (1997), for example, showed that labour market conditions appear to be associated with geographical variations in reporting of both long-term limiting illness and permanent sickness in England and Wales.

However, the interpretation of these associations between deprivation and poor mental health is problematic, since it is difficult to establish, especially from ecological studies, whether poverty is causing mental illness or is a result of mentally ill people tending to become concentrated in poor areas. The 'drift' hypothesis is plausible, since people with mental illness are often marginalized and excluded, and are likely to be forced to move to poor areas in search of low-cost housing. Once in these areas, it may then be more difficult than before for them to move out to better surroundings.

A key point emerging from some of the studies mentioned above is that the micro-level associations at the level of the individual or of the immediate local neighbourhood do not fully account for the geographical links between mental health and poverty. Social deprivation in the wider environment seems to interact with micro-level relationships, suggesting quite complex environmental impacts. Some studies suggest that living in a deprived area may be linked to health disadvantage for all its population, regardless of individual or micro-level variations in material factors like housing and employment. On the other hand, in generally more advantaged, wealthier areas, the micro-level mental health inequalities between rich and poor may be particularly stark. Thus, the experience of deprivation may be partly determined by collective aspects of disadvantage, operating at the level of the community and related to mental health. Furthermore, processes such as housing markets and labour markets, operating at the scale of geographical areas, may influence the individual level of exposure to the risk of mental illness due to material deprivation.

Anomie and social support

Several of the geographical studies referred to above have also demonstrated that there are ecological associations between mental disorder and lack of social cohesion or social support in the local community. These are often geographically correlated with measures of urban or rural deprivation, but research suggests that they have independent associations with the mental health of populations.

Thus, for example, the studies of schizophrenia by Giggs (1973) and Dean and James (1981) reported higher rates in areas where larger proportions of the population were unmarried. Congdon's (1996a) study of suicide in London showed that suicide rates at the small-area level were associated with a measure of 'anomie' that combined data on one-person households, unmarried adults, high population mobility, and privately rented accommodation (reflecting a tendency towards low residential stability in that population).

Jarman and Hirsch (1992) found psychiatric hospital admissions in English districts to be associated with district-level measures of social isolation and illegitimacy. At a finer geographical scale and for a later period, Carr-Hill *et al.* (1994) used two-stage regression modelling to analyse variation among English electoral wards in hospital admissions to psychiatric units in 1990–1992. Their approach was designed to control for the effects of supply of beds (see below). Population variables that predicted small-area rates of admission were: the proportion of single-parent households, proportion of dependants with no carer in the household, proportion of people originating from New Commonwealth countries, proportion of elderly people living alone, measures of premature mortality, and relative numbers who were permanently sick and unable to work. These variables are all suggestive of associations between social isolation, lack of family support or mobility, and demand for mental health care. Their multilevel modelling indicated that these relationships were variable between districts, suggesting the presence of effects operating at both ward and district levels.

The MINI index proposed by Glover *et al.* (1998), described above, includes measures of both unmarried adults and accommodation in boarding houses and hostels, reflecting the importance of these variables for the patterning of the use of mental health care. Also, Siegel *et al.* (2000) include a dimension of support help to explain trends over time in levels of mental health in New York. Weist *et al.* (2000) discuss the formulation of a questionnaire (MLQ) to assess protective factors against urban risks such as poverty, crime, and violence associated with behavioural problems, which was tested among youths in a school-based mental health programme. The index measured: avoiding negative peer influences, focusing on the future, and religious involvement. These elements were intended to capture aspects of the social environment thought to be important for adolescent psychological development.

These associations are probably not limited to urban areas. In fact, in rural areas, an important aspect of social deprivation is social isolation. Malmberg *et al.* (1997) reported a positive relationship between rural isolation and higher suicide rates. Research on social capital and health in communities also provides further evidence of ecological associations between social capital and health indicators. Kawachi *et al.* (1999: 1187) define social capital as 'those features of social organisation – such as the extent of interpersonal trust between citizens, norms of reciprocity, and density of civic associations – that facilitate cooperation for mutual benefit'. Information from attitudinal questions in population social surveys were used to measure these aspects of social capital and aggregated to the level of states in the USA. These authors found that individual respondents to a health questionnaire were more likely to report their health as 'fair' or 'poor' (as opposed to 'good', 'very good' or 'excellent') if they were living in states where levels of trust, reciprocity, or voluntary group membership were selectively low.

In an Australian study, Siahpush and Singh (1999) found that suicide mortality rates in Australian States were higher where levels of 'social integration' were poor – as measured by the percentage of the population living alone, divorce rate, unemployment rate, and the proportion of the labour force who were willing and available to work but had stopped seeking a job because they believed they would not find one. The association between social integration, social support, and health is further discussed in Chapter 6.

These relationships are therefore suggestive of another geographical 'risk factor' for mental illness that would be associated with lack of neighbourhood social support and the social integration of individuals into communities. However, the interpretation of these ecological associations presents several of the same difficulties encountered with statistical associations between deprivation and mental illness. First, there are potential problems of the ecological fallacy. However, social capital measured at the individual level, if its measurement is valid and reliable, has also been found to be linked to individual mental health status (Berkman & Syme, 1979; Burdine *et al.*, 1999). Berkman *et al.* (2000) proposed a theoretical model to explain behavioural, psychological, and physiological pathways by which social relationships influence the health of individuals. Social networks influence social support, social norms, social engagements, interpersonal contact, and access to resources. Through these processes, social networks are thought to influence health-related behaviour (such as alcohol consumption, adherence to medical treatment, and help-seeking). Better social networks may also promote psychological well-being in terms of, for example self-esteem, self-efficacy, and levels of depression or distress. Social relationships can also show associations with physiological variables such as immune function.

It is difficult however to establish with certainty whether lack of social support and of social integration factors precipitates mental illness, or whether the associations observed are due to a process of social disengagement on the part of people who are already mentally ill. This disengagement is particularly associated with geographical 'drift' into socially disadvantaged areas where social capital is relatively low. Again, it is likely that both processes are operating, but there are empirical and theoretical bases for assuming that social support variables can contribute to individual mental (and also physical) health. These have been comprehensively reviewed, for example by Stansfeld (1999). One of the key ways that social support may influence mental health is as a protective buffer against the impact of disruptive and negative life events, while lack of such support in the face of these events may worsen their damaging effects on mental health. Stansfeld (1999) also reviews evidence that problematic aspects of social support and interaction in the social network may exacerbate existing mental illness. A study by Ennis *et al.* (2000) illustrated the varying ways that social support may buffer the risks associated with material disadvantage. Their survey of low-income, single women in America suggests that social support plays a role in offsetting the effects of poverty, especially for certain ethnic groups. 'Mastery' (sense of control over one's circumstances) and social support were more effective in buffering against the short-term needs created by material loss. Mastery was more important for European American women and social support more significant for African American women. Social support in the workplace, as well as in wider social networks, is also protective of mental health (e.g. Stansfeld *et al.*, 1999).

Geographical factors protecting mental health: therapeutic landscapes

The preceding discussion has focused on the extensive and largely quantitative research suggesting that social deprivation and lack of social support are likely environmental risk factors for mental disorder. This can be considered in relation to the more qualitative and intensive research in geography which has sought to understand the therapeutic aspects of 'landscapes' (the places and spaces occupied by people in their daily lives). Much of this work draws on humanistic paradigms in geography (e.g. Tuan, 1974) or models based on concepts of individual psychology, rather than on approaches associated with social and spatial epidemiology.

Fullilove (1996) reviewed studies from a range of disciplines to develop a theoretical perspective on the psychology of place. Individuals require a 'good enough' environment in which to live: key psychological processes in this are attachment, familiarity, and identity. Attachment involves a mutual bond between a person and a beloved place. Familiarity involves the processes by which a detailed knowledge of a place is built up. Place identity involves derivation of a sense of self from places in which one passes one's life. As each of these processes is threatened by displacement, problems associated with nostalgia, disorientation, and alienation may ensue, with associated risks to mental health. Fullilove uses this model to consider the psychological impact of migration and displacement due to urban change and renewal, which is another fundamentally geographical aspect of risk to mental health in the population. However, the model can also be used to understand the positive or 'therapeutic' aspects of the individual's experience of place.

From a geographer's perspective, Gesler (1992) has also developed theories concerning the therapeutic nature of certain places, arising from the cultural values with which they are imbued, as well as the physical nature of the place. The idea of a 'therapeutic place' can be applied to a range of places, either in institutions or outside.

The design of hospital spaces and other psychiatric service facilities is often associated with ideas of what comprises a therapeutic environment for mental health. Gittins (1998) discusses how the structure of an American psychiatric hospital reflects changes in the treatment of mental illness over time and the sort of buildings and environment which were considered suited to these changing therapies. Pearson (1999) describes the New York Psychiatric Institute as a building that projects a modernist image of mental health care. In a rather contrasting view of what comprises a therapeutic setting, Bridgman (1999) uses ethnographic methods to explore how some of the qualities of life on the street were experienced in a positive way by homeless people with mental illness. She explains how these were incorporated into the design of innovative accommodation to help such people make a transition from life on the street to redevelop a sense of 'home'. Other studies of institutional landscapes use more Foucauldian interpretations of the 'panoptican' and focus on the power relations that have been reflected in the design and organization of institutional spaces intended to exercise control and surveillance over people with mental illness (Philo, 1989).

Geographical studies of this type also often reflect strategies of resistance to exclusion and discrimination exercised by people with mental illness. Pinfold (2000) describes how people with mental illness need to identify and have access to 'safe havens' in an often hostile environment in order to operate survival strategies and protect their often fragile mental health. Knowles (2000) explains that these may not always be in 'care facilities', and she discusses the role played by commercial public spaces such as cheap fast-food outlets in providing relatively safe and comfortable environments which have longer opening hours and are less stigmatized than mental health care institutional spaces. Parr (1995) suggests that the tendency for some people with mental illness to use urban spaces in idiosyncratic, often disruptive, ways may be associated with resistance to imposed medical identities. She discusses how patient power may be facilitated in therapeutic places. Parr (1999) also discusses the 'unboundedness' of delusional experience and the unpredictable therapeutic properties of non-medical material spaces from the perspective of people who experience delusion.

The geography of service provision and access to psychiatric care in institutions

Discussion of places that may be therapeutic for mentally ill people leads us to another set of geographical factors that relate to variations in the experience of mental illness. These concern patterns of provision of mental health care and access to services for people with mental disorder.

Some of the earliest research in medical geography, carried out by Jarvis in the nineteenth century, examined psychiatric institutions in the USA. He established what has been referred to as Jarvis' Law, which postulated a universal tendency for use of services to show a 'distance decay effect' whereby a larger proportion of patients came from areas close to the hospital and fewer from more distant areas. 'The people in the vicinity of lunatic hospitals send more patients to them than those at a greater distance' (Jarvis, 1850, cited in Hunter & Shannon, 1985).

This relationship of decreasing probability of use in relation to increasing distance to be travelled may to some extent be attributed to 'friction of distance', i.e. the disincentive associated with the 'costs' of covering greater distances to a health facility. In fact, Hunter and Shannon (1985) showed that even in Jarvis' original data, the relationship between use and distance was variable between institutions. They suggest that a number of other factors, such as ease of access by available transport routes, differences in admission policies of institutions, and variations in the cost of care probably also come into play. Thus, research in mental health care has helped to substantiate one of the recurrent messages from the geography of health care – that in aggregated populations, distance to be travelled often shows an inverse relationship with propensity to use services, but that physical distance can only be considered as one of the variables in a complex set of factors influencing access to and use of health care (see e.g. Curtis & Taket, 1996: 154–156).

Thus, one aspect of the 'drift' hypothesis concerning variation in the mental health of populations is that people with mental disorder will tend to be drawn towards areas where services are provided for them. This has implications for ecological studies in the geography of mental health discussed above, since many of them rely on information about use of mental health care to measure levels of the morbidity of affected individuals in the community. However, a problem in the interpretation of research on mental health risk that used health service activity data is that use of services depends not only on need, but also on variations in supply of and access to health care. Carr-Hill *et al.* (1994) drew attention to the fact that when patients are cared for in long-stay psychiatric institutions, they are likely, on discharge, to remain living in the area close to the hospital. This tendency for mental health facilities to 'generate' local populations of mentally ill people in their catchment areas may also result from 'revolving door' cases, when patients experience repeated admissions and also may need ongoing support and surveillance while living in the community. Such cases may gravitate towards the places from which they are receiving care. Lamont *et al.* (2000) showed a high degree of residential mobility among mental health patients admitted to hospital in London (28% had moved in the previous year). This may reflect a tendency to drift towards institutional sources of care and treatment, since patients seen by community psychiatric teams were less likely to have moved.

Some types of mental illness may be particularly associated with 'drift' towards places where care is available. Maylath *et al.* (1999) showed that in Hamburg, the risk of hospitalization for psychiatric cases was markedly variable between areas: high admission rates for schizophrenia were associated with close proximity to psychiatric units. A high risk of admission for neurosis, personality disorder, and abuse of drugs or alcohol was concentrated in areas of low social status.

Some studies suggest that resource allocation mechanisms may not be fully sensitive to variations in the need for mental health care, and that this may result in provision that is insufficient to meet demand in some areas. The King's Fund report (Johnson *et al.*, 1998) on London's mental health described a crisis situation, with services struggling to meet demands that are strongly related to social deprivation, including high rates of unemployment and of people living alone. The emergency care provided through A&E units and community services is generally not sufficient. Possible solutions include more resources, capital investment in facilities, and changes in the relationship between health and social services. Goldberg (1999) has argued that while community psychiatric care is generally preferable and is beneficial for many patients, some inpatient and residential services are essential for such services to be run efficiently and effectively. In urban areas like London, the pressure on hospital beds is particularly great, making it less likely that the community care strategy for mental health can succeed. Kisely (1998) criticized the original King's Fund report on mental health in London for making comparisons with average conditions in the UK as a whole, rather than with other major urban areas. He argued that other major cities have similar problems to London, and that it is important to ensure equity between the principal centres of population.

In areas where service provision is under pressure due to particularly high demand, services may become focused on a relatively small number of patients in the most severe need categories, leaving few resources to respond to the mental health needs of the larger numbers with less severe illnesses. In a study of English health authority areas, Glover *et al.* (1999) demonstrated that the rate of use of services for mentally disordered offenders varied by a factor of 20 between areas. This may mean that the resources of individual health authorities would be insufficient to cope with such concentrated demand for 'forensic' mental health provision, as well as general health care. Where services are most clearly insufficient to meet needs, this may be a contextual factor increasing the risk of worsening mental illness through lack of access to effective treatment.

Variation in health-care provision is therefore a contributor to 'breeder' as well as 'drift' effects.

Post-asylum geographical research

Partly overlapping with the work reviewed on therapeutic landscapes, and also related to studies of institutional psychiatric provision, is a large body of geographical research on the impacts of the deinstitutionalization of care. This has resulted in a widening of the range of places for the care and treatment of mental illness. Wolch and Philo (2000) identify three 'waves' of this research concerning the 'post-asylum' situation. The first started in the late 1960s and early 1970s with a focus on questions of the socio-spatial location of people with mental health problems and the trend towards deinstitutionalization, leading to a shift from psychiatric hospitals to community-based treatment and less structured settings such as street homelessness. As explained below, a 'second wave' of research, starting especially in the mid-1980s, has emphasized issues including control and resistance and the ways that these are reflected by and formed by the spatial contexts of mental health care at different places and at different points of time. The third thematic 'wave' in mental health geography includes studies that are more orientated towards policy issues that are relevant today, such as questions of '(dis)placement' and 'churning' (high mobility of mentally ill people resulting in rapid and frequent changes of location and type of place where they live and receive care). Wolch and Philo suggest that geographers may need to pay increasing attention to the wide range of types of places and spaces that are becoming common sites of experience of mental illness and psychiatric treatment, including the streets and prisons.

In their analysis of deinstitutionalized mental health care in the North American cities, Dear and Wolch (1987) offered a model of the 'service-dependent ghetto', that has been influential in the discussion of post-asylum geographies. They argue that deinstitutionalization has resulted in a concentration of mentally ill people in poor inner-city areas, where they rely on a range of service provision. This can be contrasted with the semi-rural location of nineteenth-century asylum institutions, designed to separate people with mental illness from the wider society and to offer what was considered a therapeutic (natural and peaceful) landscape for care. The strength of Dear and Wolch's model lies in the comprehensive way they bring together ideas about trends in urban development and the political economy of cities, the roles of the key stakeholders involved in decisions about mental health-care policy and its implementation, and the evolution of mental health services.

These authors suggest that the functioning of networks of professionals in health and social care tends to encourage spatial grouping to form a 'critical mass' of personnel who are specialized in working with groups who show 'challenging' behaviour. However, attracting clients who need to use such services into areas where these are already provided contributes to the 'service-dependent ghetto' effect. Dear and Wolch also point to the NIMBY ('not in my back yard') syndrome in negotiation over the location of facilities for socially excluded groups, who may tend to exhibit behaviour that is not socially acceptable to the majority. These groups include people who are homeless, mentally ill, or drug users. Affluent communities which are influential and articulate are successful in rejecting such facilities if they consider them undesirable, while disadvantaged communities may be in a weaker position to reject them from their neighbourhood. Furthermore, lower property prices and greater levels of population needs argue for location in poorer areas.

It is interesting to compare Dear and Wolch's model with a related perspective proposed by Wallace and Wallace (Wallace, 1990; Wallace & Wallace, 1997). The latter authors describe the concentration of pathology in inner cities as being associated with a 'desertification' (degradation) of those areas. They emphasize the political and social forces that cause degrading of some of the key services for enforcement of law and order, public safety, welfare, and health in deprived areas, where the population is disempowered in relation to democratic processes and decision-making.

These models are both useful in the way that they highlight the significance of some general social, economic, and political trends in the political economy of major cities, which influence employment, housing markets, and the rent values of space for welfare facilities. These trends are associated with increased socio-economic inequality and with growing spatial separation of rich, powerful populations from poor, disempowered ones.

Since these models were developed principally from a North American perspective, several studies in geography have considered how applicable they are to the situation in other countries. These studies show something of the international variability of trends in mental health policy and its implementation, and also highlight the significance of the local context for the development of structures for care of mental illness. For example, Milligan (1996) examined circumstances in Scotland and found that Dear and Wolch's model was reflected in the continued concentration of some non-residential facilities for mentally ill people in larger towns, but that residential provision was less concentrated in urban areas. She attributes this partly to the more powerful position of statutory planning agencies in the UK, compared with the USA. The increasing separation and dislocation of the residential and care functions of support to mentally ill people has also been noted in studies elsewhere. For example, Kearns and Joseph (2000) considered the geographies of consumption (especially in the housing market and in the increasingly privatized market of mental health care) which influence the organization of residential and care opportunities for mentally ill people in Auckland, New Zealand. Jones (2000) compared the development of policies for the deinstitutionalization of mental health care in Sheffield and Verona. While the aims of changes in mental health care in both places were similar, the pace of implementation was found to be slower in the British case. Factors such as the historical legacy of provision in each city, the degree of decentralization of health policy decisions, the role of health professionals in championing reforms and of planners exercising control over new developments, as well as the patterns of land use and the housing market, were influential on the varying trajectories reported for the two cities. Jones also comments on the fact that the situation in Sheffield did not accord with the service-dependent ghetto model proposed by Dear and Wolch. The geographical patterning of the housing stock in Sheffield led to concentrations of provision in certain more affluent areas of the city, where suitable properties were available to accommodate services, rather than in deprived inner-city areas.

One of the issues incorporated in Dear and Wolch's (1987) analysis is the role of mentally ill people themselves as one of the groups of stakeholders involved in decisions about mental health services and their location. Typically, their position is presented as one of relative weakness in negotiation, as compared with other groups such as mental health professionals, planners, and the wider society. As a wider range of settings are used to provide care to people with mental illness, the question of who makes decisions about the placement of such people becomes more complex. Social environmental factors may influence the way that decisions are made concerning the pathways of care followed by these patients. Pescosolido *et al.* (1998) identified different processes by which people come to use mental health services, which they typify as: (i) patient's 'choice', (ii) 'coercion' of the patient by family or other carers, and (iii) 'muddling through' processes, where the agency is less clear. There was some evidence that patients with larger, closer social networks were more likely to have experienced coercion. Goeres and Gesler (1999) discussed the roles of different actors and institutions in determining where people with mental illness are placed, and suggest that the mentally ill patient is often disadvantaged in the decision-making process. Parr (1995) also discussed the role of user groups in negotiation with medical professions and the wider community over the provision and location of mental health services. Although she also stresses the difficulty experienced by mental health-care users wishing to have a voice in these decisions, her account suggests a growing assertiveness on the part of user groups, associated with the introduction of consumerist objectives into the British National Health Service during the 1980s and 1990s.

Dear and Wolch's model drew upon earlier work by researchers, including geographers, concerning the tensions surrounding the location of mental health facilities. This is interesting for what it reveals about the public perception of mental illness and the social relations operating in communities, as well as for its effects on mental health facility location. Early work included studies by Smith and Hanham (1981) concerning the effect of proximity on existing mental health facilities as a factor determining public attitudes towards mental illness. They compared two neighbourhoods in Oklahoma City, USA, one of which was close to a psychiatric facility and the other more distant. Their study showed that those living close to the psychiatric hospital were in general more accepting of this disorder. However, attitudes to mental illness were strongly associated with overall attitudes to social and welfare issues, and the authors point out that those choosing to live close to the hospital may have been more inclined to be accepting of mental illness. Also, homeowners who were residentially more permanent in the area were more likely to reject the mentally ill, which the authors interpret as being due to a 'desire for greater discretion about who is to live in one's neighbourhood' (Smith & Hanham, 1981: 161). Furthermore, informants who had direct experience of serious mental illness were less likely to be accepting of the condition. This sort of research highlights the strong social stigma attached to mental disorder, which is a major issue for policies seeking greater integration of mentally ill people into communities. More recent work includes a study by Takahashi and Gaber (1998) comparing data from surveys revealing the views of the public and of planners. This takes up the idea that in the siting of controversial facilities, different roles are played by the state (especially planners), the 'shadow state' (voluntary and non-profit organizations), and interest groups (mainly community residents).

Public attitudes to mental illness often involve a balance between recognition of the importance of personal liberty for all, including the mentally ill, and concern about perceived risks associated with freer interaction between people with serious illness of this kind and the wider society. Moon (2000) explored how themes of confinement have recently re-emerged in both policy literature and popular discourse, and noted that community health services are presented as having to control the danger and risk to society that is posed by some mentally ill people. Moon commented on what this may tell us about the changing social understanding of risk and also the varying balance in society between values of individual aspiration and freedom on one hand and the importance of protective aspects of the community on the other. These geographical views of perceptions of mental illness and mental health-care policy connect with discussion in other disciplines. For example, Mossman (1997) considered the view that the growing numbers of mentally ill, homeless people encountered in public spaces in the USA result from the virtual abandonment of mentally ill people by the psychiatric profession through the process of deinstitutionalization. This widely held view is examined from an anthropological perspective, interpreting abandonment as a myth. Ducq *et al.* (1997) also consider that socio-economic disadvantage and deinstitutionalization of people with mental illness may both be causes of homelessness.

Another feature of post-asylum geographical approaches to mental health care is the growing emphasis on the roles of non-statutory agencies in the provision of care. Milligan (2000b) discussed the growing influence of the voluntary sector and the importance of voluntarism for our understanding of variations in access to care. She discussed the role of the voluntary sector and the factors that are associated with geographical variation in voluntary support. These include policies, priorities, and patterns of spending at the local level as well as at national and international levels; and the opportunistic and *ad hoc* nature of funding streams for voluntary organizations. Parr (2000) cited Wolch's (1990) commentary on the tensions of the 'shadow state' with increased bureaucratization or appropriation by the state of voluntary community resources for mental health care. This has conflicted with the revitalization of statutory service provision in response to more democratic, diverse, and responsive models developed in the voluntary sector.

Community-based models of mental health care offer a new range of less institutional settings for provision of treatment and support to mentally ill people. Some geographical work has focused on how, in these community settings, supportive and therapeutic functions are combined with control and surveillance. For example, Parr (2000) reported the use of covert ethnographic observation at a drop-in centre in Nottingham to explore the processes of inclusion and exclusion that can operate in semi-institutional spaces providing mental health care. That study traced the process of 'psychosocial boundary formation' by which certain 'unusual norms' of behaviour were accepted uncritically by others in the centre, although in 'mainstream' settings, they would be considered abnormal and perhaps unacceptable. Examples included making repeated rude gestures to others, standing in the middle of the room staring at nothing, and listening at the door. On the other hand, Parr noted that some behaviour was not accepted so readily, for example if it disrupted group activities or involved very aggressive behaviour towards others. Thus, there were differential patterns of inclusion or exclusion of members of the drop-in centre, depending on whether their behaviour transgressed the accepted psychosocial boundaries in this setting. Parr, like other geographers working in this vein, used Wilton's (1998) interpretation of the Freudian concept of *unheimlich* as the notion of something 'uncanny' that threatens our sense of a controlled and predictable environment.

The development of geographical perspectives on care outside institutions therefore contributes to our understanding of the place of mentally ill people in the wider society. Taken as a whole, the insights provided from this literature highlight the need to consider the experience of people with mental illness who move between a range of different settings, where they interact with both other mentally ill people and the general public, as well as with mental health professionals. The research described above shows that the nature and the outcome of these interactions is influenced by the psychosocial environment in which they take place. The behaviour of mentally ill people that transgresses social norms is more likely to be tolerated in some settings than in these others. Mentally ill people find 'safe havens' more readily in these places than in settings that are less tolerant and more exclusionary.

Conclusions

The geographical perspectives reviewed above have contributed to understanding of issues such as the ecological fallacy, the relationship between drift and breeder effects, and the significance of environmental ('place') effects in mental health and health care. The balance of the research suggests that both the risk of mental illness and its outcome result not only from individual factors, but also from environmental conditions that vary among areas or settings. These interactions are not merely spurious associations resulting from an ecological fallacy, since they have been identified in studies of individuals, as well as in research on aggregated populations. These 'environmental' effects contribute to an explanation of the causal pathways by which variations in mental health occur. It is also clear that the causal pathways arise from a complex interaction of 'breeder' and 'drift' effects, so that it is more useful to consider these as complementary explanatory models, rather than conflicting alternatives. These breeder and drift effects may operate variably for patients with different characteristics and in different settings.

These perspectives contribute to an interesting debate about the strategy of public health and the extent to which attention should be focused on individual variables affecting health, as opposed to collective processes. Authors such as Rose (1992) have encouraged a debate over whether public health strategies need to focus more on intervention at the individual level or at the collective level of communities and wider societies. Link and Phelan (1995) warn against over-emphasis on individually based proximal behavioural causes of diseases. Individually based risk factors must be contextualized so that we can understand what factors produce behavioural risks at this level. We need to learn more about 'fundamental causes' of disease such as socio-economic conditions and social support, which also influence access to resources and affect disease outcomes in a variety of ways. Broad-based societal interventions need to be considered as ways of producing health gain in the population. Researchers taking a geographical perspective (e.g. Curtis, 2004; Curtis & Jones, 1998; Macintyre, 1999; Macintyre *et al.*, 1993) have supported the argument that intervention at the collective level is a necessary adjunct to measures targeted at individuals. Curtis and Jones have also argued that interventions at either the individual or the collective level will need to be sensitive to variations in local context. The research reviewed here underlines the arguments that support these approaches in respect of mental as well as physical health.

References

Bardsley, M. and Jones, I. (1998) *Housing and health in London: A review by the Health of Londoners Project*. London: East London & The City Health Authority.

Barnett, P. (1995) 'Unemployment, work and health: opportunities for healthy public policy'. *New Zealand Medical Journal*, *108*, 138–140.

Bartley, M. (1994) 'Unemployment and ill health: understanding the relationship'. *Journal of Epidemiology and Community Health*, *48*, 333–337.

Bentham, C. G. (1984) 'Mortality rates in the more rural areas of England and Wales'. *Area*, *16*, 219–226.

Berkman, L. F. and Syme, S. L. (1979) 'Social networks, host resistance, and mortality: a nine-year follow-up study of Alameda County residents'. *American Journal of Epidemiology*, *109*, 186–204.

Berkman, L. F., Glass, T., Brissette, I. and Seeman, T. E. (2000) 'From social integration to health: Durkheim in the new millennium'. *Social Science and Medicine*, *51*, 843–857.

Best, R. (1995) 'The housing dimension', in Benzeval, M., Judge, K. and Whitehead, M. (eds), *Tackling inequalities of health: An agenda for action*. London: King's Fund Publishing.

Best, R. (1999) 'Health inequalities, the place of housing', in Gordon, D., Shaw, M. and Davey Smith, G. (eds), *Inequalities in health: The evidence presented to the Independent Inquiry into Inequalities in Health.* Bristol: The Policy Press.

Bolton, W. and Oatley, K. (1987) 'A longitudinal study of social support and depression in unemployed men'. *Psychological Medicine, 17,* 453–460.

Bosma, H., Peter, R., Siegrist, J. and Marmot, M. (1998) 'Two alternative job stress models and the risk of coronary heart disease'. *American Journal of Public Health, 88,* 68–74.

Bosma, H., Marmot, M. G., Hemingway, H., Nicholson, A. C., Brunner, E. and Stansfeld, S. A. (1997) 'Low job control and risk of coronary heart disease in Whitehall II (prospective cohort) study'. *British Medical Journal, 314,* 558–565.

Bourbonnais, R., Brisson, C., Moisan, J. and Vezina, M. (1996) 'Job strain and psychological distress in white-collar workers'. *Scandinavian Journal of Work, Environment and Health, 22,* 139–145.

Bridgman, R. (1999) 'The street gives and the street takes: designing housing for the chronically homeless', in Williams, A. (ed.), *Therapeutic landscapes: The dynamic between place and wellness.* New York: University Press of America.

British Medical Association (1987) 'Deprivation and ill-health: what do we know?', in BMA (ed.), *British Medical Association Board of Science and Education Discussion Paper.* London: British Medical Association.

Brown, G. and Harris, T. (1978) *The social origins of depression: A study of psychiatric disorders in women.* London: Tavistock.

Burdine, J. N., Felix, M. R., Wallerstein, N., Abel, A. L., Wiltraut, C. J., Musselman, Y. J. and Stidley, C. (1999) 'Measurement of social capital'. *Annals of the New York Academy of Sciences, 896,* 393–395.

Burridge, R. and Ormandy, D. (1993) *Unhealthy housing: Research remedies and reform.* London: E & FN Spon.

Carr-Hill, R., Hardman, G., Martin, S., Peacock, S., Sheldon, T. and Smith, P. (1994) *A formula for distributing NHS revenues based on small area use of hospital beds.* York: Centre for Health Economics, University of York.

Congdon, P. (1996a) 'The incidence of suicide and parasuicide: a small area study'. *Urban Studies, 33,* 137–138.

Congdon, P. (1996b) 'The epidemiology of suicide in London'. *Journal of the Royal Statistical Society A, 159,* 515–533.

Congdon, P. (1997) 'Bayesian models for the spatial structure of rare health outcomes: a study of suicide using the BUGS program'. *Journal of Health and Place, 3,* 229–247.

Congdon, P. (2001) 'Bayesian models for suicide monitoring'. *European Journal of Population, 16,* 251–284.

Congdon, P., Shouls, S. and Curtis, S. (1997) 'A multi-level perspective on small-area health and mortality: a case study of England and Wales'. *International Journal of Population Geography, 3,* 243–263.

Congdon, P., Smith, A. and Dean, C. (1998) 'Assessing psychiatric morbidity from a community register: methods for Bayesian adjustment'. *Urban Studies, 35,* 2323–2352.

Cummins, S. and Milligan, C. (2000) 'Taking up the challenge: new directions in the geographies of health and impairment'. *Area, 32,* 7–9.

Curtis, S. (2004) *Health and inequality: Geographical perspectives.* London: Sage.

Curtis, S. and Jones, I. (1998) 'Is there a place for geography in the analysis of health inequality?', *Sociology of Health and Illness, 20,* 645–672.

Curtis, S. and Taket, A. (1996) *Health and societies: Changing perspectives,* London: Routledge.

Dean, K. and James, H. (1981) 'Social factors and admission to psychiatric hospital: schizophrenia in Plymouth'. *Transactions of Institute of British Geographers NS, 6*, 39–52.

Dear, M. and Wolch, J. (1987) *Landscapes of despair: From institutionalization to homelessness*. Oxford: Polity Press.

Driessen, G., Gunther, N. and Van Os, J. (1998) 'Shared social environment and psychiatric disorder: a multilevel analysis of individual and ecological effects'. *Social Psychiatry and Psychiatric Epidemiology, 33*, 606–612.

Ducq, H., Guesdon, I. and Roelandt, J. L. (1997) 'Mental health of homeless persons: critical review of the Anglo-Saxon literature'. *Encephale, 23*, 420–430.

Duncan, C. and Jones, K. (1995) 'Individuals and their ecologies: analysing the geography of chronic illness within a multi-level modeling framework'. *Health and Place, 1*, 27–40.

Ecob, E. (1996) 'A multi-level approach to examining the effects of area of residence on health and functioning'. *Journal of the Royal Statistical Society A, 159*, 61–75.

Ennis, N. E., Hobfoll, S. E. and Schroder, K. E. (2000) 'Money doesn't talk, it swears: how economic stress and resistance resources impact inner-city women's depressive mood'. *American Journal of Community Psychology, 28*, 149–173.

Freeman, H. (1984a) 'Housing', in Freeman, H. (ed.), *Mental health and the environment*. London: Churchill Livingstone.

Freeman, H. (1984b) *Mental health and the environment*. London: Churchill Livingstone.

Fuller, T. D., Edwards, J. N., Vorakitphokatorn, S. and Sermsri, S. (1996) 'Chronic stress and psychological well-being: evidence from Thailand on household crowding'. *Social Science and Medicine, 42*, 265–280.

Fullilove, M. T. (1996) 'Psychiatric implications of displacement: contributions from the psychology of place'. *American Journal of Psychiatry, 153*, 1516–1523.

Gabe, J. and Williams, P. (1993) 'Women, crowding and mental health', in Burridge, R. and Ormandy, D. (eds), *Unhealthy housing: Research remedies and reform*, London: E & FN Spon.

Gesler, W. M. (1992) 'Therapeutic landscapes: medical issues in light of the new cultural geography'. *Social Science and Medicine, 34*, 735–746.

Giggs, J. (1973) 'The distribution of schizophrenics in Nottingham'. *Transactions of the Institute of British Geographers, 59*, 55–76.

Giggs, J. (1975) 'The distribution of schizophrenics in Nottingham: a reply'. *Transactions of the Institute of British Geographers, 64*, 150–156.

Giggs, J. A., Bourke, J. B. and Katschinski, B. (1988) 'The epidemiology of primary acute pancreatitis in Greater Nottingham: 1969–1983'. *Social Science and Medicine, 26*, 79–89.

Gittins, D. (1998) *Madness in its place: Narratives of Severalls Hospital 1913–1997*. London: Routledge.

Glover, G. R., Leese, M. and McCrone, P. (1999) 'More severe mental illness is more concentrated in deprived areas'. *British Journal of Psychiatry, 175*, 544–548.

Glover, G. R., Robin, E., Emami, J. and Arabscheibani, G. R. (1998) 'A needs index for mental health care'. *Social Psychiatry and Psychiatric Epidemiology, 33*, 89–96.

Goeres, M. and Gesler, W. (1999) 'Compromised space: contests over the provision of a therapeutic environment for people with mental illness', in *Therapeutic landscapes: The dynamic between place and wellness*. New York: University Press of America.

Goldberg, D. (1999) 'The future pattern of psychiatric provision in England'. *European Archives of Psychiatry and Clinical Neuroscience, 249*, 123–127.

Graycer, A. (1983) 'Informal, voluntary and statutory services: the complex relationship'. *British Journal of Social Work, 13*, 379–393.

Harvey, C. A., Pantelis, C., Taylor, J., McCabe, P. J., Lefevre, K., Campbell, P. G. and Hirsch, S. R. (1996) 'The Camden schizophrenia surveys. II. High prevalence of schizophrenia in an inner London borough and its relationship to socio-demographic factors'. *British Journal of Psychiatry*, *168*, 418–426.

Haynes, R. and Gale, S. (1999) 'Mortality, long-term illness and deprivation in rural and metropolitan wards of England and Wales'. *Health and Place*, *5*, 301–312.

Haynes, R., Bentham, G., Lovett, A. and Eimermann J. (1997) 'Effect of labour market conditions on reporting of limiting long term illness and permanent sickness in England and Wales'. *Health and Place*, *51*, 282–288.

Hays, P. and Zouari, J. (1995) 'Stress, coping and mental health among rural, village and urban women in Tunisia'. *International Journal of Psychology*, *30*, 69–90.

Higgs, G. (1999) 'Investigating trends in rural health outcomes: a research agenda'. *Geoforum*, *30*, 203–221.

Hoyt, D. R., Conger, R. D., Valde, J. G. and Weihs, K. (1997) 'Psychological distress and help seeking in rural America'. *American Journal of Community Psychology*, *25*, 449–470.

Hunter, J. M. and Shannon, G. W. (1985) 'Jarvis revisited: distance decay in service areas of mid-19th century asylums'. *Professional Geographer*, *37*, 296–302.

Jarman, B. and Hirsch, S. (1992) 'Statistical models to predict district psychiatric morbidity', in Thornicroft, G., Brewin, C. and Wing, J. (eds), *Measuring mental health needs*. London: Gaskell (Royal College of Psychiatrists).

Joelson, L. and Wahlquist, L. (1987) 'The psychological meaning of job insecurity and job loss: results of a longitudinal study'. *Social Science and Medicine*, *25*, 179–182.

Johnson, S., Ramsay, R., Thornicroft, G., Brooks, L., Lelliott, P., Peck, E., Smith, H., Chisholm, D., Audini, B., Knapp, M. and Goldberg D. (1998) *London's mental health: The report to the King's Fund Commission*. London: King's Fund Publishing.

Jones, J. (2000) 'Mental health care reforms in Britain and Italy since 1950: a cross-national comparative study'. *Health and Place*, *6*, 171–187.

Jones, K. and Moon, G. (1987) *Health, disease & society: An introduction to medical geography*. London: Routledge & Kegan Paul.

Jones, K. and Moon, G. (1993) 'Medical geography: taking space seriously'. *Progress in Human Geography*, *17*, 515–524.

Kawachi, I., Kennedy, B. P. and Glass, R. (1999) 'Social capital and self-rated health: a contextual analysis'. *American Journal of Public Health*, *89*, 1187–1193.

Kearns, R. and Gesler, W. (1998) *Putting health into place: Landscape, identity and well-being*. New York: Syracuse University Press.

Kearns, R. A. (1991) 'The place of health in the health of place: the case of the Hokianga special medical area'. *Social Science and Medicine*, *33*, 519–530.

Kearns, R. A. and Joseph, A. E. (1993) 'Space in its place: developing the link in medical geography'. *Social Science and Medicine*, *37*, 711–717.

Kearns, R. A. and Joseph, A. E. (2000) 'Contracting opportunities: interpreting post-asylum geographies of mental health care in Auckland, New Zealand'. *Health and Place*, *6*, 159–169.

Kelly, S., Charlton, J. and Jenkins, R. (1995) 'Suicide deaths in England and Wales, 1982–92: the contribution of occupation and geography'. *Population Trends*, *80*, 16–25.

Kisely, S. (1998) 'More alike than different: comparing the mental health needs of London and other inner city areas'. *Journal of Public Health Medicine*, *20*, 318–324.

Knowles, C. (2000) 'Burger King, Dunkin Donuts and community mental health care'. *Health and Place*, *6*, 213–224.

Lamont, A., Ukoumunne, O. C., Tyrer, P., Thornicroft, G., Patel, R. and Slaughter, J. (2000) 'The geographical mobility of severely mentally ill residents in London'. *Social Psychiatry and Psychiatric Epidemiology, 35*, 164–169.

Link, B. G. and Phelan, J. (1995) 'Social conditions as fundamental causes of disease'. *Journal of Health and Social Behavior, 35*, extra issue, 80–94.

Lowry, S. (1991) 'Housing'. *British Medical Journal, 303*, 838–840.

Macintyre, S. (1999) 'Geographical inequalities in mortality, morbidity and health related behaviour in England', in Gordon, D., Shaw, M., Dorling, D. and Davey Smith, G. (eds), *Inequalities in Health: The evidence presented to the Independent Inquiry into Inequalities in Health, chaired by Sir Donald Acheson*. Bristol: The Policy Press.

Macintyre, S., Maciver, S. and Soomans, A. (1993) 'Area, class and health: should we be focusing in places or people?'. *Journal of Social Policy, 22*, 213–234.

Macintyre, S., Ellaway, A., Der, G., Ford, G. and Hunt, K. (1998) 'Do housing tenure and car access predict health because they are simply markers of income or self esteem? A Scottish study'. *Journal of Epidemiology and Community Health, 52*, 657–664.

Malmberg, A., Hawton, K. and Simkin, S. (1997) 'A study of suicide in farmers in England and Wales'. *Journal of Psychosomatic Research, 43*, 107–111.

Mattiasson, I., Lindgarde, F., Nilsson, J. A. and Theorell, T. (1990) 'Threat of unemployment and cardiovascular risk factors: longitudinal study of quality of sleep and serum cholesterol concentrations in men threatened with redundancy'. *British Medical Journal, 301*, 461–466.

Maylath, E., Seidel, J. and Schlattmann, P. (2000) 'Inequity in the hospital care of patients with alcoholism and medication addiction'. *European Addiction Research, 6*, 79–83.

Maylath, E., Seidel, J., Werner, B. and Schlattmann, P. (1999) 'Geographical analysis of the risk of psychiatric hospitalization in Hamburg from 1988–1994'. *European Psychiatry: the Journal of the Association of European Psychiatrists, 14*, 414–425.

Milligan, C. (1996) 'Service dependent ghetto formation – a transferable concept?', *Health and Place, 2*, 199–211.

Milligan, C. (2000a) ' "Breaking out of the asylum": developments in the geography of mental ill-health – the influence of the informal sector'. *Health and Place, 6*, 189–200.

Milligan, C. (2000b) ' "Bearing the burden": towards a restructured geography of caring'. *Area, 32*, 49–58.

Mitchell, R., Gleave, S., Bartley, M., Wiggins, D. and Joshi, H. (2000) 'Do attitude and area influence health? A multilevel approach to health inequalities'. *Health and Place, 6*, 67–79.

Moon, G. (1990) 'Conceptions of space and community in British health policy'. *Social Science and Medicine, 30*, 165–171.

Moon, G. (2000) 'Risk and protection: the discourse of confinement in contemporary mental health policy'. *Health and Place, 6*, 239–250.

Morrell, S., Taylor, R., Quine, S., Kerr, C. and Western, J. (1994) 'A cohort study of unemployment as a cause of psychological disturbance in Australian youth'. *Social Science and Medicine, 38*, 1553–1564.

Mossman, D. (1997) 'Deinstitutionalization, homelessness and the myth of psychiatric abandonment: a structural anthropology perspective'. *Social Science and Medicine, 44*, 71–83.

Pacione, M. (1995) 'The geography of deprivation in rural Scotland'. *Transactions of Institute of British Geographers, 20*, 173–192.

Parr, H. (1995) 'Mental health, public space and the city'. *Environment and Planning D: Society and Space, 15*, 435–454.

Parr, H. (1999) 'Mental health and the therapeutic geographies of the city', in Williams, A. (ed.), *Therapeutic landscapes: The dynamic between place and wellness*. New York: University Press of America.

Parr, H. (2000) 'Interpreting the "hidden social geographies" of mental health: ethnographies of inclusion and exclusion in semi-institutional places'. *Health and Place, 6*, 225–237.

Pearson, C. A. (1999) 'New York Psychiatric Institute, New York City'. *Architectural Record, 197*, 138–141.

Pescosolido, B. A., Gardner, C. B. and Lubell, K. M. (1998) 'How people get into mental health services: stories of choice, coercion and "muddling through" from "first-timers" '. *Social Science and Medicine, 46*, 275–286.

Philo, C. (1989) 'Enough to drive one mad: the organization of space in 19th century lunatic asylums', in Wolch, J. and Dear, M. (eds), *The power of geography*. Boston: Unwin Hyman.

Philo, C. (1997) 'Across the water: reviewing geographical studies of asylums and other mental health facilities'. *Health and Place, 3*, 73–89.

Pinfold, V. (2000) ' "Building up safe havens . . . around the world": users' experiences of living in the community with mental health problems'. *Health and Place, 6*, 201–212.

Popay, J., Williams, G., Thomas, C. and Gatrell, A. (1998) 'Theorising inequalities in health: the place of lay knowledge', in Bartley, M., Blane, D. and Davey-Smith, G. (eds), *The Sociology of Health Inequalities*, pp. 59–84. Oxford: Blackwell.

Rose, G. (1992) *The strategy of preventive medicine*. Oxford: Oxford University Press.

Sainsbury, P. (1955) *Suicide in London: an ecological study*. London: Chapman and Hall.

Sanderson, T. and Langford, I. (1996) 'A study of the geographical distribution of suicide rates in England and Wales 1989–1992 using empirical Bayes estimates'. *Social Science and Medicine, 43*, 489–502.

Schwartz, S. (1994) 'The fallacy of the ecological fallacy: the potential misuse of a concept and the consequences'. *American Journal of Public Health, 84*, 819–824.

Schwefel, D. (1986) 'Unemployment, health and health services in German-speaking countries'. *Social Science and Medicine, 22*, 409–430.

Shouls, S., Congdon, P. and Curtis, S. (1996a) 'Modelling inequality in reported long term illness in the UK: combining individual and area characteristics'. *Journal of Epidemiology and Community Health, 50*, 366–376.

Shouls, S., Congdon, P. and Curtis, S. (1996b) 'Geographic variation in illness and mortality: the development of a relevant area typology for SAR districts'. *Health and Place, 2*, 139–156.

Siahpush, M. and Singh, G. K. (1999) 'Social integration and mortality in Australia'. *Australian and New Zealand Journal of Public Health, 23*, 571–577.

Siegel, C., Laska, E., Haguland, G., O'Neill, D., Cohen, N. and Lesser, M. (2000) 'The construction of community indexes of mental health and social and mental well-being and their application to New York City'. *Evaluation Programme Planning, 23*, 315–327.

Sim, D. (1984) 'Urban deprivation: not just the inner city'. *Area, 16*, 299–300.

Sloggett, A. and Joshi, H. (1998) 'Deprivation indicators as predictors of life events 1981–1992 based on the UK ONS Longitudinal Study'. *Journal of Epidemiology and Community Health, 52*, 228–233.

Smith, C. (1977) *The geography of mental health*. Washington, DC: Association of American Geographers.

Smith, C. and Giggs, J. (1988) *Location and stigma: Contemporary perspectives on mental health and mental health care*. London: Unwin Hyman.

Smith, C. and Hanham, R. (1981) 'Proximity and the formation of public attitudes towards mental illness'. *Environment and Planning A, 13*, 147–165.

Stansfeld, S. (1999) 'Social support and social cohesion', in Wilkinson, R. and Marmot, M. G. (eds), *The social determinants of health*. Oxford: Oxford University Press.

Stansfeld, S. A., Fuhrer, R., Shipley, M. J. and Marmot, M. G. (1999) 'Work characteristics predict psychiatric disorder: prospective results from the Whitehall II Study'. *Occupational and Environmental Medicine, 56*, 302–307.

Takahashi, L. and Gaber, S. (1998) 'Controversial facility siting in the urban environment – resident and planner perceptions in the United States'. *Environment and Behavior, 30*, 184–215.

Theorell, T. and Karasek, R. A. (1996) 'Current issues relating to psychosocial job strain and cardiovascular disease research'. *Journal of Occupational Health Psychology, 1*, 9–26.

Townsend, P., Phillimore, P. and Geattie, A. (1988) *Health and deprivation: Inequality in the North*. London: Croom Helm.

Tuan, Y.-F. (1974) *Topophilia*. London: Prentice Hall.

Verheij, R. A. (1996) 'Explaining urban–rural variations in health: a review of interactions between individual and environment'. *Social Science and Medicine, 42*, 923–935.

Victor, C. (1997) 'The health of homeless people: a review'. *European Journal of Public Health*, 7, 398–404.

Vorster, H., Wissing, M., Venter, C., Kruger, H., Kruger, A., Malan, N., de Ridder, J., Veldman, F., Steyn, H., Margetts, B. and MacIntyre, U. (2000) 'The impact of urbanization of physical, physiological and mental health of Africans in the North West Province of South Africa, The THUSA study'. *South African Journal of Science, 96*, 505–514.

Wallace, R. (1990) 'Urban desertification, public health and public order: "planned shrinkage", violent death, substance abuse and AIDS in the Bronx'. *Social Science and Medicine, 31*, 801–813.

Wallace, R. and Wallace, D. (1997) 'Socioeconomic determinants of health: community marginalisation and the diffusion of disease and disorder in the United States'. *British Medical Journal, 314*, 1341–1345.

Weist, M. D., Albus, K. A., Bickham, N., Tashman, N. A. and Perez-Febles, A. (2000) 'A questionnaire to measure factors that protect youth against stressors of inner-city life'. *Psychiatric Services, 51*, 1042–1044.

Williams, A. (1999) *Therapeutic landscapes: The dynamic between place and wellness*. New York: University Press of America.

Wilson, K. C., Chen, R., Taylor, S., McCracken, C. F. and Copeland, J. R. (1999) 'Socio-economic deprivation and the prevalence and prediction of depression in older community residents, the MRC-ALPHA Study'. *British Journal of Psychiatry, 175*, 549–553.

Wilton, R. (1998) 'The constitution of difference: space and psyche in landscapes of exclusion'. *Geoforum, 29*, 173–185.

Wolch, J., (1990) *The shadow state: Government and voluntary sector in transition*. New York: The Foundation Centre.

Wolch, J. and Philo, C. (2000) 'From distributions of deviance to definitions of difference: past and future mental health geographies'. *Health and Place, 6*, 137–157.

4 Urban–rural differences, socio-economic status and psychiatric disorder

Stephen Stansfeld, Scott Weich, Charlotte Clark, Jane Boydell and Hugh Freeman

Differences have been observed in the prevalence of psychiatric disorder between urban and rural environments that vary both by type of disorder and by area studied, though with generally modest effect sizes. These have been examined to try to understand variations in exposure to factors in different communities that might contribute to explaining environmental influences on aetiology. For instance, there may be variations in urban and rural areas between rates of employment, ethnicity, social support, life events, and physical illness (Bowling & Farquhar, 1991; Carpiniello *et al.*, 1989; Romans-Clarkson *et al.*, 1990). Some differences in prevalence may also be explained in terms of nosocomial factors, i.e. relating to services: including access to treatment, recognition of illness, expectations of treatment, and available resources (Sundquist *et al.*, 2004b).

Since these differences are not uniform across the great variety of urban and rural environments that exist, one may assume that any explanations for them must be multifactorial, but what constitutes an 'urban' or 'rural' environment? The answer is complex, because the boundaries between cities, suburbs, and the countryside are now less easily defined. Garden cities, the sprawl of suburbs into the country, the move away from inner cities to suburbs, and the gradual formation of shapeless 'edge cities' have reduced the homogeneity of both kinds of setting. At one time, the physical distance between town and country was accompanied by a marked cultural, social, and psychological contrast between urban and rural dwellers. Cultural traditions, the arrangements of society, social networks, and ways of thinking about health were clearly identifiable as separate in the different communities. This was especially the case in rural populations, where the pace of life was slower and there was relative isolation from other communities. Isolation in such groups, though, has always been relative; trade and traffic between them has gone on at least since the Bronze Age. However, recent ease of travel and communications has greatly reduced such isolation: urban and rural environments are becoming socially and culturally homogenized.

An inhuman environment. Subway, Slough, England, 2005 (used with permission of Dan Sparham/Rex Features).

Cities and rural areas

Cities, or the process of urbanization, are defined primarily according to the discipline involved: to the social demographer, it concerns population size, to sociologists the effect of this size on social dynamics, to anthropologists it is 'urban culture', and to economists urban patterns of trade and labour. Psychiatrists and psychologists may see cities primarily in terms of social and psychological variables, but these are not necessarily contradictory definitions. Population size is largely a macro-level variable, while 'urban culture' is a more intermediate-level one of neighbourhoods, and psychological variables act mainly at the level of the individual; these different influences have complex interrelationships.

There is enormous variation within the category of 'cities', which range from quite small towns to vast megalopolises. Because of this, urban–rural differences in mental health cannot be categorical, but more of a continuum. Sartorius (1998) points out that such agglomerations 'are not only cities grown big; they are likely to be different creatures'. This dimension of scale may have far-reaching implications for health. In 1800, 86% of the world's population lived in rural areas, but by 2000 it was estimated that more than 50% lived in urban settings. By 2030, 'more than 80% of several continents and half of Asia and Africa will probably be living in urban areas' (Vidal, 2004).

In the developing world, at least 50% of urban dwellers live in poverty with a high risk for both physical and mental illness, and for every type of social problem. Cities create a context that can foster economic growth, political security, and social networks, though with an ever greater increase in scale, it becomes more difficult to maintain conditions of 'intimacy, security, and mutuality' (Marsella, 1998), which are believed to be essential for a secure and healthy existence. There is more likelihood of social disorganization with increasing city size because of the ever greater difficulty in maintaining cohesion and public order (Wedmore & Freeman, 1984). Through its connection to urban deprivation and disorganisation, poverty is probably the greatest single predictor of ill-health and mortality.

Methodological issues

Kasl (1977: 75) (quoted in Marsella, 1998) wrote that:

> A contrast of urban versus rural places of residence is a natural extension of the urban ecology approach . . . containing not only differences in residential environment, but also factors, such as education, occupation, physical activity, diet, availability of services, etc., as well as interpersonal contacts, attitudes, values, and beliefs about medical care. Thus, information about rural–urban health differences is inherently ambiguous from a theoretical or aetiological viewpoint.

This methodological warning remains relevant when one is looking at the issues that arise in research. First, in studying urban–rural differences, there is the choice of sample: simply taking subjects from a particular area of residence may not be sufficient, since rural residence does not necessarily mean adoption of a rural lifestyle. It might seem desirable to include participation in rural life in the definition. Even then, it is not always clear that those living in rural areas necessarily subscribe to 'rural' values, particularly as the numbers of people engaged in agriculture fall continuously.

Recent studies have been concerned with the potential impact of the wider environment on rates of psychiatric disorder, progressing from exposures operating at the individual level (e.g. poverty, poor social support) to more 'contextual' factors including the built environment, income inequality (Weich *et al.*, 2001) and 'social capital' (McKenzie *et al.*, 2002). All of these are conceptualized as being 'ecological' risk factors, in the sense of being characteristics of communities or places that are independent of individual residents. 'Social capital' can be related to Durkheim's (1952) concept of 'anomie'. It is often described as community cooperation, reciprocity, and trust, manifest particularly through civic participation and engagement (Health Development Agency, 2004; Putnam, 1993) although its definition is by no means agreed. Neither is there any consensus on how such a valuable quality could be improved (Muntaner *et al.*, 2001). An American attempt to measure social capital (Kawachi *et al.*, 1997) used people's membership of voluntary groups and their level of trust in other people; associations between these and mortality rates were found in comparisons between different states. However, a concept such as 'trust' seems highly subjective.

One repeated question is the relative importance of birth versus childhood residence in either environment. Marcelis *et al.* (1999), finding that about three-quarters of people living in urban areas had also been born there, proposed that living in an urban environment in early life might increase general vulnerability later, particularly to schizophrenia. This would be more likely if exposure to any type of environment was relatively stable over time, as seemed to be generally true. Since subtle, psychosis-like experiences have been identified in 23% of people in the most urban areas of the Netherlands, compared with 13% in the most rural areas, there must be a widespread exposure to environmental influences that would have a cumulative effect over the course of development. This was independent of the increased rate of psychosis, service use, and socio-demographic factors (Van Os *et al.*, 2001). Van Os *et al.* (2004) estimated the association between urbanicity of birth and family history of schizophrenia in a large population-based Danish cohort, concluding that a proxy genetic risk factor acts synergistically with a proxy environmental factor so that between one-fifth and one-third of individuals exposed to both develop the disorder. Theoretically, therefore, elimination of the environmental factor would neutralize much of the genetic morbidity force in the general population.

'Compositional' measures – the aggregated characteristics of individuals living in particular places – are often contrasted with 'contextual' measures, which reflect the characteristics of places themselves. The latter remain largely conspicuous by their absence in the literature, notable exceptions being studies with independent observations of (typically) the built environment (Cohen *et al.*, 2000; Hembree *et al.*, 2005; Weich *et al.*, 2002). Macintyre *et al.* (2002) suggested that the distinction between the two indices may not be clear cut: 'Variables measured at the individual level (e.g. educational attainment or employment) may be partly determined by area-level characteristics (e.g. quality of local schools, job opportunities, or even public transport)'. Unfortunately, the dearth of validated contextual measures precludes empirical investigation of this work, but it represents a major theoretical and empirical advance (Cummins *et al.*, 2005). Geographical differences based on the importance of shared norms, traditions, and interests have been described as 'collective' explanations; these complement both the contextual and compositional kinds, although coming generally within the ambit of the contextual (Macintyre *et al.*, 2002).

Definitions of urbanicity

The definition of urbanicity is of fundamental methodological importance; most studies use population density for this purpose (Martin *et al.*, 2000; National Statistics, 2006; Shucksmith, 1990), with sparsely populated areas being considered 'rural' and more densely settled areas 'urban'. However, this may result in some misclassification, as not all rural areas have a low population density or urban areas a high one (Weich, 2005). Another approach is to use definitions derived from administrative sources, such as the census: these range from large-scale, such as electoral wards, to smaller-scale neighbourhood-based criteria. A UK governmental group has defined urban areas as having a population of 10,000 or more (National Statistics, 2004). Subjective ratings of urbanicity by residents or investigators have also been used (e.g. Paykel *et al.*, 2000), but may be of limited validity.

The heterogeneity within both urban and rural environments may also invalidate comparisons of one setting with another. Even if the population size is similar between communities, social processes such as stratification – the division of the community by social class, implying differences in income, occupation, and leisure interests – will vary. It is also difficult to make meaningful international comparisons if the origins and definition of urbanization differ markedly.

A further issue concerns the level of disorder to be studied. Psychiatric diagnoses, although precise, may represent too severe a degree of morbidity and be too limited for this purpose. Most environmental influences are more likely to induce subclinical health effects – on well-being, quality of life, morale/demoralization, empowerment, and feelings of threat from or control over one's surroundings – rather than clinical abnormalities. So far as possible, 'active ingredients' of positive mental health, such as coping, resourcefulness, and hardiness, should also be included. In assessing the simultaneous impact of these many different factors, sophisticated statistical techniques need to be used, which include multivariate analysis, multilevel modelling, and path analysis. It is then often feasible to separate the effects of factors that act on health at a societal level from those acting at local or individual levels.

The dearth of longitudinal research

There have been very few prospective studies in this area. This is especially problematic in the investigation of chronic or recurrent disorders such as anxiety and depression, since cross-sectional studies may conceal associations between risk factors as well as the onset or outcome of episodes of disorder. Evidence that socio-economic adversity is associated with longer episodes of the common mental disorders, but not with the onset of episodes (Hauck & Rice, 2004; Lorant *et al.*, 2003, Weich & Lewis, 1998b), suggests that episode duration should be longer in areas with the highest levels of socio-economic deprivation.

Since it is inconceivable that the effects of place on mental health are instantaneous, cross-sectional studies are arguably the least informative. Although there is little evidence to indicate the time-scale over which such effects occur, the most potent risk factors may be those operating during childhood (Gilman *et al.*, 2003). Clearly, educational and employment opportunities vary markedly between places. Therefore, adjusting for the socio-economic characteristics of residents (including their educational attainment and employment status) overlooks the fact that these are likely to be determined in part by where they live (or have lived). We know that deprived individuals live in deprived places and are less healthy than those living in affluent areas. Perhaps the question should be not whether there is an independent effect of place on health, after adjusting for individual characteristics, but why it is that this clustering should persist across generations? We need to know much more about residential mobility: who moves between areas, why they move, and what effect this has on their health. The health effects of residential mobility (or lack thereof) – like those of place more generally – may vary with individual circumstances, including health. Childhood socio-economic status is a powerful determinant of adult mental health, independent of adult socio-economic status (Poulton *et al.*, 2002). We need to establish whether place has similarly potent effects during childhood.

Rural tranquility. Near Totnes, Devon, England (used with permission of CPRE).

Common mental disorders and the environment

Socio-economic status

Robust associations have been demonstrated between individual-level socio-economic status, mortality, and many forms of morbidity, including psychiatric (Lewis *et al.*, 1998; Marmot & Wilkinson, 2001; Rodgers, 1991; Stansfeld & Marmot, 1992; Weich & Lewis, 1998a, 1998b). Much more research has been done to understand the links between socio-economic status and the most common mental disorders (CMDs) – anxiety and depression – than with schizophrenia, where individual disability and impaired social functioning are often highly evident. Earlier studies based on occupational social class – an imprecise measure of social status – resulted in inconsistent findings (Rodgers, 1991; Stansfeld & Marmot, 1992). By contrast, those using measures of material standard of living (such income, housing tenure, and car access) have demonstrated a linear gradient in morbidity analogous to that reported for cardiovascular disease and independent of occupational social class (Weich & Lewis, 1998a). One of the most intriguing findings is that the best predictor of future CMD morbidity is self-reported financial strain. This association remained highly significant even after adjusting for objective indices of standard of living such as income and baseline symptoms of anxiety and depression (Weich & Lewis, 1998b). Although unexplained, this raises the possibility that 'financial strain' might be a more accurate indication of an individual's material circumstances than indices such as income or housing tenure. This variable may also reflect personality traits such as pessimism or neuroticism, which might act as independent risk factors for future mental disorder.

Perhaps the greatest challenge to our understanding here lies in trying to define the relevant 'environment', since potentially important exposures may be found across a wide range of spatial scales. Indeed, some exposures that are considered to be 'environmental' – such as education, housing, income, and even life events – are highly heritable and may reflect intrinsic characteristics of the individual (Kendler *et al.*, 1999, 2002). Furthermore, associations with exposures that are located within individuals, such as ethnicity and past psychiatric morbidity, may well be mediated through 'environmental' exposures such as socio-economic deprivation, employment, or even racism and discrimination.

An important factor is poverty and relative social disadvantage. Both of these are risk factors for CMDs. The key aspects of poverty for mental health are largely material: low family income and the problems this entails (poor housing, heating, nutrition, clothing, and access to health care and transport; inability to maintain hygiene; and lack of choice about an area in which to live). A focus solely on material aspects of poverty, however, ignores the social implications. Poor housing can lead to overcrowding and lack of areas for positive interaction, with loss of opportunities for social support. Poor nutrition can lead to physical ill-health, apathy, and fatigue as well as interfering with the capacity to maintain social relationships and care for children. Inadequate clothing, lack of money for transport, and no housing choice can all contribute to low self-esteem. Thus, material disadvantage is tied in with psychosocial disadvantage. Also, relative social deprivation, i.e. detrimental comparison with others, may be related to anxiety and lower levels of well-being (Wilkinson, 1996).

Much recent research into environmental risks for the most common mental disorders, anxiety and depression, has been concerned with quantifying the variance in rates of these conditions at different spatial levels. However, the intuitive importance of location as a determinant of life chances (Dorling, 2001; Macintyre *et al.*, 2002) is at odds with rapidly accumulating evidence of little or no geographical variation in the prevalence of these disorders – particularly after adjusting for the characteristics of individual residents (Henderson *et al.*, 2005; McCulloch, 2001; Pickett & Pearl, 2001; Reijneveld & Schene, 1998; Ross, 2000; Wainwright & Surtees, 2004a, 2004b; Weich *et al.*, 2003a). Certainly, larger area-level effects are found for psychotic illnesses and severe depression (Boydell *et al.*, 2001; Silver *et al.*, 2002; Sundquist *et al.*, 2004a; van Os, 2004; van Os *et al.*, 2000).

The geographical scale at which contextual factors might impact on mental health remains unknown. Most studies have been based on the secondary analysis of data collected across administrative boundaries, inviting criticism of a lack of theorizing about place effects (Macintyre *et al.*, 2002; Mitchell, 2001). Studies of very large areas, such as UK regions (with hundreds of thousands of residents), are especially difficult to interpret (Duncan *et al.*, 1995; Lewis & Booth, 1992; Skapinakis *et al.*, 2005). Recent studies have examined effects over smaller areas, ranging from Amsterdam boroughs (average population 33,000) to postcode sectors (population 9500), neighbourhoods (average 8000) (Reijneveld *et al.*, 2000), UK electoral wards (average 5500) (McCulloch, 2001; Wainwright & Surtees, 2004b; Weich *et al.*, 2003a) and US census tracts (population 4000) (Ross, 2000). Effect sizes at these levels are small and rarely statistically significant. The percentage of variance in symptoms of anxiety and depression at the area level ranges from 0.5%–4% before adjusting for the characteristics of individual residents to less than 1% after doing so.

Wards may be too large and heterogeneous to detect contextual effects, and recent studies provide only limited support for the view that variance in CMD is greater for smaller areas (Reijneveld *et al.*, 2000). The significance of this remains to be determined, and there have been few studies at a very small scale. Although 'neighbourhood' is commonly used, it remains notoriously difficult to define (Burrows & Bradshaw, 2001). While some studies have defined neighbourhoods using natural boundaries (for example, areas of homogeneous housing type) (Birtchnell *et al.*, 1988; Halpern, 1995; Weich *et al.*, 2002), others have used the same term to describe administrative units such as census tracts or US city blocks (Cohen *et al.*, 2000; Hembree *et al.*, 2005; Sampson *et al.*, 1997). Other studies have avoided this uncertainty by encouraging respondents to judge the boundaries of their 'neighbourhood' or 'area' (Macintyre *et al.*, 2003).

Rural tranquility again. Crowlink Estate, Sussex, England (used with permission of CPRE).

There is a substantial between-household variation in rates of CMD in Britain, although most studies overlook household as a discrete level (McCulloch, 2001; Silver *et al.*, 2002; Wainwright & Surtees, 2004a). In a large national household panel study, over 10% of the variance in scores on the 12-item General Health Questionnaire occurred at household level, even after adjusting for the characteristics of individuals, households, and wards (Weich *et al.*, 2003). This remains unexplained, but could be due to exposures operating at a spatial level between ward and household, including factors – such as difficulties with neighbours, or fear of being burgled or mugged – operating over much smaller areas (Weich *et al.*, 2002).

Understanding place: context or composition?

Several studies have estimated associations between the characteristics of places and rates of mental disorders. Since most studies are data-driven secondary analyses (Macintyre *et al.*, 2002), places are often characterized using census-based aggregate measures of population composition. The most commonly used measures are those reflecting prevailing socio-economic circumstances, for example (un)employment, housing tenure, and the proportion of single adult households – singly or in combination (Henderson *et al.*, 2005; Reijneveld & Schene, 1998; Ross, 2000; Wainwright & Surtees, 2004a) – or income inequality (Weich *et al.*, 2001). None have been found to be associated with the prevalence of CMD to a statistically significant degree, after adjusting for individual characteristics (Weich *et al.*, 2003b). However, a recent Chilean study found that individuals living in sectors of Santiago with more desirable features of the built environment, such as better roads and more green space had less common mental disorder even adjusting for individual education and income (Araya *et al.*, 2007b).

The most common alternatives to census-based place descriptors are summary statistics derived from surveys of local residents (Cohen *et al.*, 2003; Sampson *et al.*, 1997). These are sometimes portrayed as characteristics of the local area, but little attention has been paid to possible confounding by outcomes (for example, mental health). Even where attitudes (for example, about the trustworthiness of neighbours) are from a representative sample of those living in an area and not just participants in a particular study, there is a tendency to use mean values without reference to other statistical properties. This approach is typical of social capital research, which has been criticized on both theoretical and empirical grounds (Health Development Agency, 2004; McKenzie *et al.*, 2002).

Another approach has been to classify small areas according to a particular characteristic, most commonly 'urban' or 'rural' location. UK studies have found a higher prevalence of CMDs among those living in 'urban' (compared with 'rural' or 'suburban') areas (Lehtinen *et al.*, 2003; Lewis & Booth, 1994; Meltzer *et al.*, 1995; Paykel *et al.*, 2000). Suicide rates are also higher in urban than rural areas of Britain (Saunderson *et al.*, 1998), although this gradient may be falling (Middleton *et al.*, 2003). In Sweden, a study based on the entire population aged 25–64 found a statistically significant linear association between increasing population density and rates of first admission for depression (Sundquist *et al.*, 2004a). Yet studies in New Zealand (Romans-Clarkson *et al.*, 1990), USA (Blazer *et al.*, 1985), Scandinavia (Lehtinen *et al.*, 2003), and Canada (Wang, 2004) found no evidence of statistically significant urban–rural differences in the prevalence of CMDs. These inconsistencies may be partly due to differences in methodology, including variation in the definition of 'urban' and 'rural' areas; cross-national comparisons are also problematic (Costello *et al.*, 2001). Findings based on the treated incidence of psychiatric disorders are especially difficult, given nosocomial differences.

Population density, the most common index of urbanicity (e.g. Sundquist *et al.*, 2004a; Wang, 2004), may fail to capture aspects such as geographical remoteness (Middleton *et al.*, 2004); some researchers have resorted to subjective or impressionistic definitions (Meltzer *et al.*, 1995; Paykel *et al.*, 2000). The assumption that rural residents are less deprived and healthier than their urban counterparts has also been challenged statistically. In many parts of the world, rural life is, on average, more deprived than that in cities. Rural wards (in the UK) are smaller, and have greater internal (between-individual) variability in deprivation, even over areas smaller than wards (Weich *et al.*, 2006), but there is less variation in deprivation *between* rural areas than their urban counterparts (Haynes & Gale, 2000). However, associations between area-level socio-economic deprivation and worse health emerge for rural areas when their wards are aggregated to approximate to the size of urban wards (Haynes & Gale, 2000).

Interactions between people and places

In addition to the finding that area explains little of the variance in the prevalence of CMDs, the substantial variance at the household level is little altered by specifying a host of household- and individual-level characteristics. Since this variance is unexplained, theoretical models remain incomplete. The findings at household level are consistent with spousal similarity in depressive symptoms (Dufouil & Alpérovitch, 2000), and intra-household processes certainly warrant scrutiny. Although assortative mating may play a part, genetic factors are otherwise unlikely to play a very large role, as most cohabiting individuals are not consanguineous.

The effects of place may vary with individual and household characteristics (Macintyre *et al.*, 2002). This is reflected in: (i) an urban excess of CMDs only among those who were economically inactive (Weich *et al.*, 2003b); (ii) variation in suicide rates with area-level and individual socio-economic factors, particularly unemployment (Kelly *et al.*, 1995; Saunderson & Langford, 1996); and (iii) interaction between ethnicity and urban/rural location in the association with depressive symptoms among those living in poverty in the USA (Amato & Zuo, 1992). These findings suggest that place may only affect those with specific vulnerabilities, rather than everyone living in a particular location (van Os, 2004). To date, few studies have had sufficient power to test for important interactions, particularly concerning the onset of rare conditions such as schizophrenia.

The aetiology of CMDs

Important aetiological factors in explaining urban–rural differences in psychiatric disorder may relate to: (i) the physical environment (e.g. noise, air, soil and water pollution; problems with housing or transport); or (ii) the social, cultural, and economic environment (social integration, networks, isolation, social change, employment opportunities, industrialization, acculturation and migration/immigration – forced or voluntary); or (iii) a combination of the two (e.g. overcrowding, which has both spatial and psychological components).

Another complex set of issues in which there may be urban–rural differences comprises attitudes, values, and beliefs. In spite of the changes mentioned above, some rural cultures may still differ markedly from urban ones. The generally slower pace of life, greater focus on the land, self-sufficiency, and the more interlinked nature of many rural communities could still contain elements either protective or harmful for mental health. The different patterns of life may also mean exposure to contrasts in life events, chronic difficulties, occupational exposures, physical activity, leisure, substance use, and educational opportunities. The scientific challenge is to try to disentangle the ingredients important for mental health and different rates of disorder.

Urban–rural differences in the United Kingdom

Currently, one-fifth of the UK population live in rural areas (National Statistics, 2006), though the proportion has begun to rise in recent years, after a very long decline. In contrast to the usually positive view, increased homelessness, lack of supported housing, social isolation, and poor public transport are all features of the current British rural environment (Shucksmith *et al.*, 1990).

Regional differences in psychiatric morbidity have been demonstrated in the UK through analysis of a national survey (Lewis & Booth, 1992). On the General Health Questionnaire (GHQ), all four northern regions had a higher prevalence of psychiatric morbidity than all four southern regions. These variations were less common in the Registrar-General Social Classes I and II and among those living in urban areas. In general, the rates of psychiatric disorder matched the regional overall mortality rates, though psychiatric morbidity was lower in Scotland but higher in London, while the converse was true for mortality. These variations in health are often explained in terms of social deprivation, but it is not clear that this in itself would be sufficient. A study using GHQ data from the 1984/5 Health & Lifestyle survey found regional variation in mental health, but explained this on methodological grounds (Duncan *et al.*, 1995). No north–south distinction was found and the local neighbourhood seemed to have little effect beyond that of the type of people who lived there (i.e. 'compositional effects').

More recent analyses of GHQ data from the British Household Panel Survey (BHPS), using ward-level data (mean population = 5000) to assess urbanicity, have found modest but statistically significant differences in rates of CMDs between urban and rural residents (Weich *et al.*, 2006). However, an earlier analysis found this association only for the economically inactive (Weich *et al.*, 2003b), suggesting that the effects of place may be greater for those who spend more time at home or who are vulnerable because of adversity. Furthermore, a follow-up study found that less than 1% of the total variance in CMDs and change in GHQ scores occurred at the ward level (Weich *et al.*, 2005); in comparison, household-level factors accounted for a significant 12% of the variance. It was concluded that ward-level socio-economic deprivation had little effect on either the onset or maintenance of CMDs, though associations might be observable at a smaller spatial scale. In the BHPS, household-level effects including overcrowding, household type, housing tenure, and structural problems explained 14% of the variance in GHQ scores. Nevertheless, while measured at the household level, these exposures are not independent of area influences. Individual and household influences are more proximal measures of risk, and so likely to explain more of the variance of an individual measure of mental health, but this does not rule out the possibility that area characteristics influence both kinds of effects. Thus, if area influences are in fact mediated through household and individual effects, the size of their contribution might be underestimated.

Over a five-year period, Propper *et al.* (2005) found no association between urbanicity, using census enumeration districts (500 to 800 persons), and prevalence of CMD or changes in GHQ scores. This was evidence against urbanicity being associated with common mental disorders. On the other hand, in a representative UK community sample, using the Structured Clinical Interview for DSM-IV AXIS II disorders (American Psychiatric Association, 1994), personality disorders were especially common in urban areas and highest among separated and unemployed men in cities and towns (Coid *et al.*, 2006). This suggests that any urban–rural differences may differ by diagnosis and that diagnoses that are susceptible to the social influences prevalent in cities may be more frequent there.

In the 1993 national study of psychiatric morbidity in 10,000 private households in Britain, significantly higher prevalences of depression, anxiety disorders, and phobias were found in urban areas. However, there were no significant differences in obsessive-compulsive disorder, panic, alcohol and drug dependency, or psychosis, although in the last of these, the numbers were very small (Meltzer *et al.*, 1995). The disadvantage of these comparisons was that the definition of 'rurality' was left to the many interviewers, thus allowing the possibility of bias towards a rural definition of more favourable environments (Gregoire & Thornicroft, 1998). The UK analyses of the national psychiatric morbidity survey, which also found higher rates of psychiatric morbidity, measured by the Revised Clinical Interview Schedule, in urban than in rural areas (Paykel *et al.*, 2000), was similarly limited by its definition of urbanicity.

Differences in affective disorder in Europe and North America

Early studies suggested higher rates of affective disorders in urban areas (Dohrenwend & Dohrenwend, 1974), but subsequent data have been mixed (Kasl, 1977), and definitions used in earlier work may now be out of date (Sturm & Cohen, 2004).

Data from the US National Health & Nutrition Examination Survey suggest higher rates of depression in urban compared with suburban and rural areas (Eaton & Kessler, 1981). Urban areas tended to have higher mean depression scores, though some of the rural farming residents had rates of depression not lagging far behind. Blazer *et al.* (1986), as part of the US Epidemiologic Catchment Area (ECA) Program, found urban–rural differences in 'major depressive episodes', but not in 'dysthymia'. In one site, major depressive disorders were more than twice as frequent in urban as in rural areas (2.4% vs 1.1%). In the Piedmont Health Survey, current major depression was nearly three times more frequent in urban counties (Crowell *et al.*, 1986); rural residence seemed to be especially protective for young women. Retrospective analysis of the 'Americans Changing Lives' survey also found that higher population density was associated with increased rates of depression, after adjustment for age, ethnicity, education, family income, marital status, and length of residence (Oliver, 2003).

In the 1998–9 Canadian National Health Survey, rural areas had a lower prevalence of major depression; this difference remained after adjustment for race, immigration status, occupation, and marital status (Wang, 2004). Not all studies, though, have found higher rates in urban areas (Parikh *et al.*, 1996; Sturm & Cohen, 2004). One study, based on population density, found that suburban residents reported more mental distress than either their rural or urban counterparts (Rohrer *et al.*, 2005), but this did not use validated measures of mental health.

European and North American rural areas do not appear to have exactly the same prevalence rates of psychiatric disorder. In a comparison of the Upper Bavarian Study (UBS) with the ECA, the prevalence rate for any DSM-III Axis I disorder (American Psychiatric Association, 1987) was 18.5% in UBS and 13.4% in rural ECA sites (Fichter *et al.*, 1996). However, if all five ECA sites were included, the prevalence rate became very similar at 18%; within these sites there was more alcohol and drug abuse, more major depression, and more dysthymia in the urban communities. The UBS sample had more dysthymia, but less major depression, phobias, obsessive-compulsive disorder, and substance abuse than the rural ECA sites.

In a study of the lifetime prevalence of psychiatric disorders in Iceland, rates of panic disorder and alcohol dependence were higher in urban areas, while alcohol abuse was more prevalent in rural parts (Stefánsson *et al.*, 1991). Similarly, a study of all first psychiatric admissions in the Netherlands found that individuals living in urban areas were at increased risk of admission for affective psychosis, neuroses, and personality disorders (Peen & Dekker, 2003). The first to make cross-country comparisons of the association between urbanicity and depressive disorder was the European multi-centre ODIN study; it examined prevalence rates in Dublin, Liverpool, Oslo, and Turku (Finland), finding large between-country variation. In Dublin and Liverpool only, urbanicity was associated with higher rates of depression for females, whereas there was no such association for males (Lehtinen *et al.*, 2003).

Reasons for urban–rural differences in affective disorders

Whereas many studies demonstrate urban–rural differences in affective and common mental disorders, other data have shown very little difference (Cheng, 1989; Leighton *et al.*, 1963; Parikh *et al.*, 1996). These contradictions, however, may relate to circumstances peculiar to local environments. If the rural area is impoverished and employment is possible in adjacent urban areas, there will be a tendency for a migration there of healthy workers; this process may then reduce any excess morbidity due to urban living. Levels of social deprivation, employment opportunities, and social integration may be more important than context or location (Judd *et al.*, 2002).

In the UK national psychiatric morbidity survey (Paykel *et al.*, 2000), the higher rates of urban psychiatric morbidity were thought likely to result from urban subjects tending to be both more socially deprived and exposed to more adverse living conditions and life stress. There were also higher rates of alcohol and drug dependence in urban areas. After adjustment for these socio-demographic factors, though, the urban–rural differences in psychiatric morbidity diminished and became non-significant for drug dependence, suggesting that adverse living conditions might explain the identified differences.

However, such differences are sometimes in the opposite direction and may vary by gender. Gender differences in both mood and anxiety disorders were found in urban but not rural samples from the US National Co-morbidity Study (Diala & Muntaner, 2003). Rural men reported more such disorders than urban men, thus removing the expected gender difference in rural populations. It was suggested that these relatively high rates in rural men might be due to fewer well-paid jobs being available, causing greater financial strain.

In a secondary analysis of a sample from a poor Illinois neighbourhood, an increased risk of depression was partially explained by 'compositional' factors: race, ethnicity, sex, age, education, employment, income, household structure, and urban residence (Ross, 2000). Neighbourhood disadvantage, measured as the proportion of poor mother-only households in the area, had a significant effect on individual depression scores. Even though compositional factors reduced the coefficient associated with neighbourhood disadvantage by 64%, this disadvantage effect still remained. This influence on depression became statistically non-significant after adjustment for perceptions of disorder in the local environment. Living in an area of poverty and lawlessness, where social control has broken down, seemed to increase the risk of depression beyond the influence of individual-level factors. It is accepted that such disordered neighbourhoods are much more likely to occur in urban areas.

Culture, social support, and women's roles

It may be that urban–rural differences in women's mental health are more influenced than those of men by cultural factors, the availability of social support, and the value placed on their roles. On the other hand, men's mental health may be influenced more by employment and income. The ODIN study found, in both Liverpool and Dublin, a large urban–rural difference in the prevalence of depression in women that was not found in men or in the overall sample (Lehtinen *et al.*, 2003). Adjustment for socio-demographic factors as well as lack of a confidant and having difficulties in getting practical support from neighbours – both important predictors of depressive disorder – did not explain this female difference.

A comparison of a semi-industrial suburb of Montreal, with a rural county to its north-east (Kovess *et al.*, 1987), reported that major depressive disorder was significantly more frequent in the urban sample. However, that sample had a relative excess of women, persons over the age of 65 years, and separated, divorced, and widowed individuals, while the rural subjects were less mobile and more likely to be unemployed. In men, unemployment was more strongly related to depression in urban areas, especially in the short term. Among women, the most striking difference was between the 'partnered' and 'unpartnered', rates of depression among the latter being much higher in Montreal. Rather than a pure contextual effect, this suggests an interaction between a compositional effect (single marital status) and the social context (a culture not facilitating social integration for single women). In Holland, Van Os *et al.* (2000) found an interaction between individual characteristics and the neighbourhood context; at both levels, social isolation was identified as important. In a study of psychiatric outpatient referrals in Bergen, more married, unmarried, separated, and divorced women, but not men, with affective and anxiety disorders were referred from a satellite town newly established in a rural area than from established urban communities (Andersen, 1987). The unrewarding nature of women's roles – housework, poorly paid employment, low educational attainment, social isolation, poverty, and the presence of children, which were all prevalent in these satellite communities – was a possible explanation for the higher rates in women.

By contrast, the importance of valuing women's roles was shown in a valley of Navarra, where higher rates of minor psychiatric morbidity were found in urban areas. This raised morbidity was associated with single status, age 15–24 years, being unskilled, and having poor social and educational levels (Vázquez-Barquero *et al.*, 1982). However, a lack of association between unemployment and psychopathology among women in the rural part (Vázquez-Barquero *et al.*, 1992) contradicts other urban findings (Bebbington *et al.*, 1981; Brown & Harris, 1978; Cochrane & Stopes Roe, 1980). In urban areas, this effect of unemployment has been interpreted as being due to child-care responsibilities preventing women from going out to work and finding rewarding social relationships, whereas in Spanish rural areas: 'child rearing activities do have a high social value and . . . going out to work is not so essential to guarantee interpersonal contacts and intimate relationships' (Vázquez-Barquero *et al.*, 1992).

Differences in suicide

One specific area in which geographical effects have been studied is suicide. In Sweden, the cause-specific morbidity of 60,515 farmers was compared with that of all economically active individuals living in the same areas (Thelin, 1991). Males had a lower risk of 'mental diseases' (standardized mortality ratio (SMR), males 68; females 92), and also a low relative risk of hospitalization for these disorders. Alcohol-dependent diseases and attempted suicide were also significantly less frequent than expected among both male and female farmers. These data are strikingly different from British findings of increased mental illness and suicide among farmers (Kelly & Bunting, 1998). Farmers rank fourth in the list of occupational groups at most risk of suicide, while suicide is the second most common cause of death for male farmers under 45 (accidents being the first). In numbers of suicides, farmers have the highest ranking of any occupation in the UK; these rates are related to depressive illness, financial and occupational problems, and access to firearms (Malmberg *et al.*, 1999). That Swedish farmers are said to drink modestly, have control over and variety in their work, have stable social circumstances, and low levels of 'migration and alienation' may explain their lower rates of mental illness. In the UK, though, farming is a financially precarious occupation for many, dogged by central regulation, cheap imports, and epidemics of livestock disease.

In an analysis of British rural versus urban suicide rates for young people between 1981 and 1991, the most unfavourable trends occurred in remote rural areas, especially for 15–24-year-old girls, after adjusting for the most obvious potential confounding factors (Middleton *et al.*, 2003). Access to psychiatric services for depression might be an issue here. In Arkansas, more suicide attempts were found in rural than urban residents, with fewer outpatient visits for depression in rural areas (Rost *et al.*, 1998). Singh and Siahpush (2002), using US national mortality data, found that men in the most rural group had almost twice the risk of suicide, compared with urban males. For females, however, an effect was found only in the youngest group, similar to UK findings (Middleton *et al.*, 2003). In China, the female excess in suicide is explained by high rates among women aged 20 to 34 years from rural areas, because of the 'one child' policy and rapid urbanization of the 60 per cent of the population currently living in rural areas. If, as expected, the number of 20–39-year-olds decreases, the excess suicide rate in women should decline (Yip & Liu, 2006). One possibly important factor is the availability of lethal means, e.g. pesticides and rat poison (Yang *et al.*, 2005): in the UK, firearms are generally more available in rural areas.

UK analyses of suicide by area between 1989 and 1992 used Bayes estimates that adjusted for the exaggerated effect of a small number of suicides in sparsely populated rural areas (Saunderson & Langford, 1996). The picture was complex, with some clustering in the large urban areas of Manchester, Birmingham, and London and also in sparsely populated rural areas for men aged 25–44; there were clusters in other areas for men aged 45–64. Among women aged 15–24 there were several high-risk areas but there was less spatial variation for older women. The authors suggest that unemployment and social isolation may be important risk factors, as well as living in an economically depressed area. This combination of factors is probably more likely to be found in deprived inner cities, but males also experienced a greater suicide risk in areas where dairy and hill farmers had been hit by recession. Male suicide rates are more strongly associated with rurality than female rates, which show far less spatial variation (Caldwell *et al.*, 2004; Levin & Leyland, 2005; Otsu, 2004; Singh, 2002).

Another rural factor is remoteness, particularly from support services and social networks. An Australian study (Caldwell *et al.*, 2004) found that young men in non-metropolitan areas, who had significantly less access to professional help, had a higher suicide rate, but there was no such difference in rates of mental disorder. While lack of services could explain the difference in suicide rates for males, factors such as fear of showing vulnerability, denial, and levels of sophistication might contribute to the urban–rural difference. In Scotland, the accessibility of an area – i.e. a town with 10,000 or more within a 30-minute drive – impacted on suicide rates (Levin & Leyland, 2005). Rates in either remote towns or remote rural areas were higher compared with those for males living in accessible towns. Rurality and remoteness had less of an impact on female suicide rates, though these were significantly higher for those living in accessible rural compared with urban areas. Confirming earlier studies, this difference suggests that both service accessibility and rurality have a greater impact on male than on female suicide rates.

Social isolation and difficulties integrating into rural communities may explain the higher rural rates of suicide among immigrant males to Australia than among Australian-born males (Morrell *et al.*, 1999). Similarly, in a Finnish study, risk factors tended to be associated with a different degree of importance in urban and rural suicide rates respectively (Isometsa *et al.*, 1997). Substance use disorders, personality disorders, and psychiatric comorbidity were more common in urban suicides, while rural cases more commonly had physical illness and lacked a close companion of the opposite gender.

Overall, differences between urban and rural settings in terms of suicide are affected by two kinds of factors. They are increased by unemployment, financial problems, poor social support, and access to means of suicide, but are decreased by access to treatment services. While urban–rural differences may be explained in this way, there are also variations within urban areas: London borough suicide rates were highest for the boroughs with the highest population density and a high level of deprivation (Kennedy, 1999). However, an earlier study by Sainsbury (1952) identified social isolation as the factor most strongly associated with suicide in London.

Underlying factors

The concentration of urban–rural differences in population sub-samples seems to make it more likely that such differences in depression and in CMDs are attributable to compositional differences between urban and rural populations. If these differences came primarily from ubiquitous contextual stressors, it seems more likely that the differences between residents would be found across all population groups, as with a toxic exposure. An alternative explanation is that the differences may relate to greater difficulties in achieving the roles in society that are generally expected of men and women respectively.

Less than 1% of the variance in CMDs in the British Household Panel Survey (BHPS) could be explained by area effects at ward level; this was further reduced after adjustment for individual characteristics (Weich *et al.*, 2003a). Similar findings have been shown in other UK studies (Wainwright & Surtees, 2004a). However, both these studies used wards as their definition of 'areas'. These are relatively large areas that may contain much heterogeneity of characteristics, although one study concluded that size of area had little impact on health differences related to area deprivation (Reijneveld *et al.*, 2000).

Overall, though, the evidence above emphasizes the explanation of urban–rural differences in psychiatric disorder mainly by the differential distribution of characteristics at the individual level, such as unemployment, social deprivation, and social isolation, i.e. compositional effects. Moreover, since these exposures tend to cluster, it may be the interaction between them or their cumulative effect that is actually pathogenic. As mentioned above, in analyses of the BHPS, associations between population density, urbanicity, social deprivation, and CMD were only statistically significant in the economically inactive, who would tend to spend more time at home (Weich *et al.*, 2003b), but Macintyre *et al.* (2002) pointed out that the distinction between compositional and contextual effects is by no means absolute. The characteristics of individuals, such as occupation, are likely to be modified by the nature of the local labour market; individual factors may be intervening rather than confounding influences on the effects of area on health. What is probably true for both CMD and affective disorders in adults is that there are no universal urban–rural differences. Instead, where such differences are observed, they are more likely to be due to compositional effects, though what may be particularly powerful is the interaction between contextual and compositional effects in creating pathways of risk for psychiatric disorder.

Children's mental health

In the case of children, the factors that will be important in explaining urban–rural differences in their mental health are not necessarily the same as those in adults. Indeed, the most potent risk factors for such differences may be found in childhood (Weich, 2005). Rutter (1981) compared school children in an inner London borough with others in the rural Isle of Wight, finding a highly significant excess of neurotic and conduct disorders in the urban areas. Four factors were causally related to these differences: family discord, parental deviance, social disadvantage, and school characteristics. These findings confirmed the background features identified by West and Farrington (1973) as important correlates of delinquent behaviour: low family income, large family size, parental criminality, low intelligence, and poor parental behaviour. This made up a subculture in which other antisocial conduct (e.g. drug-taking, attempted suicide, theft) also occur commonly in the late adolescent and early adult years.

A study of adolescents in Munich found that living in an urban area was associated with an increased risk for reporting at least one psychotic experience, after adjustment for socio-economic factors, but was not significantly associated with depressive symptoms or mania (Spauwen *et al.*, 2004). A study of younger children in Finland also found no urban–rural differences in rates of referral for psychiatric evaluation, after adjustment for socio-economic factors (Kumpulainen & Räsänen, 2002). In a sample of very young Turkish children, urban–rural differences were found in parental reports of behavioural and emotional problems (Erol *et al.*, 2005), but major social differences between Turkey and more industrialized countries need to be borne in mind here. Future research is needed to corroborate whether urban–rural differences in mental health are observable in very young children.

In the Great Smoky Mountains Study (Costello *et al.*, 1996) of children aged 9–13, urban–rural differences in psychiatric morbidity, measured by the Child & Adolescent Psychiatric Assessment (CAPA), became non-significant after adjustment for poverty. Rates were high only in children in the direst poverty, and overall the prevalence rates of common childhood psychiatric disorders were fairly similar to those of urban-based studies. It seems likely that material deprivation may contribute to significant psychosocial stressors such as family discord. In Jones's view (2001), 'Financial poverty in rural areas can be extreme, but may not be associated with the social isolation that can affect individuals in urban environments'. On the other hand, it might be that there is nothing specifically damaging about urban environments for children's mental health, but that these environments provide 'more objects and opportunities for delinquent behaviour and that certain features of the built environments may make key activities such as parenting more difficult' (Quinton, 1988).

Service uptake and utilization

Does the rural environment influence service uptake and utilization differently from the urban, in those with established illness? This was examined in a study of two case registers in Northern Italy (Thornicroft *et al.*, 1993). South Verona is an industrial city while Portogruaro is largely rural with similar availability of services. For schizophrenia, no differences were found in the total number of admissions, mean duration of stay, or number of long-stay patients between the two areas. However, for psychiatric diagnoses overall, Portogruaro had more community contacts, fewer admissions, but twice the treated prevalence and incidence of schizophrenia. In the urban districts, unmarried and unemployed persons were more likely to be living alone, while in Portogruaro they were more likely to be living with families. Thus, the pattern of predictors of service use differed across the two areas. For schizophrenia in South Verona, not unlike an earlier British study (Thornicroft, 1991), the combined factors of living alone, unemployment, number of dependants, and being unmarried predicted the total number of admissions, days in hospital, number of community contacts, and number of long-stay patients. Service utilization was predicted by number of dependants, living alone, and unemployment in the case of schizophrenia and by number of dependants, being unmarried, and being unemployed for all psychiatric diagnoses. None of these patterns were found in Portogruaro. It was concluded that these differences may be explained by the social isolation experienced by those with mental illness. In urban areas, patients with no work, no partner, and who live alone are clustered in relatively small portions of Verona, with inexpensive rented accommodation. In the rural districts, although similar patients are no more likely to be married or working, they more often remain living with their family and are not localized. In urban areas, patients without family or other informal carers seemed to place a disproportionate demand on psychiatric services, for want of any other source of support.

In a three-year follow-up of British general practice patients with 'conspicuous psychiatric morbidity' attending either (inner city) urban or rural general practices, urban patients were three times more likely to be admitted to psychiatric hospital, six times more likely to become psychiatric day-patients, and were more likely to attend psychiatric outpatients and take psychotropic drugs (Seivewright *et al.*, 1991). Psychiatric patients from the urban practice had greater severity of illness and were more likely to be male, unemployed, unmarried, and with more personality disorder and alcohol abuse than the rural patients. Some of these differences could be explained in terms of the easier availability of psychiatric services for the urban patients, but they also seem to have had greater levels of handicap and social deprivation.

Patients with schizophrenia and comorbid substance abuse from Arkansas, followed-up six months after discharge from hospital, fared less well in rural than in urban areas for similar reasons to do with the lack of suitable community services (Fischer *et al.*, 1996). In a sample of households in the Ontario Health Survey, there were higher rates of help-seeking for mental health problems in urban than in rural areas (Lin & Parikh, 1999). Clearly, such results are strongly influenced by the different patterns of health care between countries, as well as between areas.

Schizophrenia and the environment

Since the studies by Eaton and Weil (1955) of the Hutterites, a pastoral law-abiding community, it has been established that lack of environmental stressors is no bar to psychosis. Their conclusions did not confirm the common view that a simple and relatively uncomplicated way of life provides virtual immunity from mental disorders.

Nevertheless, the prevalence of schizophrenia is often reported to be lower in rural areas: the rate in rural Scotland was half that in Camberwell (Allardyce *et al.*, 2001). However, the many differences between two such areas make comparisons unhelpful in understanding the nature and antecedents of these widely differing prevalence rates. In this study, the major explanatory variable for the difference was ethnicity, with the urban excess of illness explained by the high rate in non-whites. There was little difference in this respect between urban and non-urban whites, despite socio-economic variations; McCreadie *et al.* (1997) found similar levels of education and occupation among people with schizophrenia in the two areas.

Recent studies have found an association (although not necessarily linear) between deprivation and incidence rates of psychosis (Croudace *et al.*, 2000), prevalence rates of schizophrenia (Moser, 2001), and admission rates for schizophrenia (Boardman *et al.*, 1997; Harrison *et al.*, 1995; Koppel & McGuffin,

1999). While it has long been recognized that individuals with established illness are more likely to be living in deprived, impoverished circumstances, the pendulum of scientific opinion has continued to swing between whether this is cause or effect. The salience of environmental factors for onset has been highlighted at the same time as evidence has emerged concerning underlying genetic and neurodevelopmental processes.

Studying such environmental factors is not easy, particularly since the effects of exposures in early life may not be manifest for many years. Changes in behaviour and (sometimes) context can happen rapidly during adolescence, while onset is not always rapid and easily dated, but may be insidious over several months. Thus, distinguishing between prodromal features of schizophrenia and risk factors for the onset of this illness can be problematic, even using longitudinal research designs. Finally, many environmental factors (like living in an urban area and low socio-economic status) are often confounded with one another.

Social selection versus social causation

For many years, the generally accepted view was that high rates of schizophrenia among those with the lowest socio-economic status – including the preponderance of this illness in inner-city areas – could be accounted for by drift of people with developing schizophrenia into urbanized and deprived areas (the 'social drift' hypothesis). A variant on this theme implied that more able people move out to better areas in the suburbs, leaving a 'residual' population in the centre with a high risk of psychiatric disorders (the 'social residue' theory). Both are forms of health-related social selection. The same processes have been invoked to explain the inverse social class gradient in the prevalence of schizophrenia. The alternative view ('social causation' or 'breeder' hypothesis) holds that environmental factors, such as socio-economic deprivation, cause schizophrenia.

'Social drift' is used to mean the migration to areas of a particular kind, where social demands on them may be less; it has been considered particularly relevant to people affected by schizophrenia, though alcoholics, drug addicts, people with marked personality disorders, and others with reduced social competence and affiliative bonds show the same tendency. Inner-city areas are the ones to which such affected individuals are most likely to migrate in Western countries, since these tend to contain both cheap, single-person accommodation and opportunities for casual but low-paid work, while lacking any well-knit social structure that would make them feel unwelcome. In many studies, the higher prevalence of schizophrenia in central city areas has been more marked in men than in women, which suggests that social influences affect the two genders differently in this disorder, for example that men may be more likely to drift centrally.

Goldberg and Morrison's theory of inter-generational 'social drift' (1963) was a hypothesis of great heuristic importance and was confirmed by Byrne *et al.* (2004), though Dauncey *et al.* (1993) raised methodological objections. Lewis *et al.* (1992) described the social drift hypothesis as having been little challenged for 25 years, in spite of the evidence for it being weak. In fact, Lapouse *et al.* (1956) examined the movement of schizophrenic patients within a city over 20 years before the onset of psychotic illness, but found little evidence of downward drift, while a control group did not move significantly up the social scale, relative to them.

The reverse of the social drift process, but a similar hypothesis, is that of 'social residue', i.e. that the mentally healthy migrate away from socially and environmentally undesirable areas, leaving the relatively incompetent behind (Freeman & Alpert, 1986a). The result of this differential migration, in which those affected by morbidity of any kind fail to participate in a general movement to better environmental areas, is that levels of morbidity rise in the central areas and remain low in suburban or new communities. One example illustrating this process is the dramatic population fall of the industrial city of Salford, beginning in 1928, which was the sharpest for any local authority in England (Freeman, 1984); this resulted predominantly from the movement outwards of smaller family groups containing employed adults. Such a differential fall tends to leave behind those who are below average in social mobility, including the mentally and physically disabled, single-parent families, the elderly, etc.; they have been described by Stromgren (1987) as a 'residual population'.

One of the most influential studies to examine the causation/selection issue investigated the relative effects of socio-economic status (measured by educational attainment) and ethnic discrimination on the risk of schizophrenia in Israel, comparing those of North African with those of European descent (Dohrenwend *et al.*, 1992). Ethnic discrimination in Israel against Jews of North African descent allowed for a test of the independent effects of two distinct types of social force. Whereas social causation predicted incrementally higher rates of schizophrenia for these individuals at every level of socio-economic status, social selection predicted the opposite, since the reduced social mobility of healthier North African Jews would 'dilute' the prevalence of schizophrenia at any level of socio-economic status. In fact, a higher prevalence of schizophrenia was found among men in the European group at each level of education, supporting the social selection hypothesis. The same trends emerged among women and college graduates. The findings for depression were in the opposite direction (and were even more convincing, given greater numbers), supporting the social causation model.

These findings have been confirmed in a case–control study from Denmark that combined data from a national psychiatric case register with administrative socio-demographic information (Byrne *et al.*, 2004). Cases were those admitted to a psychiatric facility for the first time between 1981 and 1998 with a diagnosis of schizophrenia and with known maternal identity. The risk of schizophrenia was associated with low premorbid socio-economic status among cases and, to a lesser extent, among their parents. After adjusting for parental socio-economic status, statistically significant associations with the incidence of schizophrenia were found for unemployment and low income in the year prior to first admission. While incidence was associated with lower parental socio-economic status, risk was also associated with *higher* parental education. Thus 'social disadvantage' was associated with first onset of schizophrenia, but there was little evidence that this factor was mirrored in the socio-economic status of the families. The implication is that the socio-economic gradient – even at first onset – is more a prodromal effect (drift) than a cause of illness.

In a case–control study in South London, Castle *et al.* (1993) found that people with schizophrenia were more likely to have been born in socially deprived areas and to have fathers with manual occupations. It seems unlikely that the entire urban effect can be attributed to socio-economic status, as some of the positive findings have come from countries where there is a higher standard of living in cities as a whole than in the rural areas.

Fifty years ago, Hare (1956) studied all male admissions in a UK city over five years and found a marked excess of schizophrenia among people from social classes IV and V. Reviewing early studies, Freeman (1994) demonstrated that rates of schizophrenia increased towards the centre of cities in Western societies. The classic study of Faris and Dunham (1939) showed that first-admission rates of schizophrenia were particularly high in certain areas of inner-city Chicago, and decreased towards the periphery. Furthermore, there were considerable differences within the inner city itself, with rates higher in the more disorganized 'hobohemia' area than in more cohesive working-class areas. Faris and Dunham suggested that living conditions in certain neighbourhoods were associated with social isolation and abnormalities of behaviour and mentality that subsequently led to increased rates of schizophrenia. It was also pointed out that in contrast to schizophrenia, the incidence of manic-depression was not higher in the inner city – a finding that has now been replicated by Mortensen *et al.* (1999). However, later findings in Detroit by Dunham (1965) did not confirm these findings, so that his view changed largely from a social causation to a social selection hypothesis. In later studies in Chicago, Levy and Rowitz (1973) found no clear-cut pattern for first admissions for schizophrenia; areas with high rates were scattered throughout the city. On the other hand, readmissions showed a marked excess in the poorer central areas, providing strong evidence for the 'social drift' explanation. These authors speculated that Faris and Dunham's findings might have been contaminated by the lack of general hospital psychiatric beds at the time their research was done, so that most middle-class schizophrenic patients would not have appeared in the statistics – being treated either at home or in distant private hospitals. The absence of these cases from the data might thus have led to a misleading impression of a central excess of new cases. Much of subsequent research has sought to answer whether aspects of the environment *cause* psychosis (the 'breeder' hypothesis), or whether those at risk of psychosis gravitate towards particular social environments through social selection.

Neither Dauncey *et al.* (1993), who examined where patients had lived during the five years before their first admission in Nottingham, nor Mortensen *et al.* (1999) in Denmark, who estimated that a hypothetical cohort of 'at risk' (but asymptomatic) parents of 50,000 children would have to have drifted in to the capital to explain the urban excess of schizophrenia in their offspring's generation, found evidence for the drift hypothesis. These authors also found that a family history of schizophrenia did not explain the urban–rural gradient in schizophrenia, further undermining the social drift hypothesis.

Most recent studies investigating urbanicity have come from Northern Europe, where comprehensive population records have made large-scale epidemiological studies possible. Lewis *et al.* (1992) investigated the association between place of upbringing and the incidence of schizophrenia, using data from a cohort of over 49,000 male Swedish conscripts and linking these to the national psychiatric register. There was a strongly significant linear trend, with the highest rate of clinically diagnosed schizophrenia in those who had mostly lived in cities while they were growing up. Intermediate rates were found in both large and small towns, with the lowest rates in country areas. Adjusting for family finances, parental divorce, and family psychiatric history had little effect. However, adjusting for cannabis use and any psychiatric disorder at conscription (as these may have been part of a prodrome) reduced, but did not eliminate, the associations. These findings did not distinguish between place of birth and place of upbringing. Lewis *et al.* state that their study design eliminated the possibility that geographical drift could explain any observed association between city life and schizophrenia; in that case, undetermined environmental factors, believed to be present in cities, must be assumed to have increased the risk – a return to the 'breeder hypothesis'.

Subsequently, Marcelis *et al.* (1998) found that urban birth was linearly associated with later psychosis in the Netherlands. The incidence rate ratio showed evidence of a linear trend, with an odds ratio of 1.18 for affective psychosis, 1.27 for 'other' (non-affective, non-schizophrenic) psychoses, and 1.39 for broadly defined schizophrenia. This study also found an interaction with gender, in that the effect of urbanicity on the incidence of psychosis was greater for men than for women.

Mortensen *et al.* (1999) studied a Danish population-based cohort of 1.75 million: the relative risk associated with birth in Copenhagen, compared with rural areas, was 2.40. There was a clear dose–response relationship for urbanicity, in that the larger the town of birth, the greater the risk. A family history of schizophrenia did not explain the results.

In the UK, Allardyce *et al.* (2001) compared all incident cases (admitted or not admitted) of psychosis from two areas – a largely rural part of Southwest Scotland and urban South London. The incidence of schizophrenia was 61% higher in the urban compared to the rural area; once again, the urban excess was more marked in males. The Danish case–control study by Byrne *et al.* (2004) also confirmed an urban excess in the incidence of schizophrenia after adjusting for both parental and patients' socio-economic status, and for family psychiatric history.

There is still no satisfactory explanation for this phenomenon. Biological factors such as infectious disease and obstetric complications do not seem to play a large part (Boydell & Murray, 2003). Substance abuse is also unlikely to explain these findings (especially those from very early studies), given the substantial variation in patterns of drug and alcohol use over time. The increased incidence of schizophrenia in cities is not necessarily related to social class or deprivation; some studies have attempted to control for deprivation and still found an urban excess. There are still aspects of social class and deprivation that might interact with the social environment and would be difficult to control in research. More recently, interest has turned to area or contextual effects, reflecting the characteristics of places and communities. Although these effects may be mediated by biological mechanisms, such as poor diet or overcrowding, recent work has shown that relative inequality may have an independent effect. Boydell *et al.* (2004) found that the incidence rate of schizophrenia in socio-economically deprived areas in London increased as inequality within the local area rose after adjusting for age, gender, deprivation, and ethnicity. One theory that is consistent with all of these findings is that of 'social defeat' (Selten & Cantor-Graae, 2005). The notion that social marginalization might contribute to the onset of schizophrenia is supported by animal studies. Increased levels of mesolimbic dopamine have been demonstrated in male rats introduced into the cages of other rats (which invariably leads to attack and defeat of the intruder). These effects on dopamine activity were exacerbated by isolating the defeated rat afterwards, yet ameliorated by returning it to its former group.

Theories linking increased rates of schizophrenia to the crowding and resultant stress which are regarded as typical of cities have a long history. Cooper and Sartorius (1977), seeking an explanation for the emergence of schizophrenia as a major disorder in the nineteenth century, pointed out that large populations had accumulated then on a hitherto unprecedented scale, mainly through migration. As a result, cases of severe mental illness, which would previously have remained scattered in rural societies, became aggregated in such numbers that they represented a major public health problem. Furthermore, because of the demands of industrialization, many families became unable to manage psychotic relatives at home, where conditions were often very overcrowded, although this would have been more possible in their previous agrarian settings.

Prevalence rates of schizophrenia reported from urban areas, in both Europe and the USA, have generally been significantly higher than those of rural areas, though with some marked exceptions, such as the Istrian peninsula of Croatia and isolated areas of Norway (Andersen, 1975), Iceland (Helgason, 1964), and Finland (Haukka *et al.*, 2001). Paradoxically, though, possibly the highest prevalence of schizophrenia ever measured (17.4 per thousand population) was reported from a thinly populated rural area of County Roscommon in the West of Ireland (Torrey, 1987), though there is no evidence that this represented a higher than average incidence rate. What these anomalous rural areas may have as a common factor is a high proportion of unmarried males, living as farmers or rural labourers (Keatinge, 1987). Surprisingly, therefore, a strong association appears to exist between excess prevalence of schizophrenia and some places with the opposite environmental characteristics to those of large cities. Prevalence rates are likely to be influenced by factors such as migration, infectious disease, fertility, mortality, culture, and other social processes (Eaton, 1985). More recent relevant social processes include 'deinstitutionalization', since there has been a widespread failure in Western countries to provide adequate community residences for schizophrenic patients leaving mental hospitals, so that they tend to drift into the poorest parts of cities, or even be resettled there by public services (Goldman, 1983). However, from the point of view of aetiological factors, data on incidence are more valuable than those on prevalence – if more difficult to determine. Henderson (1988) pointed out that the non-random distribution of the incidence of a disorder might be due to: (a) environmental factors having a direct effect; (b) the disorder or its prodromata influencing where people live; or (c) a third set of factors prior to both (a) and (b).

An international study of first-onset schizophrenia in urban and rural catchment areas of 12 centres in both developing and developed countries (Varma *et al.*, 1997) showed significant differences in illness variables between cases from the two types of environment. These differed in the type of onset, early manifestations, and clinical diagnosis of schizophrenia, as well as in the CATEGO classification. The Indian cases, and particularly the rural cohort there, differed strongly from those from industrialized countries. It was concluded that cultural factors, particularly urbanization, play a role in determining the onset, early manifestations, and typology of the illness.

Social isolation and social cohesion

'Social isolation', or having few social contacts (a characteristic of individuals), and 'social cohesion', meaning the community level of trust, neighbourliness, and involvement in community activities (a population characteristic), are both important aspects of the social environment. Disorganized, deprived areas with high social mobility tend to be low on social cohesion and high on social isolation. Hare (1956) reported that social isolation, as measured by proportion of single-person households in a geographical area, was associated with increased rates of schizophrenia. Movement of people into the area who had schizophrenia did not account for the data. However, it is difficult here to distinguish between cause and effect: disruption of social networks may well decrease an individual's capacity to cope with psychosocial stress and so increase the risk of developing schizophrenia.

Van Os *et al.* (2000) found that people who were single had a higher risk of developing psychosis if they lived in a neighbourhood with fewer single people: single status might give rise to perceived (or actual) social isolation if most other people are living with a partner. A similar phenomenon has been reported in the case of ethnic differences, described by Cantor-Graae and Selten (2005) as the 'protective effect of ethnic density'. Since people with a schizoid or schizotypal personality might well be less able to form social relationships, the resulting social isolation could itself be an adverse factor for their mental health. Boydell *et al.* (2001) found members of non-white ethnic minorities to be at a higher risk of admission to hospital for psychosis when living in areas with the lowest proportion of non-white residents, even though these areas were the least deprived on socio-economic measures. Jablensky and Cole (1997) showed that marriage had a protective effect against schizophrenia and was not simply a consequence of better adjusted males being able to marry. If social isolation and/or cohesion contribute to the onset of schizophrenia, these could perhaps account for some of the urbanization, social class, and deprivation findings.

Migration

A full discussion of this topic is outside the scope of this chapter (see Chapter 7), but migration and belonging to a minority group are important risk factors for psychosis. In a meta-analysis of 40 published studies, Cantor-Graae and Selten (2005) found that the relative risk for developing schizophrenia among first-generation migrants was 2.7, which rose to 4.5 in studies of second-generation migrants. These authors also found a higher incidence rate in studies where migration was from areas where the majority of the population is black. This effect seems to remain even when methodological problems are overcome (Boydell & Murray, 2003). Migrants often live initially in the most deprived areas of a city, so that the adverse social environment might increase the risk. Malzberg (1969), however, found that controlling for urbanicity reduced but did not explain the excess of psychosis among migrants to the USA. There is also growing evidence that discrimination – particularly that arising due to ethnicity – is related to the excess risk (Boydell & Murray, 2003; Boydell *et al.*, 2001; Karlsen & Nazroo, 2002).

Migration, however, is a difficult issue in relation to psychiatric morbidity, not least because there is evidence that both good and bad mental health may provoke a higher rate of mobility than the average, though for opposite reasons (Giggs, 1984) (see Chapter 7). The high prevalence of schizophrenia recorded both for inner-city Salford (Freeman & Alpert, 1986b) and for rural areas of the west of Ireland (Torrey, 1987) may well have resulted to a significant extent from migration: in both places, the population fell to half an earlier level over a period of about 50 years, though the Irish fall began much earlier. Since primarily economic migration of this kind inevitably has a differential character, it will tend to alter levels of morbidity in the populations affected by it.

Evidence from the UK

In an inner-city area of South London all first-contact cases of schizophrenia recorded between 1965 and 1984 were compared with matched non-psychotic patients (Castle *et al.*, 1993). Compared with controls, the schizophrenic cases were more likely to have been born in the socially deprived parts and to have had fathers with manual as opposed to non-manual occupations; controlling for ethnicity did not alter the trends recorded. The results suggested that individuals who develop schizophrenia are more likely than non-psychotic controls to have been born into socially deprived households. This would be associated with a greater risk of disadvantage both *in utero* and in early life. The favoured explanation was that some environmental factor of aetiological importance in schizophrenia is more likely to affect those born into households of lower socio-economic status.

In Nottingham, enumeration districts were statistically grouped into low-status and high-status clusters respectively; social deprivation emerged as mainly concentrated in the areas of post-1919 public housing and in some inner-city districts of privately rented accommodation. New cases of schizophrenia were significantly more likely to come from low-status areas, in contrast to manic-depressive cases, which were evenly distributed (Cooper *et al.*, 1987). From a first-episode cohort of cases of schizophrenia (and non-affective psychoses) from a delineated catchment area of Nottingham, the risk of developing schizophrenia was attenuated slightly for those who were not of African-Caribbean family origin (Harrison *et al.*, 2001). The conclusion was that the known association between schizophrenia and social deprivation at the time of diagnosis is not attributable entirely to inter-generational social selection and intra-generational social drift.

For Salford, in Greater Manchester, a population-based case register, linked with all specialist psychiatric agencies serving the population, recorded for each patient – on a cumulative basis – the total use of psychiatric services. Freeman and Alpert (1986a) found higher than expected prevalence rates of schizophrenia for 1974 compared with other industrialized countries (Hafner & An der Heiden, 1986; Jablensky, 1986). These differences were most marked in the middle-aged, and a relationship was proposed with selective population movements, combined with the low mortality and often chronic course of the disorder. The prevalence figures were then analysed in terms of distribution by electoral ward (Freeman & Alpert, 1986b). The data showed the city to be divided on this basis into two separate zones – an inner one, in which all wards had a rate of schizophrenia above 5 per thousand general population, and an outer one in which all wards had a rate below that figure. There was no direct relationship between prevalence of schizophrenia and social class, but the group of wards with higher rates was those closest to the centre of the whole conurbation. When this 1974 prevalence study was repeated for 1984, the point-prevalence rate of treated schizophrenia within this urban community had increased from 4.56 to 6.26 per thousand adult population during the decade (Bamrah *et al.*, 1991). Thus, in some populations at least, the prevalence rate of schizophrenia was then increasing, even if inception rates remained average. The general population fell by 25% in the decade, although by 1982–1984 some relative stability had occurred. The increased prevalence of schizophrenia may therefore have reflected a continuing selective migration of healthy individuals out of the inner city. Thus under current conditions, people suffering from schizophrenia who are left behind in the inner city might be becoming progressively older and more chronic.

Torrey and Bowler (1991) examined the distribution of 'insanity' and schizophrenia in the USA for nine separate years between 1880 and 1963. Urban/rural rates of population for the USA were compared with rates of psychosis. For all years except 1963, there were high correlations between mental illness and urbanicity. This study is important because a gradient was found between areas that would all be considered rural today and with relatively low population densities. The findings therefore suggest that the putative risk factor resulted from relative (rather than absolute) differences in living conditions.

The main methodological question raised by Torrey and Bowler's study is their criterion for 'urbanicity': the minimum population of 2500 is little more than a large village, so that the conflation of all populated areas above that size – including the largest cities – might be concealing important differences between sub-groups with different orders of population.

Evidence from Europe

Urban birth of Dutch patients first admitted for psychosis between 1970 and 1992 was associated with the later onset of schizophrenia, but less with affective and other psychoses (Marcelis *et al.*, 1998). Those born in areas with the highest level of population density were twice as likely to develop schizophrenia. Associations were stronger for men, for individuals with an early age of onset, and in more recent birth cohorts. Part of the effect could be due to differential in-migration of parents carrying psychosis genes, but since effect sizes are smaller for affective psychosis than for schizophrenia, an urban risk factor affecting vulnerable individuals around the time of birth seems possible. If high-risk groups experience more psychosocial stress around the time of illness onset, one would have expected a stronger effect of urban exposure on the rate of affective psychosis than on schizophrenia. That the effect of urbanicity was greatest in men and in younger age-groups was thought to be consistent with male sex and early onset both predicting poorer prognosis in schizophrenia. Marcelis *et al.* (1999) found that urban residence at the onset of illness did not affect the risk of developing the condition, when controlling for urban birth. However, this finding has been criticized by Pedersen and Mortensen (2001a) because the results might have been biased by the migration of pre-schizophrenic individuals.

The most sophisticated study of the putative effect of urbanicity was that of Pedersen and Mortensen (2001b). Using a Danish population-based cohort of 1.89 million people, linked to schizophrenia in cohort members and mental illness in a parent or siblings, they divided places of birth and residence into five levels of urbanization. Those who had lived their first 15 years in the highest category of urbanization had a 2.75-fold increased risk of schizophrenia. In relation to urbanicity at the fifteenth birthday, the risk increased with ever higher degrees of urbanization at birth, while the more years lived in increasingly urbanized settings, the greater was the risk. It was concluded that continuous or repeated exposures during upbringing may be responsible for the association between urbanization and the risk of schizophrenia. This was the first study that directly examined the relative importance of urbanicity at birth and during upbringing respectively. It was acknowledged that the classification of relative urbanization 'is almost certainly a wide proxy variable for the unidentified underlying risk factors and mechanism'. However, since a close relationship was found, the view that there is a causal association between urbanicity and the risk of schizophrenia was supported. The authors say that this shifts potential explanations for the urban–rural differences from factors influencing children around birth to those that occur continuously or repeatedly throughout upbringing. At the same time, very early influences might well affect the risk independently of urbanicity.

Discussion

If there is an environmental factor, or group of factors, that is present more in cities than elsewhere and that has a direct positive effect on the incidence of mental disorders, knowledge of it might provide opportunities both for primary prevention and for treatment at earlier stages. For schizophrenia, attempts to explain the uneven distribution, both in different environments and among social classes, have focused more on individual than on environmental factors, though individual genetic predisposition can be linked to the process of social segregation (Eaton, 1980). Theories emphasizing that environmental influences relate to the experience of deprived inner-city living – both psychological stressors and poor physical health – need not exclude the importance of biological factors, though. Similarly, hypotheses of a neurodevelopmental basis for schizophrenia (Castle & Murray, 1991; Murray *et al.*, 1988) are not incompatible with some environmental influence. Environmental risk factors might interact with developmental vulnerability (Marcelis *et al.*, 1998), and it is likely that complex gene–environment interactions mediate the influence of these factors on mental illness in adults. Van Os *et al.* (2003) found that both level of urbanization and positive family history increased the risk of psychotic disorder, independently of each other. The effect of urbanization on the additive scale was much larger for those who had evidence for a familial liability to psychosis, suggesting a possible biological synergism between the two factors. Pedersen and Mortensen (2001a) concluded that genetic factors may largely determine how many individuals are at risk for schizophrenia, but relatively common factors, some linked to urbanicity, may influence how many individuals develop the disease. A constantly recurring issue is that of 'stress', but van Os (2004) points out that associations between urban life and the incidence of affective disorder are much weaker than those with psychosis.

Jablensky and Sartorius (1988) pointed out the difficulty that arises from the lack of a clear-cut distinction between 'social' and 'non-social' (or biological) environmental factors. However, since the action of the latter is mediated by social circumstances, the two types are not mutually exclusive. Non-social environmental factors connected with urban living include exposure to lead or other heavy metals, air-polluting gases, toxic waste sites and industrial effluents, as well as birth complications and head injuries and a higher rate of infectious diseases, especially where there are many persons per household and/or room (Torrey & Bowler, 1991).

Second, social environmental factors that are more common in cities include stressful life-events, which represent a risk factor for the development of many psychiatric disorders including schizophrenia (Brown & Birley, 1968). The British study of Paykel *et al.* (2000) attributed greater psychiatric morbidity in urban areas to more adverse living conditions, which included stressful life events and poor social support. Other urban factors that have been implicated include social isolation, lack of control over the living environment – both isolation and overcrowding (Magaziner, 1988) – and social over-stimulation, which can provoke psychotic breakdown in vulnerable individuals (Wing, 1989).

So far as crowding is concerned, though central city areas tend to contain more crowded accommodation than peripheral districts, any such influence on schizophrenia or other psychiatric disorders remains controversial. In Western populations, there is now probably little difference between urban and rural populations in the degree of household crowding, which is largely governed by social class in both town and country. Two recent studies that examined childhood crowding in the home found no association with the later development of schizophrenia (Agerbo *et al.*, 2001; Walbeck *et al.*, 2001).

In the scientific study of these questions, the meaning of 'urban' or even 'city' also needs much clearer definition, because of the changes that have occurred worldwide. A fairly homogeneous community of 100,000 cannot be equated with a sprawling megalopolis of perhaps 15 million; settlements of the latter kind have been previously unknown in human history. Harpham (1993) pointed out that research on the social and economic characteristics of particular populations might be more productive than examination of their physical environments. Culturally, it would clearly be wrong to extrapolate Western experience to cities of the world as a whole.

In spite of the strong association between schizophrenia and a low social-class position, it has not so far been established that this is an aetiological relationship. That a relationship of schizophrenia with lower social class was demonstrated only within large American cities might be at least partly explained by a double drift of individuals with schizophrenia – into the lowest socio-economic class and into a particular kind of urban area. No studies, though, have compared socio-economic status and prevalence rates in both rural and urban areas up to now.

Several studies of the early course of schizophrenia, before first contact with mental health services, have found a prodromal phase of several years duration on average, in which there is an accumulation of negative and non-specific symptoms (Häfner, 1998). Functional impairment, social disability, and adverse social consequences tend to emerge in the pre-psychotic phase, and may convey a false impression of social disadvantage as an environmental factor of aetiological importance. Harrison *et al.* (2001) pointed out that 'Measures of socio-economic position are, at best, proxy markers for factors linked more directly to the risk of schizophrenia. As yet, there is little agreement as to what these more proximal factors are.' As discussed above, allied to the question of socio-economic position – though not identical with it – is that of deprivation.

If living in more urbanized areas is a risk factor for schizophrenia, then its prevalence might rise in developing nations that are currently undergoing rapid urbanization, though no firm evidence of such a change has yet been obtained. Similarly, if industrialization is also a major factor, one might expect prevalence to increase with modernization (Eaton, 1974), but in Taiwan, at a time when this process was occurring rapidly, Lin *et al.* (1969) found an actual *decrease* in schizophrenia over 15 years, despite an overall increase in psychiatric morbidity. It should not be assumed, though, that the full effects of urbanization are necessarily seen in the short term: an incubation period might extend over several generations, during which the environment continues to change, so that there could be a persisting cultural lag (Swedish Government, 1971). Henderson (1988) pointed out that urbanization, modernization, regional variation, and secular change have shared components, and that it is very difficult to identify clearly defined factors within them. However, unless this is done, attempting to establish independent effects for any of them must remain controversial. Similarly, Murphy (1976) emphasized that discovering the social causes of psychiatric disorder means not only developing case-finding methods for the dependent variables, but also locating those events in society that are genuinely antecedent to the disorders, and are therefore independent variables. The second task remains much more difficult. This is part of the wider issue of the role of social factors in the aetiology of psychosis. Jablensky (1986) concluded that there is only weak evidence for them having a direct effect of this kind: 'Although social stress may be a trigger of the symptoms, schizophrenia does not have the characteristics of a stress reaction, or of a pattern of learned responses to threatening social situations'. If that carefully supported view is accepted, then we would expect to see variations in prevalence between ecologically different areas for schizophrenia, but little difference in incidence.

The evidence reviewed above does not lead clearly in any one direction. Dauncey *et al.* (1993) suggest that such data are best explained as combining elements of the two social processes of 'breeding' and 'drifting', and that the support these provide for a significant relationship between schizophrenia and a tendency for patients to originate in poor urban areas points to a link between this disorder and an early environment of socio-economic deprivation. So far as immigration is concerned, Harrison *et al.* (1989) found that area of residence did not explain the higher rates of schizophrenia for African-Caribbeans in an urban setting. Furthermore, selective migration (e.g. of those with some form of abnormal behaviour) might result in a genetic risk that could act over several generations.

The view that a factor of 'urbanicity' – the nature of which so far remains unknown – could be a significant aetiological influence in schizophrenia does not seem to take adequate account of the effects of migration, though that process is less relevant to incidence than to prevalence. For instance, because of the greater mobility in Swedish society since the Second World War, it is quite possible that social residue processes would have reduced the healthy population (in all senses) within that country's cities, correspondingly raising the proportion living there who have some form of morbidity. The young men in the sample of Lewis *et al.* who were born in cities may therefore have come disproportionately from families with either genetic or environmental handicaps, or both. Lewis *et al.* (1992) refer to low socio-economic status as an 'environmental' factor, which confuses the issue. While 'inner-city' areas are nearly always characterized by a social-class composition that is skewed heavily towards the poorest groups, urban populations in many countries have a more favourable socio-economic level than rural populations. Cabot (1990) states that epidemiological studies of schizophrenia have focused so much on urban areas (and to some extent on middle-class patients) that 'We know very little about first contact rates . . . among the rural poor of any country', though it is in precisely such areas that the high schizophrenic morbidity of Ireland, for instance, is suspected to be. Furthermore, the influence of schizophrenic suicides, particularly in the younger age groups, deserves further examination. It is also likely that co-morbidity with alcohol and drug abuse occurs at a higher rate in cities. Finally, the question of urban size remains neglected: urbanicity can hardly be a common influence when the communities it describes can vary in size by a factor of 100 or more.

Yet any lack of evidence for significant urban–rural differences in psychiatric morbidity may not mean that the hypothesis of additional social stress in cities is wrong, but rather that the usual urban–rural dichotomy does not represent it (Murphy, 1976). The reason suggested by Murphy is that each large rural or urban area is now too diverse to have the same impact from this point of view on all inhabitants. For instance, 'city' residence has a totally different meaning for those who live in a middle-class suburb compared with those who live in a poor, working-class housing development. In one kind of area, the level of environmental stress is very low, while in the other it is very high. Yet they are all city residents. Again, the view that maternal infection, particularly viral, is the key mechanism in an urban excess of schizophrenia was based on population rates of infection, which have an unknown relationship to rates in mothers of children who will develop schizophrenia. However, there is some evidence that infection may still be relevant, even in a non-specific way, perhaps through delaying brain maturation and increasing the risk for schizophrenia (Rantakallio *et al.*, 1997). In Western countries, the old urban–rural dichotomy has largely broken down. Apart from fringe areas, most rural people live in similar housing, shop in the same supermarkets, and watch the same television programmes as city people. It is often hard to say where the city ends and the country begins.

Hammer *et al.* (1978) offered a warning that 'migration, social class and ethnic marginality are too gross as social variables and too complex as social phenomena to implicate any particular mechanism that would account for their association with psychopathology'. This view has been strongly confirmed by subsequent research. However, adverse change in people's social networks has been identified as a possible common mechanism underlying these processes, and this hypothesis remains to be fully examined (see above).

Until recently, findings on urban–rural differences in mental health have not been consistent, though the Swedish study based on the whole national population (Sundquist *et al.*, 2004a) seems to have shifted the evidence decisively in favour of an urban excess. Nevertheless, the mechanisms that link city life with this morbidity remain unexplained, though van Os (2004) describes its role as: 'relatively untainted in terms of inconsistencies in the findings, failure to replicate, major biases inherent to research design and heated debates about exposure measurement'. He adds that: 'there is no valid exploration as to what constitutes the true nature of the environmental exposure that poses as "urbanicity" '. The very fact that worldwide, so many people are now born and living in cities, means that it would only take a fairly small increase in risk as a result of urban living to cause a significant increase in the number who develop mental illness.

Conclusion

Evidence for an effect of the environment in the aetiology of common mental disorders and psychosis is inconclusive: some modest effects have been observed and evidence is stronger for an effect on schizophrenia than for common mental disorders. However, it has not been possible to ascertain whether an effect of the environment on either represents anything greater than an association between the characteristics of people living in certain types of environment. A purely contextual effect of the environment on psychiatric health has yet to be demonstrated and compositional factors, such as unemployment, social deprivation, and social support, along with biological factors, are important mediating factors in the association between the environment and psychiatric disorder.

Studies of urban–rural differences in these disorders are limited methodologically, which may have resulted in environmental effects being underestimated. Investigators have struggled to determine which factors distinguish urban environments from rural, and also to attain accurate measurement of them. In addition, the level of measurement of environmental factors has been problematic and is further complicated by confounding between individual-level, household-level, and area-level factors. Recent studies have moved from demonstrating varying prevalence rates for disorders in different environments to considering which specific individual, household, area, and environmental factors, along with their interactions, can account for these differences. Further use of a multifaceted approach to measuring the environment is required to assess fully the contribution of environmental influences in the aetiology of both common mental disorders and schizophrenia.

References

Agerbo, E., Fuller Torrey, E. and Mortensen, P. B. (2001) 'Household crowding in early adulthood and schizophrenia are unrelated in Denmark: a nested case–control study'. *Schizophrenia Research*, *47*, 243–246.

Allardyce, J., Boydell, J., Van Os, J., Morrison, G., Castle, D. J., Murray, R. M. and McCreadie, R. G. (2001) 'Comparison of the incidence of schizophrenia in rural Dumfries and Galloway and urban Camberwell'. *British Journal of Psychiatry*, *179*, 335–339.

Amato, P. R. and Zuo, J. (1992) 'Rural poverty, urban poverty and psychological well-being'. *Sociological Quarterly*, *33*, 229–240.

American Psychiatric Association (1987) *Diagnostic and Statistical Manual III*. Washington, DC: APA.

American Psychiatric Association (1994) *Diagnostic and Statistical Manual IV*. Washington, DC: APA.

Andersen, J. E. (1987) 'Urban environment, marital status and mental disorders – an investigation of psychiatric new referrals to outpatient clinics from a geographically defined sector'. *Acta Psychiatrica Scandinavica*, *76*, 94–100.

Andersen, T. (1975) 'Physical and mental-illness in a Lapp and a Norwegian population'. *Acta Psychiatrica Scandinavica Supplementum*, *263*, S47–S56.

Araya, R., Montgomery, A., Rojas, G., Fritsch, R., Solis, J., Signorelli, A. and Lewis, G. (2007) 'Common mental disorders and the built environment in Santiago, Chile'. *British Journal of Psychiatry*, *190*, 394–401.

Bamrah, J. S., Freeman, H. L. and Goldberg, D. P. (1991) 'Epidemiology of schizophrenia in Salford, 1974–84: changes in an urban-community over 10 years'. *British Journal of Psychiatry*, *159*, 802–810.

Bebbington, P., Hurry, J., Tennant, C., Sturt, E. and Wing, J. K. (1981) 'Epidemiology of mental-disorders in Camberwell'. *Psychological Medicine*, *11*, 561–579.

Birtchnell, J., Masters, N. and Deahl, M. (1988) 'Depression and the physical environment: a study of young married women on a London housing estate'. *British Journal of Psychiatry*, *153*, 56–64.

Blazer, D., Crowell, B. A., George, L. K. and Landerman, R. (1986) 'Urban–rural differences in depressive disorders: does age make a difference?', in Barrett, J. E. and Rose, R. M. (eds), *Mental disorders in the community*. London: Guilford.

Blazer, D., George, L. K., Landerman, R., Pennybacker, M., Melville, M. L., Woodbury, M., Manton, K. G., Jordan, K. and Locke, B. (1985) 'Psychiatric disorders: a rural/urban comparison'. *Archives of General Psychiatry*, *42*, 651–656.

Boardman, A., Hodgson, R., Lewis, M. and Allen, K. (1997) 'Social indicators and the prediction of psychiatric admission in different diagnostic groups'. *British Journal of Psychiatry*, *171*, 457–462.

Bowling, A. and Farquhar, M. (1991) 'Associations with social networks, social support, health-status and psychiatric morbidity in 3 samples of elderly people'. *Social Psychiatry and Psychiatric Epidemiology*, *26*, 115–126.

Boydell, J. and Murray, R. M. (2003) 'Urbanisation, migration and risk of schizophrenia', in Murray, R. M., Jones, P. B., Susser, E., van Os, J. and Cannon, M. (eds) *The epidemiology of schizophrenia*. Cambridge: Cambridge University Press.

Boydell, J., van Os, J., McKenzie, K. and Murray, R. M. (2004) 'The association of inequality with the incidence of schizophrenia – an ecological study'. *Social Psychiatry & Psychiatric Epidemiology*, *39*, 597–599.

Boydell, J., van Os, J., McKenzie, K., Allardyce, J., Goel, R., McCreadie, R. G. and Murray, R. M. (2001) 'Incidence of schizophrenia in ethnic minorities in London: ecological study into interactions with environment'. *British Medical Journal, 323*, 1336–1338.

Brown, G. W. and Birley, J. L. T. (1968) 'Crises and life changes and the onset of schizophrenia'. *Journal of Health and Social Behaviour, 9*, 203–214.

Brown, G. W. and Harris, T. (1978) *Social origins of depression*. London: Tavistock.

Burrows, R. and Bradshaw, J. (2001) 'Evidence-based policies and practice'. *Environment and Planning A*, *33*, 1345–1348.

Byrne, M., Agerbo, E., Eaton, W. W. and Mortensen, P. B. (2004) 'Parental socio-economic status and risk of first admission with schizophrenia – a Danish national register based study'. *Social Psychiatry and Psychiatric Epidemiology*, *39*, 87–96.

Cabot, M. R. (1990) 'The incidence and prevalence of schizophrenia in the Republic of Ireland'. *Social Psychiatry and Psychiatric Epidemiology*, *25*, 210–215.

Caldwell, T. M., Jorm, A. F. and Dear, K. B. (2004) 'Suicide and mental health in rural, remote and metropolitan areas in Australia'. *Medical Journal of Australia, 181*, S10–S14.

Cantor-Graae, E. and Selten, J. P. (2005) 'Schizophrenia and migration: a meta-analysis and review'. *American Journal of Psychiatry*, *162*, 12–24.

Carpiniello, B., Carta, M. G. and Rudas, N. (1989) 'Depression among elderly people – a psychosocial study of urban and rural populations'. *Acta Psychiatrica Scandinavica*, *80*, 445–450.

Castle, D. J. and Murray, R. M. (1991). 'The neuron-developmental basis of sex-differences in schizophrenia'. *Psychological Medicine*, *21*, 565–575.

Castle, D. J., Scott, K., Wessely, S. and Murray, R. M. (1993) 'Does social deprivation during gestation and early life predispose to later schizophrenia?'. *Social Psychiatry and Psychiatric Epidemiology*, *28*, 1–4.

Cheng, T. A. (1989) 'Urbanisation and minor psychiatric morbidity: a community study in Taiwan'. *Social Psychiatry and Psychiatric Epidemiology*, *24*, 309–316.

Cochrane, R. and Stopes Roe, M. (1980) 'Factors affecting the distribution of psychological symptoms in urban areas of England'. *Acta Psychiatrica Scandinavica*, *61*, 445–460.

Cohen, D., Spear, S., Scribner, R., Kissinger, P., Mason, K. and Wildgen, J. (2000) ' "Broken windows" and the risk of gonorrhea'. *American Journal of Public Health*, *90*, 230–236.

Cohen, D. A., Farley, T. A. and Mason, K. (2003) 'Why is poverty unhealthy? Social and physical mediators'. *Social Science and Medicine*, *57*, 1631–1641.

Coid, J., Yang, M., Tyrer, P., Roberts, A. and Ullrich, S. (2006) 'Prevalence and correlates of personality disorder in Great Britain'. *British Journal of Psychiatry*, *188*, 423–431.

Cooper, J. and Sartorius, N. (1977). 'Cultural and temporal variations in schizophrenia: a speculation on the importance of industrialization'. *British Journal of Psychiatry*, *130*, 50–55.

Cooper, J. E., Goodhead, D., Craig, T., Harris, M., Howat, J. and Korer, J. (1987)

'The incidence of schizophrenia in Nottingham'. *British Journal of Psychiatry, 151*, 619–626.

Costello, E. J., Keeler, G. P. and Angold, A. (2001) 'Poverty, race/ethnicity, and psychiatric disorder: a study of rural children'. *American Journal of Public Health, 91*, 1494–1498.

Costello, E. J., Angold, A., Burns, B. J., Stangl, D. K., Tweed, D. L., Erkanli, A. and Worthman, C. M. (1996) 'The Great Smoky Mountains Study of youth – goals, design, methods, and the prevalence of DSM-III-R disorders'. *Archives of General Psychiatry, 53*, 1129–1136.

Croudace, T. J., Kayne, R., Jones, P. B. and Harrison, G. L. (2000) 'Non-linear relationship between an index of social deprivation, psychiatric admission prevalence and the incidence of psychosis'. *Psychological Medicine, 30*, 177–185.

Crowell, B. A., George, L. K., Blazer, D. and Landerman, R. (1986) 'Psychosocial risk-factors and urban rural differences in the prevalence of major depression'. *British Journal of Psychiatry, 149*, 307–314.

Cummins, S., MacIntyre, S., Davidson, S. and Ellaway, A. (2005) 'Measuring neighbourhood social and material context: generation and interpretation of ecological data from routine and non-routine sources'. *Health and Place, 11*, 249–260.

Dalgard, O. S. and Tambs, K. (1997) 'Urban environment and mental health: a longitudinal study'. *British Journal of Psychiatry, 171*, 530–536.

Dauncey, K., Giggs, J., Baker, K. and Harrison, G. (1993) 'Schizophrenia in Nottingham – lifelong residential-mobility of a cohort'. *British Journal of Psychiatry, 163*, 613–619.

Diala, C. C. and Muntaner, C. (2003) 'Mood and anxiety disorders among rural, urban, and metropolitan residents in the United States'. *Community Mental Health Journal, 39*, 239–252.

Dohrenwend, B. P. and Dohrenwend, B. S. (1974) 'Psychiatric disorder in urban settings', in Caplan, G. (ed.), *American handbook of psychiatry*, Vol. II, 2nd edition. New York: Basic Books.

Dohrenwend, B. P., Levav, I., Shrout, P. E., Schwartz, S., Naveh, G., Link, B. G., Skodol, A. E. and Stueve, A. (1992) 'Socioeconomic status and psychiatric disorders: the causation–selection issue'. *Science, 255*, 946–952.

Dorling, D. (2001) 'Anecdote is the singular of data'. *Environment and Planning A, 33*, 1335–1340.

Dufouil, C. and Alpérovitch, A. (2000) 'Couple similarities for cognitive functions and psychological health'. *Journal of Clinical Epidemiology, 53*, 589–593.

Duncan, C., Jones, K. and Moon, G. (1995) 'Psychiatric morbidity: a multi-level approach to regional variations in the UK'. *Journal of Epidemiology and Community Health, 49*, 290–295.

Dunham, H. W. (1939) 'City core and suburban fringe distribution patterns of mental illness', in Plog, S. C. and Edgerton, R. B. (eds), *Changing perspectives in mental illness.* New York: Holt, Rinehart and Winston.

Dunham, H. W. (1965) *Community and schizophrenia.* Detroit, MI: Wayne State University Press.

Durkheim, E. (1952) *Suicide.* London: Routledge & Kegan Paul.

Eaton, W. W. (1974) 'Residence, social class, and schizophrenia'. *Journal of Health and Social Behaviour, 15*, 289–299.

Eaton, W. W. (1980) 'A formal theory of selection for schizophrenia'. *American Journal of Sociology, 86*, 149–158.

Eaton, W. W. (1985) 'Epidemiology of schizophrenia'. *Epidemiologic Reviews*, 7, 105–126.

Eaton, W. J. and Weil, R. J. (1955) *Culture and mental disorders*. Glencoe, NY: Free Press.

Eaton, W. W. and Kessler, L. G. (1981) 'Rates of symptoms of depression in a national sample'. *American Journal of Epidemiology*, *114*, 528–538.

Erol, N., Simsek, Z., Oner, O. and Munir, K. (2005) 'Behavioral and emotional problems among Turkish children at ages 2 to 3 years'. *Journal of the American Academy of Child and Adolescent Psychiatry*, *44*, 80–87.

Faris, R. E. L. and Dunham, H. W. (1939) *Mental disorders in urban areas*. Chicago: Chicago University.

Fichter, M. M., Narrow, W. E., Roper, M. T., Rehm, J., Elton, M., Rae, D. S., Locke, B. Z. and Regier, D. A. (1996) 'Prevalence of mental illness in Germany and the United States: comparison of the Upper Bavarian Study and epidemiologic catchment area program'. *Journal of Nervous and Mental Disease*, *184*, 598–606.

Fischer, E. P., Owen, R. R., Jr and Cuffel, B. J. (1996) 'Substance abuse, community service use, and symptom severity of urban and rural residents with schizophrenia'. *Psychiatric Services*, *47*, 980–985.

Freeman, H. (1984) *Mental health and the environment*. London: Churchill Livingstone.

Freeman, H. (1994) 'Schizophrenia and city residence'. *British Journal of Psychiatry*, *164* (supp. 23), 39–50.

Freeman, H. and Alpert, M. (1986a) 'Prevalence of schizophrenia in an urban population'. *British Journal of Psychiatry*, *149*, 603–611.

Freeman, H. and Alpert, M. (1986b) 'Prevalence of schizophrenia: geographical variations in an urban population'. *British Journal of Clinical and Social Psychology*, *4*, 67–75.

Giggs, J. A. (1984) 'Residential mobility and mental health', in Freeman, H. L. (ed.), *Mental health and the environment*. London: Churchill Livingstone.

Gilman, S. E., Kawachi, I., Fitzmaurice, G. M. and Buka, L. (2003) 'Socio-economic status, family disruption and residential stability in childhood: relation to onset, recurrence and remission of major depression'. *Psychological Medicine*, *33*, 1341–1355.

Goldberg, E. M. and Morrison, S. L. (1963) 'Social class and schizophrenia'. *British Journal of Psychiatry*, *190*, 785–802.

Goldman, H. H. (1983) 'International perspectives in deinstitutionalization'. *International Journal of Mental Health*, *11*, 3–165.

Gregoire, A. and Thornicroft, G. (1998) 'Rural mental health'. *Psychiatric Bulletin*, *22*, 273–277.

Hafner, H. (1998) 'Neurodevelopmental disorder and psychosis: one disease or major risk factor?'. *Current Opinion in Psychiatry*, *11*, 17–18.

Hafner, H. and An der Heiden, W. (1986) 'The contribution of European case registers to research on schizophrenia'. *Schizophrenia Bulletin*, *12*, 26–51.

Halpern, D. (1995) *Mental health and built environment*. London: Taylor & Francis.

Hammer, M., Makiesky-Barron, S. and Gutwirth, L. (1978) 'Social networks and schizophrenia'. *Schizophrenia Bulletin*, *4*, 522–545.

Hare, E. (1956) 'Mental illness and social conditions in Bristol'. *Journal of Mental Science*, *102*, 349–357.

Harpham, T. (1993) 'Urbanization and mental disorder', in Bhugra, D. and Leff, J. (eds), *Principles of Social Psychiatry*. Oxford: Blackwell.

Harrison, G., Gunnell, D., Glazebrook, C., Page, K. and Kwiecinski, R. (2001) 'Association between schizophrenia and social inequality at birth: case–control study'. *British Journal of Psychiatry*, *179*, 346–350.

Harrison, G., Holton, A., Neilson, D., Owens, D., Boot, D. and Cooper, J. (1989) 'Severe mental disorder in Afro-Caribbean patients – some social, demographic and service factors'. *Psychological Medicine, 19*, 683–696.

Harrison, J., Barrow, S. and Creed, F. (1995) 'Social deprivation and psychiatric admission rates among different diagnostic groups'. *British Journal of Psychiatry, 167*, 456–462.

Hauck, K. and Rice, N. (2004) 'A longitudinal analysis of mental health mobility in Britain'. *Health Economics, 13*, 981–1001.

Haukka, J., Suvisaari, J., Varilo, T. and Lonnqvist, J. (2001) 'Regional variation in the incidence of schizophrenia in Finland: a study of birth cohorts born from 1950 to 1969'. *Psychological Medicine, 31*, 1045–1053.

Haynes, R. and Gale, S. (2000) 'Deprivation and poor health in rural areas: inequalities hidden by averages'. *Health and Place, 6*, 275–285.

Health Development Agency (2004) *Social capital for health*. London: NHS.

Helgason, T. (1964) 'Epidemiology of mental disorders in Iceland: a psychiatric and demographic investigation of 5395 Icelanders'. *Acta Psychiatrica Scandinavica Supplementum, 173*, s1–s180.

Hembree, C., Galea, S., Ahern, J., Tracy, M., Markham Piper, T., Miller, J., Vlahov, D. and Tardiff, K. J. (2005) 'The urban built environment and overdose mortality in New York City neighborhoods'. *Health and Place, 11*, 147–156.

Henderson, A. S. (1988) *An introduction to social psychiatry*. Oxford: Oxford Medical Publications.

Henderson, C., Diez Roux, A. V., Jacobs, D. R., Kiefe, C. I., West, D. and Williams, D. R. (2005) 'Neighbourhood characteristics, individual level socioeconomic factors, and depressive symptoms in young adults: the CARDIA study'. *Journal of Epidemiology and Community Health, 59*, 322–328.

Isometsa, E., Heikkinen, M., Henriksson, M., Marttunen, M., Aro, H. and Lonnqvist, J. (1997) 'Differences between urban and rural suicides'. *Acta Psychiatrica Scandinavica, 95*, 297–305.

Jablensky, A. (1986) 'Epidemiology of schizophrenia – a European-perspective'. *Schizophrenia Bulletin, 12*, 52–73.

Jablensky, A. and Cole, S.W. (1997) 'Is the earlier age at onset of schizophrenia in males a confounded finding? Results from a cross-cultural investigation'. *British Journal of Psychiatry, 170*, 234–240.

Jablensky, A. and Sartorius, N. (1988) 'Is schizophrenia universal?', *Acta Psychiatrica Scandinavia Supplementum, 78*, s65–s70.

Jones, P.B. (2001) 'Schizophrenia: social and environmental factors: implications for aetiology'. *Current Opinion in Psychiatry, 14*, 39–43.

Judd, F. K., Jackson, H. J., Komiti, A., Murray, G., Hodgins, G. and Fraser, C. (2002) 'High prevalence disorders in urban and rural communities'. *Australian and New Zealand Journal of Psychiatry, 36*, 104–113.

Karlsen, S. and Nazroo, J. (2002) 'Relation between racial discrimination and health among ethnic minority groups'. *American Journal of Public Health, 92*, 624–631.

Kasl, S. V. (1977) *The effect of the man made environment on health and behavior*. Atlanta, GA: Centre for Disease Control.

Kawachi, I., Kennedy, B.P., Lochner, K. and Prothrow Stith, D. (1997) Social capital, income inequality, and mortality. *American Journal of Public Health, 87*(9), 1491–1498.

Keatinge, C. (1987) 'Schizophrenia in rural Ireland: a case of service over-utilisation'. *International Journal of Social Psychiatry, 33*, 186–194.

Kelly, S. and Bunting, J. (1998) 'Trends in suicide in England and Wales 1982–96'. *Population Trends, 92,* 29–41.

Kelly, S., Charlton, J. and Jenkins, R. (1995) 'Suicide deaths in England and Wales, 1982–92: the contribution of occupation and geography'. *Population Trends, 80,* 16–25.

Kendler, K. S., Gardner, C. O. and Prescott, C. A. (2002) 'Toward a comprehensive developmental model for major depression in women'. *American Journal of Psychiatry, 159,* 1133–1145.

Kendler, K. S., Karkowski, L. M. and Prescott, C. A. (1999) 'Causal relationship between stressful life events and the onset of major depression'. *American Journal of Psychiatry, 156,* 837–841.

Kennedy, H. G., Iveson, R. C. Y. and Hill, O. (1999) 'Violence, homicide and suicide: strong correlation and wide variation across districts'. *British Journal of Psychiatry, 175,* 462–466.

Koppel, S. and McGuffin, P. (1999) 'Socioeconomic factors that predict psychiatric admissions'. *Psychological Medicine, 29,* 1235–1241.

Kovess, V., Murphy, H. B. M. and Tousignant, M. (1987) 'Urban–rural comparisons of depressive-disorders in French-Canada'. *Journal of Nervous and Mental Disease, 175,* 457–466.

Kumpulainen, K. and Räsänen, E. (2002) 'Symptoms and deviant behavior among eight-year-olds as predictors of referral for psychiatric evaluation by age 12'. *Psychiatric Services, 53,* 201–206.

Lapouse, R., Monk, M. and Terris, M. (1956) 'The drift hypothesis in sociological differentials in schizophrenia'. *American Journal of Public Health, 46,* 978–986.

Lehtinen, V., Michalak, E., Wilkinson, C., Dowrick, C., Ayuso-Mateos, J. L., Dalgard, O. D., Casey, P., Vazquez-Barquero, J. L., Wilkinson, G. and the ODIN Group (2003) 'Urban–rural differences in the occurrence of female depressive disorder in Europe'. *Social Psychiatry and Psychiatric Epidemiology, 38,* 283–289.

Leighton, D. C., Harding, J. S., Macklin, D. B. and Leighton, A. H. (1963) *The character of danger: Psychiatric symptoms in selected communities.* New York: Basic Books.

Levin, K. A. and Leyland, A. H. (2005) 'Urban/rural inequalities in suicide in Scotland, 1981–1999'. *Social Science and Medicine, 60,* 2877–2890.

Levy, L. and Rowitz, L. (1973) *The ecology of mental disorder.* New York: Behavioral Publications.

Lewis, G. and Booth, M. (1992) 'Regional differences in mental health in Great Britain'. *Journal of Epidemiology and Community Health, 46,* 608–611.

Lewis, G. and Booth, M. (1994) 'Are cities bad for your mental health?'. *Psychological Medicine, 24,* 913–915.

Lewis, G., David, A., Andreasson, S. and Allebeck, P. (1992) 'Schizophrenia and city life'. *The Lancet, 340,* 137–140.

Lewis, G., Bebbington, P., Brugha, T., Farrell, M., Gill, B., Jenkins, R. and Meltzer, H. (1998) 'Socioeconomic status, standard of living, and neurotic disorder'. *Lancet, 352,* 605–609.

Lin, E. and Parikh, S. V. (1999) 'Sociodemographic, clinical, and attitudinal characteristics of the untreated depressed in Ontario'. *Journal of Affective Disorders, 53,* 153–162.

Lin, T. Y., Rin, H., Yeh, E., Hsu, C. and Chu, H. (1969) 'Mental disorders in Taiwan fifteen years later', in Caudill, W. and Lin, T. Y. (eds), *Mental health research in Asia and the Pacific.* Honolulu, HI: East-West Center Press.

Lorant, V., Deliege, D., Eaton, W., Robert, A., Philippot, P. and Ansseau, M. (2003)

'Socioeconomic inequalities in depression: a meta-analysis'. *American Journal of Epidemiology*, *157*, 98–112.

Macintyre, S., Ellaway, A. and Cummins, S. (2002) 'Place effects on health: how can we conceptualise and measure them?', *Social Science and Medicine*, *55*, 125–139.

Macintyre, S., Ellaway, A., Hiscock, R., Kearns, A., Der, G. and McKay, L. (2003) 'What features of the home and the area might help to explain observed relationships between housing tenure and health? Evidence from the west of Scotland'. *Health Place*, *9*, 207–218.

Magaziner, J. (1988) 'Living density and psychopathology – a re-examination of the negative model'. *Psychological Medicine*, *18*, 419–431.

Malmberg, A., Simkin, S. and Hawton, K. (1999) 'Suicide in farmers'. *British Journal of Psychiatry*, *175*, 103–105.

Malzberg, B. (1969) 'Are immigrants psychologically disturbed?', in Plog, S. C. and Edgerton, R. B. (eds), *Changing perspectives in mental illness*. New York: Holt, Rinehart and Winston.

Marcelis, M., Takei, N. and van Os, J. (1999) 'Urbanisation and risk for schizophrenia: does the effect operate before or around the time of illness onset?', *Psychological Medicine*, *29*, 1197–1203.

Marcelis, M., Navarro-Mateu, F., Murray, R., Selten, J. P. and van Os, J. (1998) 'Urbanisation and psychosis: a study of 1942–1978 birth cohorts in the Netherlands'. *Psychological Medicine*, *28*, 871–879.

Marmot, M. and Wilkinson, R. G. (2001) 'Psychosocial and material pathways in the relation between income and health: a response to Lynch *et al.*'. *British Medical Journal*, *322*, 1233–1236.

Marsella, A. J. (1998) 'Urbanization, mental health and social deviancy: a review of issues and research'. *American Psychologist*, *53*, 624–634.

Martin, D., Bringham, P. and Roderick, P. (2000) 'The (mis)representation of rural deprivation.' *Environment and Planning A*, *32*, 735–51.

McCreadie, R. G., Leese, M., Tilak-Singh, D., Loftus, L., MacEwan, T. and Thornicroft, G. (1997) 'Nithsdale, Nunhead and Norwood: similarities and differences in prevalence of schizophrenia and utilisation of services in rural and urban areas'. *British Journal of Psychiatry*, *170*, 31–36.

McCulloch, A. (2001) 'Ward-level deprivation and individual social and economic outcomes in the British Household Panel Study'. *Environment and Planning A*, *33*, 667–684.

McKenzie, K., Whitley, R. and Weich, S. (2002) 'Social capital and mental health'. *British Journal of Psychiatry*, *181*, 280–283.

Meltzer, H., Baljit, G., Petticrew, M. and Hinds K. (1995) *OPCS Surveys of Psychiatric Morbidity in Great Britain: Report 1: The prevalence of psychiatric morbidity among adults living in private households*. London: HMSO.

Middleton, N., Gunnell, D., Frankel, S., Whitley, E. and Dorling, D. (2003) 'Urban–rural differences in suicide trends in young adults: England and Wales, 1981–1998'. *Social Science and Medicine*, *57*, 1183–1194.

Middleton, N., Whitley, E., Frankel, S., Dorling, D., Sterne, J. and Gunnell, D. (2004) 'Suicide risk in small areas in England and Wales, 1991–1993'. *Social Psychiatry and Psychiatric Epidemiology*, *39*, 45–52.

Mitchell, R. (2001) 'Multilevel modeling might not be the answer'. *Environment and Planning A*, *33*, 1357–1360.

Morrell, S., Taylor, R., Slaytor, E. and Ford, P. (1999) 'Urban and rural suicide differentials in migrants and the Australian-born, New South Wales, Australia 1985–1994'. *Social Science and Medicine, 49*, 81–91.

Mortensen, P. B., Pedersen, C. B., Westergaard, T., Wohlfahrt, J., Ewald, H., Mors, O., Andersen, P. K. and Melbye, M. (1999) 'Effects of family history and place and season of birth on the risk of schizophrenia'. *New England Journal of Medicine, 340*, 603–608.

Moser, K. (2001) 'Inequalities in treated heart disease and mental illness in England and Wales 1994–1998'. *British Journal of General Practice, 51*, 438–444.

Muntaner, C., Lynch, J. and Smith, G. D. (2001) 'Social capital, disorganized communities, and the third way: understanding the retreat from structural inequalities in epidemiology and public health'. *International Journal of Health Services, 31*, 213–237.

Murphy, J. E. (1976) 'Social causes; the independent variable', in Kaplan, B. H., Wilson, R. N. and Leighton, A. H. (eds), *Further explorations in social psychiatry*. New York: Basic Books.

Murray, R. M., Lewis, S. W., Owen, M. H. and Foerster, A. (1988) 'The neurodevelopmental origins of dementia praecox', in Bebbington, P. and McGuffin, P. (eds), *Schizophrenia: The major issues*. London: Heinemann.

National Statistics (2004) *Rural and urban area classification 2004*. Retrieved 1 November, 2006, from www.statistics.gov.uk/geography/nrudp.asp

National Statistics (2006) Urban areas: 8 in 10 people live in an urban area. Retrieved 30 September, 2006 from *www.statistics.gov.uk/cci/nugget.asp?id=1307*

Oliver, J. E. (2003) 'Mental life and the metropolis in suburban America'. *Urban Affairs Review, 39*, 228–253.

Otsu, A., Araki, S., Sakai, R., Yokoyama, K. and Scott Voorhees, A. (2004) 'Effects of urbanisation, economic development and migration of workers on suicide mortality in Japan'. *Social Science and Medicine, 58*, 1137–1146.

Parikh, S. V., Wasylenki, D., Goering, P. and Wong, J. (1996) 'Mood disorders: rural/urban differences in prevalence, health care utilization, and disability in Ontario'. *Journal of Affective Disorders, 38*, 57–65.

Paykel, E. S., Abbott, R., Jenkins, R., Brugha, T. S. and Meltzer, H. (2000) 'Urban–rural mental health differences in Great Britain: findings from the National Morbidity Survey'. *Psychological Medicine, 30*, 269–280.

Pedersen, C. B. and Mortensen, P. B. (2001a) 'Family history, place and season of birth as risk factors for schizophrenia in Denmark: a replication and reanalysis'. *British Journal of Psychiatry, 179*, 46–52.

Pedersen, C. B. and Mortensen, P. B. (2001b) 'Evidence of a dose response relationship between urbanicity during upbringing and schizophrenia risk'. *Archives of General Psychiatry, 58*, 1039–1046.

Peen, J. and Dekker, J. (2003) 'Urbanisation as a risk factor for psychiatric admission'. *Social Psychiatry and Psychiatric Epidemiology, 38*, 535–538.

Pickett, K. E. and Pearl, M. (2001) 'Multilevel analyses of neighbourhood socio-economic context and health outcomes: a critical review'. *Journal of Epidemiology and Community Health, 55*, 111–122.

Poulton, R., Caspi, A., Milne, B. J., Thomson, W. M., Taylor, A., Sears, M. R. and Moffitt, T. E. (2002) 'Association between children's experience of socioeconomic disadvantage and adult health: a life-course study'. *Lancet, 360*, 1640–1645.

Propper, C., Jones, K., Bolster, A., Burgess, S., Johnson, R. and Sarker, R. (2005) 'Local neighbourhood and mental health: evidence from the UK'. *Social Science and Medicine, 61*, 2065–2083.

Putnam, R. (1993) *Making democracy work: Civic traditions in modern Italy*. Princeton, NJ: Princeton University Press.

Quinton, D. (1988) 'Annotation, urbanism and child mental health'. *Journal of Child Psychology and Psychiatry*, *29*, 11–20.

Rantakallio, P., Jones, P., Moring, J. and Von Wendt, L. (1997) 'Association between central nervous system infections during childhood and adult onset schizophrenia and other psychoses: a 28-year follow-up'. *International Journal of Epidemiology*, *26*, 837–843.

Reijneveld, S. A. and Schene, A. H. (1998) 'Higher prevalence of mental disorders in socioeconomically deprived urban areas in the Netherlands: community or personal disadvantage?'. *Journal of Epidemiology and Community Health*, *52*, 2–7.

Reijneveld, S. A., Verheij, R. A. and de Bakker, D. H. (2000) 'The impact of area deprivation on differences in health: does the choice of the geographical classification matter?'. *Journal of Epidemiology and Community Health*, *54*, 306–313.

Rodgers, B. (1991) 'Socio-economic status, employment and neurosis'. *Social Psychiatry and Psychiatric Epidemiology*, *26*, 104–114.

Rohrer, J. E., Borders, T. F. and Blanton, J. (2005) 'Rural residence is not a risk factor for frequent mental distress: a behavioural risk factor surveillance survey'. *BMC Public Health*, *5*, 46.

Romans-Clarkson, S. E., Walton, V. A., Herbison, G. P. and Mullen, P. E. (1990) 'Psychiatric morbidity among women in urban and rural New Zealand: psycho-social correlates'. *British Journal of Psychiatry*, *156*, 84–91.

Ross, C. E. (2000) 'Neighborhood disadvantage and adult depression'. *Journal of Health and Social Behaviour*, *41*, 177–187.

Rost, K., Zhang, M. L., Fortney, J., Smith, J. and Smith, G. R. (1998) 'Rural–urban differences in depression treatment and suicidality'. *Medical Care*, *36*, 1098–1107.

Rutter, M. L. (1981) 'The city and the child'. *American Journal of Orthopsychiatry*, *51*, 610–625.

Sainsbury, P. (1952) *Suicide in London*. London: Chapman & Hall.

Sampson, R. J., Raudenbush, S. W. and Earls, F. (1997) 'Neighborhoods and violent crime: a multilevel study of collective efficacy'. *Science*, *277*, 918–924.

Sartorius, N. (1998) 'Nearly forgotten: the mental health needs of an urbanised planet', in Goldberg, D. and Thornicroft, G. (eds), *Mental health in our future cities*, Maudsley Monograph, no. 42. Hove, UK: Psychology Press.

Saunderson, T. R. and Langford, I. H. (1996) 'A study of the geographical distribution of suicide rates in England and Wales 1989–92 using empirical Bayes estimates'. *Social Science and Medicine*, *4*, 489–502.

Saunderson, T., Haynes, R. and Langford, I. H (1998) 'Urban–rural variations in suicides and undetermined deaths in England and Wales'. *Journal of Public Health Medicine*, *20*, 261–267.

Seivewright, H., Tyrer, P., Casey, P. and Seivewright, N. (1991) 'A three-year follow-up of psychiatric morbidity in urban and rural primary care'. *Psychological Medicine*, *21*, 495–503.

Selten, J. P. and Cantor-Graae, E. (2005) 'Social defeat: risk factor for schizophrenia?' *British Journal of Psychiatry*, *187*, 101–102.

Shucksmith, M. (1990) 'A theoretical perspective on rural housing – housing classes in rural Britain'. *Sociologia Ruralis*, *30*, 210–229.

Silver, E., Mulvey, E. P. and Swanson, J. W. (2002) 'Neighborhood structural characteristics and mental disorder: Faris and Dunham revisited'. *Social Science and Medicine*, *55*, 1457–1470.

Singh, G. K. and Siahpush, M. (2002) 'Increasing rural-urban gradients in US suicide mortality, 1970–1997'. *American Journal of Public Health, 92*, 1161–1167.

Skapinakis, P., Lewis, G., Araya, R., Jones, K. and Williams, G. (2005) 'Mental health inequalities in Wales, UK: multi-level investigation of the effect of area deprivation'. *British Journal of Psychiatry, 186*, 417–422.

Spauwen, J., Krabbendam, L., Lieb, R., Wittchen, H. U. and van Os, J. (2004) 'Does urbanicity shift the population expression of psychosis?'. *Journal of Psychiatric Research, 38*, 613–618.

Stansfeld, S. A. and Marmot, M. G. (1992) 'Social class and minor psychiatric disorder in British Civil Servants: a validated screening survey using the General Health Questionnaire'. *Psychological Medicine, 22*, 739–749.

Stefánsson, J. G., Lindal, E., Bjornsson, J. K. and Gudmundsdottir, A. (1991) 'Lifetime prevalence of specific mental disorders among people born in Iceland in 1931'. *Acta Psychiatrica Scandinavica, 84*, 142–149.

Stromgren, E. (1987) 'The development of the concept of reactive psychoses'. *Psychopathology, 20*, 62–67.

Sturm, R. and Cohen, D. A. (2004) 'Suburban sprawl and physical and mental health'. *Public Health, 118*, 488–496.

Sundquist, K., Frank, G. and Sundquist, J. (2004a) 'Urbanisation and incidence of psychosis and depression: follow-up study of 4.4 million women and men in Sweden'. *British Journal of Psychiatry, 184*, 293–298.

Sundquist, K., Johansson, L. M., Johansson, S. E. and Sundquist, J. (2004b) 'Social environment and psychiatric illness'. *Social Psychiatry and Psychiatry Epidemiology, 39*, 39–44.

Swedish Government (1971) *Urban conglomerates as psycho-social human stressors.* A report to the UN Conference on the Human Environment, Stockholm.

Thelin, A. (1991) 'Morbidity in Swedish farmers, 1878–1983, according to national hospital records'. *Social Science and Medicine, 32*, 305–309.

Thornicroft, G. (1991) 'Social deprivation and rates of treated mental disorder: developing statistical models to predict psychiatric service utilization'. *British Journal of Psychiatry, 158*, 475–484.

Thornicroft, G., Bisoffi, G., De Saliva, D. and Tansella, M. (1993) 'Urban–rural differences in the associations between social deprivation and psychiatric service utilization in schizophrenia and all diagnoses: a case register study in Northern Italy'. *Psychological Medicine, 23*, 487–496.

Torrey, E. F. (1987) 'Prevalence studies of schizophrenia'. *British Journal of Psychiatry, 150*, 598–608.

Torrey, E. F. and Bowler, A. (1991) 'Geographical distribution of insanity in America: evidence for an urban factor'. *Schizophrenia Bulletin, 16*, 591–604.

Torrey, E. F., Bowler, A. and Clark, K. (1997) 'Urban birth and residence as risk factors for psychoses: an analysis of 1880 data'. *Schizophrenia Research, 25*, 169–176.

Van Os, J. (2004). 'Does the urban environment cause psychosis?'. *British Journal of Psychiatry, 184*, 287–288.

Van Os, J., Pedersen, C. B. and Mortensen, P. B. (2004) 'Confirmation of synergy between urbanicity and familial liability in the causation of psychosis'. *American Journal of Psychiatry, 161*, 2312–2314.

Van Os, J., Driessen, G., Gunther, N. and Delespaul, P. (2000) 'Neighbourhood variation in incidence of schizophrenia: evidence for person–environment interaction'. *British Journal of Psychiatry, 176*, 243–248.

Van Os, J., Hanssen, M., Bijl, R. V. and Vollebergh, W. (2001) 'Prevalence of psychotic disorder and community level of psychotic symptoms – an urban–rural comparison'. *Archives of General Psychiatry, 58*, 663–668.

Van Os, J., Hanssen, M., Bak, M., Bijl, R. V. and Vollebergh, W. (2003) 'Do urbanicity and familial liability coparticipate in causing psychosis?'. *American Journal of Psychiatry, 160*, 477–482.

Varma, V. K., Wig, N. N., Phookun, H. R., Misra, A. K., Khare, C. B., Tripathi, B. M., Behere, P. B., Yoo, E. S. and Susser, E. S. (1997) 'First-onset schizophrenia in the community: relationship of urbanization with onset, early manifestations and typology'. *Acta Psychiatrica Scandinavica, 96*, 431–438.

Vázquez-Barquero, J. L., Munoz, P. E. and Madoz Jauregui, V. (1982) 'The influence of the process of urbanization on the prevalence of neuroses: a community survey'. *Acta Psychiatrica Scandinavica, 65*, 161–170.

Vázquez-Barquero, J. L., Diez Manrique, J. F., Muñoz, J., Menendez Arango, J., Gaite, L., Herrera, S. and Der, G. J. (1992) 'Sex differences in mental illness: a community study of the influence of physical health and sociodemographic factors'. *Social Psychiatry and Psychiatric Epidemiology, 27*, 62–68.

Vidal, J. (2004) 'Beyond the city limits'. *The Guardian*, 9 September, 'Life' section, 4–6.

Wainwright, N. W. and Surtees, P. G. (2004a) 'Places, people, and their physical and mental functional health'. *Journal of Epidemiology and Community Health, 58*, 333–339.

Wainwright, N. W. and Surtees, P. G. (2004b) 'Area and individual circumstances and mood disorder prevalence'. *British Journal of Psychiatry, 185*, 227–232.

Walbeck. K., Osmond, C., Forsen, T., Barker, D. J. P. and Eriksson, J. G. (2001) 'Associations between childhood living circumstances and schizophrenia: a population-based cohort study'. *Acta Psychiatrica Scandinavia, 104*, 356–360.

Wang, J. L. (2004) 'Rural–urban differences in the prevalence of major depression and associated impairment'. *Social Psychiatry and Psychiatric Epidemiology, 39*, 19–25.

Wedmore, K. K. and Freeman, H. L. (1984) 'Social pathology and urban overgrowth' in Freeman, H. L. (ed.) *Mental health and the environment*. London: Churchill Livingstone.

Weich, S. (2005) 'Absence of spatial variation in rates of the common mental disorders'. *Journal of Epidemiology and Community Health, 59*, 254–257.

Weich, S. and Lewis, G. (1998a) 'Material standard of living, social class, and the prevalence of the common mental disorders in Great Britain'. *Journal of Epidemiology and Community Health, 52*, 8–14.

Weich, S. and Lewis, G. (1998b) 'Poverty, unemployment, and common mental disorders: population based cohort study'. *British Medical Journal, 317*, 115–119.

Weich, S., Lewis, G. and Jenkins, S. P. (2001) 'Income inequality and the prevalence of common mental disorders in Britain'. *British Journal of Psychiatry, 178*, 222–227.

Weich, S., Twigg, L. and Lewis, G. (2006) 'Rural/non-rural differences in rates of common mental disorders in Britain – prospective multilevel cohort study'. *British Journal of Psychiatry, 188*, 51–57.

Weich, S., Twigg, L., Lewis, G. and Jones, K. (2005) 'Geographical variation in rates of common mental disorders in Britain: prospective cohort study'. *British Journal of Psychiatry, 187*, 29–34.

Weich, S., Holt, G., Twigg, L., Jones, K. and Lewis, G. (2003a) 'Geographic variation in the prevalence of common mental disorders in Britain: a multilevel investigation'. *American Journal of Epidemiology, 157*, 730–737.

Weich, S., Twigg, L., Holt, G., Lewis, G. and Jones, K. (2003b) 'Contextual risk factors for the common mental disorders in Britain: a multilevel investigation of the effects of place'. *Journal of Epidemiology and Community Health*, *57*, 616–621.

Weich, S., Blanchard, M., Prince, M., Burton, E., Erens, B. and Sproston, K. (2002) 'Mental health and the built environment: cross-sectional survey of individual and contextual risk factors for depression'. *British Journal of Psychiatry*, *180*, 428–433.

West, D. J. and Farrington, D. P. (1973) *Who becomes delinquent?* London: Heinemann.

Wilkinson, R. G. (1996) *Unhealthy societies*. London: Routledge.

Wing, J. K. (1989) 'The concept of negative symptoms'. *British Journal of Psychiatry*, *155*, 10–14.

Yang, G. H., Phillips, M. R., Zhou, M.G., Wang, L. J., Zhang, Y. P. and Xu, D. (2005) 'Understanding the unique characteristics of suicide in China: national psychological autopsy study'. *Biomedical Environmental Science*, *18*, 379–389.

Yip, P. S. F. and Liu, K. Y. (2006) 'The ecological fallacy and the gender ratio of suicide in China'. *British Journal of Psychiatry*, *189*, 465–466.

5 Psychosocial processes linking the environment and mental health

Gary W. Evans and Stephen J. Lepore

The theme of this book is the role of the physical and social environment in mental health; evidence throughout suggests that the physical environment influences both psychological distress and psychiatric disorder. The specific design elements most clearly implicated include high-rise design, housing quality, crowding, and amount of natural light. Most of the data linking the physical environment to mental health are difficult to interpret, largely because people have some choice in where they live. Because of this choice, or selection bias, it is difficult to disentangle these environmental influences from other characteristics of an individual that may influence both environmental exposures and mental health. To some extent, prospective, longitudinal studies that follow the same person as environmental exposures change can help to rule out self-selection confounds. Experiments in which individuals are randomly assigned to different types of environment are even stronger in controlling selection bias, but are seldom feasible in the real world.

There are several other aspects of the debate concerning the potential role of environmental quality in health that are not as widely understood or appreciated as this selection bias or endogeny problem. For one, populations are not equal in the extent that selection bias applies. For example, relative to adults, children have significantly less control over their environmental surrounds. Institutionalized populations (e.g. patients, prisoners), where selection is often constrained or does not exist at all, present another opportunity to control for selection artifacts in the study of environmental effects on mental health.

A second under-appreciated challenge is the issue of main and interaction (i.e. moderator) effects. Given the nascent state of the endeavour, it makes sense to attempt initially to uncover overall or main effects of the environment on mental health. However, this approach presumes equivalent sensitivity and exposure to environmental conditions. Yet we know, for example, that psychologically, pre-pubescent males tend to be more vulnerable to adverse environmental conditions than girls, and that adolescents diverge in their psychological reactions to risky conditions, with boys responding more strongly in terms of externalization symptoms (e.g. aggression) and girls manifesting more internalization symptoms (e.g. depression) (Wachs, 2000). The absence of a main effect of an environmental condition on mental health may indicate just that – no effect; but such null results can obscure critical individual differences that may matter; perhaps the clearest example of this is air quality and respiratory health. What has little or minimal consequences for the general population can be devastating to an asthmatic.

A third issue has to do with measurement error that can undermine our ability to detect a true environmental effect on health. On the environment side, exposure estimates often are gross and indirect, possibly calculated from post-codes or street addresses of residence. Metrics themselves can be crude or ill-informed. For example, the US census uses the standard of more than one person per room as its official index of crowding, but there is no evidence that this is a meaningful threshold. Finally, little research on environmental exposure and mental health has considered the role of dosage (or intensity) of exposure, or of the timing and duration of exposure.

On the outcome side, measurement problems in mental health indices may also contribute to weaknesses in the literature. One common problem is reliance for the identification of symptoms on insensitive, catastrophic indices of mental health such as hospital admission or DSM-IV thresholds. Non-clinical indices of moderate anxiety or depression or low levels of frustration or hostility are missed when these definitions are restricted to more serious outcomes. This is problematic because we know that: (a) chronic low-level symptoms of psychological distress, if left untreated, tend to become more serious, and (b) we miss identification of many of the more severe mental health sequelae of poor environmental exposure, because such individuals are much more likely to drop out of studies (i.e. attrition bias). Finally, too many studies in this field use mental health outcomes with dubious or unknown validity and reliability.

A final methodological and conceptual challenge in establishing evidence of a link between environmental conditions and mental health is perhaps the most interesting one – ecological covariation. In our efforts to establish causal relations between environmental characteristics and health outcomes, we rely on the scientific method that requires isolation of the proposed causal variable from other factors that may covary with both the environmental target variable and the health outcome. However, it is possible that particular environmental characteristics affect mental health differently in isolation from the more ecologically valid context in which it typically occurs. For example, crowding often covaries with noise and may have a different effect on mental health in a noisy context than in a quiet one. There is growing evidence that exposure to cumulative risk factors in childhood leads to significantly more adverse outcomes than exposure to single risk factors (Evans, 2003). Also, since the confluence of risk also is greatest among the most disadvantaged (Evans, 2004), the environment of childhood poverty is characterized by a unique and potentially lethal combination of environmental risk factors – both social and physical.

Underlying models of environmental effects on mental health

Here we examine psychosocial pathways through which the environment might influence mental health. The overall model used as the basis for this discussion is illustrated in Figure 5.1.

We have identified in the literature four dominant pathways through which the physical environment can influence mental health, including changes in: (1) control and learned helplessness; (2) interpersonal relationships, (3) negative emotional states, and (4) physiological stress. Below, we review evidence for each of the individual arrows in Figure 5.1. However, because of a lack of empirical evidence, it will only be possible to cite a few studies that show evidence for the full causal sequence suggested above.

Control and learned helplessness

Chronic environmental conditions that are stressful and uncontrollable can diminish self-efficacy and mastery, and so lead to learned helplessness. This is defined as a psychological state in which the individual believes that the outcomes of their behaviours are independent, i.e. non-contingent, of those behaviours. Learned helplessness is thought to occur because of repeated experiences with non-contingent outcomes (Seligman, 1975). The principal index of helplessness is motivation, most often measured by task persistence.

Induction of helplessness by environmental stressors

Early studies used acute, uncontrollable noise to induce helplessness (Hiroto & Seligman, 1975). In this paradigm, participants are first exposed to noise while performing a task; for some, the noise is continuous and inescapable, whereas for others it is contingent on task performance. Next, participants are exposed to a different learning task, which enables them to avoid the noise. These studies show evidence of the induction of helplessness, as indicated by poorer performance in Phase 2 of the experiment for those participants who had experienced non-contingent exposure to the noise in Phase 1. Chronic exposure to either noise or crowding also can induce helplessness. Cohen *et al.* (1986) showed that elementary school children in zones affected by airport noise were significantly less likely to solve challenging jigsaw puzzles than well-matched children living nearby in quiet areas. Baum *et al.* (1978) found that students randomized to a crowded college residence experienced increases in helplessness over time, withdrawing during social-interaction games, whereas students randomized to

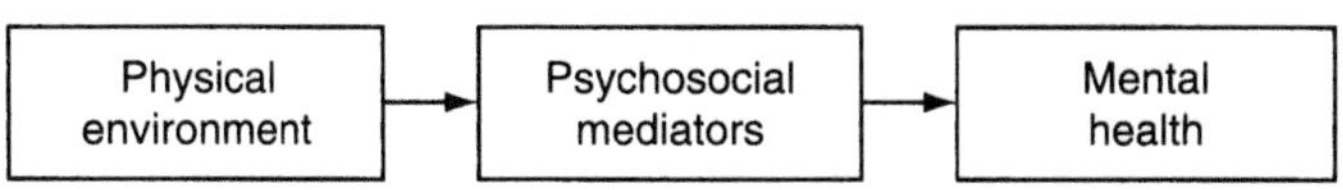

Figure 5.1 Model of psychosocial pathways.

an uncrowded residence became more socially engaged over time. The increases in helplessness over time corresponded with students' perceived inability to control social interactions in their living environments. There is also evidence that residents of high-rise buildings feel a diminished sense of control over their immediate setting, in comparison to those living in low-rise buildings (McCarthy & Saegert, 1978; Wilcox & Holahan, 1976).

Chronic exposure to uncontrollable environmental conditions appears to heighten vulnerability to the induction of helplessness. Rodin (1976) found that middle-school children living in more crowded apartments were more apt to succumb to helplessness induced by feedback of failure on a concept-formation task. Evans *et al.* (1998b) induced helplessness with an unsolvable geometrical puzzle, and then examined performance on a second similar, but soluble puzzle. Ten-to-twelve-year-olds from more crowded homes were less likely to solve the second puzzle than their less crowded counterparts; girls in particular were susceptible to chronic residential crowding. Children attending a nursery school prior to extensive sound insulation modifications took significantly longer to solve a jigsaw puzzle, following experience with an unsolvable puzzle, than those attending one year later, after the sound insulation had been completed (Maxwell & Evans, 2000). These studies had good statistical controls for the socio-demographic characteristics (e.g. income) of their participants.

Decisional control

Another way in which helplessness may be measured is to examine individual preferences for choice. Persons chronically exposed to crowding (Baum & Valins, 1977; Rodin, 1976) and noise (Cohen *et al.*, 1986) are more likely to relinquish choice than their counterparts living under uncrowded or quiet conditions, respectively. Rodin gave six-to-nine-year-olds the option of choosing a reward or allowing the experimenter to choose it for them, in an operant learning paradigm. Those who were from crowded homes, independent of income, were more likely to opt for selection of the reward by the experimenter. In another study, children chronically exposed to airport noise were more likely to let the experimenters select a reward for them at the conclusion of experimental procedures, compared with children living in quiet areas (Cohen *et al.*, 1986). Saegert (1982), however, was unable to replicate this environmental effect on children's exercise of behavioural choice.

Task persistence

Many investigators have used the Glass and Singer (1972) after-effects paradigm to assess helplessness. In a series of experiments, these authors found that following brief exposures to uncontrollable noise, adults were less likely to persist with challenging puzzles. The performance deficits occurred after the noise stimulus was removed, hence the term 'after-effect'. Interestingly, providing experimental subjects with a sense of control largely eliminates the adverse effect of noise on task persistence. Glass and Singer manipulated perceived control by providing a button and telling subjects that, if necessary, they could halt the noise by pushing the button. This effect has been widely replicated (Cohen, 1980; Evans *et al.*, 1999). These findings suggest that control is an important mediator. Parallel after-effect results have been found in the laboratory with acute exposure to crowding (Evans, 1979; Sherrod, 1974). Sherrod also showed that perceived control over crowding largely ameliorated the adverse effects on motivation of crowding in the laboratory. Rotton (1983) uncovered similar effects with laboratory exposures to malodorous pollutants.

These environmental effects on motivation are also found in community studies. Chronic exposure to noise, crowding, and traffic congestion all produce deficits on the Glass and Singer after-effects task. Stokols *et al.* (1978) and White and Rotton (1998) recorded less task persistence on the after-effect puzzles as a function of traffic congestion. The former study had good statistical controls for socio-demographic variables, and the latter incorporated random assignment of students to simulated daily car commuting. Schaeffer *et al.* (1988a) found parallel results using two different indices of task persistence, as did Wener *et al.* (2003), in relation to commuting time among rail passengers.

Independent of socio-economic status, residents of more crowded neighbourhoods persisted less on a challenging task relative to residents of nearby low-density areas (Fleming *et al.*, 1987). Evans *et al.* (2000b) found in two different samples of low-income households that elementary school children living in more crowded housing were less likely to persist with after-effects puzzles. This association held independently of income levels.

Chronic exposure to noise is also associated with deficits on the Glass and Singer task persistence measure among children. Elementary school children exposed to loud aircraft noise attempted fewer puzzles than their counterparts living in nearby quiet areas (Evans *et al.*, 1995). Evans *et al.* (2001) found similar results among girls, but not boys, in relation to neighbourhood noise levels. Both of these cross-sectional studies had good controls for socio-economic status. These same noise effects were replicated in a prospective, longitudinal study, which examined children before and after the opening of a new international airport (Bullinger *et al.*, 1999). A comparison group of children, studied over the same two-year period, did not show such changes.

Children attending kindergarten near a major airport who were insulated from external sound performed better on a standardized index of task persistence (visual search), compared with those from a kindergarten in the same airport noise-impact zone that was not sound-insulated (Moch-Sibony, 1981). The schools were closely matched on socio-economic characteristics. Wachs (1987) showed that mastery-oriented behaviour is less frequent among toddlers living in noisier homes. Corapci and Wachs (2002) have also shown that mothers of toddlers in noisier homes feel a lower sense of parental efficacy – less skilled and less capable of competently parenting their children. These results were not explicable by social class. Though Haines *et al.* (2001a) were unable to replicate the effects of aircraft noise on puzzle persistence among a group of primary school children, they administered the task in small groups, rather than individually.

Control, helplessness, and mental health

The preceding section has made clear that exposure to uncontrollable environmental stressors results in reduced perceived control, motivational deficits, and helpless behaviour. In this section, we provide a brief overview of the literature on control-relevant processes and mental health. Because this is an extensive body of research, an exhaustive account is not possible here.

People are highly motivated to maintain control over their environment (Wortman & Brehm, 1975). When deprived of control, individuals often exhibit depression and negative affect (Seligman, 1975). Both depressed persons and those exposed to unsolvable problems exhibit similarly low expectancies of control and initiation of responses. Both groups report similarly elevated feelings of hopelessness and apathy (Burns & Seligman, 1991; Maier & Seligman, 1976; Miller, 1975). In a reformulated theory of learned helplessness, Abramson *et al.* (1980) argued that individual differences in persons' attributions of the cause of negative outcomes could moderate the helpless response. Depression is likely to follow if someone attributes failure in resolving a stressor to an internal cause (e.g. incompetence). But this will not follow if a person attributes failure to external causes (e.g. fate).

Because learned helplessness is likely to decrease perceived personal control, many investigations in this area have focused on the relation between perceived control and depressive symptoms. Research has provided consistent but somewhat modest support for the theory that a perceived lack of control causes depression (see Benassi *et al.*, 1988; Coyne & Gotlib, 1983; Peterson & Seligman, 1984; Weisz, 1990). The relation between perceived control and mental health has been studied frequently in adults coping with chronic illness. Perceptions of personal control have been related to better mental health in persons suffering with rheumatoid arthritis (Nicassio *et al.*, 1985) and breast cancer (Taylor *et al.*, 1984, 1991). In a study of child outpatients in mental health clinics, Weisz *et al.* (1987) noted that children who felt competent in performing solution-relevant behaviour, and who believed they could solve (i.e. control) the problems if they tried, had lower depressive symptoms than those who felt relatively incompetent and unable to control problems. Several investigations have also revealed that low perceived control over the work environment is negatively associated with mental health (Sauter *et al.*, 1989; Stansfeld *et al.*, 1999).

Role of control in the environment and mental health

As stated at the outset, there are considerable data demonstrating each of the two linkages shown in Figure 5.1. The physical environment is linked to control, which, in turn, is linked to mental health. However, much fewer data are available to test the actual mediating effects of control in the link between the physical environment and mental health. Only two examples represent direct tests of this pathway. Both cross-sectional and longitudinal data revealed that high household density exacerbated the negative association between daily hassles in the home and psychological distress (Lepore *et al.*, 1991a). Subsequently, Lepore *et al.* (1992) showed that this significant density-by-hassles interaction on mental health in the longitudinal sample was mediated by residents' perceived control over their home environment. The interaction of household crowding and daily hassles led to diminished perceived control over the immediate environment, which in turn increased symptoms of psychological distress. Evans *et al.* (2000b) found that the ratio of people per room was associated with both helplessness and psychological distress among elementary school children, but the significant link between residential density and psychological distress in children was not mediated by learned helplessness.

Less direct evidence of control-related mediational processes is available in two traffic congestion studies. Evans and Carrere (1991) found that bus drivers' perceived levels of control over their job mediated the effects of traffic congestion on psychophysiological stress. Drivers in heavier traffic felt less control over their work, which in turn led to stress hormones becoming elevated. Kluger (1992) found that individuals driving in more congested conditions felt less control over the situation, while perceived control over traffic led to lower levels of self-reported stress. Unlike the findings of Lepore *et al.* (1992) on crowding and hassles or the study of crowding and children (Evans *et al.*, 2000b), neither of these two traffic congestion studies examined mental health as an outcome measure. The bus driver study examined only psychophysiological markers of stress, while the study of car drivers measured perceived stress.

Earlier, we noted well-documented linkages between control over the work environment and psychological health (Sauter *et al.*, 1989; Stansfeld *et al.*, 1999). The latter research group has also shown that grade-level differences in well-being can largely be explained by perceived control over the job environment. Undoubtedly, some of the elements of uncontrollable work environments are physical, although research to date has blurred distinctions between physical and psychosocial aspects of the job environment (Evans *et al.*, 1994).

Interpersonal relationships

There are multiple ways in which the physical environment can affect mental health outcomes through changes in interpersonal relationships. Our review has identified three potentially important social mediators: social support, social withdrawal, and parent–child relationships.

Social support

Several studies suggest that crowding can impair the development and maintenance of socially supportive relationships. Munroe and Munroe (1972) found that more crowded tribal groups in Kenya were less likely to hold hands in public and when tested for short-term memory of a list of words, remembered fewer affiliative words (e.g. friend, help) than members of less crowded tribes. Sundstrom (1973) manipulated density in a laboratory study and found that students exhibited lower levels of affiliative behaviour in more crowded conditions.

Studies have shown an inverse relation between residential density and perceived social support among residents in college housing, private homes, and juvenile delinquent housing (Cheung *et al.*, 1998; Evans *et al.*, 1989; Lepore *et al.*, 1991b; Ray *et al.* 1982). These studies used different but standardized social support measures, and all incorporated socio-demographic controls.

Evans and Lepore (1993) also found evidence of behavioural indications of less social support in a quasi-experimental field study of crowding. College students who lived off the campus under more crowded conditions were significantly less likely to respond positively to an offer of social support and were less likely to seek additional support when placed in need of social support in a laboratory experiment. These same students from more crowded apartments, compared to those from uncrowded apartments, were less likely to offer support to another student in need (in reality a highly trained confederate). This differential support behaviour occurred outside the subject's residence, in a standard, uncrowded laboratory setting. People who live under crowded conditions not only perceive less social support from their immediate housemates, but their affiliative behaviour towards people in general may also be altered, regardless of the immediate density conditions,

Social networks also appear to be sensitive to density: the size of informal social groups in public places is inversely related to population density (Tucker & Friedman, 1972). Residents of more crowded residencies know fewer fellow residents, have more friends outside, and are less likely to disclose personal information to someone in their accommodation, compared with students living in uncrowded accommodation (Baum & Valins, 1977).

Other aspects of the physical setting appear to influence social networks. The probability of social interaction is also influenced by the routing of pedestrian paths: residents are more likely to form friendships with those whose paths they cross (literally). Thus, variables such as the juxtaposition of doorways or the interconnectedness of walkways between residences affect the formation of friendship (Festinger *et al.*, 1950). Children who live in high-rise buildings know fewer of their neighbours and rate them as more unfriendly than do children residing in low-rise buildings (Saegert, 1982). Adults in high-rise buildings report greater anonymity (i.e. seeing people they do not know in semi-public areas of the building) (Churchman & Ginsberg, 1984; McCarthy & Saegert, 1978). College students living in high-rise buildings have fewer friends who live nearby (Holahan, 1978), feel less involved in their accommodation, and report lower levels of social support than those living in low-rise residences (Wilcox & Holahan, 1976).

Social withdrawal

One of the reasons that crowding may disrupt the development and maintenance of social support is that a common way in which people cope with crowding is by social withdrawal. Ittelson *et al.* (1970) noted that psychiatric patients who had to share a room, rather than have their own, were more likely to withdraw. In their crowding studies of student residencies, Baum and his colleagues also noted that, relative to students from uncrowded residences, crowded residents sat further away from a confederate in a waiting room and were also less likely to initiate conversation with the other person. Both Baum and Valins (1977) and others have also found that under high-density conditions, people avoid eye contact more than they do when the density is relatively low (Baxter & Rozelle, 1975; Sundstrom, 1973). This may be especially true for males (Ross *et al.*, 1973). Mothers of young children who live in more crowded homes rate themselves as less sociable than their less crowded counterparts (Wachs, 1988).

Students living in higher-density (people/room) apartments, when placed in a social interaction situation with people they do not know, manifest multiple signs of social withdrawal. These interactions occurred in uncrowded, controlled conditions outside the students' own residences (Evans & Lepore, 1993). In another study, college students in two different samples who resided in high-density housing did not pay as much attention to other students. For example, they had poorer knowledge of interpersonal information they had just been exposed to in social interactions with trained confederates (Evans *et al.*, 2000a).

A large number of studies converge in their findings of elevated social withdrawal among people interacting under more crowded conditions. Several of these studies randomly exposed people to different levels of density, rather than observing pre-existing groups. Liddell and Kruger (1989) found that residential density was associated with some degree of social withdrawal among children in a nursery school: those from more crowded homes were less actively involved in classroom activities. Wener and Keys (1988) found that fluctuations in the density of a prison dormitory affected passive, isolating behaviour, with withdrawal increasing when crowding increased. Prisoners in this study were randomly assigned to cells of varying density. Similarly, clerical workers from offices that were more crowded were more likely to spend coffee breaks alone (Oldham & Fried, 1987). Elementary school children living in high-density apartments (people/room) spent less time in the public spaces of their development, compared with children living in less crowded homes (Saegert, 1982).

Parent–child interaction

We have demonstrated that the physical environment can influence social support and social withdrawal, as well as positive social interactions such as neighbouring and altruistic behaviour. Studies showing that parent–child interaction can be adversely affected by noise, crowding, and environmental chaos in the home environment will now be reviewed.

Polluted urban slums. A district of London – Gustave Doré, 1868 (used with permission of Roger Voillet/Rex Features).

Both children and parents report more strained, negative familial interactions in high-density homes (Booth, 1976; Fuller *et al.*, 1993; Gove & Hughes, 1979; Saegert, 1982). Parents in higher-density (people/room) households do not monitor their children's behaviour as closely as those living in less crowded households (Gove *et al.*, 1979; Mitchell, 1971). These associations occur independently of social class. Moreover, parents are less responsive to their young children in more crowded homes (Bradley & Caldwell, 1984; Bradley *et al.*, 1994; Evans *et al.*, 1999; Wachs, 1989; Wachs & Camli, 1991).

Residential noise levels are inversely related to parental responsiveness to children (Wachs, 1989; Wachs & Camli, 1991). Environmental chaos – a composite measure of residential crowding, noise, and structure/routine in the household – is also negatively associated with parental responsiveness, independently of social class (Corapci & Wachs, 2002; Matheny *et al.*, 1995).

Interpersonal relationships and mental health

As discussed above, there is considerable evidence that crowding, noise, high-rise living, and certain design characteristics can influence the development and maintenance of interpersonal relationships, as well as the quality of those relationships. This section provides an overview of the evidence that the quantity and quality of interpersonal relationships have mental health implications, since the desire for close interpersonal relationships is a fundamental human motive (Baumeister & Leary, 1995; see also Chapter 6). Environmental factors that thwart the development of supportive, friendly, and healthy relationships will clearly have negative psychological effects. Likewise, environmental factors can increase mental health problems by provoking interpersonal conflicts, promoting social violence and crime, reducing privacy, and otherwise disrupting healthy social interaction.

There is a vast literature documenting the beneficial effects of supportive social ties on physical and mental health (Uchino, 2004). In particular, the perception or belief that others are available to provide emotional comfort or practical assistance in times of need appears to be greatly beneficial for mental health (Wethington & Kessler, 1986). Many studies have shown an inverse association between social support and depression (e.g. Billings *et al.*, 1983; Blazer, 1983; Cohen & Wills, 1985; Lepore *et al.*, 1996; Mitchell & Moos, 1984; Monroe *et al.*, 1986).

Although much of the psychological research tends to focus on the beneficial aspects of social relationships, investigators are increasingly documenting the negative effects of social relationships on both mental and physical health (see discussions by Coyne & Downey, 1991; Eckenrode & Gore, 1981; Lepore, 1992). Both negative social interactions and the absence of positive interaction can be highly distressing. Environmentally induced social isolation and separation can produce feelings of social deprivation, loneliness, and associated distress. Bolger *et al.* (1989) showed that emotional distress was more strongly correlated with social stressors, such as marital conflict, than with non-social stressors, such as financial problems. From studies that have compared the emotional impact respectively of positive and negative aspects of social ties, it appears that social negativity (e.g. conflict, rejection) may have adverse effects on emotional functioning that exceed the beneficial effects of positive or supportive social ties (Henderson *et al.*, 1980; Lepore, 1992; Rook, 1984; Schuster *et al.*, 1990). These findings suggest that environmental factors that contribute to negative social interaction may have a particularly strong adverse effect on mental health.

Mediating role of interpersonal relationships in the environment and mental health

Few studies have been done on the mediating role of interpersonal relationships between the physical environment and mental health. Lepore and Evans have shown both cross-sectionally (Evans *et al.*, 1989) and prospectively (Lepore *et al.*, 1991b) that the positive relationship between high-density housing and psychological distress is mediated by social support. Data were reported above showing that college students who lived under more crowded conditions were less socially supportive when they interacted with a stranger in an uncrowded laboratory

(Evans & Lepore, 1993). These same students were also shown to be more socially withdrawn, the covariance between residential density and social support being accounted for by social withdrawal. Evans *et al.* (1996b) also found evidence for the mediating effects of social withdrawal in the link between residential crowding and psychological distress. Moreover, when social withdrawal is interfered with in a laboratory experiment, the stressful effects of acute crowding are accentuated, particularly for people who live in crowded situations (Evans *et al.*, 2000a). In a laboratory study, college students interacted in very close physical proximity. Those who lived in high- or low-density apartments were randomly assigned to conditions where social withdrawal was either permitted or blocked. Independent of income levels, when withdrawal was blocked, participants who were living in crowded conditions reacted with higher levels of stress, relative to when withdrawal was not blocked. Finally, Evans *et al.* (1999) demonstrated that the link between residential density and speech complexity was mediated by parental responsiveness. In high-density homes, irrespective of social class, parents are less responsive to their children's verbalizations which, in turn, accounts for their tendency to speak more simply to their children. This series of studies clearly implicates changes in interpersonal interaction, particularly related to social withdrawal or responsiveness, as an important pathway linking residential density to mental health. Unfortunately, none of the other potent environmental characteristics of settings (chaos, noise, high-rise design, street traffic) have been tested for explanatory interpersonal processes that might help explain their respective links to mental health.

Negative affective states

One of the ways that the environment might influence mental health, including mood disorders and violent behaviour, is through its influence on emotional states. Various environmental stressors, particularly noise, crowding, traffic congestion, high temperatures, and pollutants, have all been associated with negative emotional states. Some of these negative states resemble clinical disorders, but they may not result in full-blown symptoms (e.g. depression, anxiety) unless they become intense and chronic, as can occur through repeated exposures to environmental stressors. For instance, in both laboratory and field studies, persons exposed to short-term or chronic crowding report feeling stressed, tense, anxious, nervous, irritated, and hostile (Baum & Paulus, 1987; Gove & Hughes, 1983; Sundstrom, 1978). If these feelings are repeated daily, they could well lead to mental health problems. Another common environmental stressor – commuting under congested conditions – has been associated with negative emotions (Evans, 1994; Novaco *et al.*, 1991; Stokols *et al.*, 1978; Wener *et al.*, 2003).

Annoyance is another common type of negative emotional response to untoward environmental conditions. Noise is often perceived as a source of annoyance, particularly in urban settings and those proximate to primary noise sources (e.g. heavily trafficked streets and airport impact zones; see Chapter 9).

There is little evidence that people become accustomed to very noisy ambient conditions (Fields, 1993; Job, 1988; Kryter, 1994; Lercher, 2001). For instance, children chronically exposed to aircraft noise remain annoyed and do not habituate over time (Cohen *et al.*, 1986; Evans *et al.*, 1995; Haines *et al.*, 2001a, 2001b).

Community studies also reveal that exposure to ambient air pollution and odorous pollutants are associated with heightened annoyance (Cavalini, 1992; Evans, 1994; Evans & Jacobs, 1981). Under controlled laboratory conditions, Rotton (1983) found heightened annoyance in response to malodorous pollutants. Although the quantity of this research is nowhere as large as in the case of noise, some of the same moderator variables surface: health concerns, perceived control, awareness, polluter malfeasance on the part of authorities, and economic linkages to sources all appear to alter negative reactions to ambient pollutants.

Thermal comfort – another indicator of emotional well-being – has a long history of analysis in laboratory and field studies. Negative affect is reliably increased by high temperatures (Anderson, 1989; Baron, 1978; Bell, 1992). Despite a widespread belief to the contrary, there are few regional, age, or gender differences in affective reactions to high levels of heat – it is universally experienced as negative and the preferred range of comfortable temperature is surprisingly stable across widely disparate groups of people. Adaptation to heat in terms of fatigue and performance does occur, but not thermal comfort.

Negative affective states and mental health

We have argued that negative emotional states can influence mental health if they become intense or chronic. This argument rests on the assumption that negative mood is part of a continuum of affective states that can include disorders such as anxiety or depression (Lewinsohn *et al.*, 2000). Although debatable (Coyne, 1994), this assumption seems reasonable in the light of evidence that negative affect is a risk factor for the development of mental health problems such as depressive disorder (e.g. Harrington *et al.*, 1990; Pine *et al.*, 1999; Weissman *et al.*, 1999). We also know that negative emotions trigger mental health problems (Hankin & Abramson, 2001).

In addition to mood disorders, negative emotional states – annoyance, irritability, anger – can potentially increase behavioural problems such as aggression or violence. Several investigators have documented that crowding, noise, pollution, and high temperatures are associated with greater hostility and aggression (e.g. Baum & Koman, 1976; Donnerstein & Wilson, 1976; Hutt & Vaizey, 1966; Paulus, 1988; Rotton & Frey, 1985). It also appears that negative affect is related to greater hostility and aggression (Anderson, 1989). Thus, there is some potential for negative affect to mediate the relationship between environmental stressors and aggressive behaviour.

Mediating role of negative affect in the relation between the environment and mental health

Several studies have found that annoyance from noise influences mental health reactions. Graeven (1974) found that annoyance and awareness of airport noise elevated psychosomatic symptoms, independent of actual noise levels and socio-economic status. Topf and Dillon (1988) showed that critical care nurses who were more bothered by noise at work evidenced higher levels of burnout and emotional exhaustion. Nivison and Endresen (1993) found similar trends in psychological distress among urban residents in response to street traffic noise. However, none of the above studies actually tested for the mediating role of subjective responses to noise in affecting mental health outcomes. In a series of studies, though, van Kamp (1990) demonstrated that annoyance to airport noise mediated the impacts of objective noise levels on several indices of psychological well-being. Tarnopolsky *et al.* (1978) found that rather than annoyance mediating noise and psychological distress, the direction of influence appeared to be the other way round. Persons with greater distress were more likely to be annoyed by aircraft noise. It should also be noted that one of the strongest predictors of annoyance to noise – noise sensitivity – is correlated with neuroticism (a dispositional tendency to experience negative emotions; Stansfeld, 1992; Stansfeld *et al.*, 2000).

A difficulty in interpreting the mediational data on annoyance and mental health is that both constructs are typically operationalized by self-report methods, and thus share methodological variance that could masquerade as a real relationship. Several investigators, though, have attempted to overcome this problem. Physical concentrations of malodorous pollutants have a modest relationship across several different samples to psychological distress; annoyance reactions to such pollutants mediated these relationships (Cavalini, 1992). After statistically partialling annoyance from the equation, the previously significant effect of odour onto psychological distress was no longer significant. Cavalini found parallel results for psychosomatic symptoms, and these cross-sectional findings were replicated in a longitudinal study.

Another approach is to manipulate appraisals. Vera *et al.* (1992) manipulated cognitive appraisals during exposure to noise. Some participants were given negative self-statements (e.g. 'I can't stand this horrible noise') during exposure to noise in the laboratory. These college students felt more tension and anxiety compared with others who were only exposed to noise. Rather than rely on self-reports of mental health, Arvidsson and Lindvall (1978) examined annoyance and task performance among male college students who were exposed to simulated road traffic noise at high volume. Those participants who were more annoyed manifested poorer task performance in response to noise. This study did not suffer from the problem of sole reliance on self-report measures for both annoyance and mental health, but on the other hand, task performance is not equivalent to mental health and no direct test of mediation was undertaken.

A few studies have directly examined the role of negative affect as a mediator between high temperatures and aggression. However, this area is controversial because of disagreement over the shape of the function relating heat to aggression. There is a consensus that negative affect increases linearly with temperature elevations beyond the comfort range (Anderson & De Neve, 1992; Baron, 1978; Bell & Greene, 1982), but disagreement exists over the relationship between temperature and aggression. Anderson argues that the relationship is linear, whereas Bell and Baron both claim it is curvilinear. According to the curvilinear hypothesis, initially elevated negative affect in response to heightened temperatures increases hostility, irritability, and aggression, but as temperatures continue to increase, escaping the heat becomes the primary motive, thus resulting in lower aggression.

Our focus here is on research demonstrating a mediating impact of negative affect on the relationship between heat and mental health. Most of the research on negative affect as a mediator has manipulated affect during high-temperature conditions. Baron and Bell (1976) found that providing participants with a cool drink, which lowered negative affect, in conjunction with high temperatures, led to increased aggression (for example, shocking a stranger when he made mistakes during a task). This was relative to a condition of similar high temperature wherein no drink was offered. Other experiments with different types of affect manipulations have found similar support for the curvilinear linkages between temperature and aggression (Bell & Baron, 1976; Palamarek & Rule, 1979).

Psychophysiological stress

The final psychosocial process that may mediate the relationship between the physical environment and mental health is psychophysiological stress. Below, we review evidence that crowding, commuting to work, and noise can all elevate psychophysiological parameters associated with stress. Most of this research has examined cardiovascular and neuroendocrine markers of stress.

Neuroendocrine measures

Crowding in prisons, trains, households, and neighbourhoods has been associated with elevations in catecholamines (Evans & Saegert, 2000; Fleming *et al.*, 1987; Heshka & Pylypuk, 1975; Lundberg, 1976; Schaeffer *et al.*, 1988b; Singer *et al.*, 1978). Similarly, commuting has been implicated in elevating levels of cortisol (Wener *et al.*, 2003) and catecholamines (Bellet *et al.*, 1969). In urban bus drivers, on-the-job rises in catecholamines were positively correlated with traffic congestion levels on their shift (Evans & Carrere, 1991).

Short-term noise exposure reliably elevates stress hormones, but as in the case of cardiovascular parameters, these effects may be short-lived (Evans, 2001). In a series of studies, evidence was found of airport operations elevating cortisol levels (Ising & Braun, 2000; Maschke *et al.*, 1995). Work around the Munich airport has revealed evidence of both cross-sectional and prospective longitudinal elevations in catecholamines, but not cortisol, in elementary school children exposed to noise (Evans *et al.*, 1995, 1998). The absence of effects on cortisol from airport noise has been replicated around Heathrow in London (Haines *et al.*, 2001a). In a subsequent study, Haines *et al.* (2001b) found no cortisol effects but, contrary to the Munich data, also no differences in catecholamines in relation to noise levels at Heathrow. Evans *et al.* (2001) uncovered small, cross-sectional differences in cortisol and in a cortisol metabolite among children exposed to varying levels of road and rail traffic noise in small towns and rural areas in alpine Austria. They used a more sensitive cortisol assay technique than that employed in the earlier studies.

Cardiovascular stress

Several laboratory studies have found elevated blood pressure among individuals randomly assigned to high- versus low-density settings (Epstein *et al.*, 1981; Evans, 1979; Hackworth, 1976). Skin conductance was also higher among more crowded laboratory participants (Aiello *et al.*, 1975). McCallum *et al.* (1979) found elevated skin conductance under crowded laboratory conditions, but only when subjects were motivated to maintain their task performance. When performance was allowed to deteriorate under more crowded conditions, skin conductance did not rise. This is an interesting and potentially quite important finding because it suggests that coping efforts may elevate physiological activity in response to environmental stress. As will be shown below, this same pattern has been revealed in both laboratory and field studies of noise.

Field studies of crowding in men's prisons have revealed elevated blood pressure (D'Atri, 1975; Paulus, 1988) and elevated skin conductance (Cox *et al.*, 1979). Ten- to 12-year-old boys, but not girls, who live in more crowded homes have elevated blood pressure (Evans *et al.*, 1996b). A similar pattern of results was found for skin conductance in a laboratory study of crowding among 9–17-year-old boys and girls (Aiello *et al.*, 1979). Adults who live in more crowded neighbourhoods have larger increases in blood pressure in response to a problem-solving task than others with similar backgrounds (e.g. socio-economic status) living in uncrowded neighbourhoods (Fleming *et al.*, 1987). Booth (1976) found no association between residential crowding levels and blood pressure, but did uncover a small association with cholesterol levels for adult males.

Commuting by car can elevate blood pressure and heart rate (Hoffmann, 1965; Simonson *et al.*, 1968). Levels of traffic congestion are positively associated with blood pressure measures (Schaeffer *et al.*, 1988b; Stokols *et al.*, 1978; White & Rotton, 1998). The last of these studies is particularly interesting because it incorporated random assignment of participants to different conditions of road traffic congestion.

The literature on noise and cardiovascular changes is too large to review exhaustively, but an overview will be given here. Short-term exposure to noise in the laboratory momentarily elevates cardiovascular parameters, but these rapidly habituate (Berglund & Lindvall, 1999; Kryter, 1994). This habituation effect, however, does not occur if individuals are noise-sensitive or are working on a demanding task (Evans, 2001). This interaction between noise and task demands on psychophysiological responses has also been shown in two field studies (Melamed *et al.*, 2001; Welch, 1979).

Field studies of noise exposure and blood pressure are of two major types: first, occupational and second, community studies of airport or traffic noise. The occupational literature is equivocal with respect to links between noise and blood pressure levels, as well as with rates of hypertension (Kryter, 1994; Stansfeld *et al.*, 2000; Thompson, 1993). However, mixed findings and poor methodological controls plague this literature. There is some suggestion that workers with longer durations of noise exposure may be at risk for higher blood pressure (Talbott *et al.*, 1999). These data on duration of exposure, coupled with findings indicating that task demands can play an important role in physiological responses to occupational noise, begin to suggest some reasons why this general area of inquiry has yielded inconsistent findings. Other contributing factors may be poor measurement of noise exposure and of psychophysiological outcomes (Evans, 2001; Melamed *et al.*, 1999).

Several community studies of aircraft noise have revealed evidence of small elevations in children's blood pressure (Evans, 2001). These include one prospective study (Evans *et al.*, 1998a) and mostly have good controls for sociodemographic background. Knipschild (1977) earlier reported a dose–response relationship between aircraft noise exposure and adult hypertension in communities around the Amsterdam airport. However, the link between traffic noise levels on one hand and blood pressure and other cardiovascular parameters on the other is much less clear than in the case of airport noise (Babisch, 2000; Neus & Boikat, 2000; Stansfeld *et al.*, 2000). Two recent studies, though, indicate small relationships between street traffic noise and elevated blood pressure in children (Evans *et al.*, 2001; Regecova & Kellerova, 1995). The former study also found evidence of greater cardiovascular reactivity to a test in the laboratory among children from noisier areas of the community.

Psychophysiological stress and mental health

There is growing evidence that stress-induced hormonal changes can influence mental health in both adults and children (Gunnar & Barr, 1998; Leonard, 2001). One of the most consistent findings in biological psychiatry is the existence of dysregulation of the hypothalamic-pituitary-adrenal (HPA) axis in cognitive and mood disorders. This evidence is most compelling for the link between excessive brain exposure to glucocorticoids (e.g. cortisol) and depression. Much of the basic research has been done with animals, but human studies provide convergent evidence (McEwen, 2000; Schulkin *et al.*, 1994). One robust finding is that patients with major depressive disorder have significantly higher cortisol levels than other psychiatric patients or control subjects (Bauer *et al.*, 1994; Gold *et al.*, 1996; Pitman & Orr, 1990). Longitudinal increases in cortisol during ageing may also be related to the development of depression (Lupien *et al.*, 1997). Pharmacological studies show that mood changes often accompany exposure to synthetic glucocorticoids (Boston Collaborative Drug Surveillance Program, 1972; Chrousos *et al.*, 1993; Wolkowitz, 1994).

In children, elevated cortisol has been associated with poorer control of attention, which in turn has been implicated in poor impulse control and conduct disorders (Gunnar & Barr, 1998). Granger *et al.* (1994) found that children who were more reactive (i.e. greater cortisol increases) had greater global symptoms of social anxiety and social problems and were more socially inhibited during the parent–child conflict task. In addition to altering the brain's neurochemical milieu, chronic stress may alter the brain's architecture by sustaining high levels of cortisol (Bremner *et al.*, 2000; Gunnar & Barr, 1998). Elevated glucocorticoids have been implicated in dendrite shrinkage and cell death in the hippocampus (McEwen, 2000; McEwen & Gould, 1990; Schulkin *et al.*, 1994). Neuronal damage in the hippocampus obviously has negative implications for HPA axis regulation, as well as for cognitive and emotional functioning. One implication of this is that persons may lose their ability to turn off the HPA stress response, which can then lead to even more prolonged elevations and exposures to glucocorticoids and further hippocampal damage. Because the hippocampus plays an important role in both verbal memory and memory for context, damage to this region might increase the risk for mental health problems by interfering with effective coping mechanisms (McEwen, 1998).

In addition to its direct effects, pathophysiological responses to environmental stressors might indirectly influence mental health by increasing cardiac and cardiovascular diseases (e.g. hypertension). The link between depression and CHD has been noted for many years, and it appears that the relationship is bidirectional. There is considerable evidence that depression is a risk factor for CHD (Aromaa *et al.*, 1994; Booth-Kewley & Friedman, 1987; Schwartzman & Glaus, 2000) and is a predictor of poor outcome after the onset of disease (Lesperance *et al.*, 1996; Silverstone, 1987). Furthermore, there is evidence that depression often occurs after, and in response to, CHD (Schleifer *et al.*, 1989).

Mediating role of psychophysiological stress

We are unaware of any studies directly examining the role of psychophysiological responses to environmental conditions in mediating adverse mental health consequences. Several, however, have examined the interplay between annoyance and elevated perceived stress in relation to noise and psychophysiological reactions. Lercher *et al.* (1993) found that noise annoyance in concert with job dissatisfaction doubled elevations in blood pressure associated with occupational noise annoyance alone. Men exposed to occupational noise showed higher elevations in serum cholesterol if they were also annoyed by the noise (Melamed *et al.*, 1997). Both studies included good statistical controls for standard CHD risk factors. Independent of social class, elementary school children exposed to noise around the Los Angeles airport had elevated blood pressure

(Cohen *et al.*, 1986); controlling for objective noise exposure, blood pressure elevations were greater for children who perceived the airport noise as louder. Both children and adolescents exposed to loud military over-flights who were more annoyed had greater elevations in blood pressure than those less annoyed (Schmeck & Poustka, 1993).

The role of subjective reactions in physiological responses to noise may depend in part on the level of noise. Neus *et al.* (1983) found that negative subjective reactions to road traffic noise increased the incidence of hypertension, but only at relatively low levels of noise. At higher levels, hypertension was more prevalent, but did not vary in relation to the individual responses to noise. The meaning of noise may also have physiological consequences. Atherley *et al.* (1970) demonstrated that skin conductance habituated more quickly to acute exposure to unimportant noise sources (i.e. white noise) than to more important noises (i.e. aircraft, baby, bell). In a second experiment, investigating seven-hour noise exposure periods to office, aircraft or white noise, biochemical assays of adrenal cortical activity and immunological function revealed parallel trends.

As noted earlier, Vera *et al.* (1992) manipulated mental states by exposing female university students to negative self-statements (e.g. 'This noise is making me crazy', 'My heart is pounding more and more'), while they were listening to short periods of acute noise. Muscle tension, as measured by electromyogram (EMG), in the prefrontal cortical lobe increased with noise, but only under conditions of negative self-statements. Weaker but similar effects were found for skin conductance.

Several studies indicate that when noise is more annoying or increases perceived stress, psychophysiological stress reactions are stronger. This pattern of data evidences a moderating effect of subjective reactions to noise, suggesting indirectly that physiological outcomes are influenced by cognitive appraisal. The one study to examine the mediating effect of subjective reactions on physiological stress more directly did not include, unfortunately, a mediational analysis. Cohen *et al.* (1986) demonstrated that children's perceptions of the loudness of aircraft noise significantly added to the correlation between objective noise levels and resting blood pressure. This is necessary but not sufficient to demonstrate mediation. To show full mediation, the investigators would have needed to partial-out perceived loudness from the objective noise/blood pressure relationship and show a significant reduction in that association.

A different type of physiological pathway from those discussed above which should be considered when linking noise and mental health is sleep quality. There is a large literature demonstrating negative impacts on sleep quality by ambient aircraft and road traffic noise. Sleep interference, particularly if chronic, can obviously have mental health consequences (Stansfeld *et al.*, 2000).

Conclusion

In this chapter, various psychosocial processes that may underlie linkages between the physical environment and mental health have been considered.

There was a focus on four primary mediators: control and the related process of helplessness, interpersonal relationships, negative affective states, and physiological stress. Each of these mediating linkages has documented associations with both the environmental antecedents and mental health outcomes. Because few studies satisfy all of the methodological and analytical requirements for establishing mediation (Baron & Kenny, 1986; Evans & Lepore, 1997), the primary goal has been to evaluate the plausibility of these four mediators. Much more research is needed to fully test the model suggested in Figure 5.1.

Prolonged experiences of uncontrollable stimuli are associated with the development of depression, particularly when individuals attribute their lack of mastery to their own limited ability. Further, there is good evidence that suboptimal environmental conditions such as crowding, noise, pollution, and poor housing quality undermine individuals' perceived control and increase feelings of helplessness in both adults and children. Interpersonal relationships have a profound influence on mental health; this review shows that environmental factors can shape both the quality and quantity of social ties. The third mediator to be considered was negative affective states, which appear to be a precursor to some mental health problems, such as depressive symptoms. A variety of environmental characteristics, such as noise, pollution, and high temperatures can elevate negative affect (e.g. irritation, frustration, psychological stress). The last mediator – psychophysiological stress – might influence mental health in two ways. First, environmentally induced pathophysiological states can result in physical health disorders, such as heart disease, that can increase depression and other mental health problems. However, research indicates that the relationship between depression and illnesses such as heart disease may be reciprocal. Second, psychophysiological stress might influence mental health via physiological arousal. Chronic environmental stressors affect the HPA axis, thus exposing the brain to various neuroendocrine hormones such as cortisol that can undermine both cognitive functioning (e.g. working memory, attention regulation) and mental health.

There are multiple and related biopsychological pathways linking the physical environment and mental health. Abundant evidence shows that control and social relationships are critical mediators, and there is suggestive evidence that negative affect may mediate relations between the physical environment and mental health. Physiological stress is a plausible but untested mediating process in addition. By drawing attention to these mediational pathways, we hope to enrich understanding of the role of the physical environment in mental health. Important avenues for future research have also been highlighted above. In the longer run, a better understanding of why and how the physical environment can adversely impact on mental health should also open up potential intervention strategies for helping people to cope more effectively with poor environmental conditions.

Acknowledgements

Preparation of this chapter was partially supported by the W. T. Grant Foundation and the John D. and Catherine T. MacArthur Foundation Network on Socioeconomic Status and Health.

References

Abramson, L., Garber, J. and Seligman, M. E. P. (1980) 'Learned helplessness in humans', in Garber, J. and Seligman, M. E. P. (eds), *Human helplessness*. New York: Academic Press.

Aiello, J. R., Epstein, Y. M. and Karlin, R. A. (1975) 'Effects of crowding on electrodermal activity'. *Sociological Symposium, 14*, 43–58.

Aiello, J. R., Nicosia, G. and Thompson, D. E. (1979) 'Physiological, social, and behavioral consequences of crowding on children and adolescents'. *Child Development, 50*, 195–202.

Anderson, C. A. (1989) 'Temperature and aggression: ubiquitous effects of heat on occurrence of human violence'. *Psychological Bulletin, 106*, 74–96.

Anderson, C. A. and De Neve, K. M. (1992) 'Temperature, aggression, and the negative affect escape model'. *Psychological Bulletin, 111*, 347–351.

Aromaa, A., Raitsalo, R., Reunanen, A., Impivaara, O., Heliovaara, M., Knekt, P., Joukamaa, M. and Maatela, J. (1994) 'Depression and cardiovascular diseases'. *Acta Psychiatrica Scandinavia Supplement, 377*, 77–82.

Arvidsson, O. and Lindvall, T. (1978) 'Subjective annoyance from noise compared with some directly measurable effects'. *Archives of Environmental Health, 33*, 159–166.

Atherley, G. R. C., Gibbons, S. and Powell, J. (1970) 'Moderate acoustic stimuli: the interrelation of subjective importance and certain physiological changes'. *Ergonomics, 13*, 536–545.

Babisch, W. (2000) 'Traffic noise and cardiovascular disease: epidemiological review and synthesis'. *Noise and Health, 8*, 9–32.

Baron, R. A. (1978) 'Aggression and heat: the long hot summer revisited', in Baum, A., Singer, J. E. and Valins, S. (eds), *Advances in environmental psychology*, vol. 1 (pp. 57–84). Hillsdale, NJ: Lawrence Erlbaum Associates, Inc.

Baron, R. A. and Bell, P. A. (1976) 'Aggression and heat: the influence of ambient temperature, negative affect, and a cooling drink of water on physical aggression'. *Journal of Personality and Social Psychology, 33*, 245–255.

Baron, R. M. and Kenny, D. A. (1986) 'The moderator–mediator variable distinction in social psychological research: conceptual, strategic, and statistical considerations'. *Journal of Personality and Social Psychology, 51*, 1173–1182.

Bauer, M., Priebe, S., Graf, K.-J. and Kurten. I. (1994) 'Psychological and endocrine abnormalities in refugees from East Germany. II. Serum levels of cortisol, prolactin, luteinizing hormone, follicle-stimulating hormone, and testosterone'. *Psychiatric Research, 51*, 75–85.

Baum, A. and Koman, S. (1976) 'Differential response to anticipated crowding: psychological effects of social and spatial density'. *Journal of Personality and Social Psychology, 34*, 526–536.

Baum, A. and Paulus, P. B. (1987) 'Crowding', in Stokols, D. and Altman I. (eds), *Handbook of environmental psychology*. New York: Wiley.

Baum, A. and Valins, S. (1977) *Architecture and social behavior: Psychological studies of social density*. Hillsdale, NJ: Lawrence Erlbaum Associates, Inc.

Baum, A., Aiello, J. R. and Calesnick, L. (1978) 'Crowding and personal control: social density and the development of learned helplessness'. *Journal of Personality and Social Psychology, 36,* 1000–1011.

Baumeister, R. F. and Leary, M. R. (1995) 'The need to belong: desire for interpersonal attachments as a fundamental human motivation'. *Psychological Bulletin, 117,* 497–529.

Baxter, J. C. and Rozelle, R. (1975) 'Nonverbal expression as a function of crowding during a simulated police–citizen encounter'. *Journal of Personality and Social Psychology, 32,* 40–54.

Bell, P. A. (1992) 'In defense of the negative affect escape model of heat and aggression'. *Psychological Bulletin, 111,* 342–346.

Bell, P. A. and Baron, R. A. (1976) 'Aggression and heat: the mediating role of negative affect'. *Journal of Applied Social Psychology, 6,* 1479–1482.

Bell, P. A. and Greene, T. C. (1982) 'Thermal stress: physiological, comfort, performance and social effects of hot and cold temperatures', in Evans, G. W. (ed.), *Environmental stress.* New York: Cambridge University Press.

Bellet, S., Roman, L. and Kostis, J. (1969) 'The effect of automobile driving on catecholamine and adrenocortical excretion'. *American Journal of Cardiology, 24,* 365–368.

Benassi, V. A., Sweeney, P. D. and Dufour, C. L. (1988) 'Is there a relation between locus of control orientation and depression?' *Journal of Abnormal Psychology, 97,* 357–367.

Berglund, B. and Lindvall, T. (1999) 'Community noise'. *Archives of the Center for Sensory Research, 2,* 1–195.

Billings, A. G., Cronkite, R. C. and Moos, R. H. (1983). Social-environmental factors in unipolar depression: comparisons of depressed patients and nondepressed controls. *Journal of Abnormal Psychology, 92,* 119–133.

Blazer, D. G. (1983) 'Impact of late life depression on the social network'. *American Journal of Psychiatry, 140,* 162–166.

Bolger, N., DeLongis, A., Kessler, R. C. and Schilling, E. A. (1989) Effects of daily stress on negative mood. *Journal of Personality and Social Psychology, 57,* 808–818.

Booth, A. (1976) *Urban crowding and its consequences.* New York: Praeger.

Booth-Kewley, S. and Friedman, H. S. (1987) 'Psychological predictors of heart disease: a quantitative review'. *Psychological Bulletin, 101,* 343–362.

Boston Collaborative Drug Surveillance Program (1972) 'Acute adverse reactions to prednisone in relation to dosage'. *Clinical Pharmacology, 13,* 694–698.

Bradley, R. H. and Caldwell, B. (1984) 'The HOME inventory and family demographics'. *Developmental Psychology, 20,* 315–320.

Bradley, R. H., Whiteside, L., Mundfrom, D., Casey, P., Kelleher, K. and Pope, S. (1994) 'Early indications of resilience and their relation to experiences in the home environments of low birth weight, premature children living in poverty'. *Child Development, 65,* 346–360.

Bremner, J. D., Narayan, M., Anderson, E. R., Staib, L. H., Miller, H. L. and Charney, D. S. (2000) 'Hippocampal volume reduction in major depression'. *American Journal of Psychiatry, 157,* 115–118.

Bullinger, M., Hygge, S., Evans, G. W., Meis, M. and von Mackensen, S. (1999) 'The psychological costs of aircraft noise among children'. *Zentralblatt für Hygiene und Umweltmedizin, 202,* 127–138.

Burns, M. O. and Seligman, M. E. P. (1991) 'Explanatory style, helplessness, and depression', in Snyder, C. R. and Forsyth, D. R. (eds), *Handbook of social and clinical psychology.* New York: Pergamon Press.

Cavalini, P. (1992) *It's an ill wind that brings no good*. PhD dissertation, University of Groningen, The Netherlands.

Cheung, C., Leung, K., Chan, W. and Ma, K. (1998) 'Depression, loneliness, and health in an adverse living environment: a study of bedspace residents in Hong Kong'. *Social Behavior and Personality, 26*, 151–170.

Chrousos, G. A., Kattah, J. C., Beck, R. W. and Cleary, P. A. (1993) 'Side effects of glucocorticoid treatment: experience of the optic neuritis treatment trial'. *Journal of the American Medical Association, 269*, 2110–2112.

Churchman, A. and Ginsberg, Y. (1984) 'The image and experience of high rise housing in Israel'. *Journal of Environmental Psychology, 4*, 27–41.

Cohen, S. (1980) 'After-effects of stress on human performance and social behavior: a review of research and theory'. *Psychological Bulletin, 88*, 82–108.

Cohen, S. and Wills, T. A. (1985) 'Stress, social support, and the buffering hypothesis'. *Psychological Bulletin, 98*, 310–357.

Cohen, S., Evans, G. W., Stokols, D. and Krantz, D. S. (1986) *Behavior, health and environmental stress*. New York: Plenum.

Corapci, F. and Wachs, T. D. (2002) 'Does parental mood or efficacy mediate the influence of environmental chaos upon parenting behavior?' *Merrill Palmer Quarterly, 48*, 182–201.

Cox, V. C., Paulus, P. B., McCain, G. and Schkade, J. (1979) 'Field research on the effects of crowding in prisons and on offshore drilling platforms', in Aiello, J. R. and Baum, A. (eds) *Residential crowding and design*. New York: Plenum.

Coyne, J. C. (1994) 'Self-reported distress: analog or Ersatz depression?'. *Psychological Bulletin, 116*, 29–45.

Coyne, J. C. and Downey, G. (1991) 'Social factors and psychopathology: stress, social support, and coping processes'. *Annual Review of Psychology, 42*, 401–425.

Coyne, J. C. and Gotlib, I. H. (1983) 'The role of cognition in depression: a critical appraisal'. *Psychological Bulletin, 94*, 472–505.

Cunningham, M. R. (1979) 'Weather, mood, and helping behavior: quasi-experiments with the sunshine Samaritan'. *Journal of Personality and Social Psychology, 37*, 1947–1956.

D'Atri, D. A. (1975) 'Psychophysiological responses to crowding'. *Environment and Behavior*, 7, 237–250.

Donnerstein, E., & Wilson, D. W. (1976). 'Effects of noise and perceived control on ongoing and subsequent aggressive behavior'. *Journal of Personality and Social Psychology, 34*, 774–781.

Eckenrode, J. and Gore, S. (1981) 'Stressful life events and social supports: the significance of context', in Gottlieb, B. H. (ed.), *Social networks and social support*. Beverly Hills, CA: Sage.

Epstein, Y., Woolfolk, R. L. and Lehrer, P. (1981) 'Physiological, cognitive, and nonverbal responses to repeated exposure to crowding'. *Journal of Applied Social Psychology, 11*, 1–13.

Evans, G. W. (1979) 'Behavioral and physiological consequences of crowding in humans'. *Journal of Applied Social Psychology, 9*, 27–46.

Evans, G. W. (1994) 'Working on the hot seat: urban bus operators'. *Accident Analysis and Prevention, 26*, 181–193.

Evans, G. W. (2001) 'Environmental stress and health', in Baum, A. T., Revenson, T. and Singer, J. E. (eds), *Handbook of health psychology*. Mahwah, NJ: Lawrence Erlbaum Associates, Inc.

Evans, G. W. (2003) 'A multi-methodological analysis of cumulative risk and allostatic load among rural children'. *Developmental Psychology*, *39*, 924–933.

Evans, G. W. (2004) 'The environment of childhood poverty'. *American Psychologist*, *59*, 77–92.

Evans, G. W. and Carrere, S. (1991) 'Traffic congestion, perceived control, and psychophysiological stress among urban bus drivers'. *Journal of Applied Psychology*, *76*, 658–663.

Evans, G. W. and Jacobs, S. V. (1981) 'Air pollution and human behavior'. *Journal of Social Issues*, *37*, 95–125.

Evans, G. W. and Lepore, S. J. (1993) 'Household crowding and social support: a quasi-experimental analysis'. *Journal of Personality and Social Psychology*, *65*, 308–316.

Evans, G. W. and Lepore, S. J. (1997) 'Moderating and mediating processes in environment behavior research', in Moore, G. T. and Marans, R. W. (eds), *Advances in environment, behavior, and design*. New York: Plenum.

Evans, G. W. and Saegert, S. (2000) 'Residential crowding in the context of inner city poverty', in Wapner, S., Demick, J., Hminami, H. and Yamamoto, T. (eds), *Theoretical perspectives in environment–behavior research: Underlying assumptions, research problems, and relationships*. New York: Plenum.

Evans, G. W., Bullinger, M. and Hygge, S. (1998a) 'Chronic noise exposure and physiological response: a prospective, longitudinal study of children under environmental stress'. *Psychological Science*, *9*, 75–77.

Evans, G. W., Hygge, S. and Bullinger, M. (1995) 'Chronic noise and psychological stress'. *Psychological Science*, *6*, 333–338.

Evans, G. W., Johansson, G. and Carrere, S. (1994) 'Psychosocial factors and the physical environment: inter-relations in the workplace', in Cooper, C. L. and Robertson, I. T. (eds), *International review of industrial and organizational psychology*. Chichester, UK: Wiley.

Evans, G. W., Lepore, S. J. and Schroeder, A. (1996b) 'The role of architecture in human responses to crowding'. *Journal of Personality and Social Psychology*, *70*, 41–46.

Evans, G. W., Maxwell, L. and Hart, B. (1999) 'Parental language and verbal responsiveness to children in crowded homes'. *Developmental Psychology*, *35*, 1020–1023.

Evans, G. W., Saegert, S. and Harris, R. (2000b) 'Residential density and psychological health among children in low income families'. *Environment and Behavior*, *33*, 165–180.

Evans, G. W., Allen, K., Tafalla, R. and O'Meara, T. (1996a) 'Multiple stressors'. *Journal of Environmental Psychology*, *16*, 147–174.

Evans, G. W., Lepore, S. J., Sejwal, B. and Palsane, M. N. (1998b) 'Chronic residential crowding and children's well being: An ecological perspective'. *Child Development*, *69*, 1514–1523.

Evans, G. W., Palsane, M. N., Lepore, S. J. and Martin, J. (1989) 'Residential density and psychological health: the mediating effects of social support'. *Journal of Personality and Social Psychology*, *57*, 994–999.

Evans, G. W., Lercher, P., Meis, M., Ising, I. and Kofler, W. (2001) 'Community noise exposure and stress in children'. *Journal of the Acoustical Society of America*, *109*, 1023–1027.

Evans, G. W., Rhee, E., Forbes, C., Allen, K. M. and Lepore, S. J. (2000a) 'The meaning and efficacy of social withdrawal as a strategy for coping with chronic crowding'. *Journal of Environmental Psychology*, *20*, 335–342.

Festinger, L., Schacter, S. and Bach, K. (1950) *Social pressures in informal groups*. Stanford, CA: Stanford University Press.

Fields, J. M. (1993) 'Effect of personal and situational variables on noise annoyance in residential areas'. *Journal of the Acoustical Society of America, 93*, 2753–2763.

Fleming, I., Baum, A. and Weiss, L. (1987) 'Social density and perceived control as mediators of crowding stress in high density neighborhoods'. *Journal of Personality and Social Psychology, 52*, 899–906.

Fuller, T. D., Edwards, J. D., Vorakitphokatorn, S. and Sermsri, S. (1993). 'Household crowding and family relations in Bangkok'. *Social Problems, 40*, 410–430.

Glass, D. C. and Singer, J. E. (1972) *Urban stress*. New York: Academic Press.

Gold, P. W., Wong, M. L., Chrousos, G. P. and Licinio, J. (1996) 'Stress system abnormalities in melancholic and atypical depression: molecular, pathophysiological, and therapeutic implications'. *Molecular Psychiatry, 1*, 257–265.

Gove, W. R. and Hughes, M. (1983) *Overcrowding in the household*. New York: Academic Press.

Gove, W. R., Hughes, M. and Galle, O. R. (1979) 'Overcrowding in the home: an empirical investigation of its possible pathological consequences'. *American Sociological Review, 44*, 59–80.

Graeven, D. B. (1974) 'The effects of airport noise on health: an examination of three hypotheses'. *Journal of Health and Social Behavior, 15*, 336–343.

Granger, D. A., Weisz, J. R. and Kauneckis, D. (1994) 'Neuroendocrine reactivity, internalizing behavior problems, and control-related cognitions in clinic-referred children and adolescents'. *Journal of Abnormal Psychology, 103*, 267–276.

Gunnar, M. R. and Barr, R. G. (1998) 'Stress, early brain development, and behavior'. *Infants and Young Children, 11*, 1–14.

Hackworth, J. R. (1976) 'Relationship between spatial density and sensory overload, personal space, and systolic and diastolic blood pressure'. *Perceptual and Motor Skills, 43*, 867–872.

Haines, M. M., Stansfeld, S. A., Brentnall, S., Head, J., Berry, B., Jiggins, M. and Hygge, S. (2001a) 'The West London Schools Study: the effects of chronic airport noise exposure on child health'. *Psychological Medicine, 31*, 1385–1396.

Haines, M. M., Stansfeld, S. A., Job, R. F. S., Berglund, B. and Head, J. (2001b) 'Chronic airport noise exposure, stress responses, mental health, and cognitive performance in school children'. *Psychological Medicine, 31*, 265–277.

Hankin, B. L. and Abramson, L. Y. (2001) 'Development of gender differences in depression: an elaborated cognitive vulnerability–transactional stress theory'. *Psychological Bulletin, 127*, 773–796.

Harrington, R., Fudge, H., Rutter, M., Pickles, A. and Hill, J. (1990) Adult outcomes of childhood and adolescent depression. I. Psychiatric status. *Archives of General Psychiatry, 47*, 465–473.

Henderson, S., Byrne, G., Duncan-Jones, P., Scott, R. and Adcock, S. (1980) 'Social relationships, adversity and neurosis: a study of associations in a general population sample'. *British Journal of Psychiatry, 136*, 574–583.

Heshka, S. and Pylypuk, A. (1975) *Human crowding and adrenocortical activity*. Quebec City, Canada: Canadian Psychological Association.

Hiroto, D. and Seligman, M. E. P. (1975) 'Generality of learned helplessness in man'. *Journal of Personality and Social Psychology, 31*, 311–327.

Hoffman, H. (1965) 'Medizinisch-psychologische untersuchungen zum fahrenim verkehrsfluss'. *Zeitschrift für Verkehrssicherhus, 11*, 145–160.

Holahan, C. J. (1978) *Environment and behavior*. New York: Plenum.

Hutt, C. and Vaizey, M. J. (1966) 'Differential effects of group density on social behavior'. *Nature, 209*, 1371–1372.

Ising, H. and Braun, C. (2000) 'Acute and chronic endocrine effects of noise: review of the research conducted at the Institute for Water, Soil, and Air Hygiene'. *Noise and Health*, 7, 7–24.

Ittelson, W. H., Proshansky, H. M. and Rivlin, L. G. (1970) 'The environmental psychology of the psychiatric ward', in Proshansky, H. M., Ittleson, W. H. and Rivlin L. G. (eds), *Environmental psychology*. New York: Holt, Rinehart & Winston.

Job, R. F. S. (1988) 'Community response to noise: a review of factors influencing the relationship between noise exposure and reaction', *Journal of the Acoustical Society of America, 83*, 991–1001.

Kluger, A. N. (1992) 'Commute predictability and strain'. *Journal of Organizational Behavior, 19*, 147–165.

Knipschild, P. (1977) 'Medical effects of aircraft noise: community cardiovascular Survey'. *International Archives of Occupational and Environmental Health, 40*, 185–190.

Kryter, K. D. (1994) *The handbook of hearing and the effects of noise*. New York: Academic Press.

Leonard, B. E. (2001). 'Stress, norepinephrine and depression'. *Journal of Psychiatry and Neuroscience, 26*, s11–s16.

Lepore, S. J. (1992) 'Social conflict, social support, and psychological distress: evidence of cross-domain buffering effects'. *Journal of Personality and Social Psychology, 63*, 857–867.

Lepore, S. J., Evans, G. W. and Palsane, M. N. (1991a) 'Social hassles and psychological health in the context of crowding'. *Journal of Health and Social Behavior, 32*, 357–367.

Lepore, S. J., Evans, G. W. and Schneider, M. (1991b) 'The dynamic role of social support in the link between chronic stress and psychological distress'. *Journal of Personality and Social Psychology, 61*, 899–909.

Lepore, S. J., Evans, G. W. and Schneider, M. (1992) 'Role of control and social support in explaining the stress of hassles and crowding'. *Environment and Behavior, 24*, 795–811.

Lepore, S. J., Silver, R. C., Wortman, C. B. and Wayment, H. A. (1996) 'Social constraints, intrusive thoughts, and depressive symptoms among bereaved mothers'. *Journal of Personality and Social Psychology, 70*, 271–282.

Lercher, P. (2001) 'Contextual and non-contextual perspective in research and management of noise annoyance: an environmental health perspective', in Boone, R. (ed.), *Proceedings of the 2001 Inter-noise Congress*, vol. 4 (pp. 1729–1738). The Hague, The Netherlands: Nederlands Akoestisch Genootschap (NAG).

Lercher, P., Hortnagle, J. and Kofler, W. (1993) 'Work noise annoyance and blood pressure: combined effects with stressful working conditions'. *International Archives of Occupational and Environmental Health, 65*, 23–28.

Lesperance, F., Frasure-Smith, N. and Talajic, M. (1996) 'Major depression before and after myocardial infarction: its nature and consequences'. *Psychosomatic Medicine, 58*, 99–110.

Lewinsohn, P. M., Solomon, A., Seeley, J. R. and Zeiss, A. (2000) 'Clinical implications of "subthreshold" depressive symptoms'. *Journal of Abnormal Psychology, 109*, 345–351.

Liddell, C. and Kruger, P. (1989) 'Activity and social behavior in a crowded South African township nursery: a follow up study on the effects of crowding at home'. *Merrill Palmer Quarterly, 35*, 209–226.

Lundberg, U. (1976) 'Urban crowding: crowdedness and catecholamine secretion'. *Journal of Human Stress*, *2*, 26–34.

Lupien, S. J., De Leon, M., De Santi, S., Convit, A., Tarshish, C. and Nair, N. (1997) 'Longitudinal increases in cortisol during human aging predict hippocampal atrophy and memory deficits'. *Nature Neuroscience*, *1*, 64–73.

Maier, S. F. and Seligman, M. E. P. (1976) 'Learned helplessness theory and evidence'. *Journal of Experimental Psychology*, *105*, 3–46.

Maschke, C., Ising, H. and Arndt, D. (1995) 'Stress reactions caused by night-time exposure to traffic noise'. *Bundesgesundhbl*, *38*, 130–136.

Matheny, A., Wachs, T. D., Ludwig, J. and Phillips, K. (1995) ' "Bringing order out of chaos": psychometric characteristics of the confusion, hubbub, and order scale'. *Journal of Applied Developmental Psychology*, *16*, 429–444.

Maxwell, L. and Evans, G. W. (2000) 'The effects of noise on pre-school children's pre-reading skills'. *Journal of Environmental Psychology*, *20*, 91–97.

McCallum, R., Rusbult, C., Hong, G., Walden, T. and Schopler, J. (1979) 'Effects of resource availability and importance of behavior on the experience of crowding'. *Journal of Personality and Social Psychology*, *37*, 1304–1313.

McCarthy, D. and Saegert, S. (1978) 'Residential density, social overload, and social withdrawal'. *Human Ecology*, *6*, 253–272.

McEwen, B. S. (1998) 'Protective and damaging effects of stress mediators'. *New England Journal of Medicine*, *338*, 171–179.

McEwen, B. S. (2000) 'The neurobiology of stress: from serendipity to clinical relevance'. *Brain Research*, *886*, 172–189.

McEwen, B. S. and Gould, E. (1990) 'Adrenal steroid influences on the survival of hippocampal neurons'. *Biochemical Pharmacology*, *40*, 2392–2402.

Melamed, S., Fried, Y. and Froom, P. (2001) 'The interactive effect of chronic exposure to noise and job complexity on changes in blood pressure and job satisfaction: a longitudinal study of industrial employees'. *Journal of Occupational Health Psychology*, *6*, 182–195.

Melamed, S., Kristal-Boneh, E. and Froom, P. (1999) 'Industrial noise exposure and risk factors for cardiovascular disease': findings from the CORDIS study. *Noise and Health*, *4*, 49–56.

Melamed, S., Froom, P., Kristal-Boneh, E., Gofer, D. and Ribak, J. (1997) 'Industrial noise exposure, noise annoyance, and serum lipid levels in blue collar workers – the CORDIS study'. *Archives of Environmental Health*, *52*, 292–298.

Miller, W. R. (1975) 'Psychological deficits in depression'. *Psychological Bulletin*, *82*, 238–260.

Mitchell, R. E. (1971) 'Some social implications of high density housing'. *American Sociological Review*, *36*, 18–29.

Mitchell, R. E. and Moos, R. H. (1984) 'Deficiencies in social support among depressed patients: antecedents of consequences of stress?' *Journal of Health and Social Behavior*, *25*, 438–452.

Moch-Sibony, A. (1981) 'Study of the effects of noise on the personality and certain intellectual and psychomotor aspects of children: comparison between a sound-proofed and a non-soundproofed school'. *Le Travail Humain*, *44*, 170–178.

Monroe, S. M., Bromet, E. J., Connell, M. M. and Steiner, S. C. (1986) 'Social support, life events, and depressive symptoms: a one-year prospective study'. *Journal of Consulting and Clinical Psychology*, *54*, 424–431.

Munroe, R. L. and Munroe, R. H. (1972) 'Population density and affective relationships in three East African societies'. *The Journal of Social Psychology*, *88*, 15–20.

Neus, H. and Boikat, U. (2000) 'Evaluation of traffic noise-related cardiovascular risk'. *Noise and Health*, 7, 65–78.

Neus, H., Ruddel, H. and Schulte, W. (1983) 'Traffic noise and hypertension: an epidemiological study on the role of subjective reactions'. *International Archives of Occupational and Environmental Health*, *51*, 223–229.

Nicassio, P. M., Wallston, K. A., Callahan, L. F., Herbert, M. and Pincus, T. (1985) 'The measurement of helplessness in rheumatoid arthritis: the development of the Arthritis Helplessness Index'. *Journal of Rheumatology*, *12*, 462–467.

Nivison, M. E. and Endresen, I. M. (1993) 'An analysis of relationships among environmental noise, annoyance and sensitivity to noise, and the consequences for health and sleep'. *Journal of Behavioral Medicine*, *16*, 257–276.

Novaco, R., Kliewer, W. and Broquet, A. (1991) 'Home environmental consequences of commute travel impedence'. *American Journal of Community Psychology*, *19*, 881–909.

Oldham, G. R. and Fried, Y. (1987) 'Employee reactions to workplace characteristics'. *Journal of Applied Psychology*, *72*, 75–80.

Palamarek, D. L. and Rule, B. G. (1979) 'The effects of ambient temperature and insult on the motivation to retaliate or escape'. *Motivation and Emotion*, *3*, 83–92.

Paulus, P. B. (1988) *Prison crowding*. New York: Springer-Verlag.

Peterson, C. and Seligman, M. E. P. (1984) 'Causal explanations as a risk factor for depression: theory and evidence'. *Psychological Review*, *91*, 347–374.

Pine, D. S., Cohen, E., Cohen, P. and Brook, J. (1999) 'Adolescent depressive symptoms as predictors of adult depression: moodiness or mood disorder?' *American Journal of Psychiatry*, *156*, 133–135.

Pitman, R. K. and Orr, S. P. (1990) 'Twenty-four hour urinary cortisol and catecholamine excretion in combat-related posttraumatic stress disorder'. *Biological Psychiatry*, *27*, 245–247.

Ray, D., Wandersman, A., Ellisor, J. and Huntington, D. (1982) 'The effects of high density in a juvenile correctional institution'. *Basic and Applied Social Psychology*, *3*, 95–108.

Regecova, V. and Kellerova, E. (1995) 'Effects of urban noise pollution on blood pressure and heart rate in preschool children'. *Journal of Hypertension*, *13*, 405–412.

Rodin, J. (1976) 'Density, perceived choice, and response to controllable and uncontrollable outcomes'. *Journal of Experimental Social Psychology*, *12*, 564–578.

Rook, K. S. (1984) 'The negative side of social interaction: impact on psychological well-being'. *Journal of Personality and Social Psychology*, *46*, 1097–1108.

Ross, M., Layton, B., Erickson, B. and Schopler, J. (1973) 'Affect, facial regard, and reactions to crowding'. *Journal of Personality and Social Psychology*, *28*, 69–76.

Rotton, J. (1983) 'Affective and cognitive consequences of malodorous pollution'. *Basic Applied Social Psychology*, *4*, 171–191.

Rotton, J. and Frey, J. (1985) 'Air pollution, weather, and violent crimes: concomitant time-series analysis of archival data'. *Journal of Personality and Social Psychology*, *49*, 1207–1220.

Saegert, S. (1982) 'Environment and children's mental health: residential density and low income children', in Baum, A. and Singer J. E. (eds), *Handbook of psychology and health*. Hillsdale, NJ: Lawrence Erlbaum Associates, Inc.

Sauter, S., Hurrell, J. and Cooper, C. (1989) *Job control and worker health*. New York: Wiley.

Schaeffer, M. A., Street, S., Singer, J. E. and Baum, A. (1988a) 'Effects of control on the stress reactions of commuters'. *Journal of Applied Social Psychology*, *18*, 944–957.

Schaeffer, M. A., Baum, A., Paulus, P. B. and Gaes, G. (1988b) 'Architecturally mediated effects of social density in prisons'. *Environment and Behavior, 20*, 3–19.

Schleifer, S. J., Macari-Hinson, M. M., Coyle, D. A., Slater, W. R., Kahn, M., Gorlin, R. and Zucker, H. D. (1989) 'The nature and course of depression following myocardial infarction'. *Archives of Internal Medicine, 149*, 1785–1789.

Schmeck, K. and Poustka, F. (1993) 'Psychiatric and psychophysiological disorders in children living in a military jet fighter training area', in Vallet, M. (ed.), *Proceedings of the Sixth International Congress on Noise as a Public Health Problem*, vol. 2 (pp. 477–480). Arcueil, France: INRETS.

Schulkin, J., McEwen, B. S. and Gold, P. S. (1994) 'Allostasis, amygdala, and anticipatory angst'. *Neuroscience and Behavior Review, 18*, 385–396.

Schuster, T. L., Kessler, R. C. and Aseltine, R. H. (1990) 'Supportive interactions, negative interactions, and depressed mood'. *American Journal of Community Psychology, 18*, 423–438.

Schwartzman, J. B. and Glaus, K. (2000) 'Depression and coronary heart disease in women: implications for clinical practice and research'. *Professional Psychology: Research and Practice, 31*, 48–57.

Seligman, M. E. P. (1975) *Helplessness*. San Francisco: Freeman.

Sherrod, D. R. (1974) 'Crowding, perceived control, and behavioral after-effects'. *Journal of Applied Social Psychology, 4*, 171–186.

Silverstone, P. H. (1987) 'Depression and outcome in acute myocardial infarction'. *British Medical Journal, 294*, 219–220.

Simonson, E., Baker, C., Burns, N., Keiper, C., Schmitt, O. and Stackhouse, S. (1968) 'Cardiovascular stress (electrocardiographic changes) produced by driving an automobile'. *American Heart Journal, 75*, 125–135.

Singer, J. E., Lundberg, U. and Frankenhaeuser, M. (1978) 'Stress on the train: a study of urban commuting', in Baum, A., Singer, J. E. and Valins, S. (eds), *Advances in environmental psychology*. Hillsdale, NJ: Lawrence Erlbaum Associates, Inc.

Stansfeld, S. A. (1992) 'Noise, noise sensitivity, and psychiatric disorder: epidemiological and psychophysiological studies'. *Psychological Medicine Monograph Supplement, 22*, s1–s44.

Stansfeld, S. A., Haines, M. M. and Brown, B. (2000) 'Noise and health in the urban environment'. *Reviews on Environmental Health, 15*, 43–82.

Stansfeld, S. A., Fuhrer, R., Shipley, M. and Marmot, M.G. (1999) 'Work characteristics predict psychiatric disorder: prospective results from the Whitehall II study'. *Occupational and Environmental Medicine, 56*, 302–307.

Stokols, D., Novaco, R., Stokols, J. and Campbell, J. (1978) 'Traffic congestion, Type A behavior, and stress'. *Journal of Applied Psychology, 63*, 467–480.

Sundstrom, E. (1973) 'An experimental study of crowding: effects of room size, intrusion, and goal blocking on nonverbal behavior, self-disclosure, and self-reported stress'. *Journal of Personality and Social Psychology, 32*, 645–654.

Sundstrom, E. (1978) 'Crowding as a sequential process: review of research on the effects of population density on humans', in Epstein, Y. and Baum, A. (eds), *Human response to crowding*. Hillsdale, NJ: Lawrence Erlbaum Associates, Inc.

Talbott, E. O., Gibson, L., Burks, A., Engberg, R. and McHugh, K. (1999) 'Evidence of a dose–response relationship between occupational noise and blood pressure'. *Archives of Environmental Health, 54*, 71–78.

Tarnopolsky, A., Barker, S., Wiggins, R. and Mclean, E. (1978) 'The effect of aircraft noise on the mental health of a community sample: a pilot study'. *Psychological Medicine, 8*, 219–233.

Taylor, S. E., Lichtman, R. R. and Wood, J. V. (1984) 'Attributions, beliefs about control, and adjustment to breast cancer'. *Journal of Personality and Social Psychology, 46*, 489–502.

Taylor, S. E., Helgeson, V. S., Reed, G. M. and Skokan, L. A. (1991) 'Self-generated feelings of control and adjustment to physical illness'. *Journal of Social Issues, 47*, 91–109.

Thompson, S. J. (1993) 'Review: extra-aural health effects of chronic noise exposure in humans', in Ising, H. and. Kruppa, B. (eds), *Larm und krankheit*. New York: Springer-Verlag.

Topf, M. and Dillon, E. (1988) 'Noise-induced stress as a predictor of burnout in critical care nurses'. *Heart and Lung, 17*, 567–573.

Tucker, J. and Friedman, S. (1972) 'Population density and group size'. *American Journal of Sociology, 77*, 742–749.

Uchino, B. N. (2004) *Social support and physical health: Understanding the health consequences of our relationships*. New Haven, CT: Yale University Press.

Van Kamp, I. (1990) *Coping with noise and its health consequences*. PhD dissertation, University of Groningen, The Netherlands.

Vera, M. N., Vila, J. and Godoy, J. (1992) 'Physiological and subjective effects of traffic noise: the role of negative self-statements'. *International Journal of Psychophysiology, 12*, 267–279.

Wachs, T. D. (1987) 'Specificity of environmental action as manifest in environmental correlates of infant's mastery motivation'. *Developmental Psychology, 23*, 782–790.

Wachs, T. D. (1988) 'Relevance of physical environment influences for toddler temperament'. *Infant Behavior and Development, 11*, 431–445.

Wachs, T. D. (1989) 'The nature of the physical microenvironment: an expanded classification system'. *Merrill Palmer Quarterly, 35*, 399–419.

Wachs, T. D. (2000) *Necessary but not sufficient: The respective roles of single and multiple influence on individual development*. Washington, DC: American Psychological Association.

Wachs, T. D. and Camli, O. (1991) 'Do ecological or individual characteristics mediate the influence of the physical environment on maternal behavior?'. *Journal of Environmental Psychology, 11*, 249–264.

Weissman, M. M., Wolk, S., Wickramaratne, P., Goldstein, R. B., Adams, P., Greenwald, S., Ryan, N. D., Dahl, R. E. and Steinberg, D. (1999) Children with prepubertal-onset major depressive disorder and anxiety grown up. *Archives of General Psychiatry, 56*, 794–801.

Weisz, J. R. (1990) 'Development of control-related beliefs, goals, and styles in childhood and adolescence: a clinical perspective', in Rodin, J., Schooler, C. and Schaie, K. W. (eds), *Self-directedness: Cause and effects throughout the life course*. Hillsdale, NJ: Lawrence Erlbaum Associates, Inc.

Weisz, J. R., Weiss, B., Wasserman, A. A. and Rintoul, B. (1987) 'Control-related beliefs and depression among clinic-referred children and adolescents'. *Journal of Abnormal Psychology, 96*, 58–63.

Welch, B. L. (1979) *Extra-auditory health effects of industrial noise: Survey of foreign literature*, Wright Patterson Air Force Base, DH: Aerospace Medical Research Laboratory, AHRL-TR-79–41.

Wener, R. E. and Keys, C. (1988) 'The effects of changes in jail population densities on crowding, sick call, and spatial behavior'. *Journal of Applied Social Psychology, 18*, 852–866.

Wener, R. E., Evans, G. W., Phillips, D. and Nadler, N. (2003) 'Running for the 7:45: the effects of public transit improvements on commuter stress'. *Transportation, 30*, 203–220.

Wethington, E. and Kessler, R. C. (1986) 'Perceived support, received support, and adjustment to stressful life events'. *Journal of Health and Social Behavior, 27*, 78–89.

White, S. and Rotton, J. (1998) 'Type of commute, behavioral after effects, and cardiovascular activity'. *Environment and Behavior, 30*, 763–780.

Wilcox, B. and Holahan, C. J. (1976) 'Social ecology of the megadorm in university student housing'. *Journal of Educational Psychology, 68*, 453–458.

Wolkowitz, O. M. (1994) 'Prospective controlled studies of the behavioural and biological effects of exogenous corticosteroids'. *Psychoneuroendocrinology, 19*, 233–255.

Wortman, C. B. and Brehm, J. W. (1975) 'Responses to uncontrollable outcomes: an integration of reactance theory and the learned helplessness model', in Berkowitz, L. (ed.), *Advances in experimental social psychology*. New York: Academic Press.

6 Social support, environment and psychiatric disorder

Traolach Brugha, Stephen Stansfeld and Hugh Freeman

Psychiatrists have always been concerned with the psychosocial effects of their interventions, in addition to the effect of these interventions on symptoms. They have also been increasingly aware that the kind of relationships that an individual experiences is an important factor in mental health. Social support and social networks are concepts that attempt to describe and study such relationships in a scientific way. They need to be considered in an environmental context, among others.

The concept of social support, which implies a positive quality, has had various definitions, one of the broadest being 'resources provided by other persons' (Cohen & Syme, 1985). Cobb (1976), on the other hand, saw it as 'information leading the subject to believe that he is cared for and loved, is esteemed and valued, and belongs to a social network of communication and mutual obligation'. It has also been seen as the interactive process in which emotional or material aid is obtained from one's social network – which may or may not be regarded as adequate. In practice, identifiable social support may reflect the capacity of the individual to develop social networks and to form and maintain intimate relationships. The relevant social factors that have been found to have an association with psychiatric morbidity have several aspects in common: inadequate social contacts of the individual, lack of social support, and disruption of the social network. Social support is a multidimensional rather than a unitary concept, and this makes its scientific study more difficult.

Interest in this subject has grown since the seminal papers of Cassel (1976) and Cobb (1976); it has been studied from two main perspectives: types of support and in relation to social networks. Caplan (1976) proposed that social support, which is derived from social networks, buffers the negative effects of stress. Where a stressful life event has an adverse impact on an individual's mental health, this is often mainly through the disturbance that the event causes to that person's social network.

Though access to at least one intimate, confiding relationship is claimed to be vital to the protection of health (Brown & Harris, 1978; Leaf *et al.*, 1984), these findings have not been consistent, which may be for several reasons. First, there is a great variety of measures of social support, which are based on many different conceptual models. Second, many different population samples have been studied, and these are often not representative of the community in general. Third, the outcomes measured in different studies, ranging from mild distress to severe psychiatric illness, have not been consistent; yet this should not have been surprising, since there is no reason to believe that social support has a similar effect in all types of psychiatric disorder. The origins of social support have been little studied (Champion, 1995; Gilbert, 1995) and little attempt has been made to demonstrate its 'independence' from measures of personality (Brewin, 1995) or mood, in the way that this has been done for life events (Paykel, 1994). Though most studies have been retrospective, it would be methodologically better to assess current social support, and then follow-up the cases prospectively.

Jenkins (1994) states that there are three broad mechanisms by which social support may affect mental health: 'by a direct effect on well-being regardless of whether the individual is under stress; indirectly by reducing exposure to social adversity (for example, individuals with deficient social networks may be more likely to experience stressful events and to use less effective coping strategies) and interactively by buffering the individual from the maladaptive effects of stress'.

Types of support

Types of social support have been categorized in various ways – from 'affirmation, affect and aid' (Kahn & Antonucci, 1980) to 'tangible, appraisal, self-esteem, and belonging' (Cohen & Hoberman, 1983), and 'emotional, instrumental, informational, and appraisal' (House, 1981). The different types of support include social companionship, emotional support, cognitive guidance, and material aid and services. The fluidity of these categories suggests that it is not easy to capture the complexities of such human relationships when using relatively crude research measures. Nevertheless, most studies agree that support can be divided broadly into two types – emotional or practical/instrumental. There are also three principal methods of assessing it (Henderson *et al.*, 1981). First, *availability* – whether the person considers that help could be called on from supportive others, should the need arise. Second, *perceived support* – whether they subjectively feel supported by others. Third, *received support* – whether they can report instances of support from others having actually occurred. Different types of support, e.g. emotional or financial, may come from different sources.

Social networks

Probably the greatest unresolved problem in studies of psychosocial effects of the environment is to fill in those considerable areas of *terra incognita* that represent the processes of interaction between individual personality or behaviour on one hand and the social structure of a community on the other. Concern about the 'ecological fallacy' leads to the assumption that community characteristics do not usually explain much of the variation in behaviour between individuals, and it is then easy to conclude that communities are not significant forces on individuals (Fischer, 1975). However, more detailed analysis may reveal complex and even contradictory effects that are operating on different sub-populations, e.g the young or the elderly. In Fischer's view, 'What is missing in the study of intra-community variation are compelling theories which connect settlement patterns, in terms of ecological variables, to community and personality'. He suggests that the most promising conceptual tool for this purpose is analysis of social networks.

A social network has been defined as a set of identified social relationships that surround a person (including the individual's perception of them) and have a lasting effect on his/her life, or as a set of persons, connected by relations between them. Other alternative definitions are a specific set of linkages among a defined set of persons, or an established system of transactions between a group of individuals. Networks are the people with whom an individual associates regularly, and who are significant to him or her in terms of such qualities as support and influence; within the internal fabric of a community, networks are linked but generally do not merge completely. The number of channels of communication and size of coping resources that can be mobilized by an individual in a coping process will depend on the structure of his/her network, though individuals vary greatly in the way they use whatever is supplied by their own network.

The most common, and still the most important, social networks are based in family and kinships, which in certain situations, for example, with members of minority groups, may also be ethnically based. Bott (1957) showed that when going about their daily lives, people do so in relation to an immediate social environment that contains a fairly small number of individuals. This is described as the 'primary network' – of people with whom an individual has a direct and regular personal relationship. Normative data are still relatively few, but those available suggest that generally, women's networks contain more kin than men's and that they tend to be responsible for 'kin-keeping', i.e. the maintenance of family ties. However, until such data for industrialized countries are well established, it may be premature to draw detailed conclusions about deviations from them. Networks have two principal roles: first, an instrumental one, of providing support and material help, and second, as reference groups for ideas and behaviour, playing an important part in the transmission of social norms within any society. This latter function is particularly relevant, for instance, to the views of any social group about the use of alcohol or other drugs.

It is generally believed by social biologists and anthropologists that humans have an innate propensity to form close social groups, regardless of their cultural milieu. Thus, the size and durability of networks are probably derived as much from internal biological factors as from external social influences. This implies a genetic transmission of social behaviour, needed for survival of the species, in which case the fundamental properties of social networks would not be culturally limited – 'The range of network sizes is surprisingly restricted' (Hammer,

1983). The biologist Michael Chance (1988) has proposed that, like other primates, man shows two complementary but antithetical types of social behaviour. The first, described as 'hedonic', is characterized by affiliative behaviour in groups, in which members offer mutual support, while the second ('agonic') typically occurs in hierarchically organized groups, whose members are concerned with their status and with warding off threats to it. Man appears to be both affiliative and hostile, wanting both attachment and status (Gilbert, 1995). The importance of attachment to mental health has been particularly emphasized by Bowlby (1980). However, a network is not simply a form of social integration, since it may well include transactions that involve conflict and strain, as well as support.

Little is known as to how social factors interrelate with biological ones in this respect, but susceptibility to disease may be affected indirectly, through the effect of the social environment on immune and neuroendocrine functions. As mentioned above, buffering theory proposes that strongly supporting social networks mitigate the adverse physical and emotional consequences of stress, life events, and social circumstances. Positive associations between social support and health may partly reflect the influence of other variables known to be associated with morbidity – personality, socio-economic position (SEP), and education. Also, people with psychiatric morbidity, particularly schizophrenia, may perceive their networks to be less supportive than they objectively are, though the effects of the illness may themselves reduce social support.

Network size depends on socio-demographic as well as cultural and personality factors. It includes nuclear family, kin, neighbours, friends, colleagues, etc. Larger size of network is linked to greater support and reduced mortality risk, but also to a greater likelihood of conflict, due to the number of relationships. After some maximal size, further increase may not bring any identifiable advantages, but this precise size is unknown and must vary according to both personal and social circumstances.

A number of different aspects of social networks may be measured: (i) *density* – how many individuals know each other, apart from knowing the respondent, i.e. the degree of interconnectedness; (ii) *durability* – how long they have known each other; (iii) *frequency* – how often they see or contact each other; (iv) *reciprocity* – how much they do for each other; (v) *homogeneity* – the extent to which network members are similar; and (vi) *features of the transactions* – uniform or multiplex. The advantages of such measures of social networks – compared with quality of social support – are their relative reliability (Stansfeld & Marmot, 1992) and the objectivity of the information obtained, in terms of numbers and frequency of contacts. The disadvantage is the sparseness of the information regarding the content of the contacts – whether they were mainly positive or negative and what was transacted. From the mental health point of view, such information needs to be provided, for instance, in terms of the quality and types of the support received, which usually comes from a few close persons.

Both from the scientific and clinical points of view, it is not enough to look at external social behaviour, without enquiring how the individuals perceive this

(Hinde, 1974), since some social contacts may be viewed negatively as being intrusive. Thus, simple measures of numbers and frequency of contact may yield no useful information about support systems. In terms of a possible correlation between a poor social network and mental health, the perceived adequacy of relationships to the individual seems to be more important than their availability. A depressed patient might see his network in negative terms, but unless pre-illness data for it existed, it would not be certain whether or not there had been a change.

Network analysis, which orders the data but does not explain them, can nevertheless provide valuable information. *Quantitative aspects* include size, frequency of contacts, strength of ties, homogeneity of individuals, geographical distance, and symmetry of relationships (active versus passive, etc). Killilea (1982) suggests that whereas in times of personal crisis a small, dense network with strong ties may be most valuable, at times of psychosocial transition (and perhaps of psychiatric disorder), a low-density network with relatively weak ties is possibly more helpful. This is because high-density networks may put more normative pressure on their members to maintain existing roles, and so provide less support for those who are interested in effecting major role changes (Mitchell & Trickett, 1980). There is evidence (Horwitz, 1978) that when a person suffers from a psychiatric disorder, a fairly dispersed social network is generally more helpful than a closely knit, homogeneous one in providing a greater range of information and practical advice. However, prospectively assessed recovery from depression has been reported to be greater in those with more interconnected primary social networks (Brugha *et al.*, 1997).

On the whole, those with severe mental illness tend to have restricted, impoverished networks; one reason is that members are lost as a result of repeated hospital admissions, particularly if associated with prolonged in-patient stay. Mueller (1980) concluded that whereas the network of the average person consisted of 25–40 people, of whom 6–10 were known particularly well, and was of moderate density, persons suffering from neurosis had networks of about 10–15, which were of much lower density. Those suffering from psychosis had very small and dense networks – about 4–5 people, most of whom were kin.

In a *multiplex* relationship, a member serves more than one role or provides more than one type of exchange; this can be beneficial in terms of support and satisfaction within the network. A *cluster* is a group within the network who are strongly connected with each other; thus an ideal network would consist of several clusters, with multiple relationships, and be both flexible and stable.

Relationship with psychiatric disorder

From the psychiatric point of view, these concepts may provide a framework for bringing together a number of different findings about the relationship of social factors to mental disorders. Deficiencies of social bonds are considered a regular consequence of psychiatric disorder, and although definitions of 'network' and 'support' have not been operationalized consistently, both schizophrenia and major depressive disorder have been reported to produce a significant decline in network size (Leaf *et al.*, 1984). What has often been described as 'environmental manipulation' in treating psychiatric disorder is, in fact, largely the attempt to manipulate social networks (Greenblatt *et al.*, 1982). Many patients with severe symptoms may not be capable of initiating instrumental relationships, but can maintain reciprocal interaction once there is a structural context for it, such as a strongly integrated network. From the developmental point of view, a handicapping disorder such as schizophrenia, beginning in a person's formative years, is very likely to restrict the normal social learning of interpersonal behaviour. This is because the cultural meaning of social cues is acquired from age-peers, as well as from interactions and training within the family. If social skills are not established then, in the usual informal way, they will have to be taught specifically at some later stage.

The London TAPS (Team for Assessment of Psychiatric Services) study includes a five-year follow-up of 115 long-term patients from Friern and Claybury Hospitals who went out to community placements; assessments were by the Social Network Schedule (Brugha *et al.*, 1987). After the first 12 months, the proportion of patients having contacts with people providing services in the community (e.g. shopkeepers, milkmen) increased from 14% to 30%. However, for the whole group, the total network size did not change significantly, nor the number of confidants, which is the most meaningful type of social relationship (Leff *et al.*, 1994). Hammer (1983) showed that schizophrenics have many non-reciprocal relationships, i.e. taking rather than giving, but relationships of this kind, which are mainly dependent, tend to lower self-esteem.

In the very different setting of pre-communist Laos, Westermeyer (1980) found that the chronic mentally ill had social networks that were reduced in size, in spite of the fact that they had generally lived in the same village all their lives. Without the ability to exchange goods or labour, they mostly became dependent on a few family members or altruistic others to care for them. Although schizophrenia is usually considered to run a generally benign course in non-industrialized societies, these important findings show that the more severe forms can be as disabling in developing counties as in the 'developed' world.

Depression and anxiety

Henderson *et al.* (1978) observed deficiencies in social networks in non-psychotic out-patients, though a replication in Dublin, found a deficiency only in cases of neurotic depression, not retarded depressive disorder (Brugha *et al.*, 1982). The direction of causality here is uncertain, though, since both psychiatric disorder and abnormal networks might be a consequence of a higher order factor, such as personality (Brewin, 1995). It is possible that a trait characteristic both affects social support and makes a subject more vulnerable to adverse life events. While deficiencies of social bonds are considered a regular consequence of psychiatric illness, it is also appears that some of the increased prevalence of neurotic morbidity observed in the lowest socio-economic class can be partly explained by failures of networks (Henderson, 1980). Both depression and anxiety may cause the negative distortion of social cues, so that positive stimuli are ignored.

Social support may intervene to ameliorate distress, and prevent the development of frank disorder; cross-sectional studies show a clear negative association between levels of social support and psychiatric disorder, although it is not clear that this is necessarily aetiological. Reviews of the effects of social support have tended to examine the direct effects separately from buffering effects. There is a moderate consensus that emotional support buffers the effects of life events on minor psychiatric disorder (Kessler & McLeod, 1985), and Cohen and Wills (1985) extend this to include specific support functions. Kessler and McLeod cite three cross-sectional studies (Brown & Harris, 1978; Husaini *et al.*, 1982; Kessler & Essex, 1982) and two panel studies (Henderson, 1981; Pearlin *et al.*, 1981) as supporting a pervasive buffering effect on mental health across all types of event.

A similar effect was also found in studies examining chronic stressors, as opposed to acute events (Brown & Harris, 1978; Henderson, 1981; Pearlin *et al.*, 1981). Alloway and Bebbington (1987), in a cautious review of buffering studies in minor affective disturbances, suggest that there is little evidence from cross-sectional studies of significant effects of social support in the buffering process (Cohen & Hoberman, 1983; LaRocco *et al.*, 1980). Stepping back from this very rigorous conclusion, though, they do concede that additive effects remain possible and that overall, Brown's vulnerability model 'does receive appreciable support'. None of 11 longitudinal studies demonstrated unequivocally positive results, and in highlighting many methodological difficulties, the need for better research is emphasized. It was also pointed out that the Islington study (Brown *et al.*, 1986) did not confirm Brown's original findings in this respect, though the probable complexity of buffering effects was downplayed, as well as the possibility that there are cohort effects in the manifestation and effectiveness of social support according to other socio-cultural features of the environment.

Henderson (1974) stated that lack of social relationships is an atypical state for man, and that these are not just important in the context of coping with life events; the non-availability of social ties was said to be psychologically distressing in itself. In his community study in Canberra (1981), a modest negative association was found between the availability of attachment and social integration on one hand and neurotic symptoms on the other. However, measures of perceived adequacy of support showed a much stronger negative relationship with neurotic symptoms: perceived adequacy of close relationships was important for women, while that of more diffuse relationships was important for men. This was interpreted as indicating that those who view their social relationships as inadequate were substantially more at risk of developing neurotic symptoms. The 'inadequacy' was said to result from the intra-psychic needs of respondents, in terms of dependency and anxious attachment, both of which predict perceived inadequacy of social support and (independently) neurotic symptoms.

On the other hand, objective lack of social support was not thought to be related to neurotic symptoms. This view has implications for prevention, in that increasing the availability of social support might not necessarily reduce the occurrence of neurotic symptoms. However, O'Connor and Brown (1984) disputed this model, on the grounds that there had been no differentiation between the actual support provided, in terms of confiding and frequency of contact, and attachment, since reported attachment to someone does not necessarily imply that this person is actually giving support.

In a large panel study of adult female twins, Kessler *et al.* (1994) found a buffering effect for perceived support on major depression. They found no evidence to support an underlying genetic factor influencing perception of support and accommodation to stress, nor that buffering was attributable to any improvement in coping promoted by social support. They also rejected the possibility that stress-moderating effects of perceived support are mediated by received support. They suggested the possibility that perceived availability of support may lead to cognitive appraisals that are less threatening to mental health.

There have been fewer longitudinal studies of social support where questions of causation can be better addressed. Several community studies have been completely prospective, identifying deficiencies in social support prior to the onset of depression and relating this to the onset of depression. Two studies found a buffering or interactive effect (Bolton & Oatley, 1987; Brown *et al.*, 1986). The study by Brown *et al.* (1986) found little predictive effect on mental health of 17 measures of emotional support measured at baseline in an inner-city sample of married mothers. However, they did find a greater risk of depression in women who received little crisis support, i.e. when it was needed to cope with a life event. A negative response from a partner in a crisis was also associated with a subsequent risk of depression. On the other hand, among single mothers, report of a close relationship at baseline was protective against the development of depression following a subsequent life event. The onset of postnatal depression in 507 women was predicted by lack of social support from the primary group, and lack of support in relation to becoming pregnant, adjusting for antenatal depression, neuroticism, family and personal psychiatric history, and adversity (Brugha *et al.*, 1998).

There have also been several prospective studies of social support and depression in the elderly (Henderson *et al.*, 1997; Oxman *et al.*, 1992; Prince *et al.*, 1998; Schoevers *et al.*, 2000). Lack of a relative or friend to confide in predicted late-life suicide in a North American community survey (Turvey *et al.*, 2002). Lack of contact with friends predicted depression and modified the association between depression and disability. Disability itself is also a powerful predictor of depression (Prince *et al.*, 1998). In a similar way, having a marital partner, or if unmarried having social support, significantly reduced the impact of functional disabilities on depression (Schoevers *et al.*, 2000). Hence, in a situation where provision of practical and emotional support may have a profound effect on an elderly person's quality of life and functioning, a clear protective effect of social support was found.

A further longitudinal study of British middle-aged civil servants (Whitehall II study) showed, in relation to psychological distress, a protective effect on mental health of emotional support from the closest person in men (Stansfeld *et al.*, 1998) and from the primary group in women (Fuhrer *et al.*, 1999). This was not abolished by adjusting for either hostility as a measure of personality or psychiatric disorder at baseline. This is relevant because measures of personality often confound associations between social support and mental illness. Moreover, this study showed prospectively that negative aspects of close relationships were associated with greater risk of future psychiatric disorder up to five years later. Negative aspects of close relationships were consistently associated with worse mental health in both men and women. Negative aspects of close relationships have a negative effect on mental health both directly (Burg & Seeman, 1994; Lakey *et al.*, 1994; Rook, 1984; Schuster *et al.*, 1990) and in the presence of life events.

Emotional support is what the respondent receives from the person who is close and this is associated with better mental health (Brown *et al.*, 1986). Perceived emotional support has a larger effect than tangible or practical aspects of support, as has also been found in the elderly (Oxman *et al.*, 1992). Emotional support is distinct from confiding, which requires the respondent actively to disclose information to the close person, although, of course in adaptive relationships they occur reciprocally. Some studies suggest that ill-advised confiding, asking for support from sources unable to provide it, or confiding without active emotional support may be a risk factor for depression. This may explain why confiding/emotional support from a spouse does not show a direct effect in women (Andrews & Brown, 1998).

A study of women who had been in care in childhood (Quinton *et al.*, 1984) showed how social support in adulthood may exert a positive effect on parenting problems, marital difficulties, and psychiatric disorder. Many of these women returned from care to a discordant home environment, from which they then tried to escape by early marriage, but these relationships also often turned out badly and resulted in these women becoming more vulnerable to further difficulties. However, 31% of those studied prospectively showed good parenting ability. This seemed to relate to both positive school experiences, including examination success, and good relationships with peers, but also the later presence of a supportive marital relationship, which prevented parenting difficulties and depression from occurring.

The social environment

Social support includes many of the aspects of the social environment that might relate to good mental health. Although there has been much painstaking work defining patterns of interaction within social networks in different communities, relatively little of it has attempted to relate macro-social variables (e.g. social class) to social support. It seems very likely that the social environment may either set limits to social support, provide the conditions that could facilitate its development, or define the patterns of expression of the support. It is, in fact, only by examining the relationship with social structure that the impact of social policy on the distribution and availability of this support can be predicted. Any social environment can either facilitate or inhibit social interaction, while individuals differ greatly in the way they use the same social support. It seems unlikely that any social grouping could be totally comprehensive and positive in meeting the needs of all its members.

Relationships between macro-social variables (for example, level of social integration in the local community) and mental health were claimed by the Stirling County Study (e.g. Leighton, 1959), though a deficient social network was only one of several possible indicators of poor social integration. In that population of maritime Canada, factors such as heavy outward migration, cultural confusion, secularization, and poverty were said to have led to reduced social interaction and to disintegration of the communities, subsequently increasing the risk of neurotic symptoms – mainly anxiety and depression. Because the rate of social change was believed to have exceeded the rate of adaptation to it, 'other people then appear unpredictable, and the institutions of society are no longer dependable in a society where nearly all values are in flux' (Leighton, 1981). Leighton regarded this process as occurring between the sub-systems of society, so that the larger organization then became vulnerable to cultural crises, such as those of the late 1960s in many Western countries. The coping guidelines of culture that have been passed down from previous generations then cease to work effectively, and people try many new kinds of behaviour, but these often random reactions tend to conflict with each other, and may make things generally worse. In this way the meaning, stability, coherence, and capacity to function as a whole of cultures is undermined, so that for many people, it is change itself that becomes most important in determining their behaviour. The prevailing uncertainty may even extend to the definition of mental illness (Leighton, 1981), which is one factor making it difficult to decide what constitutes allowable behaviour. Socio-cultural disintegration is said to be associated with demoralization (distress associated with subjective incompetence), but this would be less likely to occur in the presence of adequate social bonds, linking an individual to others by positive affect (de Figueiredo, 1983).

In Leighton's view, social disintegration is causally related to psychopathology through a number of factors: (a) increase in the frequency of organic disease, some of which is associated with brain damage; (b) inadequacy of child-nurturing and child-rearing patterns; (c) lack of shared values, standards, and codes of behaviour; and (d) lack of opportunity for the satisfaction of basic needs, including the sense of belonging to a worthwhile group. At the same time, the malfunctioning of their organizations decreases these societies' ability and resources to meet the needs of the population for medical and social care. Leighton linked the psychological states generated by sociocultural disintegration with psychiatric disorder through the concept of stress, but it was accepted that people may have a neurotic predisposition as a result of experiences of early life, and would then manifest disorder when exposed to a lower level of stress than others. The stressor and the individual's reaction to it – in terms of internalized standards – together form a 'stressful situation', which the person has to resolve within herself/himself (de Figueiredo, 1983). However, Cassel (1974) suggested that the main underlying mechanism may be people's lack of feedback that their actions are leading to desirable and/or anticipated consequences, particularly when these actions are designed to modify their relationships to important social groups. In addition to excess psychiatric disorder, 'social disintegration' has been related to increased rates of tuberculosis, hypertension, and death from stroke.

The social indices used by Leighton *et al.* (1963) to measure this phenomenon included poverty, cultural confusion, poor leadership, high crime rates, and fragmented communication networks. While it was thought that the higher prevalence rates of psychiatric morbidity (particularly affective and personality disorders) were related to evidence of social disintegration, the severe process was confined to a few small clusters of population in the area studied. In disintegrated districts, the probability of being a psychiatric case was lower for females, whereas the reverse was true in the county as a whole.

However, all these social phenomena lack concreteness of definition, and the causal nature of any relationship between them and psychiatric disorder is unproved. The absence of a feeling of affiliation with society is equivalent to the concept of anomie, originally proposed by Durkheim, which refers to failure of social integration in the collective rather than the personal sense, with values and norms being weak or absent; in fact, 'anomie' and 'social disintegration' are sometimes used synonymously. The concept of 'alienation' also has similar aspects. If anomie could be a factor leading to suicide (as Durkheim believed), then presumably it might also lead to psychiatric disorder in general. From their studies in northern Spain, Vazquez-Barquero *et al.* (1982) suggest that the tendency of more advanced societies to organize themselves into urban communities involves a series of sociological changes that are capable of transforming the interactions of individuals not only in their work and external environment, but also through their internal family dynamics. The negative aspects of these changes involve factors such as isolation, dehumanization, loss of pride in work, and breaking up of family ties, which 'are at the roots of social disorganisation and contain as a consequence the origins of mental illness'. This view is undoubtedly overstated, though the social processes described are very likely to have some relationship with psychiatric disorder.

Social network structure

Meltzer and colleagues (1995a) employed exactly the same set of questions about the size of social network primary groups as were used in earlier studies, referred to above, by Henderson *et al.* (1978) and Brugha *et al.* (1987). This was in a national survey throughout Great Britain of over 9,000 adults living in private households. For both men and women, the prevalence of neurotic

Traditional Jubilee street party, London, 1977 (used with permission of Albert Boulton/ Rex Features).

disorders among those with a primary support group size of nine or more was less than half that among those with one of three or fewer (Meltzer *et al.*, 1995b). A primary group size of three or fewer was also shown to be associated specifically with depressive symptoms and ideas and with panic symptoms, even when controlling for a range of socio-demographic variables including marital status, household structure, and unemployment (Brugha *et al.*, 2003) in the same household survey.

Gender may need to be taken into consideration in studying these associations with social network structure. A small primary group size assessed at presentation to a hospital service by Brugha and colleagues predicted a worse clinical outcome of depression approximately four months later in women but not in men (Brugha *et al.*, 1990). But primary group size assessed antenatally clearly showed no relation to the development of common mental disorders or depression when assessed in women in the community three months after childbirth (Brugha *et al.*, 1998), although, as mentioned above, dissatisfaction with support from others did predict postnatal disorder. In a cross-sectional community study of risks for mental distress, based on the 12-item General Household Questionnaire (GHQ), in Finland (Hintikka *et al.*, 2000), marked differences in the effects of numbers of friends were found when analyses were performed by gender. Those men who had none, one, or only some friends, had a higher risk of mental distress than men who had more friends. By contrast, the number of close friends was associated only slightly with the risk of mental distress in women. A recent prospective study in a community sample of 32 women with major depression (Wildes *et al.*, 2002) found that the total number of close confiding relationships was a significantly stronger predictor of naturalistic depression occurring approximately one year later than were life events. Both theoretical and empirical studies of loneliness also suggest that the size of the social network group in community populations is more important for men than for women (Stokes & Levin, 1986). These studies seem to show that network size may have a greater bearing on the risk of developing mental ill-health in men than in women, but that this gender effect may be reversed when we look at the future outcome of those who have become cases. Thus, the initial mental health status (or course of disorder) may need to be taken into account in studying the influence of network structure. The failure of some researchers to note gender differences in the effects of social support could also be explained if the effect of perception of social support is much the same in both sexes, as earlier epidemiological work (Meltzer *et al.*, 1995a) and work on the outcome of depression suggests (Brugha *et al.*, 1990). In line with the findings summarized here, recent data in a follow-up of 2,400 adults in the community throughout Great Britain now replicate the strong effects of primary group size on future mental health that emerge when men and women are studied separately and when subjects are categorized according to baseline mental health status (Brugha *et al.*, 2005).

Social processes

It will be evident from the earlier discussion that mental health is related not so much to the environment in its physical, structural sense as to the social processes connected to that setting. In their turn, these processes are determined not only by the structure of any environment, but also by the culture, economy, and political ideology that govern it. The relationships of all these forces are enormously complicated, therefore, and are constantly changing over time, so that scientific study of them needs to be approached with great caution. It is possible to find common factors in the absence of social support or disruption or individuals' social networks, but such situations may be specific to particular socio-demographic groups or psychiatric conditions (Mueller, 1980). Nevertheless, social network factors might be the underlying mechanism of these statistical relationships, and so provide the basis for an integrating framework in which to assess the contribution of the social environment to psychiatric disorder.

The physical environment

Features of the physical environment influence social support; housing design, for instance, may either encourage or discourage interaction between inhabitants and their neighbours. It is also to be expected that socio-environmental factors will influence the effects of the physical environment. For instance, certain design features of blocks of flats, such as outside walkways, may have a more negative effect in poverty-stricken public housing estates, with high risk of personal danger from attack or mugging, than the same features in private flats with security staff (Coleman, 1985).

Yancey (1971) reported that the architectural design of the notorious Pruit-Igoe public housing development in St Louis had an atomizing effect on the informal social networks often found in working-class neighbourhoods. Without the provision of semi-public space, around which informal networks might develop, families retreated into the internal structure of their apartments and did not have the social support, protection, and informal social control found in more traditional neighbourhoods. However, Gans (1962) pointed out that a particular architectural design will not necessarily have the same effect on all social groups; for one thing, this will depend on the importance attached to informal neighbouring relationships in any specific cultural group. In more traditional environments, such informal networks among neighbours were an important means by which the urban working class coped with poverty and deprivation. Neighbourhood networks based on physical proximity, age, sex, and ethnicity provide social norms, as well as a means of integration into larger groups; the less personal integration there is into networks of this kind, the greater the perception of human dangers in the environment is likely to be. However, geographically based networks usually require long-standing relationships, with many casual contacts in public spaces, which will eventually form a trusting community. A well-known description of these in the East End of London was given by Young and Willmott (1957).

A similar view was that of Jane Jacobs in her now classic book, *The Death and Life of Great American Cities* (1961), which argued that what is 'good' should not merely be equated with aesthetic appearance, but should focus upon what actually works to promote a stable social structure. In Jacobs' view, successful city neighbourhoods are likely to be close-textured and to be high-density areas of mixed land uses, where people live within walking distance of many destinations and there is constant movement on foot, along a network of streets. People who are passed on the pavement come to be known by sight, and this leads to public acquaintanceship, in which people's roles are known and contact can be made with them without invading their private lives. Friendships of various degrees can then mature naturally, resulting in interconnecting levels of acquaintanceship. In this way, the community accumulates informal guidelines for behaviour, which provide a framework for its social stability. This pattern, however, generally evolved in areas that were socially and culturally homogeneous to a large extent, and where the demoralization now caused by extensive drug-trafficking, for instance, was unknown.

Coleman (1985) points out that the segregation of land uses into large units such as 'business parks', shopping precincts, industrialized estates, and 'cultural complexes' means that few destinations are within walking distance. People passing each other at high speed in vehicles, on their way to and from these various destinations, have no informal opportunities to build up acquaintanceship in public. Housewives, in particular, may become very lonely, but if they are to develop any friendships, they have to invite strangers into their homes, which involves risks. 'In these circumstances, the circle of contacts tends to remain small and the prevailing atmosphere is one of anonymity. There is no accepted set of social mores, which means that some people agonise over what is acceptable behaviour.'

These environmental factors may have an important effect on the bringing-up of children. If streets contain friends and neighbours, they can keep a responsible eye on children who are playing outside, as can those people, described by Jacobs as the 'eyes on the street', who like to watch a busy scene from their windows. Such a neighbourhood was self-policing to a large extent, and children could be allowed out into it when they had got beyond infancy. This helped them to become integrated into the adult community, but entering an anonymous world of strangers is much more hazardous, and much of children's time is now spent with a very low ratio of adults to children. As Coleman (1984) suggests, children pick up most of their behaviour patterns from their peers, and will often be frustrated by constraints intended for their safety, for example through separation from traffic. In many public housing developments, children live in an environment where the distinction between public and private is blurred by shared grounds that extend right up to families' windows, and by internal common areas that extend up to their front doors. This is particularly the case with high-rise blocks of flats (see Chapter 8).

The incessant growth of motor traffic, making it dangerous for young children – particularly those living in towns and cities – to be in any streets or make any journeys without supervision, has been one of the main features producing this situation; they are now virtually confined to the home, to private gardens (where these exist), or to segregated 'play' areas, which are protected from traffic. The price of this protection is a serious limitation of the social experience that should be an essential part of maturation. For adults, the increasing unemployment and under-employment of older industrial societies, as well as the growing tendency to work at home, using electronic communication, must greatly reduce the social interaction that previously occurred in places of work. This is not a wholly negative process – the avoidance of stressful commuting may be a great relief to many people and family life may be improved, though reducing varied life experience to local shopping and watching television could make it worse again.

Another aspect of the physical environment is that of life in institutions, where social role behaviour tends to atrophy for people who remain in them over very long periods. The work of Wing and Brown (1970) showed that the negative symptoms of schizophrenia may be worsened by lack of social stimulation in traditional mental hospitals. In these settings, chronic patients tend to remain isolated individuals, rather than forming any sort of social unit.

Social intervention

At least two arguments can be made for conducting intervention development and evaluation trials in which interpersonal functioning and social support (or factors thought to buffer the effects of uncontrollable adverse life events), are modified experimentally. First, there are difficulties in accurate measurement of exposure and of outcome (Brugha *et al.*, 1999), which are of less concern in experimental studies. Second, analysis of the effects of interventions in populations and communities could lead on more rapidly to improvements in public health following widespread implementation. There continues to be optimism about the future potential of observational research to help us better understand the interplay of environmental, genetic, and developmental influences on complex mental disorders (Rutter, 2002). However, as in the rest of medicine, there can be little doubt that more reliable and potentially useful findings are unlikely to follow unless research efforts are also directed with at least equal determination to the use of ethically acceptable experimental research designs.

Both laboratory experiments and field trials have been described in the literature. Laboratory experimental studies on normal volunteers have shown reduced anxiety (Bowers & Geston, 1986) and enhanced performance at a problem-solving task (Sarason & Sarason, 1986) following a series of supportive statements, and reduced perceived stressfulness of such a laboratory task (Lakey & Heller, 1988) when it was completed in the presence of a friend.

In the first reported study designed to use social support to improve mental health (Parker & Barnett, 1987), a controlled experimental intervention study was undertaken on highly anxious primiparous mothers, identified during a survey. The experimental treatment consisted of either lay or professional assistance, in the expectation that improvement in the treated mothers would be attributable to the therapeutic ingredient of social support. Social support was assessed by means of the ISSI – a standardized interview (Brugha *et al.*, 1987). The intervention cases did show a significant improvement on state and trait anxiety, in contrast to the controls. But there was no evidence that this was due to a change in the reported levels of social support. In another pioneering preventive intervention study, only those subjects (middle-aged and working-class women in the community) who responded to 'network stimulation', whereby they were encouraged to develop new contacts and sources of support in their community, seemed to benefit (Benum *et al.*, 1987).

Sandler argues that the development and evaluation of theory and empirically based preventive interventions should be based on a solid foundation of observational research on risk factors (Sandler & Barrera, 1984; Sandler *et al.*, 1997). Sandler's theory-based preventive intervention for divorced families, a programme for mothers, and a dual-component mother–child programme have all been experimentally evaluated (Wolchik *et al.*, 2000). Intervention development took several years, and was theoretically driven in that: (a) the programme includes multiple components designed to modify empirically and theoretically supported mediators; and (b) the putative mediators, as well as children's mental health problems, were all assessed. Empirical or theoretical justification for the selection of each mediator was provided (Wolchik *et al.*, 2000).

The necessity for extensive pre-trial intervention development comes from examining unsuccessful programmes: a community intervention that failed to get elderly persons to improve their social support systems (Heller *et al.*, 1991); and shortcomings in developing effective preventive interventions for postnatal depression. To reduce risk factors for postnatal depression previously verified in a cohort survey of 507 women in their first pregnancy (Brugha *et al.*, 1998), an existing parental support-enhancing manualized intervention programme was adapted for pregnant women who were at increased risk of postnatal depression; 209 pregnant women were then randomized to receive the adapted intervention 'Preparing for Parenthood' (PFP) antenatally (Brugha *et al.*, 2000). In intention-to-treat analyses, assignment to PFP had no significant impact on the score levels of the main risk factors, which included a measure of social support networks (Brugha *et al.*, 1987), nor on depression at three months postnatally (Brugha *et al.*, 2000).

According to a recent meta-analysis to determine whether group-based parenting programmes are effective in improving maternal psychosocial health (Barlow *et al.*, 2002), the potential success of such programmes may be attributable to effects on dyadic relationships. Barlow and colleagues showed using meta-analysis that there were statistically significant results favouring the intervention group for depression, anxiety/stress, self-esteem, and relationship with partner (−0.4, 95% CI = −0.7 to −0.2). However, the meta-analysis of social support data showed no overall evidence of effectiveness (−0.04, 95% CI = −0.3 to 0.2). It appeared that the studies with greater effects on mental health were carried out on clinical as opposed to volunteer samples, suggesting that high-risk groups may benefit more.

A randomized controlled experiment with 928 unemployed respondents in Michigan, who agreed to be randomized either to receive an information pack (control group) or to participate in eight three-hour group training sessions over a two-week period, was designed to prevent the development of depression and to increase re-employment levels (Price *et al.*, 1992). Analyses were based on 'intention to treat', and although many respondents declined to participate in the interventions, there was a significant beneficial effect on depression at one, four, and 28 months post-intervention. Explicit social support aspects of the training package were described as supportive behaviour by trainers, such as expressions of empathy, validation of participants' concerns and feelings, and encouragement of coping; group exercises were designed to 'provide opportunities and reinforcement of participants' supportive behaviour toward each other' (Price *et al.*, 1992). However, as the intervention contained many different components, this rendered less certain any final inference about the treatment specificity of a social support effect (the other ingredients being a job search skill training component and an emphasis within the group on the anticipation of possible setbacks or barriers to job seeking, termed 'inoculation against setbacks').

Psychological therapy approaches

Psychological therapy approaches have a more successful track record and it has been suggested that a common underlying effect may be by enhancing social support levels, possibly by altering the perception and interpersonal behaviour of the patient or client. A detailed training manual has been published that describes Interpersonal Psychotherapy of depression (IPT) (Klerman *et al.*, 1984). By providing the patient with a social relationship that is safe to learn within, IPT may also lead to enhanced skills in obtaining additional sources of support from others. IPT was developed by workers who had previously found that exit life events were associated with an increased risk of depression. IPT is undertaken in a one-to-one, psychotherapeutic setting, with timetabled sessions, in which exploratory and interpretative rather than prescriptive (as in cognitive and behavioural therapies) techniques are employed. Thus, it is based on traditional psychotherapy, which emphasizes the importance of the client–therapist relationship, or transference, but its subject matter is of particular relevance. The initial assessment focuses on the frequency and quality of social interaction, personal expectations of key social relationships, areas of dissatisfaction and, finally, on what the patient wants from each social relationship. Many of these variables are covered in standard social network inventories (Brugha *et al.*, 1987). Grief and loss, disputes, and changes in roles and deficits such as loneliness are also examined.

The IPT process has been shown to overlap very little with cognitive psychotherapeutic methods (Elkin *et al.*, 1989) but there appear to be no significant differences in their relative effects on outcome (Beckham, 1990). In a report on the efficacy of IPT as a maintenance treatment for recurrent depression, the process of therapy was studied through ratings of audiotaped sessions with the guidance of a Therapy Rating Scale, which rated, for example, the therapist's exploration of the patient's social network with respect to a particular problem (such as depression) (Frank *et al.*, 1991). When the patient and therapist were successful in maintaining a high level of interpersonal focus, monthly maintenance sessions of IPT were found to have had substantial prophylactic benefit. Prior analyses from the National Institute of Mental Health Treatment of Depression Collaborative Research Program also indicated that patients' expectancies of effectiveness of treatment and quality of the therapeutic relationship predicted clinical improvement. These data were reanalysed to examine the hypothesis that the link between treatment expectancies and outcome would be mediated by patients' contribution to the therapeutic alliance (Meyer *et al.*, 2002). Among 151 patients who completed treatment, this hypothesis was supported, suggesting that patients who expect treatment to be effective tend to engage in it more constructively, which helps bring about symptom reduction (Meyer *et al.*, 2002).

A 16-week bilingual controlled clinical trial compared a group receiving interpersonal psychotherapy for ante-partum depression with those receiving a parenting education control programme (Koh *et al.*, 2002; Spinelli & Endicott, 2003). Fifty outpatient ante-partum women who met DSM-IV criteria for major depressive disorder were randomly assigned to one intervention or the other. Recovery criteria were met in 60% of the women treated with interpersonal psychotherapy, according to a CGI score of <2 but only in 15.4% of control women.

Interpersonal psychotherapy may also protect against the risk of recurrence due to stressful life events (Harkness *et al.*, 2002). A study compared the role of life events in predicting time to the onset of the index episode, under conditions of no or variable treatment, versus the role of life events in predicting time to recurrence during maintenance interpersonal psychotherapy. Eighty-three women with recurrent major depression participated in acute IPT treatment, followed by two years of maintenance IPT. Although severe life events were significantly associated with time to the onset of the index episode, there was little evidence of an association between events experienced during maintenance treatment and time to recurrence. These results provide evidence that IPT may decrease the potency of life events in provoking recurrence.

The content of cognitive behavioural therapy (CBT) for depression does focus frequently on cognitions about the self, in relation to other key persons. Classic examples of faulty cognitions are rating oneself as less able than others (in the absence of confirmatory evidence), and thinking, for example, that 'they wouldn't be interested in me or they wouldn't like me anyway'. In an open, process study of 17 depressed and anxious patients undergoing CBT that was designed to disaggregate the interpersonal and technical effects of cognitive therapy (countering negative cognitions), Persons and Burns (1985) found that changes both in automatic thoughts and in the patient's relationship with his therapist made significant contributions to mood changes. Burns and Nolen-Hoeksema (1992) found that therapeutic empathy has a moderate-to-large causal effect on recovery from depression in a group of 185 patients treated with CBT. Patients of therapists who were the warmest and most empathic improved significantly more than those of therapists with the lowest empathy ratings, when controlling for initial depression severity, homework compliance, and other factors. The possible use of CBT in treating problems of social support has been discussed by Parry (1995). In addition to identifying and challenging cognitions that may lead to support from others being devalued, unused, or abused, this form of CBT focuses specifically on teaching new skills in eliciting and making use of support from others.

Conclusions

The methodological difficulties inherent in trials of social support should not be underestimated. It is difficult in trials to replicate the complex and sophisticated way in which support is provided in close relationships, and modified in response to need. Interventions to improve mental health by enhancing provision of social support have generally not shown the positive expectations suggested by non-experimental studies. But interventions that modify interpersonal functioning to improve the way people perceive and value support from others seem more promising. Until the underlying processes are better understood, closer collaboration between psychological therapy and public health researchers could prove to be a more promising route for research on interpersonal functioning and depression and common mental disorder.

Overall, the evidence from observational studies suggests that social support is an important protective factor in relation to the development of common mental disorder. Despite this, it is often difficult to identify the effects of social support on mental health specifically and consistently. Partly, this is because social support does not act independently of other factors relating to mental health. On the one hand, personality factors may both encourage or discourage the development and maintenance of relationships. Additionally, the provision of support may moderate the impact of adversity or even prevent exposure to adversity. At the same time, at a societal level, physical and social structures can both encourage and discourage the development of support. The impact of many of these broader societal influences on mental health may be mediated, in the final analysis, through effects on social interaction and support. One side-effect of current social trends is increasing social isolation; thus, there is some urgency in specifying and understanding the effects of social support on health in order to avoid higher levels of mental ill-health in the future.

References

Alloway, R. and Bebbington, P. (1987) 'The buffer theory of social support: a review of the literature'. *Psychological Medicine*, *17*, 91–108.

Andrews, B. and Brown, G. W. (1988) 'Social support, onset of depression and personality: an exploratory analysis'. *Social Psychiatry and Psychiatric Epidemiology*, *23*, 99–108.

Barlow, J., Coren, E. and Stewart-Brown, S. (2002) 'Meta-analysis of the effectiveness of parenting programmes in improving maternal psychosocial health'. *British Journal of General Practice*, *52*, 223–233.

Beckham, E. E. (1990) 'Psychotherapy of depression research at a crossroads: directions for the 1990s'. *Clinical Psychology Review*, *10*, 207–228.

Benum, K., Anstorp, T., Dalgard, O. S. and Sorenson, T. (1987) 'Social network stimulation: health promotion in a high risk group of middle-aged women'. *Acta Psychiatrica Scandinavica Supplementum*, *76*, 1–41.

Bolton, W. and Oatley, K. (1987) 'A longitudinal study of social support and depression in unemployed men'. *Psychological Medicine*, *17*, 453–460.

Bott, E. (1957) *Family and social network*. London: Tavistock.

Bowers, C. A. and Geston, E. L. (1986) 'Social support as a buffer of anxiety: an experimental analogue'. *American Journal of Community Psychology, 14*, 447–451.

Bowlby, J. (1980) *Attachment and loss: Vol. 3. Loss.* New York: Basic Books.

Brewin, C. R. (1995) 'Cognitive aspects of social support processes', in Brugha, T. S. (ed.), *Social support and psychiatric disorder: Research findings and guidelines for clinical practice.* Cambridge: Cambridge University Press.

Brown, G. W. and Harris, T. O. (1978) *Social origins of depression: A study of psychiatric disorder in women.* London: Tavistock.

Brown, G. W., Andrews, B., Harris, T., Adler, Z. and Bridge, L. (1986) 'Social support, self-esteem and depression'. *Psychological Medicine, 16*, 813–831.

Brugha, T. S., Bebbington, P. E. and Jenkins, R. (1999) 'A difference that matters: comparisons of structured and semi-structured diagnostic interviews of adults in the general population'. *Psychological Medicine, 29*, 1013–1020.

Brugha, T. S., Bebbington, P. E., Stretch, D. D., MacCarthy, B. and Wykes, T. (1997) 'Predicting the short-term outcome of first episodes and recurrences of clinical depression: a prospective study of life events, difficulties, and social support networks'. *Journal of Clinical Psychiatry, 58*, 298–306.

Brugha, T. S., Bebbington, P. E., MacCarthy, B., Sturt, E., Wykes, T. and Potter, J. (1990) 'Gender, social support and recovery from depressive disorders: a prospective clinical study'. *Psychological Medicine, 20*, 147–156.

Brugha, T. S., Sturt, E., MacCarthy, B., Potter, J., Wykes, T. and Bebbington, P. E. (1987) 'The Interview Measure of Social Relationships: the description and evaluation of a survey instrument for assessing personal social resources'. *Social Psychiatry, 22*, 123–128.

Brugha, T. S., Morgan, Z., Bebbington, P., Jenkins, R., Lewis, G., Farrell, M. and Meltzer, H. (2003) 'Social support networks and type of neurotic symptom among adults in British households'. *Psychological Medicine, 33*, 307–318.

Brugha, T. S., Weich, S., Singleton, N., Lewis, G., Bebbington, P. E., Jenkins, R. and Meltzer, H. (2005) 'Primary group size, social support, gender and future mental health status in a prospective study of people living in private households throughout Great Britain'. *Psychological Medicine, 35*, 705–714.

Brugha, T. S., Sharp, H. M., Cooper, S. A., Weisender, C., Britto, D., Shinkwin, R., Sherrif, T. and Kirwan, P. H. (1998) 'The Leicester 500 Project: social support and the development of postnatal depressive symptoms, a prospective cohort survey'. *Psychological Medicine, 28*, 63–79.

Brugha, T. S., Wheatley, S., Taub, N. A., Culverwell, A., Friedman, T., Kirwan, P. H., Jones, D. R. and Shapiro, D. A. (2000) 'Pragmatic randomised trial of antenatal intervention to prevent postnatal depression by reducing psychosocial risk factors'. *Psychological Medicine, 30*, 1273–1281.

Brugha, T., Conroy, R., Walsh, N., Delaney, W., O'Hanlon, J., Dondero, B., Daly, L., Hickey, N. and Burke, G. (1982) 'Social networks, attachments and support in minor affective disorders: a replication'. *British Journal of Psychiatry, 141*, 249–255.

Burg, M. M. and Seeman, T. E. (1994) 'Families and health: the negative side of social ties'. *Annals of Behavioral Medicine, 16*, 109–115.

Burns, D. and Nolen-Hoeksema, S. (1992) 'Therapeutic empathy and recovery from depression in cognitive behavioral therapy: a structural equation model'. *Journal of Consulting and Clinical Psychology, 60*, 441–449.

Caplan, G. (1976) 'The family as support system', in Caplan, G. and Killilea, M. (eds), *Support systems and mutual help: Multidisciplinary explorations.* New York: Grune & Stratton.

Cassel, J. (1976) 'The contribution of the social environment to host resistance: the Fourth Wade Hampton Frost Lecture'. *American Journal of Epidemiology*, *104*, 107–123.

Cassel, J. C. (1974) 'Psychiatric epidemiology', in Caplan, G. (ed.), *American handbook of psychiatry*. New York: Basic Books.

Champion, L. (1995) 'A developmental perspective on social support networks', in Brugha, T. S. (ed.), *Social support and psychiatric disorder: Research findings and guidelines for clinical practice*. Cambridge: Cambridge University Press.

Chance, M. R. A. (1988). *Social fabric of the mind*. Hillsdale, NJ: Lawrence Erlbaum Associates, Inc.

Cobb, S. (1976) 'Presidential Address – 1976: social support as a moderator of life stress'. *Psychosomatic Medicine*, *38*, 300–314.

Cohen, S. and Syme, S. L. (1985) *Social support and health*. London: Academic Press.

Cohen, S. and Wills, T. A. (1985) 'Stress, social support and the buffering hypothesis'. *Psychological Bulletin*, *98*, 310–357.

Cohen, S. and Hoberman, H. M. (1983) 'Positive events and social supports as buffers of life stress'. *Journal of Applied Social Psychology*, *13*, 99–125.

Coleman, A. (1985) *Utopia on trial: Vision and reality in planned housing*. London: Hilary Shipman.

de Figueiredo, J. M. (1983) 'The law of sociocultural demoralization'. *Social Psychiatry*, *18*, 73–78.

Elkin, I., Shea, T., Watkins, J. T., Imber, S. D., Sotsky, S. M., Collins, J. F., Glass, D. R., Pilkonis, P. A., Leber, W. R., Docherty, J. P., Fiester, J. S. and Parloff, M. B. (1989) 'National Institutute of Mental Health Treatment of Depression Collaborative Research Program: general effectiveness of treatments'. *Archives of General Psychiatry*, *46*, 971–982.

Fischer, C. S. (1975) 'The study of urban community and personality'. *Annual Review of Sociology*, *1*, 67–89.

Frank, E., Kupfer, D. J., Wagner, E. F., McEachran, A. B. and Cornes, C. (1991) 'Efficacy of interpersonal psychotherapy as a maintenance treatment of recurrent depression: contributing factors'. *Archives of General Psychiatry*, *48*, 1053–1059.

Fuhrer, R., Stansfeld, S. A., Chemali, J. and Shipley, M. J. (1999) 'Gender, social relations and mental health: prospective findings from an occupational cohort (Whitehall II study)'. *Social Science and Medicine*, *48*, 77–87.

Gans, H. J. (1962) 'Urbanism and suburbanism as ways of life: a re-evaluation of definitions', in Rose, A. M. (ed.), *Human behavior and social processes*. New York: Houghton-Mifflin.

Gilbert, P. (1995) 'Attachment, cooperation and rank: the evolution of the need for status and social support', in Brugha, T. S. (ed.), *Social support and psychiatric disorder: Research findings and guidelines for clinical practice*. Cambridge: Cambridge University Press.

Greenblatt, M., Becerra, R. M. and Serafetinides, E. A. (1982) 'Social networks and mental health: on overview'. *American Journal of Psychiatry*, *139*, 977–984.

Hammer, M. (1983) ' "Core" and "extended" social networks in relation to health and illness'. *Social Science and Medicine*, *17*, 405–411.

Harkness, K. L., Frank, E., Anderson, B., Houck, P. R., Luther, J. and Kupfer, D. J. (2002) 'Does interpersonal psychotherapy protect women from depression in the face of stressful life events?'. *Journal of Consulting and Clinical Psychology*, *70*, 908–915.

Heller, K., Thompson, M., Trueba, P. E., Hogg, J. R. and Vlachos-Weber, I. (1991) 'Peer support telephone dyads for elderly women: was this the wrong intervention?'. *American Journal of Community Psychology*, *19*, 1–74.

Henderson, A. S. (1981) 'Social relationships, adversity and neurosis: an analysis of prospective observations'. *British Journal of Psychiatry, 138*, 391–398.

Henderson, S. (1974) 'Care-eliciting behavior in man'. *Journal of Nervous and Mental Disease, 159*, 172–181.

Henderson, S. (1980) 'A development in social psychiatry: the systematic study of social bonds'. *Journal of Nervous and Mental Disease, 168*, 63–69.

Henderson, S., Duncan Jones, P., McAuley, H. and Ritchie, K. (1978) 'The patient's primary group'. *British Journal of Psychiatry, 132*, 1–86.

Henderson, S., Jorm, A., Jacomb, P., Korten, A. and Easteal, S. (1997) 'Molecular genetics and the epidemiology of common mental disorders: new opportunities'. *Epidemiologia e Psichiatria Sociale, 6*, 167–172.

Hinde, R. A. (1974) *Biological bases of human social behaviour*. New York: McGraw-Hill.

Hintikka, J., Koskela, T., Kontula, O., Koskela, K. and Viinamaki, H. (2000) 'Men, women and friends – are there differences in relation to mental well-being?'. *Quality of Life Research, 9*, 841–845.

Horwitz, A. (1978) 'Family, kin and friend networks in psychiatric help seeking'. *Social Science and Medicine, 23*, 297–304.

House, J. S. (1981) *Work stress and social support*. Reading, MA: Addison-Wesley.

Husaini, B. A., Neff, J. A., Newborough, J. R. and Moore, M. C. (1982) 'The stress-buffering role of social support and personal competence among the rural married'. *Journal of Community Psychology, 10*, 409–426.

Jacobs, J. (1961) *The death and life of great American cities*. New York: Random House.

Jenkins, R. (1994) 'Principles of prevention', in Paykel, E. S. and Jenkins, R. (eds), *Prevention in psychiatry* (pp. 11–24). London: Gaskell.

Kahn, R. L. and Antonucci, T. C. (1980) 'Convoys over the life course: attachment, roles and social support', in Baltes, P. B. and Brim, O. G. (eds), *Life span development and behavior*, Vol. 3. New York: Academic Press.

Kessler, R. C. and Essex, M. (1982) 'Marital status and depression: the role of coping resources'. *Journal of Community Psychology, 61*, 484–507.

Kessler, R. C. and McLeod, J. D. (1985) *Social support and mental health in community samples*. New York: Academic Press.

Kessler, R. C., Kendler, K. S., Heath, A., Neale, M. C. and Eaves, L. J. (1994) 'Perceived support and adjustment to stress in a general population sample of female twins'. *Psychological Medicine, 24*, 317–334.

Killilea, M. (1982) 'Interaction of crisis theory, coping strategies and social support systems', in Schulberg, H. C. and Killilea, M. (eds), *The modern practice of community mental health*. San Francisco: Jossey-Bass.

Klerman, G., Weissman, M., Rounsaville, B. J. and Chevron, E. S. (1984) *Interpersonal psychotherapy of depression*. New York: Basic Books.

Koh, K. B., Kim, C. H. and Park, J. K. (2002) 'Predominance of anger in depressive disorders compared with anxiety disorders and somatoform disorders'. *Journal of Clinical Psychiatry, 63*, 486–492.

Lakey, B. and Heller, K. (1988) 'Social support from a friend, perceived support, and social problem solving'. *American Journal of Community Psychology, 16*, 811–824.

Lakey, B., Tardiff, T. A. and Drew, J. B. (1994) 'Negative social interactions: assessment and relations to social support, cognition, and psychological distress'. *Journal of Social and Clinical Psychology, 13*, 63–85.

LaRocco, J. M., House, J. S. and French, J. R. P. (1980) 'Social support, occupational stress and health'. *Journal of Health and Social Behaviour, 21*, 202–218.

Leaf, P. J., Weissman, M. M., Myers, J. K., Tischler, G. L. and Holzer, C. E. (1984) 'Social factors related to psychiatric disorder: the Yale Epidemiologic Catchment Area Study'. *Social Psychiatry and Psychiatric Epidemiology, 19*, 53–61.

Leff, J., Thornicroft, G., Coxhead, N. and Crawford, C. (1994) 'The TAPS Project. 22: a five-year follow-up of long-stay psychiatric patients discharged to the community'. *British Journal of Psychiatry, 165* (suppl. 25), 13–17.

Leighton, A. H. (1959) *My name is legion.* New York: Basic Books.

Leighton, A. H. (1981) 'Culture and psychiatry'. *Canadian Journal of Psychiatry, 26*, 522–529.

Leighton, D. C., Harding, J. S., Macklin, D. B., Macmillan, A. M. and Leighton, A. H. (1963) *The character of danger: Psychiatric symptoms in selected communities.* New York: Basic Books.

Meltzer, H., Gill, B., Petticrew, M. and Hinds, K. (1995a) *OPCS Surveys of Psychiatric Morbidity in Great Britain. Report 1: The prevalence of psychiatric morbidity among adults living in private households.* Appendix B. Algorithms for production of ICD-10 diagnoses of neurosis from the CIS-R. Office of Population Censuses & Surveys Social Survey Division, pp. 101–103. London: HMSO.

Meltzer, H., Gill, B., Petticrew, M. and Hinds, K. (1995b) *OPCS Surveys of Psychiatric Morbidity in Great Britain. Report 3: Economic activity and social functioning of adults with psychiatric disorders.* Office of Population Censuses & Surveys Social Survey Division, p. 168. London: HMSO.

Meyer, B., Pilkonis, P. A., Krupnick, J. L., Egan, M. K., Simmens, S. J. and Sotsky, S. M. (2002) 'Treatment expectancies, patient alliance, and outcome: further analyses from the National Institute of Mental Health Treatment of Depression Collaborative Research Program'. *Journal of Consulting and Clinical Psychology, 70*, 1051–1055.

Mitchell, R. E. and Trickett, E. J. (1980) 'Task force report: social networks as mediators of social support'. *Community Mental Health Journal, 16*, 18–27.

Mueller, D. (1980) 'Social networks: a primary direction for research in the relationship of the social environment to psychiatric disorder'. *Social Science and Medicine, 14A*, 147–161.

O'Connor, P. and Brown, G. W. (1984) 'Supportive relationships: fact or fancy?'. *Journal of Social and Personal Relationships, 1*, 159–175.

Oxman, T. E., Berkman, L. F., Kasl, S., Freeman, D. H., Jr and Barrett, J. (1992) 'Social support and depressive symptoms in the elderly'. *American Journal of Epidemiology, 135*, 356–368.

Parker, G. and Barnett, B. (1987) 'A test of the social support hypothesis'. *British Journal of Psychiatry, 150*, 72–77.

Parry, G. (1995) 'Social support processes and cognitive therapy', in Brugha, T. S. (ed.), *Social support and psychiatric disorder: Research findings and guidelines for clinical practice.* Cambridge: Cambridge University Press.

Paykel, E. S. (1994) 'Life events, social support and depression'. *Acta Psychiatrica Scandinavica Supplementum, 377*, 50–58.

Pearlin, L. I., Lieberman, M. A., Menaghan, E. G. and Mullan, J. T. (1981) 'The stress process'. *Journal of Health and Social Behaviour, 22*, 337–56.

Persons, J. and Burns, D. (1985) 'Mechanisms of action of cognitive therapy: the relative contributions of technical and interpersonal interventions'. *Cognitive Therapy and Research, 9*, 539–551.

Price, R. H., van Ryn, M. and Vinokur, A. D. (1992) 'Impact of a preventive job search intervention on the likelihood of depression among the unemployed'. *Journal of Health and Social Behaviour, 33*, 158–167.

Prince, M. J., Harwood, R. H., Thomas, A. and Mann, A. H. (1998) 'A prospective population-based cohort study of the effects of disablement and social milieu on the onset and maintenance of late-life depression. The Gospel Oak Project VII'. *Psychological Medicine, 28*, 337–350.

Quinton, D., Rutter, M. and Liddle, C. (1984) 'Institutional rearing, parenting difficulties and marital support'. *Psychological Medicine, 14*, 107–124.

Rook, K. S. (1984) 'The negative side of social interaction: impact on psychological well-being'. *Journal of Personality and Social Psychology, 46*, 1097–1108.

Rutter, M. (2002) 'The interplay of nature, nurture, and developmental influences: the challenge ahead for mental health'. *Archives of General Psychiatry, 59*, 996–1000.

Sandler, I. N. and Barrera, M. J. (1984) 'Toward a multi-method approach to assessing the effects of social support'. *American Journal of Community Psychology, 12*, 37–52.

Sandler, I. N., Wolchik, S. A., MacKinnon, D., Ayers, T. S. and Roosa, M. W. (1997) 'Developing linkages between theory and intervention in stress and coping processes', in Wolchik, S. A. and Sandler, I. N. (eds), *Handbook of children's coping: Linking theory and intervention*. New York: Plenum.

Sarason, I. G. and Sarason, B. R. (1986) 'Experimentally provided social support'. *Journal of Personality and Social Psychology, 50*, 1222–1225.

Schoevers, R. A., Beekman, A. T., Deeg, D. J., Geerlings, M. I., Jonker, C. and Van Tilburg, W. (2000) 'Risk factors for depression in later life; results of a prospective community based study (AMSTEL)'. *Journal of Affective Disorders, 59*, 127–137.

Schuster, T. L., Kessler, R. C. and Aseltine, R. H., Jr (1990) 'Supportive interactions, negative interactions, and depressed mood'. *American Journal of Community Psychology, 18*, 423–438.

Spinelli, M. G. and Endicott, J. (2003) 'Controlled clinical trial of interpersonal psychotherapy versus education program for depressed pregnant women'. *American Journal of Psychiatry, 160*, 555–562.

Stansfeld, S. A. and Marmot, M. G. (1992) 'Deriving a survey measure of social support: the reliability and validity of the Close Persons Questionnaire'. *Social Science and Medicine, 35*, 1027–1035.

Stansfeld, S. A., Fuhrer, R. and Shipley, M. J. (1998) 'Types of social support as predictors of psychiatric morbidity in a cohort of British Civil Servants (Whitehall II Study)'. *Psychological Medicine, 28*, 881–892.

Stokes, J. and Levin, I. (1986) 'Gender differences in predicting loneliness from social network characteristics'. *Journal of Personality and Social Psychology, 51*, 1069–1074.

Turvey, C. L., Conwell, Y., Jones, M. P., Phillips, C., Simonsick, E., Pearson, J. L. and Wallace, R. (2002) 'Risk factors for late-life suicide: a prospective, community-based study'. *American Journal of Geriatric Psychiatry, 10*, 398–406.

Vazquez Barquero, J. L., Munox, P. E. and Madoz, J. V. (1982) 'The influence of the process of urbanization on the prevalence of neurosis: a community survey'. *Acta Psychiatrica Scandinavica, 65*, 161–170.

Westermeyer, J. (1980) 'Psychosis in a peasant society: social outcomes'. *American Journal of Psychiatry, 137*, 1390–1394.

Wildes, J. E., Harkness, K. L. and Simons, A. D. (2002) 'Life events, number of social relationships, and twelve-month naturalistic course of major depression in a community sample of women'. *Depression and Anxiety, 16*, 104–113.

Wing, J. K. and Brown, G. W. (1970) *Institutionalism and schizophrenia: A Comparative study of three mental hospitals 1960–1968*. Cambridge: Cambridge University Press.

Wolchik, S. A., West, S. G., Sandler, I. N., Tein, J. Y., Coatsworth, D., Lengua, L., Weiss, L., Anderson, E. R., Greene, S. M. and Griffin, W. A. (2000) 'An experimental evaluation of theory-based mother and mother–child programs for children of divorce'. *Journal of Consulting and Clinical Psychology*, *68*, 843–856.

Yancey, W. (1971) 'Architecture, interaction and social control: the case of a large-scale public housing project' *Environment & Behavior*, *3*, 3–26.

Young, M. and Wilmott, P. (1957) *Family and kinship in East London*. London: Routledge & Kegan Paul.

7 Migration and mental health

Kamaldeep Bhui

ODYSSEUS: And now some god has flung me on this shore, no doubt to suffer more disasters here. For I have no hope that my troubles are coming to an end: Pity me my queen, you are the first person I have met after all I have been through, and I do not know a soul in this city or this land.

WHITE ARMED NAUSSICA: Your manners prove that you are no rascal, or fool, and as for these ordeals of yours, they must have been sent you by Olympian Zeus, who follows his own will in dispensing happiness to people whatever their merits. You have no choice but to endure. But since you have come to our country and our city here, you certainly shall not want for clothing or anything else that an unfortunate outcast has the right to expect from those he approaches. I will show you the town and tell you who we are.

(Homer: *The Odyssey*, Rieu, 1946)

One of the oldest tales known to mankind is that of Odysseus on his travels, encountering many hazards during his journey. Danger was found in the form of peoples and monsters, as well as natural disasters and acts of Gods. This rich account includes vivid descriptions of the physical and psychological hurdles facing travellers, albeit on a fictional journey. The challenges were both psychological and physical and were overcome by endurance and resilience, as well as by assistance from people and the 'Gods'. Odysseus's tenacity, attitude to the world, and willingness to make sacrifices all played a role in his survival. Nonetheless, from Homer's account, it appears that he and his men almost certainly suffered mental anguish that we would now label as post-traumatic stress disorder (PTSD). Odysseus was never considered to have a mental illness or psychological problems, although the intensity of his anguish and suffering, including vivid recall of war-related memories, might, in the modern world, be interpreted as indicators of depression or PTSD. If Odysseus's experiences were universal among travellers, few would take up the challenge, but he was fortunate to encounter white armed Naussica, who welcomed him, trusted him, and educated him to her people's customs and mores. Migration and geographical mobility often include life events and stressors over which the individual has little control. Like Odysseus, many migrants in the modern world have to face loss of home, family, and lifestyle, and have to overcome a series of barriers and new challenges in a world of events that are seemingly outside their control. Although this chapter will attend to the impact of these issues on mental well-being, they can only be appreciated within the broader context of migration trends and typologies of geographical mobility.

Globalization and growth in migration

According to United Nations estimates, in 1990 there were about 120 million foreigners or foreign-born persons living in 214 countries and territories in the world. This means that 2.3% of the world's population would have been international migrants, living outside their country of citizenship or birth for 12 months or more (*Migration News*, 2002). There were 76 million international migrants in 1965, 84 million in 1975, 106 million in 1985, and 120 million in 1990. The United Nations reports that in 1990, 5% of European and 9% of North American inhabitants were foreigners. This compares with 6% in the UK and 10% in France. Although some migration controls are usually in place to restrict immigration, so as to limit the perceived drain on scarce resources, data compiled by the Home Office show that, in the UK, migration may actually be profitable for host nations (Dobson *et al.*, 2001). This report draws on studies from Germany, the USA and the UK, which agree that foreign-born people contribute more to the state in taxation than they consume in benefits and social security. The median earnings for migrants are higher than for native populations, but this disguises extreme distributions of wealth, with a marked over-representation of migrants both in the highest earners and the lowest income groups (Dobson *et al.*, 2001). This also obscures the reality that specific sub-groups of migrants, for example from Bangladesh and Pakistan, have the lowest incomes in the UK and the poorest chances of employment, compared both with other migrants and with non-migrant British residents. The employment prospects of Bangladeshi, Pakistani, and African-Caribbean people remain generally poor, and appear to affect the next generation adversely (Platt, 2003). This applies not only to adults but also to children of migrants, sometimes decades after migration. For example, the Child Poverty Action Group reported that 63% of Black African and 40% of African-Caribbean children were living in poverty, defined by a family income not more than 60% of the national average (Platt, 2003).

Foreign students are contributing more and more to the world market in higher and further education, with current plans by the UK government to extend the national share of this expenditure from 17% to 25%. The latest and most accurate figures – for 1998 – showed that 100,000 work permits were issued in the year 2000, while 266,000 students were given leave to study in the UK. In addition, in 1999, 71,000 'asylum seekers' came to Britain and 65,000 family members of UK citizens settled in the country. In 1998, 16,500 illegal migrants are reported to have arrived in the UK, but these numbers are notoriously difficult to establish with certainty, so that official figures are very likely to be an underestimate. In general, though, the European Union is set to make it easier for European migrants to travel, work, and settle in other nations.

People migrate for differing reasons, with marked variations in their motivations, aspirations, capacity to generate income, and likelihood of success. Faced with global cultures and migration for economic reasons, together with concerns about the health and well-being of migrants themselves, it is surprising that more attention has not been paid to unravelling the role of movement and resettlement on the health and mental health of those involved. A recent mapping exercise across Europe (Watters, 2002) found that policies and services for migrants' health and social care were not only rather patchy, but mostly absent. Where services existed, they were not designed specifically for the migrant population. There is also marked variation in services for settled migrants and refugees who have been recognized by the state as citizens.

This chapter explores the mental health experiences of migrants, taking account of the differing types of international movement and the 'health risks' of their children, as well as the impact of forced migration on asylum seekers and refugees. It considers the phenomenon in terms of the individual's life stage, as well as that of reception at a particular point of historical and political development in Britain since the Second World War. Although genetic factors have an aetiological role in determining vulnerability to mental disorders – most specifically major affective and psychotic disorders – each of these conditions still has significant non-genetic risk factors. These social and environmental determinants are the main theme of what follows.

Definitions

The term 'migrants' is usually applied to people who belong to different ethnic groups or people with different places of birth, when compared with the host population. British, American, and European immigration policies classically aimed to exclude people from other racial groups, although such distinctions now make little sense in terms of actual variations in the risks of health and illness. Classifications based on ethnic group or place of birth are useful in the early stages of migration, where specific risk factors of the country of origin may be carried into the new environment. However, two factors may influence the value of ethnic-based classification. First, with the globalization of communications, economic strategies and access to goods, the differences between culturally distinct regions of the world are greatly diminishing. This is more so in industrialized and developed countries, where average levels of wealth allow for goods from remote parts of the world to be locally available and for this process to be economically viable. Second, recent years in the UK have seen businesses moving abroad, not only to other parts of Europe but to the Indian subcontinent and the Far East, where skilled labour is available for a fraction of the cost of that in the West. This in turn influences the local cultures there and at a later stage, may even make it easier for their economic migrants to pursue employment elsewhere.

Following migration, both individuals and groups shift their cultural values, language preferences, and styles of social interaction. To some extent, this is necessary to make effective use of the opportunities in a new country. Classifying people on the basis of their cultural identity, after migration to a new environment, may be a better way of thinking about risks to mental well-being than identifying any specific ethnic group as a risk factor. A single ethnic group often includes a rich mixture of social classes, educational achievements, aspirations, and even countries of origin. If the purpose is to define cultural risk factors, such as religious practice, diet, lifestyle, or family networks and size, then subculture-based classifications are more meaningful.

'Foreigners' are usually defined by place of birth, country of origin, or parental country of origin. In some countries, birthplace does not automatically confer citizenship rights. In the UK, routine census, health, and social care information is now collected in terms of ethnic category, occasionally including place of birth, and more recently asylum and refugee status. Few data exist, however, about the effects of migration on sense of belonging and cultural identity, and how this in turn affects emotional well-being. To distinguish those with more or less acculturation and either a greater or lesser sense of belonging to the host culture, some studies use age of migration, place of early education, place of birth, and/or newly developed acculturation scales to classify cultural belonging. Acculturative experiences may be understood as a web of life events, starting with the intention to migrate and persisting for decades after the move. How an individual reacts to and masters (or fails to master) the challenges faced during and after migration is shaped by vulnerability factors, as well as by determinants of resilience. These factors themselves will be differently constituted in varying cultural groups. For example, if family cohesion and social support are more prevalent among South Asian cultures, in which members of larger and extended families are contained under one roof, this may make them less vulnerable to mental disorder by providing greater social support. However, extended families and less private space and autonomy may also limit their ability to migrate in the first place.

Migration involves separation from the wider family unit, and may be opposed to a greater extent by an extended family that values unity over individual autonomy, compared with a nuclear family. Alternatively, where the migrant must send funds home, an extended family can actually encourage migration as a way of increasing its total income. For migrants, irrespective of the nature of their family of origin, there is a 'bereavement' process with loss of the family unit, social support, and networks that were previously taken for granted. While such a process of bereavement will be present in all such families, the experience of loss and the meaning attached to the separation will vary according to cultural values, expectations, and the specific reasons for migration. Motivations to migrate, for example, may challenge local cultural conventions, break family traditions of employment, or threaten local communities that are trying to persuade younger people to remain in their local centres, whether rural or urban.

Typologies and motivations

Although the evidence base about the aetiology of mental disorders is constantly evolving, there is a general consensus that certain characteristics of both the individual and the environment are important. Mental health is known to vary with socio-economic position, locus of control, unemployment, life events (including discrimination), income levels, and social networks. Resiliency factors such as having good confidants, the population density of ethnic groups, and social capital are also influential.

Whereas physical capital refers to physical objects and human capital refers to the properties of individuals, 'social capital' refers to connections among individuals – social networks and the norms of reciprocity and trustworthiness that arise from them (Putnam, 2000; see Chapter 6).

There is a lack of data with which to formulate an overarching model of migration and its risks and benefits that would be suited to all groups and contexts, yet it is generally understood that both risk and resiliency are differentially prevalent within any one ethnic or cultural group. Furthermore, culturally specific risk or resiliency factors make it unlikely that a single general theory can encompass all cultural groups, unless we were to postulate that there is a finite number of such factors. In that case, we would also have to posit that it is the prevalence of these universal processes that varies, rather than that the processes themselves are distinct in each ethnic group, as might be expected from the different psychosocial and historical experiences of each. To date, health research has not included any comprehensive prospective study addressing three separate factors: (i) the characteristics of both source and destination countries, (ii) intervening obstacles, and (iii) the interaction of personality and socio-cultural influences. Longitudinal studies of immigrants to Canada, New Zealand, Australia, and the USA have grappled with these methodological challenges; some have excluded asylum seekers and refugees to ensure reasonable response rates, but none have examined health outcomes in a comprehensive manner (Black *et al.*, 2003). A study of 'integration' commissioned by the Home Office showed that only 81 out of 619 publications between 1996 and 2001 actually dealt with health issues (Castles *et al.*, 2002). It was concluded that the British debate on immigration and integration was dominated by race relations terminology that lacked conceptual clarity, and that it was rarely sustained with adequate data.

Migrating populations can be classified on the basis of the distance travelled, the temporary or permanent nature of migration, the causes and selectivity of migration, and whether it is international or internal. Although this chapter is concerned with international migration, some of the issues involved are similar for internal migrants.

Peterson (in Greenwood & Hunt, 2003) specified a typology of migration: nomadic pastoralism, abduction and transport of slaves, impelled migration, free migration, and mass movement. Within each category, migration was classified as innovative or conservative. Innovative migration aimed to improve living standards and total position, whereas the conservative form aimed to maintain existing standards of living. Guinness (2002) referred to 'active migrants' as people who are risk-takers and who follow lines of communication between rural and urban areas. International migration involves taking risks, as well as incurring economic costs and uncertainty, especially where there are no open channels of communication between the destination and the home country. Passive migrants – peoples who are not in control of their destinies and migrate to survive persecution, wars, torture, or at the behest of governments – may not wish to settle permanently. They find themselves in another country without prior planning. Other theories posit that the intensity of the distress and difficulties of migration are linked to differences in socio-economic development between the societies between which migration takes place (Zelinsky, 1971).

There are few generalizations or overarching models of this experience, not least because the reasons for migration and its contexts differ so much between people and countries. However, in a paper in the *Journal of the Royal Statistical Society* in 1885, Ravenstein, a Fellow of the Royal Geographical Society, outlined a series of 'laws of migration' that attempted to explain and predict its pattern, both within and between nations (Ravenstein, 1876, 1885, 1889). Ravenstein's laws state that: (1) most migrants travel a short distance; (2) migration occurs in a series of steps; (3) the process of dispersion is the inverse of absorption; (4) each migration stream has a counter-stream; (5) the longer the distance travelled, the greater the likelihood of the destination being an industrial or commercial centre; (6) families rarely migrate, but single adults do so more often (Greenwood & Hunt, 2003; Guinness, 2002). The laws are most relevant to the period of time prior to recent trends in international travel and the ease of communication and shared information about destinations across the globe. Nonetheless, for less privileged travellers or for passive migrants, they may still be relevant and useful ways of understanding the experience. Even for modern-day modelling of geographical and spatial movements, they remain a starting point.

A common way of understanding the process is to consider 'push' and 'pull' factors, as well as the intervening obstacles, and opportunities, all of which influence the direction and volume of a migration stream (Lee, 1966). More recent analysis of urban-to-rural population movement in Africa offered a more systemic approach. This work identifies local networks of agencies, peoples, and influences within the home area; similar local knowledge and economies operate at the destination. These systems are connected, and inform and are influenced by migrating populations. Their knowledge and successes are transmitted to sustain a reflexive communication process between destination and home country. This process influences expectations and available supports, both before and after migration.

Economic, sociological, and anthropological analyses each bring a particular model to bear on the motivations and consequences of migration. One popular paradigm is the basic 'human capital' model. This suggests that foreign-born migrants are generally able, despite adverse socio-economic conditions, to make gains in the housing and labour markets. Migration is seen as an investment decision that increases productivity, so that family and individual lifetime benefits are increased. This model posits a continuous evaluation or trade-off between staying at the current residence and the economic utility of moving. Migrants may develop this approach to life in the host country, and for some groups, where this links up with greater economic rewards, repeated international migration may become the norm. In the face of uncertainty, however, migration may precipitate a particular attitude to the process, which itself may mimic severe mental illness, but which essentially is an adaptive coping response. For example, 'dream travel' has been described among Somali refugees as a state of mind in which the future destination is said to hold all sorts of rewards. However, this destination never arrives, leaving the individual with continued restlessness to keep travelling in order to find an imagined destination that would offer an adequate trade-off for the sacrifices made *en route*. This state appears to be like a psychosis, but essentially is an adaptive stage, though one in which these refugees can become trapped.

Economic migration favours those who have some resources to allow them to exercise choice, and to plan for a short-term disruption to economic gains. It is not welcomed, though, by those whose economic situation is so stable and rewarding that migration might add little to their lifetime gains. This model favours migration at a younger age, before people are established in a specific occupation, and while lifetime earnings are modest or opportunities limited at home. Migration is then motivated by expectations of better economic and social rewards and opportunities. Such a model is supported by the current trends in world movement, which are generally away from the developing world towards industrialized countries. These expectations are important in achieving emotional well-being and allowing personal appraisal of the benefits and hazards of migration. However, such perceptions and trade-off decisions may only result in the individual discovering that the decision to move was based on over-optimistic expectations. For example, in the 1950s, promises of employment and notions of Empire attracted many from the Caribbean to their 'mother country'; the early cohorts found employment, but a number of social stressors that they encountered were unexpected. Subsequent cohorts often found limited labour markets in deprived inner-city areas, with limited opportunities to find more lucrative work (Dustmann *et al.*, 2003).

In addition, some migrants who are forced to leave war-torn countries or who migrate to flee persecution may not have expected other adversities such as discrimination, social isolation, linguistic isolation, and challenges to their cultural beliefs and practices. They are likely to have arrived in the country of refuge with little planning or informed anticipation of what life might be like and how they might manage there. Language problems, illness, discrimination, dispersal, and lack of appropriate skills may limit access to labour markets.

For asylum-seekers, immigration and asylum laws (in the UK) do not allow employment until immigration decisions are concluded. During the period immediately after arrival, poverty and unemployment may compound efforts to secure necessary skills, and make use of opportunities that may be more open to those with regular income, and those who were able to make use of training and education. It is not uncommon that refugees with the relevant qualifications, good histories of employment, and high social status in their home countries, find unemployment and poverty to be sustained on arrival in the UK (Bhui *et al.*, 2003).

Mental illness or distress

This section deals with the mental health experiences of migrants, taking account of the differing types of international movement, and the 'health risks' of their children, as well as the impact of forced migration on asylum-seekers and refugees.

Migration is related to a 'grief process', although this is not always a morbid process that amounts to a mental illness. Losses include one's home, country, friends, familiar places and finally the hope of return. Fried (1963, cited in Freeman, 1972) outlines grief following forced local migration associated with the fragmentation of individuals' spatial identity, group identity, and social networks. Specifically, affective investment in these offers a feeling of continuity that is contingent on a sense of familiarity. This familiarity is hard won, perhaps taking decades or a lifetime, and follows a personal commitment to an area, country, or region. Fostering a new sense of belonging and of continuity in a new environment can only follow with time, acceptance, and the gradual recognition that the country of origin is no longer the place that was left. Edward Said (1983) described how his origins as a Palestinian exile, and a practising Christian, and how his situation between Palestine and his new home in New York offered him the opportunity for intellectual freedom to examine the assumptions found within host nations about migrants. So he condemned the anti-Islamic rhetoric found in his new country, considering himself isolated, perhaps personally condemned for holding sympathetic views about a *demonized* people and religion. Yet he preferred to live in New York, which became his home, but still referred to himself as a 'Palestinian in exile'. For Said, this challenge formed the cutting edge of academic studies; it provided him with material to challenge and reconsider conventional and stereotypical notions of identity, migration, and movement. Although formal mental illness does not enter into his discourse, his subject matter includes conflict, distress, integration, and culture clashes. The mental health costs of such processes are now becoming a major focus for social and health policy and research.

Acculturation will have transformed the migrant's identity and sense of belonging. During this process, many migrants will experience normative grief – perhaps a sense of confusion and of not belonging. This is acutely felt as anxiety, depression, sleeplessness, and loneliness while adjustments are made, for example by learning a new language or changing education systems for their children (Furnham & Bockner, 1986; Mumford, 1998). This 'culture shock' usually lasts for about 12–18 months, marking the initial adjustment period, following which successful resettlement may often be expected. Nonetheless, the process of displacement and of the distress associated with being dislocated from a place of belonging are under-studied. Some post-migration reactions may become more intractable forms of mental distress, culminating in mental disorder. On the other hand, many individuals will adapt well, seeking out new markets and perhaps developing new economic networks based on commodities to which they have unique access (Dobson *et al.*, 2001). For example, in the UK, the Indian and Chinese restaurant businesses provided migrants with a potential monopoly of such activity. However, the process of following-up a cohort of migrants and assessing risk factors for either persistent or transient disorders has not been undertaken on a large enough scale, or on sufficiently representative groups. If that were done, better predictions about risk and vulnerability could be made.

It is difficult to make general statements about the well-being of migrants or to identify general risk factors for them, as each group has a unique historical and cultural profile of experiences. Within each group, there are individual characteristics that contribute to distinct coping styles, personality dispositions, and resiliency factors. What we may describe as a psychological reaction to migration may, to migrants, simply be considered as 'home-sickness'. Home-sickness compounded by poverty, unemployment, social isolation, and discrimination is more persuasively linked with the development of social disabilities and functional impairments that may constitute key characteristics of mental illness. Migrants may have anticipated a period of emotional and practical difficulties while resettlement takes place, especially if they have little knowledge of their destination. It is more likely, though, that migration to any destination will be often accompanied by a counter-stream, bringing with it knowledge about that place, as well as consumer goods and stories of success and opportunities. Furthermore, internal migrants usually rely on friends and relatives to assist them on arrival, and the same process is not uncommon among international migrants. This knowledge and assistance will mitigate the impact of culture shock, especially if other migrants from the same source are living in same area, with some transformation of the local built environment to include elements from their culture of origin. This reasserts a sense of belonging and familiarity in the new home. For example, mosques in East London, sari shops in Wembley, and African hair product and cosmetic shops in Brixton, together with restaurants serving foods from throughout the world, all help to foster a sense of belonging, and a reorientation of identity in terms of familiar landmarks.

Even when it comes to more severe depressive and anxiety reactions, mental health professionals may be labelling distress experiences that are not accepted as illness or disorder by the cultural groups under study. It is known that South Asians feel a more interpersonal sense of distress, rather than seeing this as an isolated embodied piece of pathology akin to a mental disorder (see Beliappa, 1991). Also, somatic presentations are said to be more common among Asian peoples, whether in their home countries or as immigrants (Mumford, 1989, 1998). More recent critiques, however, suggest that such somatic symptoms are ubiquitous (Kirmayer, 1992; Piccinelli & Simon, 1997), representing both an idiomatic expression of distress and its physiological correlates. Such expressions of distress as somatic symptoms are more common among women, those on low incomes, the unemployed, and immigrants. Perhaps somatic symptoms are one example of non-psychological manifestations of difficulties of living, powerlessness, and dependency needs. Each of these basic needs may be seen in the use of health and social care services, through mechanisms of stress and distress.

Stress is often invoked as a mediator between environment and individual reactions, manifested in both psychological and physiological components. A comprehensive analysis of how the environment can lead to distress and stress is beyond the scope of this chapter. However, putative factors include social networks, population density, crowding, stimulus overload, noise, urban malaise, social disintegration, social rigidity, social isolation, and social class (see Freeman, 1984, for an earlier comprehensive review, and other chapters in this book). The prevailing culture influences expected norms of crowding, personal space, noise levels, and aspirations. Stress is also linked through neuro-physiological mechanisms with physical ill-health, most notably heart disease (Stansfeld & Marmot, 2002). The stress-vulnerability hypothesis invokes stressors, be they life events, maladaptive psychological coping strategies, or physical illness, as factors contributing to mental disorders. Stress related to migration, mediated through vulnerabilities of individual personalities – some perhaps self-selected among migrants – may culminate in mental disorders. Thus, high risk-takers or those who are over-optimistic may be more likely to migrate, but may also make poorer decisions about employment, friendships, and coping with stressors. Of course, some who develop more severe mental disorders may be more likely to have been confident about travelling and taking risky decisions, with little thought of the consequences. Such an excesively optimistic outlook is not uncommon among people with manic disorders, characterized by grandiosity and excessively high goal-directed drives that can include travel (Akiskal & Benazzi, 2005). Certainly, the suggestion that mania may predispose people to migrate when in states of hyperactivity and poor reality testing is not a new one (see Freeman, 1984, pp. 331–332). My work in inner London with the homeless frequently brings me into contact with people with long-standing manic disorders, though with their personality remaining relatively intact, so that they can still function. However, their life histories are characterized by travels across the globe, sometimes with rather heroic stories of stowing away on ships and planes, perhaps for over a decade.

Migration and mental illness: the UK literature

Migration and the genesis of psychoses and neuroses

The earliest formal research study of migration and psychiatric disorder focused on severe mental illness, particularly schizophrenia. Odegaard (1932) found that the treated incidence of schizophrenia among Norwegians migrating to

Minnesota before the 1930s was twice as high as that among native-born Americans or the general population of Norway. The raised incidence occurred some ten years after migration and not in the immediate post-migration period. Odegaard concluded that Norwegians with a schizoid character were more likely to migrate, though Rosenthal *et al.* (1974) concluded that people with schizophrenia were less likely to do so. As mentioned above, severe mental illness when characterized by manic symptoms may explain increased migration, and recent evidence suggests that manic mental states are more common among some ethnic groups with mental illness (Kirov & Murray, 1999; Mukherjee *et al.*, 1983).

Studies of mental illness among ethnic minorities usually utilize data from service contacts (Bhui & Bhugra, 2002a; Bhugra & Bhui, 2001; Sharpley *et al.*, 2001). The incidence of schizophrenia in the Caribbean appears to be substantially lower or the same as that among African-Caribbeans in Britain (Bhugra *et al.*, 1997). While African-Caribbean people living in the UK have higher rates of schizophrenia than the indigenous white population, this effect is more marked in the second generation. These data suggest that genetic–biological inheritance alone is insufficient as an explanation. Similarly, other biological factors such as obstetric complications, *in-utero* viral infection, and birth complications are no more prevalent among African-Caribbean groups in Britain. South Asian groups have not shown such high rates of schizophrenia, but some studies suggest that similar trends to those in the African-Caribbean population may be emerging among them (King *et al.*, 1994). Immigrant status may confer particular disadvantages on specific groups, as discussed above, but their resiliency, intermediate steps in the causal pathways, and moderating risk factors can operate in the other direction. Social support mechanisms, social cohesion, and financial success may all contribute. These may explain the different levels of mental disorders found across ethnic groups, but to date there is no coherent general model of migration and mental illness that can accommodate these differences in predictable and replicable ways. In part, the lack of data reflects difficulties of classifying different degrees and types of mental disorder in varying populations. An additional problem is the lack of agreed operational definitions of 'social cohesion', 'acculturation', 'neighbourhood support', and even 'discrimination'. Any such definition carries the assumption that it applies to all cultural groups equally, and to all forms of migration. In fact, migration typologies are multiple and overlapping, rather than being discrete entities that are easily mapped on to definitions of mental illness or adjustment experiences.

African-Caribbean people are also more likely to be detained in hospital against their will, and treated under the provisions of the Mental Health Act during their contact with services, compared with other ethnic groups. The higher rates of schizophrenia were put forward to explain a greater use of legal compulsion, but more recent studies have shown that even among all those with a psychosis and in contact with mental health services, non-white people are more likely to be detained under the Act (Davies *et al.*, 1996). If such detention is more likely, the question remains why this should be so. Are there communication difficulties that culminate in decisions to detain, or are assessments affected by cultural issues such as trust, perceived stigma, and fear of mental health services? If there is less empathy or poorer communication and uncertainty about the risks encountered in the assessment, these will affect the quality of mental health assessment and management plans. This of course will affect judgements about the suitability of compulsory or voluntary treatments.

Is language an issue? Most African-Caribbean people speak English, although maybe with an accent. Is the presence of accent alone sufficient to remove empathy, or are remnants of accent, alongside differences in racial appearance, and a lack of knowledge of 'the other', sufficient to lead to a lack of empathy?

Another possibility is that the actual presentation of mental distress is associated with more 'escape behaviour' that is responded to with detention under the Act. Escape behaviour may be understandable in terms of a history of oppression, and efforts to assert individual autonomy and independence. If unjust decisions are feared as an everyday reality, then such behaviour can be rationally understood. It is widely reported that black people fear mental health services, but that service providers also fear black people (Sainsbury Centre for Mental Health, 2002). Socially excluded groups may fear loss of what little autonomy they have, especially if they fear the consequence of 'mental hospital' and police involvement. Another explanation is that there are more paranoid presentations among African-Caribbeans (Littlewood & Lipsedge, 1988), and these may involve professional efforts being invested with malevolent intent, thus leading to escape behaviour and a lack of co-operation with suggested treatment plans. Each of these may operate to reduce civil liberties and sustain notions of pathology of the migrant, especially where racial stereotypes abound.

A final possibility is that clinicians are unable to convince themselves that their African-Caribbean patients will adhere to the treatment plan voluntarily, and perceive greater risks than in a comparable situation with white patients. In support of this explanation, a vignette study concluded that British pychiatrists were not 'racist', but that they were more likely to label black people in the vignettes as being violent, in comparison with white people (Lewis *et al.*, 1990). This may arise from a real and informed reluctance by potential patients to accept psychiatric interventions that are feared by the public; it might also reflect insufficient empathy or attunement in the clinical encounter. A possibly more troubling explanation is that the manifestations of distress found among African-Caribbean people, such as more religious presentations, perhaps more paranoid symptoms, and even first-rank symptoms, are not as specific to schizophrenia as they would be in a white English-speaking patient (Ndetei, 1988; Ndetei & Vadher, 1984). However, this explanation is contested, one study showing diagnostic consistency over a 13-year follow-up (Takei *et al.*, 1998), while another showed that African-Caribbeans with a diagnosis of schizophrenia have a better prognosis (McKenzie *et al.*, 1995). Nonetheless, recovery is influenced by the culture in which the patient lives (Harrison *et al.*, 2001) and the sorts of psychoses developed by different ethnic and cultural groups are not necessarily the same, in terms of prognosis, as those among the white majority.

The notion of brief reactive psychoses being more prevalent among migrant and minority groups is under question, but these probably do not explain the higher rates of non-affective psychosis found among some groups of African-Caribbeans (Takei *et al.*, 1998).

We recently completed a systematic review of studies examining ethnicity and access to services in the UK (Bhui *et al.*, 2003). South Asians required less use of the Mental Health Act and were admitted for shorter periods than either white or black patients. A few studies were found to have investigated the presentation and assessment of mental health problems among ethnic minorities in primary care. These suggest a differing pattern of assessments and referral to specialist services by GPs depending on the ethnic and cultural origin of the patient (Bhui & Bhugra, 2002a). The only population-based study recruiting sufficient numbers of ethnic minority members shows that the prevalence of psychoses (on a screening instrument) among African-Caribbean people is almost twice that found among white people, and that this excess is confined to women (Nazroo, 1997). This contrasts sharply with the service-based data, which show an incidence of schizophrenia between 6 and 13 times higher. Thus, there is a marked discrepancy between rates from population-based and service-based studies. This suggests that there are service-related factors that specifically increase the numbers of African-Caribbean patients, in contrast with white patients. This finding is not explained by immigration, even though studies on migrants in other countries have also found higher rates of admission and treatment episodes for immigrants. However, white migrants to Jamaica do not have a higher incidence of schizophrenia (Hickling, 1996), but they do experience better than average social conditions on settlement there. Schrier *et al.* (2001) found that the treated prevalence of schizophrenia in Holland was highest among men from Surinam and Morocco and in women from Surinam, Antilles, and Cape Verde. Another Dutch study found higher rates of schizophrenia, schizophreniform disorder or schizo-affective disorder for those born in Morocco, Surinam, Antilles, and other non-Western countries. Again, these studies were based on service-use data, and so may reflect hospital and specialist service engagement for immigrants, compared with more primary care service interventions delivered for other groups, presumably with success.

A meta-analysis of the effect sizes for data showing a relationship between migration and incident schizophrenia, published between 1977 and 2003, indicated that a personal or family history of migration was an important risk factor for schizophrenia. 'The differential risk pattern across subgroups suggests a role for psychosocial adversity in the etiology of schizophrenia' (Cantor-Graae & Selten, 2005). Cooper (2005) gives a balanced review of socio-economic factors interacting with migration experiences to produce potentially higher risks of mental disorders among immigrants. However, although the literature reviewed suggests that social factors are important in the generation of schizophreniform states, specifically social class, the specific factors that might cause schizophrenia among African-Caribbean immigrants remain uncertain. African-Caribbean immigrants were not necessarily poor when they first migrated, but may become so in the face of thwarted aspirations. However, why should poor African-Caribbean people of the second and subsequent generations have a higher risk of schizophrenia than poor white British people? There must be risk factors specific to status as African-Caribbean people, perhaps 'lower social status' and obstacles faced by those who are racially different. This suggests a unique role for racial and culturally specific risk factors such as discrimination, racism, isolation, and ethnic density. These are discussed below.

Ethnic density has also been linked to rates of psychosis among immigrants, a higher density of the same ethnic group conferring some protection (Boydell *et al.*, 2001). Therefore, migrants who arrive in the UK and resettle within the vicinity of people from their own country are likely to be less vulnerable to psychosis. Although understood as a population-density phenomenon, this effect may be mediated by social cohesion, since familiarity with people around can lead to a sense of belonging again. Sustaining one's own cultural mores is easier if there is a critical mass of people who share the same values and lifestyles.

Common mental disorders: psychoses or neuroses?

Part of the problem within any analysis of vulnerability to psychosis among migrants is that psychoses are not uniform in their genesis or prognosis and are mostly considered to be remarkably abnormal experiences. Yet interpersonal sensitivity, ideas of reference, and transient paranoia occur, for example, in states of sensory deprivation (Cooper, 1976; Hayashi *et al.*, 1992; Kennedy *et al.*, 1994), but also in the early stages of migration during the period of culture shock. Being unable to communicate, have needs met, find employment, or secure a safe home may all feed interpersonal suspicion; in a sense, this serves as a protective mechanism. If psychosis is then seen as a common phenomenon, but spiralling into persistence in the face of adversity, social factors can be plausible aetiological candidates (van Os *et al.*, 1999; Verdoux *et al.*, 2003). Thus adverse life events, perceived discrimination, and poor self-esteem, with little social support, may all lead to the persistence of what would otherwise be transient self-limiting disorders (Chakraborty & McKenzie, 2002). This proposition is more easily accepted for depressive and neurotic conditions, but meets with resistance when put forward to explain psychoses. In part, this is due to the gravity assigned to the presence of psychotic phenomena in Euro-American societies. Psychosis is seen as a disorder that emerges as an illness with a natural history of its own, and with a fixed set of aetiological attributes and prognostic indicators. In some other societies, 'psychoses' – especially transient episodes – are considered less severe, not necessarily pathological, and as having cultural meaning (Sharpley *et al.*, 2001).

Western notions of normality aver that we exist in an embodied self, and experiences that violate these boundaries, such as thoughts being put into the mind or hearing voices from outside the head, are abnormal. In societies with less emphasis on individual autonomy, and more diffuse boundaries between the supernatural and the earthly world, such phenomena may be considered within the normal range of experience. Persistence of psychosis, related to a loss of function, would then locate such phenomena to the realms of abnormality. Despite these reservations, most societies do recognize 'madness' as existing and being an illness, with specific local explanatory models of how it should be treated (Patel, 1995). The disabilities associated with psychosis, where this is chronic, are substantial. Industrialized nations emphasize individual self-sufficiency, productivity, and employment, but these expectations also vary according to the nation, society, and culture within which disability arises. This may explain the better prognosis found among people who develop psychoses in developing countries, where such demands are not so prominent, and there is more tolerance of less individual economic productivity. In Eastern societies, even in the presence of disability, individuals may experience more social support from families and friends, who invoke fewer attributions of pathology. These considerations are especially relevant when considering the plight of migrants who had developed a mental illness before immigration, and then find themselves facing even greater demands, while being less able to meet those demands.

The bulk of the research evidence has reported that depression and anxiety are less common among South Asian and African-Caribbean people than among whites, although more recent work suggests that significant measurement errors due to the cultural bias of current instruments may be responsible. Though two surveys in Rawalpindi and the Himalayas reported high rates of mental disorder among Pakistani peoples (Mumford *et al.*, 1997, 2000), most studies in the UK have indicated a lower prevalence of anxiety and depression among Pakistani and Bangladeshi peoples (Bhui, 1999). These people share a religion, but are also the poorest and perhaps the most traditional of the South Asian communities. Again, measurement problems might be very prominent among the most traditional societies, but this does not explain the findings in Pakistan (Mumford *et al.*, 1997, 2000). Nazroo (1997) suggested that English-speaking South Asians had profiles of common mental disorders that more closely resembled the findings among white Britons than those of other immigrants. It would be surprising if measurement problems alone account for the lower prevalence estimates in the UK, since interviewers were matched for language, ethnicity, and gender. Another possibility is that there are genuinely lower rates of disorder among these groups, or that despite the onset of more depressive and anxious episodes, these communities are more resilient, due to better social cohesion and support from a more traditional and religious cultural lifestyle (Sproston & Bhui, 2002). We know that mental distress is shaped by the cultural milieu and that expectations of treatment, part of the individual's explanatory model of distress, determine the form or subjective construction of the experience (Bhui & Bhugra, 2002b). This in turn will shape the form in which mental distress becomes manifest. For example, the higher rates of deliberate self-harm among South Asian women may be explained by similar representations of distress in Asian cultures, for example, in cinema and Indian mythology.

Poor conditions for migrants. Shanty town built by Bulgarian immigrants, Paris, 2006 (used with permission of Paul Cooper/Rex Features).

Specific risk factors and future research

Cultural identity and protective factors

The assimilation perspective that historically has dominated policies on immigration urges that new immigrants adopt the practices and beliefs of host society. That is, they give up their own beliefs and practices to adopt those in the host country. In part, this is an understandable requisite to function effectively in another country. Thus language acquisition, knowledge of local economies, and networks of potential business partners and customers demand considerable acquaintance with the host community. In the meantime, that community learns about the immigrants and adopts certain of their foods, dress, and practices, perhaps even envying the family cohesion of South Asian people, while being particularly critical of single mothers among African-Caribbean groups. The assimilation agenda makes great demands on immigrants to give up their preferred historical and identity-nurturing ways of living for unfamiliar practices. Coupled with discrimination and poorer social conditions for black and ethnic minorities, this situation encourages minorities to continue to hold on to cherished sources of cohesion and support. However, the children of migrants, as well as some first-generation migrants themselves, have adopted other solutions including bicultural proficiencies. Berry (1980) suggested that the assimilation option of 'identity change' was not reflecting real life events. He described four identity types: (i) marginalized, being associated with neither host nor own culture; (ii) traditional, among those who remain strongly identified only with their own culture; (iii) assimilated, among those who have given up their own culture; and (iv) bicultural, where people are strongly identified both with their own and with host cultures. The existence of the last group shows that the assumption that one must adopt a new cultural lifestyle by giving up the old is unnecessary. Cultures which are more similar, e.g. English and French, will clearly offer the possibility of developing bicultural proficiency more quickly than two that are markedly different, e.g. Somali and English.

Cultural identity and associated changes in social support, world view, and coping responses may explain why some ethnic groups have lower reported rates of mental illness despite socio-economic disadvantages. Bangladeshi people in the UK (Nazroo, 1997), Mexican-born immigrants to the USA (Escobar *et al.*, 2000; Holman *et al.*, 2000), and immigrant children to Australia (Davies & McKelvey, 1998) are examples of deprived populations who have such lower rates. The reasons for this include traditionalism, which protects against the potential mediating influence of substance misuse (Alderete *et al.*, 2000; Escobar *et al.*, 2000). Although some studies contend that migration is not related to psychological morbidity (Klimidis *et al.*, 1994), the majority show a significant effect (Ritsner *et al.*, 1996). The problem may be partly that the classification of migration-related mental disorder is not straightforward, because of cultural factors that influence its expression and detection. For example, Bauer and Priebe (1994) could not always assign definite diagnoses to migrants in Germany. Alternatively, as mentioned above, some psychological phenomena that are part of an adaptive process during migration may be interpreted as psychopathologies. Migrants may also be vulnerable to continuing psychological problems, even on return to their home country. For example, Tseng *et al.* (1993) found that over one-fifth of Asians who migrated from China to Taiwan developed psychiatric complications, mainly depression, when returning for a brief unexpected visit. Hickling (1991) showed that black migrants returning to Jamaica had higher rates of mental hospitalization than controls. Moilanen and Myhrman (1989) studied school-age children and adolescents who had returned from Sweden to Finland between 1984 and 1985. These subjects more often lacked a father than did the controls, and returning migrant boys more often had psychiatric disorders in their teachers' estimations than did the controls, but no such difference was found among the girls. Reviewing the literature on migration and mental health among adolescents, this research group concluded:

> When successful adaptation is not achieved, acculturative stress may arise and somatic or mental disorders may develop. The finding of individual differences in people's responses to environmental conditions has led to a search for vulnerability factors that increase people's susceptibility to

stressors and for buffering influences that serve a protecting function under the same circumstances.

(Moilanen & Myhrman, 1989)

This captures the necessary complexity of any model attempting to summarize the main factors that account for mental illness among migrants. In a related paper, Vuorenkoski *et al.* (2000) concluded that successful adaptation is contingent on effective use of two main languages – the parent tongue and the language of the host country. A striking finding was that children who spoke to their parents in one language and their friends in another were healthier and performed better on language tests at school. However, those speaking both Swedish and Finnish to their mothers, having no single parental language, were at higher risk of depression and somatic symptoms. Those who spoke to parents in one language, and whose parents spoke back to them in a different one, were more at risk of antisocial behaviour. Although these issues could be reduced to factors common to good parenting, for example, communication and containment, migration does introduce new languages and challenges to both children and parents. Through language use, therefore, migration may either increase or reduce vulnerability to mental health problems. Any identity crisis following migration will be shaped by and expressed through the use of specific languages.

Protective factors for migration-related mental disorder include family relationships, peer relationships, verbalization ability, cognitive abilities, assertiveness, school achievement, and clear linguistic identity (Moilanen & Myhrman, 1989). Marriage, female gender, absence of traumatic events (Holman *et al.*, 2000), professional occupations, satisfaction with family, having children and friendships (Koh, 1998) are all protective. A buffering social environment is also protective; for example, white mentally ill immigrants to Jamaica move to higher social class positions faster than in their home countries (Hickling, 1996). Previous knowledge of English among Greek Cypriots in London was found to be an important protective factor (Mavreas & Bebbington, 1990). Although employment is protective, the conditions of employment are more critical for migrant mental well-being. Thus, Rosmond *et al.* (1996) found that immigrants employed in Sweden were more affected by impaired working conditions than local non-immigrants in similar types of employment. Thus, risk factors may not be universally important for both migrant and non-migrant groups, and depending on the context of migration, may actually be differentially significant for different groups of immigrants.

Little is written on personality and ethnicity. This may arise because judgements of abnormal personality require more care when applied across cultures, thus deterring the assignment of such labels. In addition, there may be actual differences in socially defined abnormalities of personality between different migrant groups. Shen *et al.* (1998) found obsessionality, interpersonal sensitivity, and phobias to be more common among migrant workers. The data pointed to a complex interaction between migration and resettlement experiences, conditions before and after migration, community resources, personal coping styles, and reactions to the migrant's group. Cultural identity shifts following migration may be expressions of adaptive paths taken by migrants irrespective of ethnic origin, or of material circumstances, or else may reflect personality attributes and preparedness for change. These variables offer one way of analysing the relationships between migration and psychological coping (Figure 7.1).

Refugees and asylum seekers

Refugees are especially vulnerable to psychiatric disorders including depression, suicidality, and PTSD (Gorst-Unsworth & Goldenberg, 1998; Ramsay *et al.*, 1993). The needs for health care are therefore significant. King *et al.* (1994), when measuring the incidence of psychosis among ethnic groups in North London, found that 11% of their hospital or community contact patients were refugees, compared to only 5% of the population of the catchment area. There is now more concerted research interest in tackling the inadequacies of existing diagnostic categories and models of mental disorders in relation to refugees and asylum seekers. For example, PTSD criteria are challenged as being applied too rigidly and not recognizing the existential and moral dilemmas facing refugees fleeing from war experiences. Similarly, some refugees, despite horrific experiences, appear to suffer less from formal psychiatric problems, so that there is a need to understand how they cope or why they do not develop more symptoms and functional disabilities. There are few data on refugee children and their rates of mental disorder. Children, either as victims or as passive observers of violence, are often neglected as a necessary focus of therapeutic attention, yet such neglect can result in PTSDs, depressive reactions, and somatic symptoms (Hodes, 1998). Children and adolescents in post-war situations can develop existential dilemmas of distrust. If not identified early, these problems can escalate into crises of identity and personality development.

Could migration simply be one of many possible stressors, which alone has some impact, but is not sufficient to cause mental illness? European networks investigating the subject recently proposed a 'Ulysses syndrome' to describe the experience of a state of multiple and chronic stressors that are not necessarily associated with depression and anxiety or any formal psychiatric illness (http://migra-salut-mental.org/Ulises/Ulysses%20text%202%20english-1.pdf or http://www.migrantwatch.org/Activities/PICUMHealthCareConfrep 2007-EN.pdf). However, social distress is evident, while bereavement, unemployment, and relationship problems form the backdrop against which residential instability then needs to be understood as an additional stressor.

Residential instability and urban environments

How does residential instability affect mental health? Is there a relationship between distances travelled and mental health, or between levels of deprivation and propensity to move house, or does deprivation trap individuals within

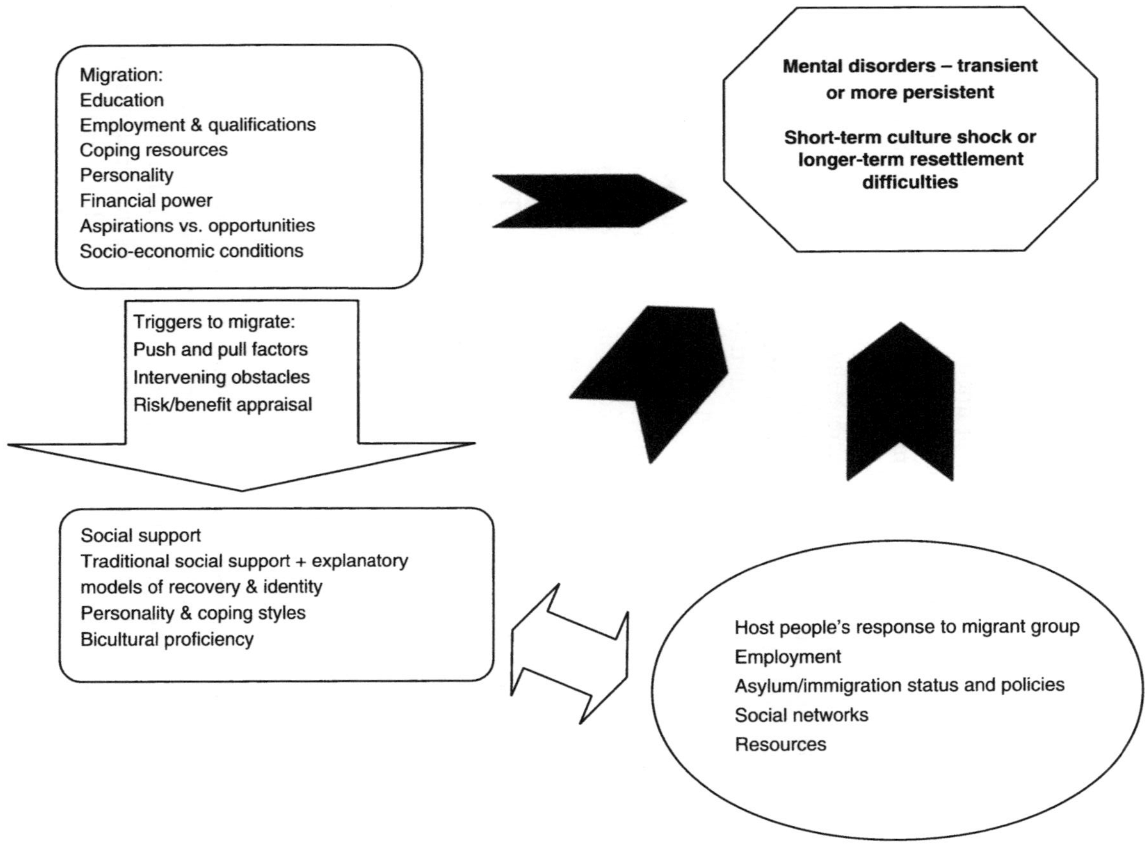

Figure 7.1 Complex variables that contribute to the risk of mental disorder among migrants.

aversive social environments? While these questions are important for internal migrants, international migrants may encounter specific pressures to move residence. For example, public housing may be the only accommodation available, and this may not offer much choice about place of residence. Public housing schemes are not renowned for quality of accommodation, safety or stability. Migrants may be more likely to continue to undergo substantial residential moves while searching for more settled accommodation in an area in which they feel safe, and into which they can integrate. Each residential move may be welcomed as an escape from intolerable living conditions in unsafe residential areas, alongside lack of opportunities to secure employment. Those spending more time at home, perhaps because of unemployment, are more likely to be affected by their accommodation and the area in which they live; there is no strong evidence for independent contextual risk factors for common mental disorders (Weich *et al.*, 2003a, 2003b; see Chapter 4).

People with mental illness are differentially distributed in urban areas and reside mainly in the inner city; both social drift and social causation have been proposed to explain this pattern (Giggs, 1986; Giggs & Cooper, 1987). The latter authors showed that the geographical distribution of foreign-born people with schizophrenia was different from that of native-born cases. It is known that most migrants live and work in inner-city areas, and 45% of the UK's minority ethnic groups are concentrated within the greater London area (Peach, 1996). These two sets of data suggest opposite constraints and forces on the internal migration of migrants, but more detailed research is necessary. An additional issue, not fully addressed in this chapter, is the higher level of international migration among migrants who make the UK their home. This includes holidays, but also regular cycles of visits to see family and friends in their countries of origin, so sustaining some contact with the homeland, and some allegiance to traditional values. Future work will need to concentrate more carefully on such variables, to increase our limited understanding of migration processes and mental health.

Discrimination and prejudice

One social risk factor proposed to explain country-to-country variability in the frequency of mental disorders is prejudice and discrimination. Discrimination is associated with common mental disorders (Bhui *et al.*, 2005) and may be manifest not only as directly prejudicial attitudes, but also in thwarted aspirations. These occur despite migrants' efforts to overcome obstacles to employment, education, improved status, and general well-being in a new community. For some, each residential move may be perceived as a forced event, from a place that, despite its faults, does feel like 'home'. Refugees to London, for example, often seek out people from their country of origin, but may be required to move to other parts of the UK in order to share the costs of care. However, other more remote parts of the country are isolated from familiar cultural landmarks and sources of support such as friendships, voluntary organizations, and communities that are familiar with and tolerant of diversity. The processes that make up perceived discrimination experiences and the pathways to poor mental health need further mapping and investigation, especially using longitudinal study designs.

Conclusions

Thus, migration is associated with mental illness through many pathways; people who migrate or people who develop mental illness are not all so similar that all risk factors and influences can be captured by a single neat theory. Typologies of migration, including motivations, interact with conditions and circumstances of migration and the post-migration period. These events are important because of the stress associated with migration in general, and the stressors associated specifically with certain migration histories, for example among refugees. Individual variables such as personality, religious beliefs, and coping strategies can moderate the impact of stressors. However, for those in unfortunate circumstances that perpetuate their distress, and if such stressors are sustained, there can be more permanent and major changes to personality and ability to recover. Candidate risk factors include cultural identity, discrimination, traumatic experiences, and within-country residential mobility, as well as migration across continents.

References

Akiskal, H. S. and Benazzi, F. (2005) 'Toward a clinical delineation of dysphoric hypomania – operational and conceptual dilemmas'. *Bipolar Disorder*, *7*, 456–464.

Alderete, E., Vega, W. A., Kolody, B. and Aguilar-Gaxiola, S. (2000) 'Lifetime prevalence of and risk factors for psychiatric disorders among Mexican migrant farmworkers in California'. *American Journal of Public Health*, *90*, 608–614.

Bauer, M. and Priebe, S. (1994) 'Psychopathology and long-term adjustment after crises in refugees from East Germany'. *International Journal of Social Psychiatry*, *40*, 165–176.

Beliappa J. (1991) *Illness or distress*. London: Confederation of Indian Organisations.

Berry, J. W. (1980) 'Acculturation as varieties of adaptation', in Padilla, A. M. (ed.), *Theory, models and some findings* (pp. 9–26). Boulder, CO: Westview.

Bhugra, D. and Bhui, K. (2001) *Cross-cultural psychiatry: A practical guide*. London: Arnold.

Bhugra, D., Leff, J., Mallett, R., Der, G., Corridan, B. and Rudge, S. (1997) 'Incidence and outcome of schizophrenia in whites, African-Caribbeans and Asians in London'. *Psychological Medicine*, *27*, 791–798.

Bhui, K. (1999) 'Common mental disorders among people with origins in or immigrant from India and Pakistan'. *International Review of Psychiatry*, *11*, 136–144.

Bhui, K. and Bhugra, D. (2002a) 'Mental illness in black and Asian ethnic minorities: pathways to care and outcomes'. *Advances in Psychiatric Treatment*, *8*, 26–33.

Bhui, K. and Bhugra, D. (2002b) 'Explanatory models for mental distress: implications for clinical practice and research'. *British Journal of Psychiatry*, *181*, 6–7.

Bhui, K., Stansfeld, S., Hull, S., Priebe, S., Mole, F. and Feder, G. (2003) 'Ethnic variations in pathways to and use of specialist mental health services in the UK: systematic review'. *British Journal of Psychiatry*, *182*, 105–116.

Bhui, K., Stansfeld, S., McKenzie, K., Karlsen, S., Nazroo, J. and Weich, S. (2005) 'Racial/ethnic discrimination and common mental disorders among workers: findings from the EMPIRIC Study of Ethnic Minority Groups in the United Kingdom'. *American Journal of Public Health, 95*, 496–501.

Black, R., Fielding, T., King, R., Skeldon, R. and Tiemoki, R. (2003) *Longitudinal studies: An insight into current studies and the social and economic outcomes for migrants*. Brighton, UK: Sussex Centre for Migration Research, University of Sussex.

Boydell, J., van Os, J., McKenzie, K., Allardyce, J., Goel, R., McCreadie, R. G. and Murray, R. M. (2001) 'Incidence of schizophrenia in ethnic minorities in London: ecological study into interactions with environment'. *British Medical Journal, 323*, 1336–1338.

Cantor-Graae, E. and Selten, J. P. (2005) 'Schizophrenia and migration: a meta-analysis and review'. *American Journal of Psychiatry, 162*, 12–24.

Castles, S., Korac, M., Vasta, E. and Vertovec, S. (2002) *Integration: Mapping the field*. London: Home Office Immigration Research and Statistics Service (IRSS).

Chakraborty, A. and McKenzie, K. (2002) 'Does racial discrimination cause mental illness?'. *British Journal of Psychiatry, 180*, 475–477.

Cooper, A. F. (1976) 'Deafness and psychiatric illness'. *British Journal of Psychiatry, 129*, 216–226.

Cooper, B. (2005) 'Immigration and schizophrenia: the social causation hypothesis revisited'. *British Journal of Psychiatry, 186*, 361–363.

Davies, L. C. and McKelvey, R. S. (1998) 'Emotional and behavioural problems and competencies among immigrant and non-immigrant adolescents'. *Australian and New Zealand Journal of Psychiatry, 32*, 658–665.

Davies, S., Thornicroft, G., Leese, M., Higginbotham, A. and Phelan, M. (1996) 'Ethnic differences in risk of compulsory psychiatric admission among representative cases of psychosis in London'. *British Medical Journal, 312*, 533–537.

Dobson, J., Koser, K., McLaughlin, G. and Salt, J. (2001) *International migration and the United Kingdom: Recent patterns and trends*. Research Development and Statistics Directorate Occasional Paper No. 75. London: Home Office.

Dustmann, C., Gabbri, F., Preston, I. and Wadsworth, J. (2003) *Labour market performance of immigrants in the UK labour market*. London: Home Office.

Escobar, J. I., Hoyos, N. C. and Gara, M. A. (2000) 'Immigration and mental health: Mexican Americans in the United States'. *Harvard Review of Psychiatry, 8*, 64–72.

Freeman, H. (1972) 'Mental health and new communities', in Nossiter, T., Hanson, A. and Rokkan, S. (eds), *Imagination and precision in the social sciences* (pp. 181–209). London: Faber and Faber.

Freeman, H. (1984) *Mental health and the environment*. London: Churchill Livingstone.

Furnham, A. and Bockner, S. (1986) *Culture shock: Psychological reactions to unfamiliar environments*. London: Methuen.

Giggs, J. A. (1986) 'Mental disorders and ecological structure in Nottingham'. *Social Science and Medicine, 23*, 945–961.

Giggs, J. A. and Cooper, J. E. (1987) 'Ecological structure and the distribution of schizophrenia and affective psychoses in Nottingham'. *British Journal of Psychiatry, 151*, 627–633.

Gorst-Unsworth, C. and Goldenberg, E. (1998) 'Psychological sequelae of torture and organised violence suffered by refugees from Iraq: trauma-related factors compared with social factors in exile'. *British Journal of Psychiatry, 172*, 90–94.

Greenwood, M. and Hunt, G. L. (2003) 'The early history of migration'. *International Regional Science Review, 26,* 3–37.

Guinness, P. (2002) *Migration.* London: Hodder & Stoughton.

Harrison, G., Hopper, K., Craig, T., Laska, E., Siegel, C., Wanderling, J., Dube, K. C., Ganev, K., Giel, R., Van der Heiden, W., Holmberg, S. K., Janca, A., Lee, P. W., Leon, C. A., Malhotra, S., Marsella, A. J., Nakane, Y., Sartorius, N., Shen, Y., Skoda, C., Thara, R., Tsirkin, S. J., Varma, V. K., Walsh, D. and Wiersma, D. (2001) 'Recovery from psychotic illness: a 15- and 25-year international follow-up study'. *British Journal of Psychiatry, 178,* 506–517.

Hayashi, M., Morikawa, T. and Hori, T. (1992) 'EEG alpha activity and hallucinatory experience during sensory deprivation'. *Perceptual and Motor Skills, 75,* 403–412.

Hickling, F. W. (1991) 'Double jeopardy: psychopathology of black mentally ill returned migrants to Jamaica'. *International Journal of Social Psychiatry, 37,* 80–89.

Hickling, F. W. (1996) 'Psychopathology of white mentally ill immigrants to Jamaica'. *Molecular and Chemical Neuropathology, 28,* 261–268.

Hodes, M. (1998) 'Refugee children'. *British Medical Journal, 316,* 793–794.

Holman, E. A., Silver, R. C. and Waitzkin, H. (2000) 'Traumatic life events in primary care patients: a study in an ethnically diverse sample'. *Archives of Family Medicine, 9,* 802–810.

Kennedy, B. R., Williams, C. A. and Pesut, D. J. (1994) 'Hallucinatory experiences of psychiatric patients in seclusion'. *Archives of Psychiatric Nursing, 8,* 169–176.

King, M., Coker, E., Leavey, G., Hoare, A. and Johnson–Sabine, E. (1994) 'Incidence of psychotic illness in London: comparison of ethnic groups'. *British Medical Journal, 309,* 1115–1119.

Kirmayer, L. J. (1992) 'Cross cultural measures of functional somatic symptoms'. *Transcultural Psychiatric Research Review, 29,* 37–45.

Kirov, G. and Murray, R. M. (1999) 'Ethnic differences in the presentation of bipolar affective disorder'. *European Psychiatry, 14,* 199–204.

Klimidis, S., Stuart, G., Minas, I. H. and Ata, A. W. (1994) 'Immigrant status and gender effects on psychopathology and self-concept in adolescents: a test of the migration-morbidity hypothesis'. *Comprehensive Psychiatry, 35,* 393–404.

Koh, K. B. (1998) 'Perceived stress, psychopathology, and family support in Korean immigrants and non-immigrants'. *Yonsei Medical Journal, 39,* 214–221.

Lee, E. S. (1966) 'Theory of migration'. *Demography, 3,* 347–357.

Lewis, G., Croft-Jeffreys, C. and David, A. (1990) 'Are British psychiatrists racist?'. *British Journal of Psychiatry, 157,* 410–415.

Littlewood, R. and Lipsedge, M. (1988) 'Psychiatric illness among British Afro-Caribbeans'. *British Medical Journal, 297,* 135–136.

Mavreas, V. and Bebbington, P. (1990) 'Acculturation and psychiatric disorder: a study of Greek Cypriot immigrants'. *Psychological Medicine, 20,* 941–951.

McKenzie, K., van Os, J., Fahy, T., Jones, P., Harvey, I., Toone, B. and Murray, R. (1995) 'Psychosis with good prognosis in Afro-Caribbean people now living in the United Kingdom'. *British Medical Journal, 311,* 1325–1328.

Migration News (2002) 'Foreign born, poverty & education'. *Migration News, 9,* 1.

Moilanen, I. and Myhrman, A. (1989) 'What protects a child during migration?'. *Scandinavian Journal of Social Medicine, 17,* 21–24.

Mukherjee, S., Shukla, S., Woodle, J., Rosen, A. M. and Olarte, S. (1983) 'Misdiagnosis of schizophrenia in bipolar patients: a multiethnic comparison'. *American Journal of Psychiatry, 140,* 1571–1574.

Mumford, D. B. (1989) 'Somatic sensations and psychological distress among students in Britain and Pakistan'. *Social Psychiatry and Psychiatric Epidemiology, 24*, 321–326.

Mumford, D. B. (1998) 'The measurement of culture shock'. *Social Psychiatry and Psychiatric Epidemiology, 33*, 149–154.

Mumford, D. B., Minhas, F. A., Akhtar, I., Akhter, S. and Mubbashar, M. H. (2000) 'Stress and psychiatric disorder in urban Rawalpindi: community survey'. *British Journal of Psychiatry, 177*, 557–562.

Mumford, D. B., Saeed, K., Ahmad, I., Latif, S. and Mubbashar, M. H. (1997) 'Stress and psychiatric disorder in rural Punjab: a community survey'. *British Journal of Psychiatry, 170*, 473–478.

Nazroo, J. (1997) *Ethnicity and mental health*. London: Policy Studies Institute.

Ndetei, D. M. (1988) 'Psychiatric phenomenology across countries: constitutional, cultural, or environmental?' *Acta Psychiatrica Scandinavica Supplementum, 344*, 33–44.

Ndetei, D. M. and Vadher, A. (1984) 'A comparative cross-cultural study of the frequencies of hallucination in schizophrenia'. *Acta Psychiatrica Scandinavica, 70*, 545–549.

Odegaard, O. (1932) 'Emigration and insanity: a study of mental disease among the Norwegian born population of Minnesota'. *Acta Psychiatrica Neurologica*, Suppl. IV, 1–206.

Patel, V. (1995) 'Spiritual distress: an indigenous model of nonpsychotic mental illness in primary care in Harare, Zimbabwe'. *Acta Psychiatrica Scandinavica, 92*, 103–107.

Peach, C. (1996) *Ethnicity in the 1991 census, volume 2: The ethnic minority populations of Great Britain*. London: HMSO.

Piccinelli, M. and Simon, G. (1997) 'Gender and cross-cultural differences in somatic symptoms associated with emotional distress: an international study in primary care'. *Psychological Medicine, 27*, 433–444.

Platt, L. (2003) *Poverty among ethnic minority groups in Britain*. London: Child Poverty Action Group.

Putnam, R. (2000) *Bowling alone: The collapse and revival of American community*. New York: Simon & Schuster.

Ramsay, R., Gorst-Unsworth, C. and Turner, S. (1993) 'Psychiatric morbidity in survivors of organised state violence including torture: a retrospective series'. *British Journal of Psychiatry, 162*, 55–59.

Ravenstein, E. G. (1876) 'The birthplace of the people and the laws of migration'. *The Geographical Magazine, 3*, 173–177.

Ravenstein, E. G. (1885) 'The laws of migration'. *Journal of the Royal Statistical Society, 48*, 167–235.

Ravenstein, E. G. (1889) 'The laws of migration'. *Journal of the Royal Statistical Society, 52*, 241–305.

Rieu, E. V. (1946) *Homer: The Odyssey*. Harmondsworth, UK: Penguin Books.

Ritsner, M., Ponizovsky, A., Chemelevsky, M., Zetser, F., Durst, R. and Ginath, Y. (1996) 'Effects of immigration on the mentally ill – does it produce psychological distress?'. *Comprehensive Psychiatry, 37*, 17–22.

Rosenthal, D., Goldberg, I., Jacobsen, B., Wender, P. H., Kety, S. S., Schulsinger, F. and Eldred, C. A. (1974) 'Migration, heredity, and schizophrenia'. *Psychiatry, 37*, 321–339.

Rosmond, R., Lapidus, L. and Bjorntorp, P. (1996) 'A comparative review of psychosocial and occupational environment in native Swedes and immigrants'. *Scandinavian Journal of Social Medicine, 24*, 237–242.

Said, E. (1983) *The world, the text, and the critic*. Cambridge, MA: Harvard University Press.

Sainsbury Centre for Mental Health (2002) *Breaking the circles of fear*. London: Sainsbury Centre for Mental Health.

Schrier, A. C., van de Wetering, B. J., Mulder, P. G. and Selten, J. P. (2001) 'Point prevalence of schizophrenia in immigrant groups in Rotterdam: data from outpatient facilities'. *European Psychiatry*, *16*, 162–166.

Sharpley, M., Hutchinson, G., McKenzie, K. and Murray, R. M. (2001) 'Understanding the excess of psychosis among the African-Caribbean population in England: review of current hypotheses'. *British Journal of Psychiatry Supplement*, *40*, s60–s68.

Shen, Q., Lu, Y. W., Hu, C. Y., Deng, X. M., Gao, H., Huang, X. Q. and Niu, E. H. (1998) 'A preliminary study of the mental health of young migrant workers in Shenzhen'. *Psychiatry and Clinical Neurosciences*, *52*, S370–S373.

Sproston, K. and Bhui, K. (2002) 'Coping mechanisms', in O'Connor, W. and Nazroo, J. (eds), *Ethnic differences in the context and experience of psychiatric illness: A qualitative study* (pp. 41–50). London: National Centre for Social Research.

Stansfeld, S. and Marmot, M. (2002) *Stress and the heart: Psychosocial pathways to coronary heart disease*. London: British Medical Journal Books.

Takei, N., Persaud, R., Woodruff, P., Brockington, I. and Murray, R. M. (1998) 'First episodes of psychosis in Afro-Caribbean and White people: an 18-year follow-up population-based study'. *British Journal of Psychiatry*, *172*, 147–153.

Tseng, W. S., Cheng, T. A., Chen, Y. S., Hwang, P. L. and Hsu, J. (1993) 'Psychiatric complications of family reunion after four decades of separation'. *American Journal of Psychiatry*, *150*, 614–619.

van Os, J., Verdoux, H., Maurice-Tison, S., Gay, B., Liraud, F., Salamon, R. and Bourgeois, M. (1999) 'Self-reported psychosis-like symptoms and the continuum of psychosis'. *Social Psychiatry and Psychiatric Epidemiology*, *34*, 459–463.

Verdoux, H., Sorbara, F., Gindre, C., Swendsen, J. D. and van Os, J. (2003) 'Cannabis use and dimensions of psychosis in a nonclinical population of female subjects'. *Schizophrenia Research*, *59*, 77–84.

Vuorenkoski, L., Kuure, O., Moilanen, I., Penninkilampi, V. and Myhrman, A. (2000) 'Bilingualism, school achievement, and mental wellbeing: a follow-up study of return migrant children'. *Journal of Child Psychology and Psychiatry*, *41*, 261–266.

Watters, C. (2002) 'Migration and mental healthcare in Europe'. *Journal of Ethnic and Migration Studies*, *28*, 153–172.

Weich, S., Holt, G., Twigg, L., Jones, K. and Lewis, G. (2003a) 'Geographic variation in the prevalence of common mental disorders in Britain: a multilevel investigation'. *American Journal of Epidemiology*, *157*, 730–737.

Weich, S., Twigg, L., Holt, G., Lewis, G. and Jones, K. (2003b) 'Contextual risk factors for the common mental disorders in Britain: a multilevel investigation of the effects of place'. *Journal of Epidemiology and Community Health*, *57*, 616–621.

Zelinsky, W. (1971) 'The hypothesis of the mobility transition'. *The Geographical Review*, *61*, 219–249.

8 Housing and mental health

Hugh Freeman

From the common-sense point of view, housing seems to represent the part of the physical environment that should be most important for any person's mental health and, since it usually contains the immediate family, also relates to the most significant aspect of the social environment. Though people obviously prefer good accommodation to bad when there is a choice, relatively little is known about the specific effects of aspects of housing on psychiatric morbidity. Johnson (2005) has emphasized that the impact of poor housing on mental health has yet to be systematically studied, though there are indications that the social environment is a critical factor. This social environment itself is related to the design and conditions of people's housing, in so far as it promotes or inhibits social relationships.

However, it is certainly an over-simplification to assume a dichotomy whereby unsatisfactory physical conditions impair only physical health, while poor psychological or social conditions specifically impair mental health, since all these constantly interact (Carstairs & Brown, 1958). In a study of housing in three cities, Hunt (1990) found escalating levels of mental disorders in residents as adverse conditions increased. The factors giving rise to this distress were largely social, such as poverty, unemployment, and lack of support, with which poor housing is almost always associated. People in damp and mouldy houses were more likely to report a variety of symptoms, including those of poor mental health. The interaction between bodily and mental health was also shown in a study (Hopton & Hunt, 1996) in a public housing estate on the outskirts of Glasgow. Although the economic and housing conditions of the sample as a whole were poor, reporting a problem with dampness was significantly and independently associated with poorer mental health. A technical survey of this accommodation confirmed overall the problems of dampness. Poor housing conditions impose additional stress on the task of daily living in a number of ways, but dampness seems to be the worst of these.

This subject needs to be considered, therefore, in relation to social processes such as rapid change, while the relationship of any housing to its own environmental context is also most important, and should be examined in both social and structural terms. Much of the research undertaken in this field has focused on residential movement, which is then used as a point of reference for investigating changes in mental health status; it is not ideal as such since, as Kasl and Rosenfield (1980) pointed out, what is being studied then is not a selected and well-defined housing variable, but 'a broad-based socio-residential experience with uncertain components and boundaries'.

A further methodological problem is to identify the mechanisms that link housing experience to mental health status. The nature of the surrounding community, with its institutions that constitute 'social capital', has often been seen as important here. Halpern (1995) concluded that while there is an independent effect of the built environment on mental health, this effect is multifactorial and the impact of each factor may operate only at the margins of health status. Mediating between the built environment and the individual is the social environment, which can be supportive or disabling. In New Zealand, Smith *et al.* (1993) found that living in a substandard dwelling was an independent and additive source of stress for low-income residents. Perceptions of social support could reduce these symptoms, but only if the housing stress was no more than moderate. In a further study (1994) by the same authors of mentally ill people living in the general community, housing was found to be generally not their main problem, compared with the maintenance of social support.

The complexity of investigating the relationship between housing conditions and psychological stress was emphasized in a study of council estate tenants in Manchester by Thomas *et al.* (2005). A major refurbishment scheme was carried out in one estate, but not in the adjacent one. Disappointingly, most residents saw the housing improvements as cosmetic compared with nearby private housing, and regarded them as below their expectations. Stress was experienced particularly in relation to the bad reputation of the area, lack of safety at night, and poor play and leisure facilities for the young. There appeared to be strong individual variation in the degree to which adverse circumstances were expressed as symptoms of distress. Mental distress correlated more with psychosocial events than with environmental conditions, so that efforts to reduce psychosocial risks might be the best way of reducing such mental ill-health, in the authors' view.

Hopton and Hunt (1996) identified three different approaches through which the impact of 'poor' housing on people might be examined. The first of these is 'ecological', whereby the health of residents in different areas is compared, but this involves the difficulty of controlling directly for other social and economic factors. Second, there is measurement of individuals' satisfaction with their housing, but here there is the methodological problem that dissatisfaction may be the consequence of emotional distress, rather than the cause. An example of this kind of study is that of Birtchnell *et al.* (1988) of young women on a London housing estate (see below). Third, there can be examination of the effects of specific adverse features, such as noise or dampness. Hopton and Hunt (1996) state that four studies – two of them directly controlled for other social and economic factors – showed a harmful effect of damp housing on mental health. Otherwise, there had been relatively little research on the mental health impact of different features of poor housing and no study had examined the relative effects of these features.

In developed countries, residential mobility since the Second World War has been predominantly out of cities and into new communities – expanded towns, new towns, and suburbs or peripheral housing estates. Among these, new towns were a particularly British development, and the failure to examine the effects of moving to them was nothing short of disastrous, since there is still hardly any information in human terms as to whether or not the whole effort was worthwhile. At that time, enormous numbers of people moved out of the central areas of British cities; in the decade 1966–1976, half a million left London, 200,000 Glasgow, 150,000 Liverpool, and 100,000 Manchester; Salford, near Manchester, fell from a population of 247,000 in 1928 to 131,000 in 1971. In this process, the great inward migration of the Industrial Revolution was to some extent reversed, but some of the vacated inner-city accommodation was then reoccupied, often by minorities or those with socially marginal characteristics. In this process, the nature of urban communities changed fundamentally, associated with an increase in a series of major social problems such as crime and drug abuse. It was doubly unfortunate that this coincided with economic decline and deindustrialization, causing much unemployment.

The present topic is also important because of sociological and anthropological evidence of the significance of community structure or 'social capital', which plays a significant part in shaping individual attitudes, values, and behaviour patterns. Because of the speed of contemporary social and structural changes, physical communities within cities may go through more than one transformation within a single generation. Urban residents may therefore have to adjust more than once to this restructuring around them, causing obvious risks to mental health. For many years, higher concentrations of people with psychiatric disorders have been found in inner-city areas, where defective housing, multi-occupancy, and a high proportion of high-rise accommodation are common (Macpherson *et al.*, 2003). It hardly needs to be argued that mental health difficulties are likely to worsen in such a milieu (see also Chapter 4).

New communities

Expanded towns

Considered in a British context, the category of expanded towns related to the major cities. While a doubling in size must have had profound effects on a provincial community, its basic identity remained intact, and some of the changes involved – such as replacement of long-established local businesses by multiple stores – were taking place throughout the country in any case. One can assume that some tensions existed between the original residents and the newcomers, though never becoming a major public issue, and it is known that a significant number of the latter eventually went back (Evans *et al.*, 1969). This does not mean, however, that the expanded town policy was necessarily right. It grew out of the planning clichés of the time, embodied in legislation of the 1940s, which assumed that conurbations were grossly overcrowded, that they had a severe shortage of land for development, and that it was economically and socially desirable to move business and industry out.

Much anecdotal evidence suggests that people who moved to expanded towns would generally not have done so if they could have found reasonable accommodation within the city. Many would have preferred to remain there, especially if they could have had houses rather than flats. The same seems to be true of many higher up the social scale, who have moved to newly developed private housing well outside the city; in the case of London, this process has caused large increases of population in areas up to almost 100 miles from the centre. Ironically, though, there was in fact always much unused land in cities, for example from obsolete railways and docks, and this increased steadily with deindustrialization. There were also many adequate houses available, which could have been rehabilitated rather than being demolished as 'twilight areas', but this was not politically acceptable. Finally, the dispersal of business and industry should have been resisted rather than encouraged, if the enormous problems of urban social and structural decay were to have been avoided. So far as mental health is concerned, kinship and other social networks would then have been preserved, much stressful daily travel would not have been necessary, many long-established urban communities would have remained in being instead of disappearing, and many employers who went out of business when they lost their premises would have continued if left alone.

It would also have been much better if grandiose road developments had not been ruthlessly imposed on communities, bringing them few benefits and enormous costs; Ward (1981) describes this as 'official vandalism', whose victims are usually well down the social scale. These changes make it more difficult for pedestrians and cyclists to move around, since they now often have to negotiate subways, ramps, footbridges, or pedestrian crossings, while previously compact neighbourhoods become broken up and dispersed. Existing communities and residential units are ignored by highways, whose vastness and flow of vehicles cause the subdivision of urban areas into artificial, segregated cells in contrast to the congested but vital and human atmosphere of what was cleared away. A wiser principle for public authorities would have been one of improvement, but of minimal interference with people and places. From knowledge of London's East End, Willmott (1982) concluded that the decline of British cities would not have gained the momentum it did, nor would its effects have been as tragic, if public policy had been more soundly based on what people themselves so clearly wanted.

New towns

Most of the above considerations also apply to the new towns, though these embodied a much more conscious element of social engineering, and were designed to become balanced and self-sufficient communities, with their own

Housing estate in South-East London, 1997 (used with permission of Times Newspapers Ltd/Rex Features).

sources of employment, as opposed to being merely dormitory areas. In this, they were the successors of the Garden City movement, which was inspired by Ebenezer Howard, and produced not only Letchworth and Welwyn but the industrial estate villages of Port Sunlight and Bournville. They remain today aesthetically pleasing to the eye and (from most points of view) good places in which to live, yet clearly offering no general solution to the problem of working-class housing. In fact, the new towns of the 1950s and 1960s continued a selective choice of residents, which protected them for some time from the worst social problems of the inner cities and from the burdens of the elderly and chronically sick, including those with psychiatric disabilities. As time went on, though, all these advantages were to diminish.

The new towns were built on the principle of the neighbourhood unit, making the assumption that this would establish social values, and that residents would have a positive feeling of relationship towards it. Nicholson (1961) stated that planned neighbourhoods:

> have come nearest to success [where] they are either based on natural features, which would probably have created some degree of a sense of belonging anyhow, or are strongly reinforced by locally grouped services. If they are seen to have a meaning and a function, they can become a reality [but] they must first satisfy felt needs – including the need to belong to some place which is recognisably different from the places where others belong.

No other country produced on a comparable scale such deliberately planned and large new communities, with a theoretical basis that was always clear and coherent.

How that requirement of identity can be met is a problem that has continued to plague all large-scale contemporary developments, and may be unanswerable without some return to characteristic features such as local building styles. Silver (1968) believed new towns must be unsatisfactory because 'there is no built-in steady change of state, just an all-at-once end state'; they have also suffered from planners' obsession with the compartmentalization of functions, which tends to give their environments a ghostly quality even during the day, in contrast with the human muddle of organic communities. The new towns were alien implants so far as the surrounding rural areas were concerned, and it is likely that something of a cultural gulf existed between the two, at least initially.

After the early years, residents were affected by the 'baby boom'; this time of young parenthood often strained the personal and financial resources of married couples, particularly when they were separated from previous family and friendship networks. The new towns failed, in fact, to become balanced communities of the kind that was originally planned, mainly as a result of the prevailing housing arrangements, whereby young married couples had special difficulties in getting accommodation anywhere else, particularly if their housing requirements changed with a growing family.

New towns contained few middle-class people, since there were few private houses available, few of the lowest socio-economic groups, and very little special housing for the elderly. During the 1960s, their populations showed a marked degree of upward social mobility, but the communities were socially unbalanced, through having a high proportion of the population within a narrow income range. It was assumed then (as is human nature) that this economic advance would go on indefinitely, and the new city of Milton Keynes was designed for a working population that would be relatively affluent and car-owning. The circumstances of subsequent years, though, made these assumptions completely invalid. One alarming aspect of the skewed age-structure came to light during 1967 in Crawley, which then had 41 per cent of its population of 62,000 aged under 20 (comparable with a developing country); de Alarcon and Rathod (1968) found about 90 cases of heroin abuse, aged 15–20, representing 2.7% of the entire male population in this age group.

Soon after the first new towns were established, there were reports of 'new town blues', mainly among women with small children at home, whereas the men generally benefited from the social support of the workplace. This was confirmed to some extent in a study of psychiatric out-patients from Crawley by Sainsbury and Collins (1966). However, the first major investigation was that by Taylor and Chave (1964), who compared measures of mental ill-health in Harlow New Town with data from a peripheral housing estate (Martin *et al.*, 1957), and also from an inner area of London from which many of the Harlow people had come. They distinguished a constitutionally vulnerable group (with the 'sub-clinical neurosis syndrome'), which was of about the same size in all three areas. In the new town, this group made relatively more demands on both general practice and hospital care, needed more help from public authorities, and generally showed much more difficulty in adapting to the local conditions than other people. Their symptoms of psychiatric ill-health, usually multiple, included 'nerves', depression, excessive irritability, and poor sleep.

However, in contrast to the peripheral estate, fewer people from Harlow in this study than in the general population were under specialist psychiatric care. Yet taking general practice consultation rates for neurosis, Harlow gave a higher figure than the national average; the explanation accepted for this was that there was an exceptionally good family doctor service, which people were more ready to consult. It was also found that neurotic illness did not become less with length of residence in Harlow, which was held to confirm the view that such illness is mainly of constitutional origin. The neurotic group showed a greater tendency to be dissatisfied with their environment and to complain of loneliness, which was considered to result mainly from their vulnerable personalities. Finally, the rate of psychosis was found to be well below the national average (in contrast to the peripheral estate) and this was held to remain true even when corrections were made, for example for the age- and income-structure of the Harlow population.

Throwing epidemiological scruples to the winds, Taylor and Chave then postulated that environment has a markedly determining effect on the manifestation and course of psychotic illness and that good social planning could reduce its incidence. This highly optimistic view ignored the fact that schizophrenia is a long-term disorder, with a low rate of incidence, but relatively high prevalence in settled populations. They were on firmer ground in pointing out that 'The full measure of the success or failure of a new town will come only in the children who have been born and brought up in an environment which differs markedly from that which their parents knew'. It would have been even more interesting to look at this next generation if any of the new towns had experimented boldly with medical, social, or educational services; apart from Harlow's particularly good GP service, though, that did not take place.

Many years after it was established, the Milton Keynes local administration consulted its residents about the way they saw their community (Bishop, 1986). Although they used the whole area extensively, they regarded it more as a series of villages and were strongly focused on their own house and its immediate surroundings. They did not see the new city as anything very special, but rather as being a little better than most usual environments. They wanted a house to look like a house and rejected the imagery of contemporary architects, who appeared more fixated on some overall design than on people's needs for living space. Like many grand designs, it seemed by then to have passed into a phase of disillusionment. Though there were no epidemiological studies of Milton Keynes, anecdotal reports from local psychiatrists spoke of marital and family breakdown in almost epidemic proportions. Perhaps this was predictable from the fact the 80,000 immigrants to it (by that date) had mostly been separated from their networks of family and social support. But in scientific terms, it was no 'experiment'.

British new towns, in fact, presented an almost unique population laboratory for systematic research, as well as a fairly concrete social situation, within which various parameters could have been manipulated. Satellite communities were also developed on the periphery of some European cities and several countries created new capitals, including Brasilia. No systematic information has been available about mental health from any of these situations, though anecdotal reports, perhaps best expressed in Jean-Luc Godard's film *Alphaville*, spoke of malaise and rootlessness in them. In 2005, social disturbance was serious in peripheral communities around Paris.

Impersonal high-rise. Teenagers standing on balcony (used with permission of Image Source/Rex Features).

Housing estates and suburbs

In Britain, peripheral housing estates or suburbs received by far the largest proportion of people moving to new homes after the First World War, and this has since been the case in virtually every industrialized country, as well as in many developing ones. This process resulted in four million houses being built in Britain within 20 years, involving over eight million people, predominantly of upper working- or lower middle-class status. Though these mostly semi-detached houses seem highly conventional today, they offered, in fact, a totally new living situation for people who had generally come from nineteenth-century terraced houses within the city, which were without such amenities as bathrooms and hot running water. The density of the new environment was on average about one-third that of the old. The greater part of this huge resettlement was carried out by private enterprise, making little use of architects or planners, though there were also some large municipal schemes, such as London's at Dagenham and Manchester's at Wythenshawe. Building was all by conventional methods, and that of the local authorities has generally stood the test of time very well, though some private developers had lower standards.

One significant fact, though, from the psychological point of view, was that local materials and styles were almost completely abandoned between the wars, so that a residential road or shopping parade anywhere from Land's End to John O'Groats took on an almost identical appearance, particularly as 'Modern' and Art Deco styles filtered down in the 1930s. Landmarks tended to become submerged in the tide of 'semis', and the combination of large built-up areas with unrelieved uniformity of style and layout produced a peculiarly disorienting effect. Lynch (1960) had pointed out that strong physical features are essential to a city's imageability; a network of paths, landmarks, edges, and districts allows people to process their movement mentally through an environment, but such features need to exist in an intelligible way. In many suburbs, this has not happened.

Considering the size of this migration, it would seem that the suburb and peripheral estate offered most people in Britain what they wanted – usually a separate family house with a garden (Oliver *et al.*, 1981). The significance of these developments was overshadowed in the 1930s by the Great Depression, yet the standard of housing being provided compared very favourably with that in almost any other country – a fact rarely acknowledged within Britain itself. It was not until 20 or 30 years later that people of comparable socio-economic level in other parts of Western Europe generally gained a similar level of housing amenity.

The dormitory suburb has generally had a poor press; Lewis Mumford called it 'an asylum for the preservation of illusion' and said it was based on a childish view of the world. Values of its society were described by Willmott (1982) as 'a blend of class-consciousness, patriotism, conservatism, ambition . . . and basic decency'; it has been despised by Marxists as representing myriad individual choices and private ownerships, rather than 'democratically controlled public housing' (whatever that might be). In sociological terms, the suburb has been described as an open community, in which 'control' mechanisms are not induced by a web of kinship ties, but by accepted patterns of work and leisure and by social expectations, for example on the role of women or children's educational achievements (Frankenberg, 1969). Unlike in closed communities, domestic privacy and 'keeping oneself to oneself' are part of the social climate of the suburbs.

In the USA, mass migration occurred mainly since the Second World War; in Newman's view (1980) the problem is that:

> new suburban communities house few extended families and facilitate little contact with one's neighbours or between different ethnic and income groups. They are spread over too large areas and provide little incentive [for] residents in one group to seek out the community or institutions of another, when both are identical. Each . . . is intentionally designed to be self-contained, and because of the small size of its population, each can support only the most mundane of communal and commercial facilities.

Also, each family has to spend a large percentage of its earnings to provide on its own property what should be the community's collective amenities. Suburban residential areas become fluid and transient, rather than developing firm social networks, while the immediate family takes on an increasingly important role and inward focus, replacing the traditional role of the community. Newman states that flight to the suburbs involves a loss of belief in that urban culture that had provided a ladder of upward mobility in the past for the poor and minorities – often including the parents of suburban residents. There is also loss of the 'rich interactive milieus' of social and economic heterogeneity that occur in cities.

Interest in the mental health aspects of suburban and peripheral communities began with Taylor's now classic paper on 'Suburban neurosis' in 1938. He recorded the stresses that commonly occurred after removal from a central city area to a housing estate, i.e. higher expenses, social isolation, distance from employment, and loss of familiar surroundings. These changes seemed to result in a higher incidence of neurotic disturbances, particularly in women. As mentioned above, in 1957 Martin *et al.* surveyed a housing estate 12 miles from London. The mental hospital admission rate from there was higher than the national average at all ages, but particularly for females aged 45 and over; consultation rates with GPs for neurosis and similar conditions greatly exceeded those found in a national sample, and the proportion of persons with nervous symptoms found in a sample of the estate population was nearly twice that in a nationwide survey. Incorporating other data on juvenile delinquency and the use of child guidance clinics, it was found that mental ill-health (particularly neurosis) in the estate population was higher than the national average. Explanations included the shock of rehousing and the poor social facilities, which led to a degree of loneliness and social isolation incompatible with good mental health. However, GP consultation rates for neurotic disorders vary nationally, being generally much higher in urban areas than outside them, and though people in good houses tend to have better physical health than those in bad ones, the good housing is not necessarily responsible for the better health. Other factors such as income, age, or heredity, which tend to cluster in a positive or negative direction, could also be influential.

Hare and Shaw (1965) compared the health of people in a peripheral housing estate in Croydon with those in an older, central area of the town. There was a marked association between mental ill-health and physical ill-health, and a similar association between nervous disturbance and attitudes of general dissatisfaction with the neighbourhood. Although more people in the new estate complained about lack of amenities than in the old area, attitudes of general dissatisfaction with the environment were no commoner. In the central area, in fact, over half the sample complained of the physical discomforts associated with industrialization and old housing. It was concluded that every population contains a vulnerable group who are more prone to the development of illness, both mental and physical. This group will tend to complain of their surroundings – wherever they are. Hare and Shaw believed this was probably because such complaints are mostly a projection of their poor health; such a view was very similar to the one developed by Taylor and Chave in their survey of Harlow.

Subsequently, Hare (1966) suggested that mental health might be expected to improve from moving to a new development, since the houses there would be better designed and easier to run, and the greater space and privacy should reduce fatigue, irritability, and resentments within the family. On the other hand, housewives who had grown up among a tradition of neighbourliness, with ready help and advice from relatives and others, might have been bewildered to find these missing in the artificially derived population of a new town or peripheral estate. On the whole, Hare believed that the conditions of life in new communities have no long-term influence on the mental health of adults who move there, though the process of moving (i.e. rapid cultural change) might cause a temporary exacerbation of symptoms in those who were already vulnerable. This might have related to increased social isolation in the early stages after moving. However, children in the new towns already then seemed to be showing evidence of improved physical health, and this gave grounds to hope that when they grew up, their mental health also might be better than that of their parents. Later social processes, though, particularly drug abuse, tended to negate this optimistic view.

Hare concluded that the apparent precipitants of mental ill-health in new communities might be no more than fairly small additional influences, which could tip the scales over to illness, when other conditions were equally balanced. Since it is a vain hope to prevent neurosis by trying to exclude minor misfortunes from life, he suggested that the causal factors of common mental disorders must be looked for in the human constitution, and that the only feasible way of improving this in future adults would be by reducing environmental factors that may damage it in infancy. Hare's view of the role of the residential environment is somewhat similar to that of Kasl and Rosenfield (1980), who considered that this is best seen as a facilitator, permitting certain outcomes to take place, but not initiating or stimulating them. A survey of young mothers in Auckland, New Zealand (Werry & Carlielle, 1983) showed little evidence of 'suburban neurosis' in terms of social isolation, chronic mild depression, use of tranquillizers, or dissatisfaction with the current lot; their level of ill-health was low. While the circumstances of life for this population were relatively favourable, it was suggested that unfavourable views of family stress, motherhood, or medical practice should not be generalized too widely from particular situations.

Redevelopment and housing

Recent times have been marked by massive world-wide processes of population growth, spread of industrialization and urbanization to previously underdeveloped regions, decline of old central city areas, and migration of urban residents to dispersed suburbs. Cooper and Sartorius (1977) put forward some intriguing hypotheses as to how industrialization, with these accompanying processes, could lead to a greater prevalence of chronically handicapped schizophrenic people in a community. Urbanization clearly involves some form of migration, which in itself is likely to be associated with an increased risk of psychiatric disorder (see Chapter 7).

Another form of migration, though over relatively short distances, is the enforced rehousing or 'relocation' resulting from clearance and redevelopment of old urban areas. This has occurred on an enormous scale in Britain since the Second World War, displacing three million people in the period 1955–1975, but there was hardly a single research study of its possible adverse psychological and emotional effects. That such effects might occur was quite likely, considering that many of the cleared areas were long-established communities, with a characteristic culture of their own and important networks of kinship and mutual help, which can never be reproduced artificially. Halpern and Reid (1992) investigated the impact of the unexpected announcement of the demolition of a housing area on its residents. In consultation with them, alternative plans for refurbishment had been prepared by a local housing association, but these were finally rejected. The outcome measure was weekly consultation rates with GPs: these showed a relative increase of 29% compared with neighbouring estates. The results were similar to those among workers threatened with redundancy and were consistent with the hypothesis that extra stress increases the probability of illness. Planners and politicians need to be constantly reminded that their decisions have human consequences of this kind.

The demolition of a neighbourhood, in fact, is not just the destruction of buildings, but also that of a functioning social system: 'slum areas not only provide cheap housing but also offer the kinds of social support that poor people need to keep going in a crisis-ridden existence' (Gans, 1967). Furthermore, most of the social problems found in slums cannot be traced to the area itself – a point that has often been forgotten in planning and redevelopment. Kasl (1977) concluded that rehousing 'represents to many individuals a major life change which, can be stressful and have definite health consequences'. Similarly, Willmott (1974) emphasized that the whole process of redevelopment can take as long as ten years, during which people are worried about their future, watch the decay of the neighbourhood around them, and may finally be compulsorily moved to a home they do not want. Willmott (1982) added that 'Redevelopment inside the cities has been a disaster, destroying established communities and creating a kind of housing that is almost universally detested'. In this process, the boundaries and spatial arrangements which different ethnic or social groups have established over time are wiped out, and with them often their *modus vivendi* with society in general. At the same time, the decline of both religious and civic rituals, which, as Durkheim said, 'affirm the moral superiority of the community over its individual members', may mean that there is eventually no 'community' left with any values to affirm (Howes, 1983). The religious Whit Walks of Manchester and patronal festivals of Italian communities are examples of these mostly disappearing events, which can be seen as an aspect of 'social capital'.

One of the few systematic accounts of the social effects of moving people from one spatial milieu to another is Young and Willmott's (1957) study of the Bethnal Green area of East London, from which large numbers were then being rehoused in a new peripheral estate. Like most others, this development was designed on the assumption that undesirable features of the old community could be planned away, and that life would be better in an environment consisting only of adequate housing, together with a few essential shops. But as Hillier and Hanson (1984) pointed out, virtually none of the anticipated benefits of achieving this 'spatial correspondence to social grouping' was actually shown to have occurred – 'the spatial hierarchy completely failed in its purpose of supporting social integration'. They related this to the fact that 'it is a physically discrete spatially identifiable enclave, not well-embedded in a more global system of space. The layout . . . seemed to have engendered suspicion, rather than sociability, and the pattern of hostility was repeated at the level of integration of the estate into the wider community.' So far as social networks were concerned, 'Kin ceased to play the vital role . . . of making relationships carry across space, while the local neighbour network, so characteristic of the old way of life, seemed to have disappeared entirely'.

This view contrasted with the more medical one of Hare and Shaw (see above), which emphasized the benefits of good physical accommodation. In the case of nearly every peripheral estate, though, provision of essential services lagged far behind the building of houses or flats, so that there was sometimes not even a post-box; this lack resulted in severe stress for residents in the earlier years of the development. Hird (1966) referred to a high rate of suicide in one estate outside Birmingham, which was nine times the national average; there was also a disproportionately high rate of night calls to GPs in the early years, often reflecting the panic of social isolation more than medical emergencies.

The first specific study of the consequences of relocation for mental and physical health was that of Wilner *et al.* (1962) in Baltimore, USA. Out of 600 families who were very poorly accommodated, half were to be rehoused on a new estate; the health of both groups was then observed for a follow-up period of two years. At the end of this time, the children who had moved showed less physical ill-health than those who had not, and as a result, their school attendance was more regular and their results better. Adults in the new area were more ready to invite friends into their house, to form friendships with neighbours, and to help them in practical ways; they were also more interested in caring for their houses and gardens, and were more optimistic in their outlook. On the other hand, there was no difference between the two groups in the amount of friction and quarrelling among family members or in the amount of irritability, nervousness, and depression in individuals, so that in terms of mental health, the effects of rehousing over this period were relatively unimpressive. Since the study dealt with a group of people living originally in a very poor environment, its results may not be generally applicable, and it is possible that non-housing variables such as poverty may have prevented the relocated residents from gaining as much benefit from the move as they might otherwise have done. Marris (1974) suggested that 'We should not burden ourselves with so many simultaneous changes that our emotional resilience becomes exhausted'.

Commenting on this Baltimore study, Kasl and Rosenfield (1980) pointed out that it had been criticized for not including wider dimensions of the social environment. But if the operational definition of the 'residential environment' combined physical and psychosocial components, it might no longer be possible to tell how the two interact with each other, or whether the observed impact of change might not be due solely to the social dimensions.

Probably the first psychiatric report relating to this problem was by Thorpe (1939) from Sheffield, where slum clearance was beginning to displace long-settled city residents into new peripheral estates. He observed cases of severe depression in which the onset seemed clearly related to this compulsory change, and attributed it to 'a profound emotional shock' when elderly people were compelled to leave a residence in which they might have lived for many years to move to a new estate of lonely roads, which they found strange and empty. The main aetiological factors of this depression, affecting particularly women and older people, were considered to be: first, dispossession from a home to which a strong emotional attachment had often developed; and second, inability of older people to adapt to new surroundings, where the neighbours were strange and the cost of living higher.

However, the most important study of the psychiatric sequelae of relocation is still that of Fried (1963) on people who had been moved from the West End of Boston, a long-established, mainly Italian working-class community. It was found that among women, 26% reported that they still felt sad and depressed two years after moving, and another 20% reported having had these feelings, related to the move, for at least six months. Among men, the percentage showing long-term grief reactions was only slightly smaller. These affective reactions had most of the characteristics of grief and mourning for a lost person, but in addition, many other subjects indicated less severe depressive feelings. The two most important components of the grief reaction were found to be fragmentation of the sense of spatial identity and dependence of group identity on stable social networks. These components were critical foci for the sense of continuity which, in such a working-class community, appeared to be dependent on the external stability and familiarity of places and people.

Fried went on to point out that any severe loss disrupts a person's sense of continuity, which is an important framework for everyday functioning. In long-established working-class communities of Europe and North America, the local area around the dwelling unit was seen as an integral part of home, and contained interlocking sets of social networks – in marked contrast to the 'trans-spatial' orientation of the middle-class person. Greenbie (1974) suggested that 'For sophisticated urban men, conceptual territories may be provided by professions, hobbies, and religious or political organisations, which can substitute for physical territory. The poor and cultural minorities will be most likely to need secure physical–cultural boundaries'. The Boston study showed that following enforced removal, marked grief was more likely the more a person had been committed to that community in terms of liking it, feeling that it had been his real home, and being very familiar with it. 'Largely because of the importance of external stability, dislocation from a familiar residential area has so great an effect on fragmenting the sense of spatial identity' (Fried, 1963).

A related study (Fried & Gleicher, 1961) showed that slum areas have in fact many sources of satisfaction for their residents, but these are mostly invisible to outside people, who do not share the same culture and value-system. Marris (1974) concluded that it was in situations where slum clearance is confused with broader ambitions of social reform that it characteristically provokes reactions akin to bereavement, for it is then that it most threatens the residents' sense of identity.

Rather different conclusions about intra-urban migration were reached by Hall (1966), studying patients in Sheffield who had attributed their symptoms to a change of home. These included a sub-group of young women who mostly had neurotic symptoms and poor marital relationships. While their clinical features seemed to have no relationship to the kind of new housing they had received, complaints about this environment were numerous and usually vague. They seemed to be mostly a projection of other problems. A group of older women presented depressive symptoms, and complaints about their new housing mostly ceased when the depression had been treated. Hall therefore suggested that a new housing environment forms a matrix for the projection of personal difficulties by neurotic patients. Complaints about housing often disappeared in the course of psychotherapy, and there was no case of illness being clearly precipitated by moving house in anyone of previously well-adjusted personality. Though social planning of new public housing schemes ought to be concerned with relieving the unhappiness and isolation felt by some incoming tenants, the psychiatric contribution might be in identifying such vulnerable individuals, and providing support and counselling at an early stage of their migration. Yet any intervention of this kind would be extremely difficult in practical terms, unless the people concerned were already under medical care.

Similar results were obtained by Johnson (1970), who analysed applications for rehousing on psychiatric grounds to the local authority in Salford, and followed-up the individuals concerned. In respect of their necessity for psychiatric treatment, no difference was found between the group who were actually rehoused and those who were not, and the same similarity was found for change in severity of symptoms. It is difficult to reconcile these findings with those of Fried, for instance, but they do suggest that whatever contribution environmental factors may make to psychiatric disorder, clinical diagnosis and treatment along established lines remain very worthwhile, and should certainly not be regarded as irrelevant in any patient. A later study in the same area (Elton & Packer, 1986) made a randomized comparison of people rehoused or not rehoused on the grounds of common mental disorders. After about a year, those rehoused showed a much greater evidence of clear improvement. Their previous housing problems included noise, vandalism, lack of immediate access to the outside world, and being in a multi-storey flat. In 1990, Smith pointed out that rehousing on medical grounds in fact accounted for only a small proportion of allocations to accommodation in the public sector. Medical advisers had no agreed clinical basis on which to assign priority (for example, bronchitis versus depression), while housing managers had no rules as to how to deal with medical recommendations. When the amount of public or 'social' housing began to shrink, there was an increasing tendency for it to be used only for the benefit-dependent poor or homeless – a process described as 'residualization'.

If research on the effect on mental health of moving one's home has so far failed to produce a clear picture, the reasons may be, as Kasl and Rosenfield (1980) suggested, that nearly all studies have been opportunistic. This has resulted in the 'sporadic and spotty accumulation of scientific knowledge', while the effect of a particular physical residential parameter probably varies with different sub-groups of residents. Their own study of the impact of the residential environment on the mental health of the elderly concluded that this did not seem to be overwhelming; it was greatest in respect of housing satisfaction (not surprisingly), less on social and leisure activities, and least on the more traditional indicators of mental health. Since many housing interventions are also, in fact, social interventions, the strongest negative impact of the residential environment seemed to be associated with certain life experiences, which have a residential change embedded in them. Generally, residential moves for the elderly are likely to be stressful, even if the new home is of a better standard, unless the move is away from an urban area with great social stress. However, Carp (1975) found that when old people in a Texas city were moved to purpose-built flats, mostly from poor accommodation, they nearly all became happier and more satisfied with life. These benefits remained stable over eight years' follow-up (see also Chapter 1).

Physical structure

A general characteristic of new communities is their relatively low density of population compared to older urban areas; this may be significant in the development of neurotic disorders because of the greater amounts of open space and unfamiliar visual patterns in new districts. From the ethological point of view Marks (1969) concluded that 'agoraphobic behaviour in hamsters, is mainly a response to illumination above the level optimal for the animal, rather than a response to the openness of the situation'. Normally, excessively bright light causes avoidance responses, which are dissipated by searching behaviour, but if the latter is blocked, the animal shows evidence of increased stress. Similarly, human agoraphobics tend to feel easier in the dark and, if crossing an open space, feel less anxious if they can skirt the edge. Marks suggested that innate mechanisms probably do not produce phobias of themselves, but rather select as targets certain situations, which may then be affected by other conditions, for example space and light perception, through optokinetic reflexes. This is also seen in the fact that many people feel uncomfortable in high flats with exterior walls of glass, while Hayden (1978) reported that agoraphobics are likely to find pedestrian bridges over main roads terrifying, particularly when a corner has to be turned, high in the sky. The same situation occurs when a lift in a high block of flats opens on to a dimly lit balcony; stepping out of this may give the phobic person the feeling that he is walking straight into space.

While there is no firm evidence yet for direct connections between particular forms of urban development and the emergence of neurotic illnesses, it does seem likely that there are psychological advantages in more traditional forms, such as arcaded streets or enclosed markets. Gradidge (1981) referred to the pleasure obtained from 'the sense of enclosure given by a small room . . . warmed with a wood fire, womb-like and protective while outside the storms howl or the fog drips'. In fact, people will often find ways of recreating a sense of cosiness in circumstances where this would seem almost impossible, such as open-plan offices; in this way, there is a kind of constant guerrilla warfare against the designs of architects and planners, perhaps indicating that stable behaviour and social institutions must rest on an innate biological basis. Leyhausen (1965) suggested that 'the human species is adapted to social life in a small group . . . having need for larger social gatherings from time to time . . . feeling a need to be by himself quite often, and reacting to continued oversocialisation with all sorts of frustrations, repressions, aggressions, and fears'.

Such a view perhaps ignored cultural differences, but those who plan and build should surely have a greater sense of humility, which would prevent them, for instance, from simply abolishing such a fundamental aspect of human society as the street, particularly when this change is imposed on people who have no choice as to where they live. Hillier *et al.* (1987) pointed out that the arrangement of built space determines to a large extent the degree to which people are made aware of the presence of others, both neighbours and strangers; thus, if people are likely to be in a place because of its relationship to other places, then it will probably remain busy (and so relatively safe). But new environments, which have generally broken away from established patterns of movement, tend to consist mostly of dead space – 'urban wastelands, through which people dash between their homes and places of work or leisure'. Disappearance of the street was primarily associated in Britain with the spread of high-rise blocks of flats; Gardiner (1982) considered that: 'The street is the most important single element in neighbourhood design . . . its loss produced a desert; [it] performs so many useful duties you scarcely notice it, and only appreciate its importance when it's not there . . . It establishes continuity, connects different parts of a neighbourhood and provides a link in a network of varying heights, materials, activities and landmarks. Streets which bring people together in terraces, or on the sides of a square looking across a garden, probably make the ideal community form'. However, this question of urban form now requires consideration of the high-rise issue as a whole.

One of the most trenchant critics of public housing policy was a geographer, Professor Alice Coleman, in the book *Utopia on Trial* (1985). This was a heady mixture of polemic, research reports, policy, and practical recommendations; it had a scientific basis but revealed the author's strong feelings. In her view, large-scale redevelopments not only had been failures, but had created a set of new and overwhelming social problems. She devised a series of indices to measure environmental disadvantage or social malaise in housing: litter, graffiti, vandal damage, presence of urine or faeces, and the number of children in social service care. While the first four of these were objective data, the last was scientifically very questionable.

From research in London, these social indicators were reported to have a direct relationship (of worsening) against five design variables, as these increased: dwellings per entrance, dwellings per block, number of storeys, number of overhead walkways, and adverse spatial organization. Crime levels showed a similar relationship. However, it was emphasized that 'bad design does not determine anything, but it increases the odds against which people have to struggle . . . the worst designs bring out the worst behaviour in children'. In her view, 'the demand for more play areas in estates is misconceived', since it removed children from the informal control of adults. Similarly, people in public housing had had 'disastrous designs chosen for them, creating a needless sense of social failure'.

Coleman shared with Oscar Newman (1972) the concept of 'defensible space'. In her view, the single family dwelling restored to people the responsibility of caring for their own homes and (within limits) the important power to make their mark on territory that is identifiably their own. It also helps to free them from the shackles of vast, unresponsive, and outrageously expensive bureaucracies. Her work almost certainly helped to turn the architectural tide so that small-scale housing began to be reintroduced even into the inner cities, sometimes by reducing and subdividing existing structures. Ironically, any new high-rise blocks would now be in expensive private developments.

High-rise

The tide of high-rise blocks of flats, which eventually began to sweep over Britain in the late 1950s, and which came to house over a million people, has to be seen against the historical background of housing in the country. Town walls had largely lost their importance by the sixteenth century, so that a growing population did not have to be squeezed into very small areas after that, as was still the case in most of Europe. Also, since the cost of building land in the nineteenth century was very much lower than that in Germany, for instance, instead of urban housing in England and Wales consisting of dense blocks of tenements and apartments, the terraced home became almost universal, housing almost 90% of the population at the beginning of the twentieth century (Muthesius, 1982). For all its drawbacks, it had the virtue of compactness; in 1914, the half-million people of Leeds were mostly housed within 2.5 kilometres of the city centre. The tenement was fairly common in Scotland, though, up to a height of four storeys, and not unknown in English cities; but it always seems to have been considered something of an aberration. Therefore, when high-rise blocks began to appear, they were generally regarded as quite foreign to the accepted tradition of urban housing in Britain – as indeed they still are.

Between the two World Wars, local authorities started to build homes for the working class, the great majority being single-family houses, and usually semi-detached. When this process began, in 1919, 90% of British homes were privately rented, yet this figure was to fall to 14% by 1971, and steadily after that. The remaining Council homes in the inter-war period were walk-up flats, usually not exceeding four floors and following in the tradition of the Victorian philanthropic tenements, such as those of the Peabody Trust. In this period, the benefits of craftsmanship, good-quality materials and traditional methods produced 'the last generation of multi-storey housing to weather well' (Esher, 1981). Very large numbers of urban houses were destroyed or damaged during the Second World War, and many more fell into disrepair as a result of wartime neglect, rent control, or simply the ageing of poor-quality buildings. Great demand for new housing then resulted not only from these factors, but also from the large number of new households that were being formed in the post-war period, and from higher expectations about standards of accommodation. Working-class couples no longer accepted, as their parents had done, that they should bring up a family in four rooms, with no bathroom, inside WC, or running hot water, and no garden. Nor did young adults of any social class continue to expect to remain in the parental home until marriage, as they continued to do in Italy, for instance.

This great demand for new homes coexisted with a climate of opinion in local authorities and the professions that was governed by the architectural and planning clichés referred to above, particularly regarding a 'shortage of land' in urban areas. It came to be felt that traditional building methods, based on brick or stone, were too slow, too expensive, and in any case out of date. Furthermore, there was little satisfaction for the new generation of architects and engineers in further variations on the endlessly repeated semi. In the immediate post-war period, single-storey prefabricated houses helped to meet some of the most urgent need for homes, and although small, they did contain the most essential modern conveniences. Their success, in the short term at least, turned attention to the possibility of a 'quick technological fix', which would be in tune with the general ethos of the period and solve a problem that otherwise seemed likely to go on indefinitely. Yet at the same time, successive social surveys had shown that the overwhelming majority of the working population preferred a house to a flat, if the rents were the same (Self, 1957).

Waiting in the wings was the architectural Modern Movement, represented particularly by Le Corbusier and by Walter Gropius and the Bauhaus; their ideas had reached Britain in the 1930s, but had only resulted in the appearance of a relatively small number of structures, mostly in or near London. When building resumed after the Second World War, the neo-Georgian and Arts and Crafts traditions that had strongly influenced local authority designs up to then were largely discredited among architects. Instead, Le Corbusier taught that there could be vertical garden cities in the sky, surrounded by plentiful open space, and containing pleasant and efficient living accommodation. These would not only put an end to the squalid housing of the last century, but also to the urban sprawl of the inter-war period, while the visual effect of towers rising from the ground was considered altogether more aesthetically exciting than that of a cottage estate, and could be a source of pride to both local authority officers and their political masters. The combination seemed irresistible, and to add to it, large building contractors promised the enormous benefits of new prefabricated systems, which would both discard the structural limitations of traditional methods and speed up the delivery of homes ready to be occupied. Because everything was so new, such claims could be made 'in the absence of experience or of any firm theoretical basis for prediction' (Cooney, 1974). In the prevailing euphoria, Glasgow's city fathers promised that the notorious Gorbals slums would be replaced by something more akin to the Hanging Gardens of Babylon. The situation was clinched when the government became convinced that high-rise building was the only practical answer to large-scale housing needs, and arranged its policy on subsidies accordingly; the higher a housing authority built, therefore, the more money it received relatively.

Not everyone was convinced, though; most local authority housing managers knew well enough that flats were unpopular as homes for families, but they were ignored as being men of little faith. Before long, it became clear that very large sites were needed for the new construction methods, and this usually required clearing them of existing buildings, although most of these were not really unfit for further use. So 'Twilight Areas' was the slogan devised to provide an excuse for demolishing huge tracts of existing housing and of industrial or commercial premises. When the occupants of these naturally protested at what was being done, they were told that they were being 'selfish' or 'behind the times'. Before long, the whole process had become a juggernaut that seemed to have gone totally out of control and that was wiping out a large proportion of the urban structure of Britain. A corresponding process was going on in relation to shops and offices, whereby the familiar high streets and small office blocks were being demolished to make way for large new structures, often occupying much of the central area of a town. With few exceptions, these new developments were tasteless, shoddy, and totally without character; their effect on many of Britain's historic towns was devastating and, in the case of one cathedral city, rightly described as 'the sack of Worcester'. As one urban area after another disappeared under a forest of tower blocks and megastructures, 'many architects stood appalled . . . in the position of the sorcerer's apprentice' (Cooney, 1974). However, by then it was too late. Regrettably, the whole story began to be repeated in 2003, when large urban areas in the north of England were scheduled for wholesale demolition. They were generally well built, many had been greatly improved by their occupants, and few of these had any wish to leave their homes. These views, however, counted for nothing in the political process (OPDM, 2003).

At no point in the story had there been any attempt to examine the needs or wishes of those who were to occupy this new Babylon; the whole political process, in so far as it purported to represent the views of the public, had in fact failed to operate, both at national and local levels (Dunleavy, 1981). Neither did the medical profession cover itself in glory, since public health doctors almost invariably declared as 'unfit' any houses that their authority wanted to demolish, even when this was clearly a travesty of the facts. It was not long, however, before both GPs and psychiatrists became aware of the ill-effects of what was going on, as a result of the dispersal of well-integrated communities and through the unsuitability of the new flats for families with young children. It did not help that wider social and cultural changes were happening at the same time, leading to a situation that could be described in many areas as 'social disintegration' (see Chapter 6). The consequences in one city were described by Gardiner (1981) as 'a panoramic picture of towers and slabs looming above an eerie wasteland of unkempt grass. Their designs' total loss of contact with people shows in acres of grey concrete and black tarmac and in the seemingly arbitrary location of identical blocks . . . [with] horrific vandalism, graffiti, violent crime, abandoned buildings'.

In 1983, when the Maiden Lane estate was completed for the Council in Camden, North London, it was described by the *Architectural Review* as 'representing the very best in British Housing care and as civilised as any recent European solution'. Within four years, though, it had attained social breakdown. As Stamp (1988) described it, its 'reference to ocean liners' had produced dangerously steep staircases, a mugger's paradise of tunnels, and rubbish collections that eluded the dustmen. So much for the legacy of Le Corbusier.

On the personal level, many people felt remote in high flats, cut off from the general life of the community, having no real neighbourly contact, yet at the same time lacking privacy because of the failure to provide sound insulation (Lowenstein, 1982); radio and television were then a poor substitute for real-life interactions. Such disadvantaged groups as the elderly and physically disabled found the situation hazardous and stressful because of their dependence on lifts, rubbish chutes, or other services that did not always work, because of their isolation (compared with conventional housing), and because they were often severely harassed by gangs of adolescents who tended to hang around the communal areas and surroundings (Cook & Morgan, 1982).

Many social disabilities have resulted from the fact that a multi-storey flat is excessively self-contained. Jephcott (1971) pointed out that it has none of the neutral areas, such as doorsteps, backyards, or gardens, 'which help people to build up their dossiers on each other without necessarily exchanging a word. And it is blind in that its windows afford no two-way link with the outside world. This turns the block and estate into eventless places, short of those goings-on of life that tempt people out of their homes, give them shared interests and help them strike up acquaintance should they so wish'. She added that 'Any community needs some spots that lend themselves to a bit of gossiping', but the usually inhuman atmosphere of entrance lobbies and landings removed them from this category, and such new outside assets as lawns and relative freedom from traffic are not made use of unless there is positive encouragement to do so.

Medical and psychiatric research

One of the first medical attempts to examine the question scientifically was that of Fanning (1967), who compared the health of British service families living in low-rise flats in Germany with similar families living in houses. Measured by medical consultation rates, flat dwellers showed 57% more morbidity than people in houses. The higher rates were most marked in the case of allergic, neurological, respiratory, dermatological, genito-urinary, and neurotic conditions, the last of these especially for young married women. The largest group of cases was that of respiratory illness in the flat dwellers, which might have been due to lack of open-air exercise, or (perhaps more likely) to emotional stress. From the subjective standpoint, boredom, isolation, and difficulty in coping with young children were certainly reported to a significant extent by those living in flats, and it is quite likely that the threshold for medical consultation was lower in this group because their life was less satisfactory.

Comparisons of similar groups, but also including residents of one tower block, were made by Moore (1974, 1975, 1976), who found that the indoor, though not outdoor social life of the flat dwellers was inferior, but that psychiatric illness was no more prevalent among them. It was concluded that for those of neurotic personality, flat dwelling was sufficient stress to cause some increase in clinical psychiatric illness, but this did not produce an overall level significantly greater than that of all house dwellers. As in Fanning's investigation, though, the flats were mostly low-rise, and the subjects did not cover an age range comparable to that of the general population. In contrast, Reynolds and Nicholson (1969), investigating the prevalence of neurotic symptoms in women living on six council estates in London and Sheffield, most of whom were in high-rise dwellings, found that although these symptoms were very frequent, their distribution showed no relationship to building form, height above the ground, or estate density. These results are very different from those of other, comparable studies, however.

A similar investigation in Bristol by Ineichen and Hooper (1974) found that women living in houses in a redeveloped central area reported more neurotic symptoms than those in high-rise flats or in maisonettes (which had the lowest rate). The wives in houses generally had poor health – both mental and physical – as well as relatively the largest number of children, often including a problem child. Selection of these large families for houses may have had some influence on the women's high rate of symptoms. Their dissatisfaction with the environment centred around derelict buildings, inflow of immigrants, noisy neighbours, and children (often resulting in conflict between the parents), high rents, and the powerlessness of tenants to get anything done. For families in flats, the number of children considered by their mothers to present behaviour problems was almost double that in any of the other groups; loneliness and isolation were significant complaints among these women. Families in any kind of accommodation in the central area who had no car (50%) found difficulty in maintaining contact with their relatives, when these had been rehoused in outer suburbs. Environmental 'problems', as these central area families perceived them, were many-layered, the 'solution' of one often merely revealing the next beneath it. Similarly, Bagley (1973) compared a random sample of women living in a 12-storey block of flats with a control group living in houses on a pre-war council estate. As measured by the Eysenck Personality Inventory, the house dwellers were significantly less neurotic, and they consulted their general practitioners significantly less often for 'nervous illness'. The control women complained significantly less about housing and environmental matters, including adequacy of play space.

Jephcott (1971) suggested that high-rise living is particularly hard on those who are below average in social assets, since the support that they might expect from neighbours and friends in a traditional street is much less likely to exist, in view of the large numbers of people involved, and the isolation of individual flats. On the other hand, those who are better off can afford such compensations as the use of a car, seaside holidays or outdoor sports. From his studies of crowding, Freedman (1975) concluded that if a social situation is initially unfavourable, living in a high-rise building with hundreds of other families is likely to exaggerate feelings of fear, suspicion and isolation.

It seems likely that young children in high flats tend to lead a more passive existence, cooped up with their mothers, who are often socially isolated themselves, and tend to develop compulsive fears (by no means unreasonable) about the children falling out of windows or off balconies (Stewart, 1970). In fact, coroners' records for England and Wales 1973–1977 showed that children living above the first floor were 57 times more likely to be killed by falling from their homes than other children. Such restrictions of stimuli and personal interactions, together with those imposed outside by traffic dangers and urban sprawl, could well hinder children's social and perceptual development, which may now largely occur at second hand, through television. For school-age children, the high-rise estate is lacking in environmental interest, is deprived of the supervisory care of adults, and is more vulnerable to damage, compared with the traditional street. Because of this, sport facilities are particularly important, yet exist hardly anywhere in the way that is needed. Stewart also found that mothers in high flats with young children, though not of teenage children, were particularly likely to show symptoms of psychiatric disorders.

Three matched groups of families, each with two very young children, living respectively in Council high-rise flats, low-rise flats and houses, in the same London borough, were compared by Richman (1974). She found that the children might spend most of the day isolated in a flat with their mother, so that the resulting boredom and irritation could well lead to tension and strained relationships; this was particularly the case when children were at the toddling stage or able to run about, but could not safely be left on their own. Since contact with neighbours might only be by chance, when entering or leaving, flat life seemed to exacerbate the inherent difficulties of women who were poor mixers, and to increase the problems of isolation and restriction to the home experienced by many mothers of young children. Depression of moderate-to-severe extent was found in 41 per cent of the mothers, and was more marked among those living in flats. Psychiatric problems in the mothers tended to be associated with behaviour problems in the children. Richman concluded that depression, loneliness, and dissatisfaction with accommodation affect a high proportion of mothers with young children who live in flats; she also suggested that some of the differences between families in different kinds of accommodation might have been obscured by the number of those who had moved out of high-rise flats in the previous year. This view was confirmed by Ineichen and Hooper (1974), who re-interviewed their sample after 18 months, finding that 40% of the total, but 60% of the flat dwellers, had moved by then, thus causing an ironing-out of the differences between the groups in prevalence of symptoms – at least temporarily.

A study in Edinburgh by Gilloran (1968) concluded that the outstanding problem of family life in high flats was isolation: 'to have forgotten a couple of items in a shopping list may produce a major crisis'. Though a safe place in which to play outside the dwelling has been part of small children's natural environment for many centuries, there is usually no possibility of this in tower blocks. There, the usual separation from relatives and established friendship networks means that young mothers are never free of the responsibility of child-minding.

In Canada, Gillis (1977) studied parents with children, living in rented public flats; finding that women, but not men, showed more psychological stress the higher up they lived. Gillis suggested that those on the ground floor might feel vulnerable in respect to crime, though this would not necessarily be true in private housing schemes. In Glasgow, Hannay (1981) found a significant correlation between residence in high flats and an increased prevalence of psychiatric symptoms; in particular, those on the fifth floor and above had twice the prevalence, compared with those on the lower floors or those living in houses.

There may well be a fundamental difference in respect of high-rise living between single people – who generally like it, as do many childless couples – and families, who generally do not. However, the fact that so many high-rise tenants vote with their feet may have prevented some research from arriving at positive conclusions, because those showing evidence of adverse effects may not remain long enough to appear in a sample. Almost all research material, in fact, is derived from residents of the public housing sector, but in recent years, these have become a vulnerable minority, which tends to result in a feeling of powerlessness to control their immediate environment. The fact that many high-rise developments are often drab, impersonal, or brutal will worsen this feeling, as do bad design or maintenance.

The basic problem of all such research, though, is that large effects from changes in housing variables could only be expected 'If the whole package of poverty, illness, and social problems could be unravelled into a single long causal chain with housing as one of the early links', but instead, 'residential variables [are] richly embedded in a large matrix of individual and social variables that condition and attenuate the impact of the residential environment' (Kasl *et al.*, 1982). These authors pointed out that the 'meaning' of housing needs to be understood in the experiential, rather than just in the physical sense, and that 'poor housing is an obstacle to well-being and self-fulfilment, but remedying only poor housing is not enough'. They also considered it undesirable to take a particular residential parameter, such as persons per room, and translate it into a specific psychological construct, because of the many ways in which different psychosocial variables can alter the effects of these processes in sub-groups of the population. As mentioned above, it is not possible to identify a single intervening process between such a factor and human experience or behaviour.

Methodologically, as mentioned elsewhere (see Chapter 1), there is a problem in many such housing studies over the direction of causality. For instance, Birtchnell *et al.* (1988), screening a large sample of young women on a London housing estate, found a disproportionate number of those with high depression scores in dwellings with the highest scores for environmental disadvantage. These high scorers also had homes with interiors that were significantly poorer in appearance than were the homes of the low scorers. However, the location of those women in the estate might have been influenced by their inherent vulnerability. Nevertheless, the authors were surely reasonable in suggesting that 'the accommodation itself also played a part in the development and maintenance of their depression'.

Maintaining the structure

One of the fundamental points about tower block accommodation, in fact, is that it is a high-technology environment, involving large maintenance costs (mostly ignored in the original calculations), and only successful when there is money to ensure that all the mechanical aspects are working, and that the communal areas are clean and free from crime. But most housing authorities in Britain, like those in many other countries, built large developments on a scale that went far beyond their capacity to maintain these satisfactorily. It was not long before essential services were breaking down, while the many faults that occurred with new and sometimes untried building systems might stay uncorrected for months or even years. Some, like dampness, have remained incurable, yet the complexity of the problem means that the tenants themselves can do nothing about it. Their personal freedom and opportunities for choice and self-expression are also restricted in such matters as keeping pets, making adaptations to the home, and having any outside space in which to potter about. Vint and Bintliff (1983) pointed out that if there are risks associated with technical change and new building methods, the costs of these should be accepted by housing authorities or by the building industry – not by the tenants, as has usually been the case.

In Britain, the 'Right to Buy' for Council tenants, introduced in the 1980s, has greatly changed the profile of ownership in public housing, though not invariably to the new owners' advantage. Ellaway and Macintyre (1998) examined data on adults from two socially contrasting neighbourhoods in Glasgow. Though residents' self-reports of housing conditions were thought to be influenced by disadvantaged people having lower expectations, tenants were found to be more exposed than owners to stresses that were directly damaging to health in both their housing and neighbourhood. This relationship was independent of income. The health effects were seen in levels of chronic illness and symptoms of anxiety and depression. The conclusion was that housing tenure may have an effect on health not only because it is associated with income, but also because of association with housing stressors and type of area, which are themselves directly health-damaging.

Quite apart from the lack of resources for maintenance, the administrative structure of many housing departments, with their rigidly bureaucratic habits, virtually collapsed under the weight of complaints and of appeals for things to be put right. Yet as soon as any chill economic wind blew (which seemed to happen frequently from the time these developments were finished), maintenance, cleaning and repairs invariably bore the first brunt of any financial cuts. As the quality of these services fell, so vandalism, crime, and despoiling of the environment escalated, increasing further when respectable working-class families with young children began to find more suitable accommodation elsewhere, and to be replaced by 'difficult' people on the waiting list. A vicious circle of environmental deterioration then began, in which the chief sufferers were those already disadvantaged, whose plight was now compounded by being trapped in often dirty, dangerous, noisy, and incomprehensible living situations. Old houses certainly had their problems, but this was on a different scale. Littlewood and Tinker (1981) found little evidence of attempts by housing departments to alleviate the problems of high-rise tenants; three-quarters of mothers with children under five were unhappy living above ground level, whereas after rehousing, two-thirds reported their own emotional health to be better, and most said that their children were better behaved.

Finally, there is the question of how an environment looks. Though this has not generally been regarded as significant from the point of view of health, and though virtually impossible to study scientifically, it has certainly been dramatically affected by the advent of high-rise buildings. The previously familiar British townscapes of terraced housing or suburban semis, like comparable areas of many North American and European cities, were not on the whole aesthetically pleasing, yet still had some very positive aspects – for instance, the intimate scale of a traditional street, or flowering trees of a suburb in the spring.

But tower blocks and other megastructural forms of housing, as well as giant shopping centres, overwhelm the human environment in ways that seem almost wholly bad. Jephcott (1971) describes how tower blocks mostly rear up fortuitously and in unrelated chunks.

> Traditionally . . . the tall, eye-catching building . . . has been an expression of the community's concept of something pre-eminent, a church, town hall, or university. Apart from deliberately introduced landmarks of this nature, buildings have mostly flowed close to the contours of the ground. Moreover the lofty silhouette has normally had some affinity with natural forms [but] . . . The rearing rectangular outline of the multi-storey block is hard on the eye. And it is inescapable. [These towers] dwarf everything, important public buildings, trees, humans. They also shut off and shut in. A single block can become a giant stopper, keeping out what used to be a pleasant glimpse of the sky at the end of a dull street. Or a line of blocks may slash across a dramatic view of snow-capped hills. They also diminish the pleasantness of city parks and public gardens since their prodigious height dispels the illusion of rural things . . . They likewise steal the nearer sky, lessening the chance of small pleasures like a fine sunset or a new moon. And any house or garden lying alongside a multi-storey block suffers drastically from the overshadowing of this cold and concrete wing.

What is more, none of the claimed advantages of high-rise housing proved to be true in practice. It did not save land (if one excludes special cases such as Hong Kong, where separation between buildings is minimal); it was not necessarily quicker, especially when new building methods went wrong; it was certainly not cheaper – both construction and maintenance turned out to be enormously more expensive than for low-rise homes; and finally, the idea that it would bring a better quality of life was the opposite of most residents' experience. Perhaps most fundamental of all is a widespread feeling among people – at least in Britain – not to be dismissed because it is difficult to define, that tower blocks are somehow an offence against the natural order of human habitation. When very large numbers are gathered into one settlement, there has to be a trade-off between the benefits of proximity and the costs of overcrowding; but the general answer to this dilemma is surely not to be found in high-rise housing. Kennan (1974) asks 'How long will it take city planners to realize that what people want in an urban community is . . . variety and intimacy? The search for grandeur . . . attempts to remove man from the reassuring disorder of nature, in which he once had his habitat, and in which he was accustomed, over millions of years, to look for his security.' Similarly, Callard (2005) points out the dangers of 'rigid visions of utopia in which the reorganisation of space is assumed to produce particular transformations in the bodies, minds and societies for which they are designed'. Such expectations will inevitably be disappointed.

At the same time, 'environment' should not be interpreted too exclusively in visual terms. Davidson (2000) argued for a more holistic view, including the efficiency with which local resources are used. Rehabilitation of existing buildings, recycling of waste, all forms of energy-saving, and greening schemes such as 'urban farms' can help jobless and disheartened people to regain vitality. Among other things, this revitalization of urban communities is very important for the resettlement of people with chronic disabilities who are leaving psychiatric and other hospitals. Generally, they tend to be placed in inner-city areas because these are the only ones that have both empty accommodation and an absence of community resistance to such incomers. Both of these features, though, also indicate the poor level of social integration in such environments, which is unlikely to be helpful to disabled people as they seek to re-establish their lives.

Very recent developments in England indicate an attempt by official agencies to provide an alternative to both high-rise blocks and sprawling suburbs. At Northampton, the new development of Upton is based on 18 homes per acre – three times the ratio of a typical American suburb. Its design code required certain features (for example, painted front doors, at least 75 cm wide), yet ensures that the buildings vary in height and design, as in a traditional village. Instead of cul-de-sacs, there are interconnected streets, encouraging people to walk past each others' home on the way to the shops, while informed surveillance is helped by windows that overlook streets and courtyards (*Economist*, 2006). Similarly, alongside the Thames in Kent, a seven-year programme of redevelopment on 'Crownfield' land is constructing eight district areas, of varying density, using regional materials. There will be 250 homes – both houses and flats – as well as shops, working space, and a new school. Its good design and prioritization of the needs of people above those of transport have already gained an award from the Commission for Architecture and the Built Environment (*Countryside Voice*, 2006). However, the extent to which such schemes can reduce the dependence of residents on car travel remains to be seen.

Finally, while there is no need to try to question the value of good housing, a review of the evidence by Thomson *et al.* (2001) showed that claims for its direct effects on health need to remain cautious. They identified 18 studies of the health effects of housing improvements, starting in 1936; the quality of these was described as 'generally poor'. Only two were prospective controlled studies, including mental health. Methodologically, the main problem was that poor housing often exists alongside other forms of deprivation, so that specifying the health gain that may result from a specific housing improvement becomes very difficult. In any of the concepts involved – whether housing, health, or deprivation – causality is a multifactorial process, while little is known about the effects of poor housing over an individual's lifecourse. The conclusion of this review was that large-scale studies, which include the wider social context, are needed to show what health gains can be achieved from investment in better housing. Ideally, the multiple factors involved would be confronted simultaneously, but in the real world such a broad approach is hardly ever possible, since expenditure tends to be tied to specific objectives. At the same time, public policy should not forget that housing is only one aspect of life in adverse circumstances, which may well include among others poverty, unemployment, crime, and drug abuse.

References

Bagley, C. (1973) 'The built environment as an influence on personality and social behaviour: a spatial study', in Canter, D. and Lee, T. R. (eds), *Psychology and the built environment*. Tonbridge: Architectural Press.

Birtchnell, J., Masters, N. and Deahl, M. (1988) 'Depression and the physical environment: a study of young married women on a London housing estate'. *British Journal of Psychiatry, 153*, 56–64.

Bishop, J. (1986) *Milton Keynes – The best of both worlds?* Bristol: SAUS.

Callard, F. (2005) 'Editorial'. *Journal of Public Mental Health, 4*, 2–5.

Carp, F. M. (1975) 'Impact of improved housing on morale and life satisfaction'. *Gerontologist, 15*, 511–515.

Carstairs, G. M. and Brown, G. W. (1958) 'A census of psychiatric cases in two contrasting communities'. *Journal of Mental Science, 104*, 72–81.

Coleman, A. (1985) *Utopia on trial*. London: Hilary Shipman.

Cook, D. A. and Morgan, H. G. (1982) 'Families in high-rise flats'. *British Medical Journal, 284*, 846.

Cooney, E. W. (1974) 'High flats in local authority housing in England and Wales since 1945': in Sutcliffe, A. (ed.), *Multi-storey living: The British working class experience*. London: Croom Helm.

Cooper, J. and Sartorius, N. (1977) 'Cultural and temporal variations in schizophrenia: a speculation on the importance of industrialization'. *British Journal of Psychiatry, 130*, 50–55.

Countryside Voice (2006) 'Ingress Park, Kent'. London: CPRE.

Davidson, J. (2000) '". . . The world was getting smaller": women, agoraphobia and bodily boundaries'. *Area, 32*, 31–40.

De Alarcon, R. and Rathod, N. H. (1968) 'Prevalence and early detection of heroin abuse'. *British Medical Journal, 2*, 549–553.

Dunleavy, P. (1981) *The politics of mass housing in Britain 1945–1975*. Oxford: Clarendon Press.

Dyos, J. (1982) 'The slums of Victorian London', in Cannadine, D. and Reeber, S. (eds), *Exploring the urban past*. Cambridge: Cambridge University Press.

Economist, The (2006) 'Field of dreams'. 29 July, 27–28.

Ellaway, A. and Macintyre, S. (1998) 'Does housing tenure predict health in the UK because it exposes people to different levels of housing related hazards in the home or its surroundings?' *Health and Place*, *4*, 141–150.

Elton, P. J. and Packer, J. M. (1986) 'A prospective randomised trial of the value of rehousing on the grounds of mental ill-health'. *Journal of Chronic Diseases*, *39*, 221–227.

Esher, L. (1981) *A broken wave*. London: Allen Lane.

Evans, J. W., Lovel, T. W. and Eaton, K. K. (1969) 'Social workers and general practice'. *British Medical Journal*, *1*, 44–46.

Fanning, D. M. (1967) 'Families in flats'. *British Medical Journal*, *4*, 382–386.

Frankenberg, R. (1969) *Communities in Britain*. London: Routledge & Kegan Paul.

Freedman, J. L. (1975) *Crowding and behavior*. San Francisco: W. H. Freeman.

Freeman, H. L. (1972) 'Mental health and new communities in Britain', in Nossiter, T. J., Hanson, A. H. and Rokkan, S. (eds), *Imagination and precision in the social sciences*. London: Faber.

Fried, M. and Gleicher, P. (1961) 'Some sources of residential satisfaction in an urban slum'. *Journal of the American Institute of Planners*, *27*, 305–315.

Fried, M. (1963) 'Grieving for a lost home', in Duhl, L. J. (ed.) *The urban condition*. New York: Basic Books.

Gans, H. J. (1967) 'Planning and city planning for mental health', in Eldredge, H. W. (ed.), *Taming megalopolis*, Vol. 2. New York: Doubleday.

Gardiner, S. (1981) 'Slabs in a wasteland'. *The Observer*, 2 August.

Gillis, A. R. (1977) 'High-rise housing and psychological strain'. *Journal of Health and Social Behaviour*, *18*, 418–431.

Gilloran, J. L. (1968) 'Social health problems associated with "high living" '. *The Medical Officer*, *120*, 117–118.

Gradidge, R. (1981) *Dream houses*. London: Constable.

Greenbie, B. B. (1974) 'Social territory, community health and urban planning'. *Journal of the American Institute of Planners*, *40*, 74–82.

Hall, P. (1966) 'Some clinical aspects of moving house as an apparent precipitant of psychiatric symptoms'. *Journal of Psychosomatic Research*, *10*, 59–70.

Halpern, D. S. (1995) *Mental health and the built environment*. London: Taylor & Francis.

Halpern, D. S. and Reid, J. (1992) 'Effect of unexpected demolition announcement on health of residents'. *British Medical Journal*, *304*, 1229–1230.

Hannay, D. R. (1981) 'Mental health and high flats'. *Journal of Chronic Diseases*, *34*, 431–432.

Hare, E. H. (1966) 'Mental health in new towns: what next?'. *Journal of Psychosomatic Research*, *10*, 53–58.

Hare, E. H. and Shaw, G. K. (1965) *Mental health on a new housing estate*. London: Oxford University Press.

Hayden, E. W. (1978) 'Agoraphobia and the role of the architect'. *Building Design*, *1*.

Hillier, B. and Hanson, J. (1984) *Social logic of space*. Cambridge: Cambridge University Press.

Hillier, B., Burdett, R., Peponis, J. and Penn, A. (1987) 'Creating life: or, does architecture determine anything?', *Architecture and Behavior*, *3*, 233–250.

Hird, J. F. (1966) 'Planning for a new community'. *Journal of the College of General Practitioners*, *12*, 33–41.

Hopton, J. L. and Hunt, S. M. (1996) 'Housing conditions and mental health in a disadvantaged area in Scotland'. *Journal of Epidemiology & Community Health, 50,* 56–61.

Howes, G. A. K. (1983) *Policing and social policy in multi-ethnic areas in Europe – the social context.* Paper to Sixth Cranfield Conference, Cambridge, UK.

Hunt, S. M. (1990) 'Emotional disasters and bad housing'. *Health & Hygiene,* 72–79.

Ineichen, B. and Hooper, D. (1974) 'Wives' mental health and children's behaviour problems in contrasting residential areas'. *Social Science and Medicine, 8,* 369–374.

Jephcott, P. (1971) *Homes in high flats.* Edinburgh: Oliver & Boyd.

Johnson, D. A. W. (1970) 'Rehousing and psychiatric illness'. *The Medical Officer, 124,* 225–228.

Johnson, R. (2005) 'Mental health and housing: making the links in policy, research and practice'. *Journal of Public Mental Health, 4,* 21–28.

Kasl, S. V. (1977) 'The effect of the residential environment on health and behavior: a review', in Hinkle, O. E. and Loring, W. C. (eds), *The effect of the man-made environment on health and behaviour.* Washington, DC: Government Printing Office.

Kasl, S. V. and Rosenfield, S. (1980) 'The residential environment and its impact on the mental health of the aged', in Birren, J. E. and Sloane, R. B. (eds), *Handbook of mental health & ageing.* Englewood Cliffs, NJ: Prentice Hall.

Kasl, S. V., Will, J., White, M. and Marcuse, P. (1982) 'Quality of the residential environment and mental health', in Baum, A. and Singer, J. E. (eds), *Advances in environmental psychology.* Hillsdale, NJ: Lawrence Erlbaum Associates, Inc.

Kennan, G. F. (1974) *The New Yorker,* 29 April.

Lee, T. R. (1976) *Psychology and the environment.* London: Methuen.

Leyhausen, P. (1965) 'The sane community – a density problem'. *Discovery, 26,* 27–33.

Littlewood, J. and Tinker, A. (1981) *Families in flats.* Department of Environment. London: HMSO.

Lowenstein, L. F. (1982) 'Psychological effects of high rise living'. *British Journal of Clinical & Social Psychiatry, 1,* 39–41.

Lynch, K. (1960) *The image of the city.* Cambridge, MA: MIT Press.

Macpherson, R., Haynes, R., Summerfield, L., Foy, C. and Slade, M. (2003) 'From research to practice: a local mental health services needs assessment'. *Social Psychiatry & Psychiatric Epidemiology, 38,* 276–281.

Marks, I. M. (1969) *Fears and phobias.* London: Heinemann.

Marris, B. (1974) 'Challenging rubbish'. *New Society.*

Martin, F. M., Brotherston, J. H. and Chave, S. P. (1957) 'Incidence of neurosis in a new housing estate'. *British Journal of Preventive and Social Medicine, 11,* 196–202.

Moore, N. C. (1974) 'Psychiatric illness and living in flats'. *British Journal of Psychiatry, 125,* 500–507.

Moore, N. C. (1975) 'Social aspects of flat dwelling'. *Public Health, 89,* 109–115.

Moore, N. C. (1976) 'The personality and mental health of flat dwellers'. *British Journal of Psychiatry, 128,* 259–261.

Muthesius, S. (1982) *The English terraced house.* London: Yale University Press.

Newman, O. (1972) *Defensible space.* New York: Macmillan.

Newman, O. (1980) *Community of interest.* New York: Anchor Doubleday.

Nicholson, J. H. (1961) *New communities in Britain.* London: National Council of Social Service.

Oliver, P., Davis, I. and Bestley, I. (1981) *Dunromin.* London: Barrie and Jenkins.

OPDM (2003) *The Sustainable Communities Plan.* London: OPDM.

Reynolds, I. and Nicholson, C. (1969) 'Living off the grounds'. *Architects Journal, 34*, 150–154.

Richman, N. (1974) 'Effects of housing on preschool children and their mothers'. *Developmental Medicine & Child Neurology, 10*, 1–9.

Sainsbury, P. and Collins, J. (1966) 'Some factors relating to mental illness in a new town'. *Journal of Psychosomatic Research, 10*, 45–51.

Self, P. (1957) *Cities in flood*. London: Faber.

Silver, N. (1968) 'Against new towns'. *New Statesman*, 2 August, 149.

Smith, C. A., Smith, C. J., Kearns, R. A. and Abbott, M. W. (1993) 'Housing stressors, social support and psychological distress'. *Social Science and Medicine, 37*, 603–612.

Smith, C. A., Smith, C. J., Kearns, R. A. and Abbott, M. W. (1994) 'Housing stressors and social support among the seriously mental ill'. *Housing Studies, 9*, 245–261.

Smith, S. J. (1990) 'Health status and the housing system'. *Social Science and Medicine, 31*, 753–762.

Stamp, G. (1988) 'Modern estate nears "complete breakdown" '. *The Independent*, 30 May.

Stewart, W. F. R. (1970) *Children in flats – a family study*. London: NSPCC.

Taylor, S. (1938) 'Suburban neurosis'. *Lancet, i*, 759–761.

Taylor, S. L. and Chave, S. P. W. (1964) *Mental health and environment*. London: Longmans.

Thomas, R. (1969) *Aycliffe to Cumbernauld*. London: PEP.

Thomas, R., Evans, S., Huxley, P., Gately, C. and Rogers, A. (2005) 'Housing improvement and self-reported mental distress among council estate residents'. *Social Science and Medicine, 60*, 2773–2783.

Thomson, H., Petticrew, M. and Morrison, D. (2001) 'Health effects of housing improvement: systematic review of intervention studies'. *British Medical Journal, 323*, 187–190.

Thorpe, F. T. (1939) 'Demolition melancholia'. *British Medical Journal, ii*, 127–128.

Vint, J. and Bintliff, J. (1983) 'Tower blocks: the economics of high rise housing'. *Social Policy & Administration, 17*, 118–129.

Ward, C. (1981) 'Pitfalls of punditry'. *New Society*, 357–358.

Werry, J. S. and Carlielle, J. (1983) 'The nuclear family, suburban neurosis, and iatrogenesis in Auckland mothers of young children'. *Journal of the American Academy of Child Psychiatry, 22*, 172–179.

Willmott, P. (1974) 'Population and community in London'. *New Society, 30*, 206–209.

Willmott, P. (1982) 'Support for suburbia'. *Times Higher Education Supplement*, 13 March, 13.

Wilner, D. M., Walkley, R. P., Pinkerton, T. C. and Tayback, M. (1962) *The housing environment and family life*. Baltimore: Johns Hopkins University Press.

Young, M. and Willmott, P. (1957) *Family and kinship in East London*. London: Routledge & Kegan Paul.

9 Noise and psychiatric disorder

Stephen Stansfeld and Charlotte Clark

One of the ubiquitous features of urban, and increasingly rural, environments is exposure to environmental noise. This kind of noise – predominantly from aircraft, road traffic, and neighbours – is a type of stressor that might be expected on common-sense grounds to have a deleterious effect on mental health. It is generally hypothesized that noise will cause disturbance of activities and communication, as well as annoyance, and that these will lead to stress responses, symptoms, and possibly overt illness (Van Dijk *et al.*, 1987). The association between noise and mental health has been examined in community surveys, using a variety of outcomes including (at the simplest level), individual symptoms, as well as psychiatric hospital admission rates, use of health services and psychotropic medication, and screening measures of common mental disorders. There has been research interest in this area for about 35 years and many of the most influential studies on risk of adult psychiatric disorder were carried out some time ago.

Definition of noise

Noise is generally defined as unwanted sound and is perceived as a pollutant and a type of environmental stressor. The physical property of 'sound' is necessary but not sufficient to produce noise. Thus, the concept of noise involves a significant psychological component ('unwanted') as well as a physical component (perceived by the ear and then transmitted by the auditory nerve to the temporal lobe in the brain) (Bell *et al.*, 1996). Noise is a disturbing phenomenon precisely because it is an unwanted component of the environment, although it is also possible for sound to be harmful for health without subjective disturbance. Recurrent or persistent ambient noise, which is frequently part of people's 'background', could be more harmful for human health because it is more likely to cause long-term reactions than a one-off environmental event (Bell *et al.*, 1996).

The measurement of sound is based on its physical components. Physically, sound is perceived by rapidly changing air pressure at the eardrum. The description of sound is typically characterized by intensity or sound pressure level (measured in decibels (dB)), frequency (pitch), periodicity (continuous or intermittent), and duration (acute or chronic). Other characteristics, which are not related to its physical components, are also important in determining the interpretation of perceived sound. These include: the predictability of noise; episodes (random or fixed interval); attitudes to the noise source; the meaning of the noise and degree of personal control over it. In general, it has been concluded that intermittent, higher-frequency, short-duration, intense sounds have greater effects on health than do those that are continuous, low-frequency, long-duration and low-intensity (Baker & Holding, 1993). It is difficult to isolate the effect of particular sound frequencies on health because they rarely occur in isolation, but increasing attention is being paid to the effects of persistent low-frequency noise that may elicit feelings of annoyance and helplessness (Berglund *et al.*, 1996).

Noise exposure and symptoms

Symptoms reported among industrial workers regularly exposed to high noise levels in settings such as weaving mills and factories (Melamed *et al.*, 1988) include nausea, headaches, argumentativeness, changes in mood, anxiety, post-work irritability, and sexual impotence. More self-reported illness and illness-related absenteeism (Cameron *et al.*, 1972), social conflicts at work and home (Jansen, 1961), and actual absenteeism (Cohen, 1976) have been found in noisy rather than quiet industries. Many of these industrial studies are difficult to interpret, however, because workers were exposed to other stressors such as physical danger and heavy work demands, in addition to excessive noise, and these may be more potent than noise in causing symptoms. There may also be a differential selection of individuals working in noisy areas: jobs in such areas may be less desirable, more difficult to fill, and hence may attract individuals with health problems that have prevented them from attaining more desirable employment. Alternatively, health factors may operate in the selection of personnel for jobs in high noise-exposure areas, which may be dangerous, demanding toughness and resilience not required for those in quieter areas (for example, few symptoms were found among men working in high noise on aircraft carriers (Davis, 1958)). Also, choice of coping strategies by individuals may influence whether noise actually causes symptoms: evasive coping strategies were related to higher scores on the Hopkins Symptom Check List in areas of high exposure to aircraft noise (Altena, 1989, cited in Passchier-Vermeer, 1993). In some studies, the increase in symptoms with noise level was only found for those who were highly annoyed (Melamed *et al.*, 1992).

Environmental noise experienced outside work settings, though less intense, tends to be more difficult for the ordinary citizen to avoid. Community surveys have found that high percentages of people reported 'headaches', 'restless nights', and 'being tense and edgy' in high-noise areas (Finke *et al.*, 1974; Kokokusha, 1973; Öhrström, 1989). An explicit link between aircraft noise and symptoms emerging in such studies raises the possibility of a bias toward over-reporting of symptoms (Barker & Tarnopolsky, 1978). Notably, a study around three Swiss airports (Grandjean *et al.*, 1973), did not mention that it was related to aircraft noise and did not find any association between the level of exposure to this noise and symptoms. In the West London Survey, 'tinnitus', 'burns, cuts and minor accidents', 'ear problems', and 'skin troubles' were all more common in areas of high-noise exposure (Tarnopolsky *et al.*, 1980). However, apart from 'ear problems' and 'tinnitus', 20 out of 23 chronic symptoms were more common in low-noise environments. These results may be related both to more social disadvantage and associated ill-health among residents in low aircraft noise exposure areas and to the possible unwillingness of chronically unhealthy individuals to move into potentially stressful high-noise exposure areas. Nevertheless, it would not exclude an effect of noise in causing some acute psychological symptoms.

Noise exposure and mental hospital admission rates

Much of the concern with the possible effects of noise on mental health began with the study of admissions to psychiatric hospitals from noisy areas. Early studies found associations between the level of aircraft noise and psychiatric hospital admissions, both in London (Abey Wickrama *et al.*, 1969) and Los Angeles (Meecham & Smith, 1977). These results have been criticized on methodological grounds (Chowns, 1970; Frerichs *et al.*, 1980) and a replication study by Gattoni and Tarnopolsky (1973) failed to confirm the findings. Jenkins *et al.* (1979) found that age-standardized admission rates to a London psychiatric hospital over four years were higher as the level of noise of an area decreased, but lower noise areas were also central urban districts, where high admission rates would be expected. In a further extensive study of three hospitals (Jenkins *et al.*, 1981), high aircraft noise was associated with higher admission rates in two hospitals, but in all three of them, admission rates seemed to follow non-noise factors more closely; the effect of noise, if any, could only be moderating that of other causal variables but not overriding them. Kryter (1990), in a re-analysis of the data, found 'a more consistently positive relation between level of exposure to aircraft noise and admissions rates'. Undoubtedly, the route to hospital admission is influenced by many psychosocial variables that are more potent than exposure to noise. Therefore, whether or not noise causes psychiatric disorder would be more suitably examined by studying a community sample.

Noise exposure and psychiatric morbidity in the community

In a community pilot study carried out in West London, Tarnopolsky *et al.* (1978) found no association between aircraft noise exposure and either General Health Questionnaire (GHQ) scores (Goldberg, 1972) (dichotomized 4/5, Low scorers/High scorers) or estimated psychiatric cases (Goldberg *et al.*, 1970). This was so even when exposure to road traffic noise was controlled for, except in three subgroups: persons 'aged 15–44 of high education', 'women aged 15–44', and those in 'professional or managerial occupations'. The authors expressed the guarded opinion that noise might have an effect in causing morbidity within certain vulnerable subgroups.

In the subsequent West London Survey of Psychiatric Morbidity (Tarnopolsky & Morton-Williams, 1980), 5885 adults were randomly selected from within four aircraft noise zones. No overall relationship was found between aircraft noise and the prevalence of psychiatric morbidity either for GHQ scores or for estimated numbers of psychiatric cases, using various indices of noise exposure. However, there was an association between noise and psychiatric morbidity in two subgroups: 'finished full-time education at age 19 years +' and 'professionals'. These two categories, which had a strong association with each other, were combined and then showed a significant association between noise and psychiatric morbidity measured by the GHQ. The authors concluded that their results 'show so far that noise *per se* in the community at large, does not seem to be a frequent, severe, pathogenic factor in causing mental illness but that it is associated with symptomatic response in selected subgroups of the population'.

One potential criticism of the cross-sectional study around Heathrow airport is that it represented a study of a population of 'noise survivors'; those most susceptible to noise effects would either have moved away or avoided living in the area. This methodological concern may be exaggerated, but it could be informative to carry out further studies where selection by noise exposure is not an issue. The possible relationship between noise and psychiatric disorder was examined in a population unlikely to have been selected by noise exposure by examining the association between road traffic noise exposure and psychological distress, in a study of the small town of Caerphilly, South Wales. In the cross-sectional results, no association was found between the initial level of road traffic noise based on traffic noise maps, and minor psychological distress, again measured by the GHQ, after adjustment for socio-demographic factors (Stansfeld *et al.*, 1993). In longitudinal analyses, no association was found between road traffic noise and psychological distress, after adjustment for socio-demographic factors and baseline psychological distress, although there was a small non-linear association of noise with increased anxiety scores (Stansfeld *et al.*, 1996). A recent Sardinian study compared subjects living close to an airport with control subjects living in other areas matched by sex, age, and employment status. This showed that exposed subjects had a higher frequency of diagnosis for 'generalized anxiety disorder' and 'anxiety disorder not otherwise specified'. This is one of the first studies finding an association between aircraft noise exposure and psychiatric diagnoses (Hardoy *et al.*, 2005). This study, which did not measure noise levels and had a response rate of 64%, is interesting and needs replication.

Exposure–effect relationships between noise exposure and mental health

One of the criteria for judging whether an association is causal is the demonstration of dose–response or exposure–effect associations, where the degree of mental health disturbance increases with the intensity and duration of noise exposure. This was not found in the Caerphilly study, but some others have found exposure–effect associations. Exposure to higher levels of military aircraft noise around the busy Kadena military airport in Japan was related in an exposure–effect association to 'depressiveness' and 'nervousness' measured by questionnaire, using the Todai Health Index, based on the Cornell Medical Index (Hiramatsu *et al.*, 1997; Ito *et al.*, 1994). Clear exposure–effect relationships were not found between scale scores and noise exposure, as expressed in five-unit steps. However, an exposure–effect association was evident between the highest noise-exposure group and lower exposure groups, indicating a threshold effect rather than a linear relationship. A further Japanese study of 5963 inhabitants around two air bases in Okinawa also found that those exposed to noise levels of Ldn 70 or above had higher rates of 'mental instability' and 'depressiveness' (Hiramatsu *et al.*, 2000). A further survey, using similar methodology on 6486 respondents, found exposure–effect associations between aircraft noise exposure, nervousness, and mental health (Miyakita *et al.*, 1998). These are important studies because of the opportunity to examine the effect of high noise-exposure levels and the probability that out-migration of vulnerable persons from noisy areas biasing the sample was small.

In a secondary analysis of a large British road traffic noise study, the noise level in dB(A) exceeded for 10% of the time (a measure of peak noise level) was weakly associated with a five-item mental health symptoms scale adjusting for age, gender, income, and length of residence (Halpern, 1995). The findings may be questioned, though, as the scale included some clear mental health items, but also some that were less obviously related to mental health. Adjustment for the amount of 'noise heard' reduced the association very little, suggesting no causal association with noise. Noise is only one aspect of traffic 'stress' and it may be difficult to separate the effects of noise from other hazardous aspects of road traffic. 'Traffic stress' comprising of 'traffic', 'auto maintenance', and 'accidents' was cross-sectionally associated with depressive symptoms in a Chinese-American sample in Los Angeles, adjusting for individual social class and neighbourhood poverty (Gee & Takeuchi, 2004). The effects of traffic noise on depression were worse in areas with more vehicle use.

Similar to the Japanese military aircraft studies, one community study of 366 Japanese women suggests that road traffic noise only has effects on depression, fatigue, and irritability above a threshold of 70 dB(A) (Yoshida *et al.*, 1997). However, it is difficult to be confident of the results of these analyses, as they were unadjusted for age or social deprivation. In a road traffic noise study in Belgrade, 253 residents exposed to road traffic noise levels of >65 dB(A) experienced significantly more fatigue, depression, nervousness, and headaches compared with residents exposed to <55 dB(A) (Belojevic & Jakovljevic, 1997). A great methodological advantage of this study was that the high- and low-noise exposure areas were homogeneous for age, gender, employment, and subjective noise sensitivity. Further support for effects at higher noise levels comes from a study that found higher ratings on the Hamilton Depression Scale in 70 steel tube factory workers exposed to industrial noise of 101 dB, compared with 71 non-noise-exposed workers in the same factory (Bing-shuang *et al.*, 1997). Overall, environmental noise seems to be linked more convincingly to psychological symptoms than to clinical psychiatric disorder. However, there may be a link to psychiatric disorder at much higher noise levels.

Noise exposure and quality of life

As environmental noise predicts annoyance and psychological symptoms, but does not seem to be associated with more severe health problems such as clinically definable psychiatric disorder, it might be that noise exposure is associated with milder conditions, such as those measured by scales of well-being and health functioning. Psychosocial well-being has been shown to be reduced in areas exposed to high traffic noise, but the results have not been especially consistent and may be mediated through disruptive effects on sleep (Öhrström, 1989, 1993).

Health functioning and well-being were also examined at the first stage of an intervention study on the effect of introducing a bypass to relieve traffic congestion in a small town in North Wales (Stansfeld *et al.*, 2000). Health functioning was measured by the SF-36 General Health Survey (Ware & Sherbourne, 1992), including dimensions of general health status, physical functioning, general mental health, and social functioning. Ninety-eight respondents were studied who lived on a busy high street with traffic noise levels varying between 72 and 75 dB(A) outdoor Leq. These respondents were compared with 239 control subjects living in adjacent quieter streets (noise level 55–63 dB(A) outdoor Leq). Although subjects were well matched on age, gender, housing insulation, car ownership, and employment status, they were not so well matched on proportion of manual workers, household crowding, deprivation, and home ownership. There was no evidence that respondents exposed to higher levels of road traffic noise had worse health functioning than those exposed to lower levels, adjusting for levels of deprivation. In addition, the introduction of the bypass did not lead to an improvement in levels of psychological distress, although the reduction in noise levels was modest. Noise has also been reported to affect well-being in office workers, with stronger effects reported than for many other nuisances (Klitzman & Stellman, 1989). However, in such cross-sectional studies it is difficult to be certain of the direction of causation and the contribution of other stressors.

Noise, health services, and medication use

The use of health services has also been taken as a measure of the relationship between noise and psychiatric disorder. Grandjean *et al.* (1973) reported that the proportion of the Swiss population taking drugs was higher in areas with high levels of aircraft noise, while Knipschild and Oudshoorn (1977) found that the purchase of sleeping pills, antacids, sedatives, and antihypertensive drugs all increased in a village newly exposed to aircraft noise, but not in a 'control' village where the noise level remained unchanged. Both studies also found an association between the rate of contact with general practitioners and level of noise exposure. In the Heathrow study (Watkins *et al.*, 1981), no association was found between levels of noise and a range of health-care indicators – use of drugs, particularly psychiatric or self-prescribed, visits to the general practitioner, attendance at hospital, and contact with various community services.

In a study of five rural Austrian communities exposed to road traffic noise, levels above 55 dB(A) were associated with increased risk of taking sleeping tablets (OR = 2.22 [95%CI 1.13–4.38]) and overall prescriptions (OR = 3.65 [95%CI 2.13–6.26]), relative to road traffic noise exposure less than 55 dB(A) (Lercher, 1996). This suggested that effects were present at fairly low noise levels. In this case, mental ill-health may be secondary to sleep disturbance, which is likely to occur at lower nocturnal noise levels than mental health symptoms resulting from daytime noise exposure. As this occurred in a rural setting, where road traffic was the predominant source of noise, it would be interesting to replicate these findings in other settings. Results from the Health Impact Assessment at Schiphol Airport, Amsterdam, suggested that there was higher use of non-prescribed sedatives, but not prescribed sedatives, in areas exposed to aircraft noise than in quieter areas (Franssen *et al.*, 2004).

Effects of noise on performance and potential mechanisms of noise effects

What might the mechanism be for the effects of noise on mental health? One way to approach this is through the effects of noise on cognitive performance, where the laboratory evidence of effects is fairly robust (Smith & Broadbent, 1992). There is evidence that noise impairs aspects of human functioning, such as performance (Loeb, 1986) and sleep, which are important in maintaining normal functioning, and that it causes adverse emotional reactions such as annoyance. In general, it seems that noise exposure increases arousal, and decreases attention through distraction (Broadbent, 1953), increases the need for focusing, or avoiding attention to irrelevant stimuli (Cohen & Spacapan, 1978), as well as altering choice of task strategy (Smith & Broadbent, 1981). Individuals' perception of their degree of control over noise may also influence whether it impairs memory (Willner & Neiva, 1986), while perception of lack of control over environmental conditions may be an important mediator of health effects.

Studies of acute noise exposure (100–110 dB, wide band frequency for 30 minutes) in rhesus monkeys showed impaired performance of a spatial memory task dependent on the prefrontal cortex (Arnsten & Goldman-Rakic, 1998). No deficits were found in noise-exposed monkeys for a visual pattern discrimination task that might show impairments, were this effect to be due to decreased motivation or motor performance. The authors concluded that acute mild noise stress produces deficits resembling prefrontal cortex lesions, and that this implied a reversion in stressful situations to more instinctual behaviour regulated by subcortical rather than higher structures. This may have survival value, but may be maladaptive in human society where higher functions are necessary for behavioural regulation. Treatment with clonidine and naloxone, which decrease stress-induced dopamine release, reduced these noise-induced effects on the prefrontal cortex, suggesting that noise stress elicits excessive dopamine release, which may be responsible for these deficits.

Noise may also affect social performance: (1) as a stressor causing unwanted aversive changes in affective state; (2) by masking speech and impairing communication; and (3) by distracting attention from relevant cues in the immediate social environment (Jones *et al.*, 1981). It may be that people whose performance strategies are already limited for other reasons (for example through high anxiety) and who are faced with multiple tasks may be more vulnerable to the masking and distracting effects of noise.

The mechanism for the effects of noise on health is generally conceptualized as fitting the stress-diathesis model, in which noise exposure increases arousal, and chronic exposure leads to chronic physiological change and subsequent health effects. It is not clear, though, whether this model is a complete explanation for mental health effects. A more sophisticated model (Biesiot, 1989; Passchier-Vermeer, 1993) incorporates the interaction between the person and their environment. In this model, the person readjusts their behaviour in noisy conditions to reduce exposure. An important addition is the inclusion of both the appraisal of noise (in terms of danger, loss of quality, meaning of the noise, challenges for environmental control, etc.) and coping (the ability to alter behaviour to deal with the stressor). This model emphasizes that dealing with noise is an active rather than a passive process.

Noise and sleep disturbance

Sleep disturbance is a symptom of common mental disorder and could plausibly be a mediating factor between noise exposure and psychiatric disorder. There is both objective and subjective evidence for sleep disturbance by noise (Öhrström, 1982; Öhrström *et al.*, 1998). Exposure to noise during sleep has shown sleep disturbance to be proportional to the amount of noise experienced, in terms of an increased rate of changes in sleep stages and in the number of awakenings. Habituation occurs with an increased number of sound exposures, both per night and across nights. It seems that the probability of awakening increases with the number of noise stimuli in the night, but levels off. In the laboratory, there was no habituation during 14 nights of exposure to noise at maximum noise level exposure (Öhrström, 1982). Objective sleep disturbance is likely to occur if there are more than 50 noise events per night, with a maximum level of 50 dBA or more indoors. In contrast to laboratory studies, there is a low association between outdoor noise levels and sleep disturbance.

In the Civil Aviation Authority Study (1980) around Heathrow and Gatwick airports, the relative proportion of total sleep disturbance *attributable to noise*, but not the level of total sleep disturbance, increased in noisy areas. This suggested a symptom reporting or attribution effect, rather than a real noise effect. In a subsequent actigraphy study around four UK airports, sleep disturbance was studied in relation to a wide range of aircraft noise exposure over 15 consecutive nights (Horne *et al.*, 1994). Although there was a strong association between both sleep EEGs and actigram-measured awakenings and self-reported sleep disturbance, none of the aircraft noise events were associated with awakenings detected by actigram; the chance of sleep disturbance with aircraft noise exposure of <82 dB was not significant. Although it is likely that the population studied was one already adapted to aircraft noise exposure, this study is also likely to be closer to real life than laboratory studies, which have subjects newly exposed to noise.

Road traffic noise at 50–60 dB(A) maximum increases the time taken to fall asleep. In particular, the number of noise events seems important in this effect (Öhrström & Rylander, 1990). The first third of the night is the time most vulnerable to sleep disturbance. Living less than 20 metres from a busy road has been found to predict insomnia in a study of Japanese women, after adjusting for many relevant confounding factors (Kageyama *et al.*, 1997).

Insomnia is a symptom of many psychiatric disorders, especially depression and anxiety. In studies of depressed patients compared to control subjects, there was prolonged latency to sleep, increased wakefulness during sleep, early morning wakening, decreased sleep efficiency, and reduced total sleep time.

Mental health consequences of insomnia

Transient insomnia is usually accompanied by reports of daytime sleepiness and performance impairment the next day, while chronic insomnia is generally associated with poorer emotional and physical health. Several large-scale epidemiological studies of the general adult population have shown that between one-third and one-half of people who complain of chronic insomnia are also diagnosable with primary psychiatric disorders, mostly anxiety and mood disorders (Ford & Kamerow, 1989; Mellinger *et al.*, 1985).

Breslau *et al.* (1996) found a strong correlation between lifetime prevalence of sleep problems and psychiatric disorders, with anxiety, depression, and substance abuse being the most common. Similar results have been found by Vollrath *et al.* (1989), Dryman and Eaton (1991), and Chang *et al.* (1997). In a large-scale European population-based study (Ohayon & Roth, 2003), it was found that insomnia more often precedes than follows incident cases of mood disorders.

Insomniacs not only have higher rates of psychiatric disorders, but not surprisingly, also have increased rates of various kinds of psychological symptoms: patients with insomnia reported increased psychological stress and/or decreased ability to cope with stress (Kim *et al.*, 2000; Roth & Ancoli-Israel, 1999). Even people whose insomnia was due to identified medical factors showed elevated signs on the MMPI, suggesting a possible causal relationship or specific association between insomnia and psychiatric symptomatology.

Does insomnia lead to depression?

There is also evidence that insomnia may be a risk factor for developing depression (Riemann *et al.*, 2001; Roberts *et al.*, 2002). This raises the question whether prolonged noise exposure leading to insomnia provokes the onset of depression in susceptible people. Though this seems theoretically possible, there is little evidence to support it. In a longitudinal study of adolescents, it was the other way round – depressive symptoms preceded the onset of insomnia (Patton *et al.*, 2000). Delayed sleep latency in children has been linked to increased externalizing symptoms, including aggressive behaviour, and impaired attention and social problems (Aronen *et al.*, 2000). In this cross-sectional study, the direction of association was uncertain, but it seems most plausible that the sleep disturbance was a feature of the behavioural disturbance rather than a cause of it. Three criteria have been suggested for sleep disturbance to be environmentally determined: (1) the sleep problem is temporally associated with the introduction of a physically measurable stimulus or definable set of environmental circumstances; (2) the physical rather than the psychological properties of the environmental factors are the critical causative elements; and (3) removal of the responsible factors results in an immediate or gradual return to normal sleep and wakefulness (Kraenz *et al.*, 2004). Most studies do not fulfil these criteria. Further longitudinal research is needed to ascertain whether noise-induced insomnia is likely to lead on to overt psychiatric disorder.

Noise exposure during sleep may increase blood pressure, heart rate, and finger pulse amplitude, as well as body movements (Muzet & Eberhardt, 1980). Noise may also have after-effects during the day following a disturbed night. In a community study of exposure to road traffic noise, perceived sleep quality, mood, and performance in terms of reaction time were all decreased following sleep disturbed by road traffic noise (Öhrström, 1982). Studies on noise abatement show that by reducing the indoor noise level, the amount of REM and slow-wave sleep can be increased (Vallet *et al.*, 1983). It does seem that although there may be some adaptation to sleep disturbance by noise, complete habituation does not occur, particularly for heart rate. Thus, there may be potential long-term health effects of noise-disturbed sleep, although critics of this hypothesis maintain that these physiological changes in response to noise are within the normal range of such responses to environmental triggers.

Noise annoyance

The most widespread and well-documented subjective response to noise is annoyance, which may include fear and mild anger, related to a belief that one is being avoidably harmed (Cohen & Weinstein, 1981). Noise is also seen as intrusive into personal privacy, while its meaning for any individual is important in determining whether that person will be annoyed by it (Gunn, 1987). Annoyance reactions are often associated with the degree of interference that any noise causes in everyday activities, which probably precedes and leads to annoyance (Hall *et al.*, 1985; Taylor, 1984). In both traffic and aircraft noise studies, noise levels have been found to be associated with annoyance in a dose–response relationship (Griffiths & Langdon, 1968; Miedema & Vos, 1998; Schultz, 1978). Annoyance is also dependent on the context in which the noise is heard. Overall, it seems that conversation, watching television, or listening to the radio (all involving speech communication) are the activities most disturbed by aircraft noise (Hall *et al.*, 1985), while traffic noise, if present at night, is most disturbing for sleep.

Levels of annoyance may be influenced by major aircraft-related events such as air crashes. The Amsterdam air disaster increased levels of annoyance in the local area, which was maximal shortly after flights were resumed at Schiphol Airport, but there was no evidence of an increase in psychological distress measured by the General Health Questionnaire (Reijneveld, 1994). Annoyance is generally transient and is not a very severe psychological symptom. However, in the context of noise causing arousal, could prolonged annoyance be an intervening step between noise and psychiatric disorder?

Near Heathrow Airport, London (courtesy of the *Hounslow Chronicle* newspaper).

Noise, noise annoyance, symptoms, and psychiatric morbidity

Noise annoyance is associated on one hand with noise level, and on the other with symptoms and psychiatric disorder (Tarnopolsky & Morton Williams, 1980). Against expectation, although there was a strong link between noise and annoyance, and those who were highly annoyed showed the greatest number of symptoms, symptoms were not more common in high- rather than low-noise areas. This apparent paradox has been explained by the 'Vulnerability Hypothesis' (Tarnopolsky *et al.*, 1980). According to this explanation, noise is not directly pathogenic, but sorts individuals into annoyance categories according to their vulnerability to stress. Tarnopolsky *et al.* (1978) found that noise and minor psychiatric disorder were the strongest predictors of annoyance and that psychiatric morbidity led to annoyance, rather than vice versa. Moreover, annoyance does not seem to act as an intervening variable between noise and morbidity; at any particular level of exposure there is wide individual variation in the degree of annoyance that is expressed. Individual variance in annoyance can be explained largely in terms of noise sensitivity and attitudes to the source of the noise (Evans & Tafalla, 1987; Job, 1988). This suggests that people with existing psychiatric morbidity may be more disturbed and annoyed by noise and potentially more sensitive to any noise-related effects.

Noise sensitivity and vulnerability to psychiatric disorder

Noise sensitivity, based on attitudes to noise in general (Anderson, 1971; Stansfeld, 1992), is an intervening variable that explains much of the variance between exposure and individual annoyance responses (Fields, 1994; Griffiths & Langdon, 1968; Weinstein, 1978). Individuals who are noise-sensitive are also likely to be sensitive to other aspects of the environment (Broadbent, 1972; Stansfeld *et al.*, 1985; Thomas & Jones, 1982; Weinstein, 1978). This raises the question as to whether noise-sensitive individuals are simply those who complain more about their environment. Certainly, there is an association between noise sensitivity and neuroticism (Belojevic & Jakovljevic, 1997; Jelinkova, 1988; Öhrström *et al.*, 1988; Smith, 2003; Thomas & Jones 1982), although it has not been found in all studies (Broadbent, 1972). Weinstein (1980) hypothesized that noise sensitivity is part of a critical–uncritical dimension, showing the same association as noise sensitivity to measures of noise, privacy, air pollution, and neighbourhood reactions. The most critical subjects are not uniformly negative about their environment, but more discriminating than the uncritical group, who comment uniformly on their environment.

Noise sensitivity has also been related to current psychiatric disorder (Bennett, 1945; Iwata, 1984; Tarnopolsky & Morton-Williams, 1980). Stansfeld *et al.* (1985) found that high noise sensitivity was associated with phobic disorders and neurotic depression, measured by the Present State Examination (Wing *et al.*, 1974). Similar to this association with phobic symptoms, noise sensitivity has also been linked to a coping style based on avoidance, which may have adverse health consequences (Pulles *et al.*, 1990) and a tendency to report health complaints rather than take a more active coping approach to noise (Lercher & Kofler, 1996). Noise sensitivity may be partly secondary to psychiatric disorder: depressed patients followed-up over four months became less noise-sensitive as they recovered (Stansfeld, 1992). 'Objective' psychophysiological laboratory investigation of reactions to noise in a sub-sample of depressed patients found that noise-sensitive people tended to have higher levels of tonic physiological arousal, more phobic and defence/startle responses, and slower habituation to noise (Stansfeld, 1992). Thus, noise-sensitive people attend more to noises, discriminate more between noises, find noises more threatening and out of their control, and adapt to noises more slowly than people who are less sensitive. Noise sensitivity may be an indicator of vulnerability to minor psychiatric disorder, although not necessarily psychiatric disorder *caused by noise* (Stansfeld, 1992).

In the analysis of a subset of noise-sensitive women, compared with less sensitive women in the West London survey, aircraft noise exposure did not predict psychiatric disorder in the sensitive women (Stansfeld *et al.*, 1985). In the Caerphilly study, noise sensitivity predicted psychological distress at follow-up after adjusting for baseline psychological distress, but did not interact with the noise level, suggesting that noise sensitivity does not specifically moderate the effect of noise on psychological distress (Stansfeld *et al.*, 1993). However, in further analyses, a statistically significant association between road traffic noise exposure and psychological distress, measured by the General Health Questionnaire, was found in noise-sensitive men but not in men of low noise sensitivity (Stansfeld *et al.*, 2002). In the original analyses, after adjusting for trait anxiety at baseline, the effect of noise sensitivity was no longer statistically significant, suggesting that much of the association between noise sensitivity and psychological distress may be accounted for by the confounding association with trait anxiety. Constitutionally anxious people may be both more aware of threatening aspects of their environment and more prone to future psychiatric disorder.

In a UK community study, associations were examined between noise exposure, noise sensitivity, subjective symptoms, and sleep disturbance in a random sample of 543 adults (Smith *et al.*, 2000). Perceived noise exposure was related to subjective health, but this association became non-significant after adjustment for negative affectivity. In a similar way, adjustment for negative affectivity eliminated the association between noise sensitivity and subjective health. Thus, it was suggested that noise sensitivity was merely a proxy measure of negative affectivity or neuroticism. However, although this would mean that noise sensitivity is not specific to noise, more recent analyses mentioned above suggest that high levels of trait anxiety or neuroticism may be an indicator of vulnerability to noise effects and could put people at risk of adverse psychological effects from noise, even if they do not increase the risk of physical ill-health (Stansfeld *et al.*, 2002).

Noise and mental health in children

Environmental noise exposure affects health and cognition in children, who may be especially vulnerable to noise effects because they have less capacity than adults to anticipate or cope with stressors. The few studies examining noise and psychological disorders in children have had mixed results. Nurmi and von Wright (1983) found that noise during learning impaired the subsequent recall performance of children with high neuroticism scores and with a high score on state-anxiety. Poustka *et al.* (1992) studied the psychiatric and psychosomatic health of 1636 children aged 4 to 16 in two geographical regions that differed according to the noise made by jet fighters frequently exercising at low altitude. Psychological and neurological outcomes were not related to noise exposure: associations between noise exposure and depression and anxiety could be demonstrated, but only beneath the threshold of clinical significance. These results are less convincing because the areas differed socio-economically, which was not adjusted for in the analyses, and there was a lack of precision of the measures of noise exposure.

In Munich, children living in areas exposed to high aircraft noise had lower levels of psychological well-being than children living in quieter environments (Evans *et al.*, 1995). The longitudinal data from around Munich showed that after the inauguration of the new airport, the newly noise-exposed communities demonstrated a significant decline in self-reported quality of life, measured on the Kindl scale, after being exposed to the increased aircraft noise for 18 months, compared with a control sample (Evans *et al.*, 1998). Impairment of 'quality of life' is a less severe disturbance than impairment of mental health. These studies suggest that noise does not influence children's mental health, though it may affect their stress responses and sense of well-being.

Further studies have examined the effects of noise on child psychiatric disorder. Child self-reported mental health on a standard scale and teacher ratings of classroom adjustment in response to motorway, road, and rail noise were studied in a large sample of 8–11-year-old Austrian primary school children. Noise exposure was significantly associated with classroom adjustment scores but, intriguingly, child self-reported mental ill-health was only impaired in noisy settings for children of low birth weight and preterm birth (Lercher *et al.*, 2002). In the Schools Health & Environment Study around Heathrow Airport (Haines *et al.*, 2001a), chronic aircraft noise exposure was not associated with anxiety and depression (measured with psychometrically valid scales), after adjustment for socio-economic factors. In a larger study of children's health around Heathrow Airport – the West London Schools Study (Haines *et al.*, 2001b) – an association was found between aircraft noise exposure level and increased hyperactivity scores measured by the Strength & Difficulties Questionnaire (SDQ) (Goodman, 1997).

These analyses were revisited in the RANCH Study of 2844 9–10-year-old children living around Schiphol Airport in the Netherlands, Barajas Airport near Madrid and Heathrow Airport in the United Kingdom. There were no overall effects of aircraft noise or road traffic noise on children's mental health, measured by the SDQ. However, an association was found between higher levels of aircraft noise and the hyperactivity subscale of the SDQ. There was also an inverse association between exposure to road traffic noise and the conduct problems subscale. The hyperactivity findings in the RANCH Study replicated the earlier findings from the West London Schools Study, and suggest that this is not due to chance. In addition, the analyses were adjusted for a wide range of socio-demographic, environmental, and parental factors, suggesting that this result is not indicative of confounding. What does this association mean, therefore?

Children with attention deficit hyperactivity disorder (ADHD) are distractible, with a short attention span, and it might be expected that external stimuli, such as aircraft noise, could specifically interfere with their attention. Children with ADHD exhibit reduced ability to process auditory information when required to divide and focus their attention for a sustained period of time (Riccio *et al.*, 1996). They show problems with signal recognition, as well as poorer auditory discrimination and poorer speech discrimination in noisy situations (Corbett & Stanczak, 1999; Pillsbury *et al.*, 1995). It is a common complaint that these children are distracted by background noise (Gray *et al.*, 2002), and it seems likely that aircraft noise exposure may be exacerbating these children's difficulties. Certainly, it seems less likely that aircraft noise is causing hyperactivity than that it is making an existing tendency towards hyperactivity worse. Further investigation of cognitive responses to noise in children with ADHD is warranted. Altogether, noise exposure in children may impair well-being, and biologically vulnerable children may be especially at risk.

Complaints about noise in the clinical setting

In clinical practice, it is not uncommon to see patients who complain of considerable disturbance by noise, often made by neighbours. Noise from neighbours is the commonest source of these complaints to local authorities in the UK (Chartered Institute of Environmental Health, 1999). Noise that is continuous and apparently indefinite, of uncertain cause or source, that is emotive or frightening, or apparently due to thoughtlessness or lack of consideration, is most likely to elicit an adverse reaction (Grimwood, 1993). In the 1991 BRE survey, people most objected to barking dogs, banging doors, noise from radio, television, or hi-fi and human voices (Grimwood, 1993). Two types of emotional response to noise were observed: outwardly directed aggression, characterized by feelings of annoyance, aggravation, bitterness, and anger towards the source of the noise, and a more emotional response of tension, anxiety, and feelings of pressure. These responses are reminiscent of the distinction between internalizing and externalizing disorders. Whether noise from neighbours can induce psychiatric disorder has been little studied in community research, but this is an area that deserves further study (Stansfeld *et al.*, 2000).

In some instances in clinical consultations, on taking a more detailed history, it becomes apparent that complaints of noise disturbance are related to persecutory delusions and may be a symptom of paranoid psychosis, schizophrenia, or in the elderly, paraphrenia. In such cases, disturbance by noise is often part of a wider system of persecutory ideas about neighbours in which noise is only one of many afflictions that the patient believes the neighbours are causing them. An accurate history and further information from a close relative or friend will often reveal the fantastic nature of the complaint.

On the other hand, the clinician should not be too ready to dismiss the reality of complaints about noise. Undoubtedly, prolonged exposure to noise can be very upsetting, intrusive, and interfering for sleep and everyday activities. In poorly built dwellings, especially apartments, even low-intensity noises may be clearly audible through walls, floors, or ceilings (Raw & Oseland, 1991). In this situation, noise is destructive of privacy, especially for those living alone, and may be associated with perceptions of threat or increase a sense of isolation. This may be especially the case among people who are chronically anxious and likely to complain of sensitivity to noise; prolonged noise exposure may make them more anxious and unhappy. Often this leads to arguments with neighbours, leading to a breakdown of neighbourly relationships and further isolation, which may well in itself have a bad effect on mental health. Occasionally, this may tragically result in violence and homicide, either in those with overt psychotic illness, as mentioned above, or in those with personality disorders. In the latter group, the expression of hostile feelings, which may relate to internal conflicts, can be triggered by the person causing the noise, with disastrous consequences.

Conclusions

The evidence for effects of environmental noise on health is strongest for annoyance, sleep, and performance, with effects on cognitive performance in children (Stansfeld *et al.*, 2000). Occupational and to a lesser extent environmental noise exposure also shows some association with raised blood pressure. The effects of noise are strongest for those outcomes that, like annoyance, can be classified under 'quality of life' rather than illness. What they lack in severity is made up for in numbers of people affected, as these responses are very widespread. Current evidence does seem to suggest that environmental noise exposure, especially at higher levels, is related to mental health symptoms and possibly raised anxiety and consumption of sedative medication, but there is little evidence that it has more serious effects. Further research is needed on the mental health effects at very high noise levels, where there is some evidence of effects. Existing studies may be confounded either by prior selection of subjects out of (or into) noisy areas as a result of noise exposure, or by confounding between noise exposure, socio-economic deprivation, and psychiatric disorder. It is also possible that people underestimate or minimize the effects of noise on health through optimism bias (Hatfield & Job, 1998) and that this is particularly protective for mental health.

So much of the world is now assailed by environmental noise: it is becoming difficult to find truly tranquil, quiet areas for comparison with noisy areas for research purposes. Such quiet areas may be beneficial in reducing stress and providing physical and psychological restoration – the positive health virtue of quiet areas needs to be explored.

It may be that the risk of developing mental or physical illness attributable to environmental noise is quite small, although in terms of the progress of research, it is too soon to be certain of this. Part of the problem is that the interaction between people, noise, and ill-health is a complex one. Humans are not usually passive recipients of noise exposure and can develop coping strategies to reduce its impact. If people don't like noise, they may take action to avoid it by moving away from noisy environments or, if they are unable to move away, by developing coping strategies. Active coping with noise may be sufficient to mitigate any ill-effects (van Kamp, 1990). Perception of control over the noise source may reduce the threat of noise and the belief that it can be harmful. It may also be that noise is more harmful to health in situations where several stressors interact and the overall burden may lead to chronic autonomic arousal or states of helplessness.

Adaptation to long-term noise exposure needs further study. Most people exposed to chronic noise, for instance from major airports, seem to tolerate it. Yet questionnaire studies suggest that high levels of annoyance do not decline over time. Another possibility is that adaptation to noise is only achieved with a cost to health. Evans and Johnson (2000) found that maintaining task performance in noisy offices was associated with additional physiological effort and hormonal response. McEwen (1998) coined the term 'allostasis' to describe the body's response to chronic stress, in which there is a patho-physiological cost to maintaining health. The possibility of such a response to noise and other environmental stressors deserves further enquiry.

Scope for further research

Undoubtedly, there is a need for further research to clarify this complex area, including better measurement of noise exposure and health outcomes. Ideally, further studies investigating the association between environmental noise and psychiatric disorder should be carried out longitudinally, either in populations in whom there is a change to lower noise exposure or, better still, where baseline measurements are carried out in low-noise conditions and follow-up measurements at a time when the noise exposure has increased. In this way, the population will not be pre-selected to include only those less affected by noise, and migration of subjects out of the study sample can be followed, to assess whether noise-sensitive subjects tend to move away as the noise increases. Careful assessment of socio-economic differences between areas of high and low exposure is needed. In many studies, it is not clear whether noise effects on health are a component part of the effects of social disadvantage on health or whether the effects of noise on health are confounded by social disadvantage, in which case noise exposure is merely an indicator of social disadvantage, and is not on the causal pathway.

Field studies suggest that multiple stressors have greater combined effects than simply summing individual stressors (Rutter, 1979). It might be the case that noise will show more effects on health in individuals already exposed to other stressors. These might include other physical stressors (e.g. air pollution, poor housing conditions), psychosocial stressors (e.g. crowding, social isolation, fear of crime, perception of lack of control over the environment), and adverse material conditions (low income, unemployment). There may be either additive or multiplicative interactions with noise exposure. So far, few studies have attempted to examine the effects of multiple environmental stressors (Cohen *et al.*, 1976). This is an important new area for the development of noise research.

The breadth of psychiatric outcomes studied should be enlarged to include well-being, hostility, depression, anxiety disorders, and phobias, while also measuring relevant aspects of personality, such as neuroticism and negative affectivity, that may influence reporting of symptoms. This needs to be combined with measurement of the appraisal of noise sources and evaluation of coping mechanisms (Lercher, 1996). It would also be interesting to combine mental health measures and hormonal measures to assess psychological and physiological responses to stress concurrently. Ultimately, evidence of the mental health effects of noise is more likely to be believed if accompanied by measurable physiological changes.

Implications for public health

Noise is disturbing, particularly of activities that require concentration and freedom from distraction. A good case can be made that places where people carry out mental work, such as schools, hospitals, offices, and libraries, should be free from noise distraction. This requires that, ideally, schools and hospitals should not be built in excessively noisy areas or, at least, there should be sound insulation in the buildings – although the efficiency of sound insulation in schools has not yet been fully empirically tested in terms of responses to noise. Good sound insulation is especially important in flats where inadequate building quality may inflict neighbours' noise most on those who are also coping with other areas of social disadvantage.

There are increasing calls for restriction of night-time noise, particularly restriction of night flights so as to limit more when most people are sleeping. Access to quiet areas and unspoilt natural areas may be beneficial for mental health and attempts should be made to protect and preserve these areas. Children exposed to high aircraft noise levels have been shown to have lower annoyance levels to noise if they have access to quiet areas where they can get psychological restoration (Gunnarsson *et al.*, 2003). In a noisy world, quietness should become a virtue.

References

Abey-Wickrama, I., A'Brook, M. F., Gattoni, F. E. and Herridge, C. F. (1969) 'Mental-hospital admissions and aircraft noise'. *The Lancet, 2,* 1275–1277.

Anderson, C. M. B. (1971) *The measurement of attitude to noise and noises,* Ac 52. Teddington, UK: National Physical Laboratory Acoustics Report.

Arnsten, A. F. and Goldman-Rakic, P. S. (1998) 'Noise stress impairs prefrontal cortical cognitive function in monkeys: evidence for a hyperdopaminergic mechanism'. *Archives of General Psychiatry, 55,* 362–368.

Aronen, E. T., Paavonen, E. J., Fjallberg, M., Soininen, M. and Torronen, J. (2000) 'Sleep and psychiatric symptoms in school-age children'. *Journal of the American Academy of Child & Adolescent Psychiatry, 39,* 502–508.

Baker, M. A. and Holding, D. H. (1993) 'The effects of noise and speech on cognitive task performance'. *Journal of General Psychology, 120,* 339–355.

Barker, S. M. and Tarnopolsky, A. (1978) 'Assessing bias in surveys of symptoms attributed to noise'. *Journal of Sound and Vibration, 59,* 349–354.

Bell, P. A., Greene, T. C., Fisher, J. D. and Baum, A. (1996) *Environmental psychology.* Fort Worth, TX: Harcourt Brace & Co.

Belojevic, G. and Jakovljevic, B. (1997) 'Subjective reactions to traffic noise with regard to some personality traits'. *Environment International, 23,* 221–226.

Bennett, E. (1945) 'Some tests for the discrimination of neurotic from normal subjects'. *British Journal of Medical Psychology, 20,* 271–277.

Berglund, B., Hassmen, P. and Job, R. F. (1996) 'Sources and effects of low-frequency noise'. *Journal of the Acoustical Society of America, 99,* 2985–3002.

Biesiot, W., Pulles, M. P. J. and Stewart, R. E. (1989) *Environmental noise and health.* GA-DR-03–03, Leidschendam, The Netherlands: VROM.

Bing-shuang, H., Yue-lin, Y., Ren-yi, W. and Zhubao, C. (1997) 'Evaluation of depressive symptoms in workers exposed to industrial noise'. *Homeostasis in Health and Disease, 38,* 123–125.

Breslau, N., Roth, T., Rosenthal, L. and Andreski, P. (1996) 'Sleep disturbance and psychiatric disorders: a longitudinal epidemiological study of young adults'. *Biological Psychiatry, 39,* 411–418.

Broadbent, D. E. (1953) 'Noise, paced performance and vigilance tasks'. *British Journal of Psychology, 44,* 295–303.

Broadbent, D. E. (1972) 'Individual differences in annoyance by noise'. *Sound, 6,* 56–61.

Cameron, P., Zaks, J. and Robertson, D. (1972) 'Sound pollution, noise pollution, and health: community parameters'. *Journal of Applied Psychology, 56,* 67–74.

Chang, P. P., Ford, D. E., Mead, L. A., Cooper-Patrick, L. and Klag, M. J. (1997) 'Insomnia in young men and subsequent depression: the Johns Hopkins Precursors Study'. *American Journal of Epidemiology, 146,* 105–114.

Chartered Institute of Environmental Health (1999) *Environmental health report 1997/8.* London: CIEH.

Chowns, R. H. (1970) 'Mental-hospital admissions and aircraft noise'. *The Lancet, 1,* 467.

Civil Aviation Authority (1980) *Aircraft noise and sleep disturbance: Final report.* DORA Report 8008. London: CAA.

Cohen, A. (1976) 'The influence of a company hearing conservation program on extra-auditory problems in workmen'. *Journal of Public Safety, 8,* 146–161.

Cohen, S. and Spacapan, S. (1978) 'The after effects of stress: an attentional interpretation'. *Environmental Psychology and Non-verbal Behaviour, 3,* 43–57.

Cohen, S. and Weinstein, N. (1981) 'Non-auditory effects of noise on behavior and health'. *Journal of Social Issues, 37,* 36–70.

Cohen, S., Evans, G. W., Stokols, D. and Kranz, D. (1976) *Behavior, health and environmental stress.* New York: Plenum Press.

Corbett, B. and Stanczak, D. E. (1999) 'Neuropsychological performance of adults evidencing attention-deficit hyperactivity disorder'. *Archives of Clinical Neuropsychology, 14,* 373–387.

Davis, H. (1958) Project Anehin 7, Project NM 130199. Subtask 1, Pensacola, Florida USN School of Aviation Medicine.

Dryman, A. and Eaton, W. W. (1991) 'Affective symptoms associated with the onset of major depression in the community: findings from the US National Institute of Mental Health Epidemiologic Catchment Area Program'. *Acta Psychiatrica Scandinavica, 84,* 1–5.

Evans, G. W., Hygge, S. and Bullinger, M. (1995) 'Chronic noise and psychological stress'. *Psychological Science, 6,* 333–338.

Evans, G. W. and Johnson, D. (2000) 'Stress and open-office noise'. *Journal of Applied Psychology, 85,* 779–783.

Evans, G. W. and Tafalla, R. (1987) 'Measurement of environmental annoyance', in Koelaga, H. S. (ed.), *Developments in toxicology and environmental science* (pp. 11–25). Amsterdam: Elsevier.

Evans, G. W., Bullinger, M. and Hygge, S. (1998) 'Chronic noise exposure and psychological response: a prospective study of children living under environmental stress'. *Psychological Science, 9,* 75–77.

Fields, J. M. (1984) 'The effect of numbers of noise events on people's reactions to noise: an analysis of existing survey data'. *Journal of Acoustic Society of America, 75,* 447–467.

Finke, H. O., Guski, R., Martin, R., Rohrmann, B., Schumer, R. and Schumer-Kohrs, A. (1974) 'Effects of aircraft noise on man'. *Proceedings of the Symposium on Noise in Transportation,* Section III, paper 1. Southampton, UK: Institute of Sound and Vibration Research.

Ford, D. E. and Kamerow, D. B. (1989) 'Epidemiologic study of sleep disturbances and psychiatric disorders: an opportunity for prevention?' *Journal of the American Medical Association, 262,* 1479–1484.

Franssen, E. A., van Wiechen, C. M., Nagelkerke, N. J. and Lebret, E. (2004) 'Aircraft noise around a large international airport and its impact on general health and medication use'. *Occupational and Environmental Medicine, 61,* 405–413.

Frerichs, R. R., Beeman, B. L. and Coulson, A. H. (1980) 'Los Angeles Airport noise and mortality – faulty analysis and public policy'. *American Journal of Public Health, 3,* 357–362.

Gattoni, F. and Tarnopolsky, A. (1973) 'Aircraft noise and psychiatric morbidity'. *Psychological Medicine, 3,* 516–520.

Gee, G. C. and Takeuchi, D. T. (2004) 'Traffic stress, vehicular burden and well-being: a multilevel analysis'. *Social Science and Medicine, 59,* 405–414.

Goldberg, D. P. (1972) *The detection of psychiatric illness by questionnaire.* London: Oxford University Press.

Goldberg, D. P., Cooper, B., Eastwood, M. R., Kedward, H. B. and Shepherd, M. (1970) 'A standardized psychiatric interview for use in community surveys'. *British Journal of Preventive and Social Medicine, 24,* 18–23.

Goodman, R. (1997) 'The Strengths and Difficulties Questionnaire: a research note'. *Journal of Child Psychology and Psychiatry and Allied Disciplines, 38,* 581–586.

Grandjean, E., Graf, P., Cauber, A., Meier, H. P. and Muller, R. (1973). 'A survey of aircraft noise in Switzerland', in Ward, E. D. (ed.), *Proceedings of the International Congress on Noise as a Public Health Problem*. Dubrovnik (pp. 645–659). Washington, DC: Environmental Protection Agency Publications.

Gray, L. C., Breier, J. I., Foorman, B. R. and Fletcher, J. M. (2002) 'Continuum of impulsiveness caused by auditory masking'. *International Journal of Pediatric Otorhinolaryngology, 66*, 265–272.

Griffiths, I. D. and Langdon, F. J. (1968) 'Subjective response to road traffic noise'. *Journal of Sound and Vibration, 8*, 16–32.

Grimwood, C. (1993) *Effects of environmental noise on people at home*, BRE Information Paper IP22/93. Watford, UK: Building Research Establishment.

Gunn, W. J. (1987) 'The importance of the measurement of annoyance in prediction of effects of aircraft noise on the health and well-being of noise exposed communities', in Koelaga, H. S. (ed.), *Developments in toxicology and environmental science* (pp. 237–255). Amsterdam: Elsevier.

Gunnarsson, A. G., Berglund, B., Haines, M. M., van Kamp, I., Lopez Barrio, I., Nilsson, M. and Stansfeld, S. A. (2003) 'Psychological restoration in noise-exposed children across three Europeon countries: the RANCH study', in de Jong, R. G., Houtgast, T., Franssen, E. A. M. and Hafman, W. F. (eds), *Proceedings of the 8th International Congress on Noise as a Public Health Problem*, Rotterdam, The Netherlands, 29 June–3 July, pp. 159–160.

Haines, M. M., Stansfeld, S. A., Job, R. F., Berglund, B. and Head, J. (2001a) 'Chronic aircraft noise exposure, stress responses, mental health and cognitive performance in school children'. *Psychological Medicine, 31*, 265–277.

Haines, M. M., Stansfeld, S. A., Job, R. F., Berglund, B. and Head, J. (2001b) 'A follow-up study of the effects of chronic aircraft noise exposure on child stress responses and cognition'. *International Journal of Epidemiology, 30*, 839–845.

Hall, F. L., Taylor, S. M. and Birnie, S. E. (1985) 'Activity interference and noise annoyance'. *Journal of Sound and Vibration, 103*, 237–252.

Halpern, D. (1995) *Mental health and the built environment*. London: Taylor & Francis.

Hardoy, M. C., Carta, M. G., Marci, A. R., Carbone, F., Cadeddu, M., Kovess, V., Dell'Osso, L. and Carpiniello, B. (2005) 'Exposure to aircraft noise and risk of psychiatric disorders: the Elmas survey – aircraft noise and psychiatric disorders'. *Social Psychiatry and Psychiatric Epidemiology, 40*, 24–26.

Hatfield, J. and Job, R. F. S. (1998) 'Evidence of optimism bias regarding the health effects of exposure to noise', in Carter, N. and Job, R. F. S. (eds), *Proceedings of Noise Effects 1998. 7th International Congress on Noise as a Public Health Problem*. Sydney, Australia: Noise Effects 1998., Vol. 1 (pp. 251–254).

Hatfield, J. and Job, R. F. S. (2001) 'Optimism bias about environmental degradation: the role of the range of impact of precautions'. *Journal of Environmental Psychology, 21*, 17–30.

Health Council of the Netherlands (2004) *The influence of night-time noise on sleep and health*. Publication No. 2004/14E. The Hague: Health Council of the Netherlands.

Hiramatsu, K., Yamamoto, T., Taira, K., Ito, A. and Nakasone, T. (1997) 'A survey on health effects due to aircraft noise on residents living around Kadena airport in the Ryukyus'. *Journal of Sound and Vibration, 205*, 451–460.

Hiramatsu, K., Minoura, T., Matsui, T., Miyakita, T., Osada, Y. and Yamamoto, T. (2000) 'An analysis of the general health questionnaire survey around airports in terms of annoyance reaction'. *Proceedings of the 29th International Congress on Noise Control Engineering*, Vol. 4 (pp. 2089–2093). Nice, France: Inter-noise 2000.

Horne, J. A., Pankhurst, F. L., Reyner, L. A., Hume, K. and Diamond, I. D. (1994) 'A field study of sleep disturbance: effects of aircraft noise and other factors on 5,742 nights of actimetrically monitored sleep in a large subject sample'. *Sleep*, *17*, 146–159.

Ito, A., Hiramatsu, K., Taira, K., Nakasone, T. and Yamamoto, T. (1994) 'Health effects on the residents due to aircraft noise around Kadena US Airbase in the Ryukyus' (pp. 247–250). *Proceedings of Internoise 1994*, Yokohama, Japan.

Iwata, O. (1984) 'The relationship of noise sensitivity to health and personality'. *Japanese Psychological Research*, *26*, 75–81.

Jansen, G. (1961) 'Adverse effects of noise on iron and steel workers'. *Stahl und Eisen*, *81*, 217–220.

Jelinkova, A. (1998) 'Coping with noise in noise sensitive subjects', in Berglund, B., Berglund, U., Karlsson, J. and Lindvall, T. (eds), *Noise as a public health problem, Vol 3: Performance, behaviour, animal, combined agents and community responses* (pp. 27–30). Stockholm, Sweden: Swedish Council for Building Research.

Jenkins, L., Tarnopolsky, A. and Hand, D. (1981) 'Psychiatric admissions and aircraft noise from London Airport: four-year, three-hospitals' study'. *Psychological Medicine*, *11*, 765–782.

Jenkins, L. M., Tarnopolsky, A., Hand, D. J. and Barker, S. M. (1979) 'Comparison of three studies of aircraft noise and psychiatric hospital admissions conducted in the same area'. *Psychological Medicine*, *9*, 681–693.

Job, R. F. S. (1988) 'Community response to noise: a review of factors influencing the relationship between noise exposure and reaction'. *Journal of the Acoustical Society of America*, *83*, 991–1001.

Jones, D. M., Chapman, A. J. and Auburn, T. C. (1981) 'Noise in the environment: a social perspective'. *Journal of Applied Psychology*, *1*, 43–59.

Kageyama, T., Kabuto, M., Nitta, H., Kurokawa, Y., Taira, K., Suzuki, S. and Takemoto, T. (1997) 'A population study on risk factors for insomnia among adult Japanese women: a possible effect of road traffic volume'. *Sleep*, *20*, 963–971.

Kim, K., Uchiyama, M., Okawa, M., Liu, X. and Ogihara, R. (2000) 'An epidemiological study of insomnia among the Japanese general population'. *Sleep*, *23*, 41–47.

Klitzman, S. and Stellman, J. M. (1989) 'The impact of the physical environment on the psychological well-being of office workers'. *Social Science and Medicine*, *29*, 733–742.

Knipschild, P. and Oudshoorn, N. (1977) 'VII medical effects of aircraft noise: drug survey'. *International Archives of Occupational and Environmental Health*, *40*, 97–100.

Kokokusha, D. (1973) *Report of investigation of living environment around Osaka International Airport*. Osaka, Japan: Aircraft Nuisance Prevention Association.

Kraenz, S., Fricke, L., Wiater, A., Mitschke, A., Breuer, U. and Lehmkuhl, G. (2004) 'Prevalence and stress factors of sleep disorders in children starting school'. *Praxis Kinderpsychologie und Kinderpsychiatrie*, *53*, 3–18.

Kryter, K. D. (1990) 'Aircraft noise and social factors in psychiatric hospital admission rates: a re-examination of some data'. *Psychological Medicine*, *20*, 395–411.

Lercher, P. (1996) 'Environmental noise and health: an integrated research perspective'. *Environment International*, *22*, 117–129.

Lercher, P. and Kofler, W. W. (1996) 'Behavioral and health responses associated with road traffic noise exposure along alpine through-traffic routes'. *The Science of the Total Environment*, *189/190*, 85–89.

Lercher, P., Evans, G. W., Meis, M. and Kofler, W. W. (2002) 'Ambient neighbourhood noise and children's mental health'. *Occupational and Environmental Medicine, 59*, 380–386.

Loeb, M. (1986) *Noise and human efficiency*. Chichester, UK: Wiley.

McEwen, B. S. (1998) 'Stress, adaptation, and disease: allostasis and allostatic load'. *Annals of the New York Academy of Sciences, 840*, 33–44.

Meecham, W. C. and Smith, H. G. (1977) 'Effects of jet aircraft noise on mental hospital admissions'. *British Journal of Audiology, 11*, 81–85.

Melamed, S., Luz, J. and Green, M. S. (1992) 'Noise exposure, noise annoyance and their relation to psychological distress, accident and sickness absence among blue-collar workers – the Cordis Study'. *Israel Journal of Medical Sciences, 28*, 629–635.

Melamed, S., Najenson, T., Luz, T., Jucha, E. and Green, M. (1988) 'Noise annoyance, industrial noise exposure and psychological stress symptoms among male and female workers', in Berglund, B., Berglund, U., Karlsson, J. and Lindvall, T. (eds), *Noise as a public health problem, Vol. 2: Hearing, communication, sleep and nonauditory physiological effects* (pp. 315–320). Stockholm, Sweden: Swedish Council for Building Research.

Mellinger, G. D., Balter, M. B. and Uhlenhuth, E. H. (1985) 'Insomnia and its treatment: prevalence and correlates'. *Archives of General Psychiatry, 42*, 225–232.

Miedema, H. M. and Vos, H. (1998) 'Exposure–response relationships for transportation noise'. *Journal of Acoustic Society of America, 104*, 3432–3445.

Miyakita, T., Matsui, T., Ito, T., Tokuyama, T., Taira, K., Hiramatsu, K., Osada, Y. and Yamamoto, T. (1998) 'General Health Questionnaire survey around Kadena US airfield in the Ryukyus – an analysis of their 12 scale scores', in Carter, N. and Job, R. F. S. (eds), *Proceedings of Noise Effect 1998. 7th International Congress on Noise as a Public Health Problem*, Vol. 2 (pp. 608–612). Sydney Australia: Noise Effects 1998.

Muzet, A. and Eberhart, J. (1980) 'Habituation of heart rate and finger pulse responses to noise in sleep', in Tobias, J. V., Jansen, G. and Ward, W. D. (eds), *Noise as a public health problem*. Rockville, MD: ASHA.

Nurmi, J. E. and von Wright, J. (1983) 'Interactive effects of noise, neuroticism and state-anxiety in the learning and recall of a textbook passage'. *Human Learning, 2*, 119–125.

Ohayon, M. M. and Roth, T. (2003) 'Place of chronic insomnia in the course of depressive and anxiety disorders'. *Journal of Psychiatric Research, 37*, 9–15.

Öhrström, E. (1982) *On the effects of noise with special reference to subjective evaluation and regularity*. Göteborg, Sweden: Department of Environmental Hygiene.

Öhrström, E. (1989) 'Sleep disturbance, psychosocial and medical symptoms – a pilot survey among persons exposed to high levels of road traffic noise'. *Journal of Sound and Vibration, 133*, 117–128.

Öhrström, E. (1993) 'Long-term effects in terms of psychosocial wellbeing, annoyance and sleep disturbance in areas exposed to high levels of road traffic noise', in Vallet, M. (ed.), *Noise and man: Noise as a public health problem*. Bron, France: Institut National De Recherche sur les Transports et leur Securite.

Öhrström, E. and Rylander, R. (1990) 'Sleep disturbance effects of traffic noise – a laboratory study on after effects'. *Journal of Sound and Vibration, 84*, 87–103.

Öhrström, E., Bjorkman, M. and Rylander, R. (1988) 'Noise annoyance with regard to neurophysiological sensitivity, subjective noise sensitivity and personality variables'. *Psychological Medicine, 18*, 605–613.

Öhrström, E., Rylander, R. and Bjorkman, N. (1998) 'Effects of night time road traffic noise – an overview of laboratory and field studies on noise dose and subjective noise sensitivity'. *Journal of Sound and Vibration, 127*, 441–448.

Passchier-Vermeer, W. (1993) *Noise and health*. Leiden, The Netherlands: TNO Institute of Preventive Health.

Passchier-Vermeer, W., Vos, H., Steenbekkers, J. H. M., van der Ploeg, F. D. and Groothmis-Oudshoorn, K. (2002) *Sleep disturbance and aircraft noise: Exposure–effect relationships*. Leiden, The Netherlands: TNO Institute of Preventive Health.

Patton, G. C., Coffey, C., Posterino, M., Carlin, J. B. and Wolfe, R. (2000) 'Adolescent depressive disorder: a population-based study of ICD-10 symptoms'. *Australian and New Zealand Journal of Psychiatry, 34*, 741–747.

Pillsbury, H. C., Grose, J. H., Coleman, W. L., Conners, C. K. and Hall, J. W. (1995) 'Binaural function in children with attention-deficit hyperactivity disorder'. *Archives of Otolaryngology – Head and Neck Surgery, 121*, 1345–1350.

Poustka, F., Eckermann, P. and Schmeck, K. (1992) 'Effect of aircraft noise and psychosocial stressors on mental disturbances of children and adolescents: an epidemiological study in Westphalia', in Remschmidt, H. and Schmidt, M. H. (eds), *Developmental psychopathology*. Gottingen, Germany: Hogrefe and Huber.

Pulles, T., Biesiot, W. and Stewart, R. (1990) 'Adverse effects of environmental noise on health: an interdisciplinary approach', in Berglund, B., Berglund, U., Karlsson, J. and Lindvall, T. (eds), *Noise as a public health problem, Vol. 4: New advances in noise research* (pp. 337–348). Stockholm, Sweden: Swedish Council for Building Research.

Raw, G. J. and Oseland, N. A. (1991) 'Subjective response to noise through party floors in conversion flats'. *Applied Acoustics, 32*, 215–231.

Reijneveld, S. A. (1994) 'The impact of the Amsterdam aircraft disaster on reported annoyance by aircraft noise and on psychiatric disorders'. *International Journal of Epidemiology, 23*, 333–340.

Riccio, C. A., Cohen, M. J., Hynd, G. W. and Keith, R. W. (1996) 'Validity of the Auditory Continuous Performance Test in differentiating central processing auditory disorders with and without ADHD'. *Journal of Learning Disabilities, 29*, 561–566.

Riemann, D., Berger, M. and Voderholzer, U. (2001) 'Sleep and depression – results from psychobiological studies: an overview'. *Biological Psychology, 57*, 67–103.

Roberts, R. E., Roberts, C. R. and Chen, I. G. (2002) 'Impact of insomnia on future functioning of adolescents'. *Journal of Psychosomatic Research, 53*, 561–569.

Roth, T. and Ancoli-Israel, S. (1999) 'Daytime consequences and correlates of insomnia in the United States: results of the 1991 National Sleep Foundation Survey. II'. *Sleep, 22*, S354–S358.

Rutter, M. L. (1979) 'Primary prevention of psychopathology', in Kent, M. M. and Rolf, J. E. (eds), *Primary prevention of psychopathology* (pp. 610–625). Hanover, NH: University of Press of New England.

Schultz, T. J. (1978) 'Synthesis of social surveys on noise annoyance'. *Journal of Acoustic Society of America, 64*, 377–405.

Smith, A. (2003) 'The concept of noise sensitivity: implications for noise control'. *Noise and Health, 5*, 57–59.

Smith, A., Hayward, S. and Rich, N. (2000) Perceptions of aircraft noise exposure, noise sensitivity, sleep disturbance and health: results from the Bristol noise, sleep and health study. *Inter-noise 2000, The 29th International Congress and Exhibition on Noise Control Engineering* (pp. 984–987). Nice, France: Internoise 2000.

Smith, A. P. and Broadbent, D. E. (1981) 'Noise and levels of processing'. *Acta Psychologica, 47*, 129.

Smith, A. P. and Broadbent, D. E. (1992) *Non-auditory effects of noise at work: A review of the literature*, HSE Contract Research Report No. 30/1991, Vol. 30. London: HMSO.

Stansfeld, S. A. (1992) 'Noise, noise sensitivity and psychiatric disorder: epidemiological and psychophysiological studies'. *Psychological Medicine Monograph Supplement 22*. Cambridge: Cambridge University Press.

Stansfeld, S., Haines, M. and Brown, B. (2000) 'Noise and health in the urban environment'. *Reviews on Environmental Health, 15*, 43–82.

Stansfeld, S. A., Clark, C. R., Jenkins, L. M. and Tarnopolsky, A. (1985) 'Sensitivity to noise in a community sample: I. Measurement of psychiatric disorder and personality'. *Psychological Medicine, 15*, 243–254.

Stansfeld, S., Gallacher, J., Babisch, W. and Shipley, M. (1996) 'Road traffic noise and psychiatric disorder: prospective findings from the Caerphilly Study'. *British Medical Journal, 313*, 266–267.

Stansfeld, S. A., Matsui, R., Gallacher, J. E. J. and Babisch, W. (2002) 'Longitudinal effects of noise, noise sensitivity and psychosocial factors on men's psychological distress'. *Epidemiology, 13*, S90.

Stansfeld, S. A., Sharp, D. S., Gallacher, J. and Babisch, W. (1993) 'Road traffic noise, noise sensitivity and psychological disorder'. *Psychological Medicine, 23*, 977–985.

Tarnopolsky, A. and Morton-Williams, J. (1980) *Aircraft noise and prevalence of psychiatric disorders, research report*. London: Social and Community Planning Research.

Tarnopolsky, A., Watkins, G. and Hand, D. J. (1980) 'Aircraft noise and mental health: I. Prevalence of individual symptoms'. *Psychological Medicine, 10*, 683–698.

Tarnopolsky, A., Barker, S. M., Wiggins, R. D. and McLean, E. K. (1978) 'The effect of aircraft noise on the mental health of a community sample: a pilot study'. *Psychological Medicine, 8*, 219–233.

Taylor, S. M. (1984) 'A path model of aircraft noise annoyance'. *Journal of Sound and Vibration, 96*, 243–260.

Thomas, J. R. and Jones, D. M. (1982) Individual differences in noise annoyance and the uncomfortable loudness level. *Journal of Sound and Vibration, 82*, 289–304.

Vallet, M., Gagneux, J. M., Clairet, J. M., Laurens, J. F. and Letisserand, D. (1983) 'Heart rate reactivity to aircraft noise after a long-term exposure', in Rossi, G. (ed.), *Noise as a public health problem* (pp. 965–975). Milan, Italy: Centro Recherche e Studio Amplifon.

van Dijk, F. J., Ettema, J. H. and Zielhuis, R. L. (1987) 'Non-auditory effects of noise in industry. VII. Evaluation, conclusions and recommendations'. *International Archives of Occupational and Environmental Health, 59*, 147–152.

Van Kamp, I. (1990) *Coping with noise and its health consequences*. Groningen, The Netherlands: Styx and PP.

Vollrath, M., Wicki, W. and Angst, J. (1989) 'The Zurich study. VIII. Insomnia: association with depression, anxiety, somatic syndromes, and course of insomnia'. *European Archives of Psychiatry and Neurological Sciences, 239*, 113–124.

Ware, J. E., Jr and Sherbourne, C. D. (1992) 'The MOS 36-item short-form health survey (SF-36). I. Conceptual framework and item selection'. *Medical Care, 30*, 473–483.

Watkins, G., Tarnopolsky, A. and Jenkins, L. M. (1981) 'Aircraft noise and mental health: II. Use of medicines and health care services'. *Psychological Medicine, 11*, 155–168.

Weinstein, N. D. (1978) 'Individual differences in reactions to noise: a longitudinal study in a college dormitory'. *Journal of Applied Psychology, 63*, 458–466.

Weinstein, N. D. (1980) 'Individual differences in critical tendencies and noise annoyance'. *Journal of Sound and Vibration, 68*, 241–248.

Willner, P. and Neiva, J. (1986) 'Brief exposure to uncontrollable but not to controllable noise biases the retrieval of information from memory'. *British Journal of Clinical Psychology*, *25*, 93–100.

Wing, J. K., Cooper, J. E. and Sartorius, N. (1974) *The measurement and classification of psychiatric symptoms*. London: Cambridge University Press.

Yoshida, T., Osada, Y., Kawaguchi, T., Hoshiyama, Y., Yoshida, K. and Yamamoto, K. (1997) 'Effects of road traffic noise on inhabitants of Tokyo'. *Journal of Sound and Vibration*, *205*, 517–522.

10 Seasonality and mental health

Mood disorders, suicide, and schizophrenia

John McGrath and Gordon Parker

Links between the seasons and health have long been an object of scrutiny and speculation. The ancient Greeks linked the four seasons with each of the vital humours (black bile, yellow bile, blood, phlegm) and then developed elaborate theories related to temperament and disease. Indeed, Hippocrates (1992) felt that the study of seasonal variations should underpin medical research:

> Whoever wishes to investigate medicine properly, should proceed thus: in the first place to consider the seasons of the year, and what effects each of them produces for they are not at all alike, but differ much from themselves in regard to their changes.

In a book about the environment and mental illness, it seems appropriate to pay homage to the long tradition of exploring seasonal correlates of health and behaviour. This chapter has several aims. It will first introduce the reader to the general rationale underpinning this field of research. Reflecting the biases of the coauthors, the chapter will then focus on mood disorders, suicide, and schizophrenia. These fields have been covered in several narrative reviews over recent years (Deisenhammer, 2003; Hakko *et al.*, 2002; Magnusson & Boivin, 2003; Tochigi *et al.*, 2004; Torrey *et al.*, 1997), and it is not our intention to assess systematically all aspects of this literature in this chapter. We will, however, examine a selection of recent publications to demonstrate how the field is progressing and what challenges remain.

Why study seasonal variations in psychiatric epidemiology?

The core business of epidemiology is to describe gradients in features of a disorder across place and time. These features include incidence (a key measure of the force of morbidity of a disorder within a population), prevalence (a feature related to both incidence and duration of an illness), and the course of illness. Gradients in the incidence of a disorder allow us to construct an 'epidemiological landscape', which is vital for the generation of both candidate genetic and non-genetic risk factors (Jablensky, 2003; McGrath, 2003). Seasonal variations in features of a disease reflect gradients across time (within-year variation). Seasons provide a type of natural experiment, where certain factors fluctuate in a regular fashion across time, while, at the group level, other environmental and genetic factors will have remained relatively stable. Thus, if seasonal fluctuations are linked to a disorder, they can then provide important clues to help generate new candidate exposures. No-one would suggest that seasonally fluctuating factors are necessary or sufficient to cause a serious mental disorder like depression or schizophrenia. However, understanding these risk factors can provide a mechanism of enquiry that can help generate disease models.

While research examining seasonal variations can be heuristic, it is important to keep the limited value of this type of investigation in perspective. The aim is to understand the factors that contribute to the cause or course of a disorder. If such research does not translate into a deeper understanding of risk factors, it is hard to justify. Looking at the field of seasonality research, there has been a tendency for investigators to undertake replication studies that contribute little, if anything, to a deeper understanding of the risk-modifying factors underlying the seasonal fluctuations. In this sense, seasonality research can be characterized as the 'donkey' of psychiatric epidemiology – it can be mindless and stubborn. Kuller has characterized this phenomenon as 'circular epidemiology', where research perseverates at the ecological level, and fails to move to more analytic methods or experimental studies (Kuller, 1999).

One of the challenges for those interested in seasonality and mental illness is to shift through the highly intercorrelated maze of variables that have regular, within-year variation. Ultimately, most of these variables are downstream consequences of biometeorological variables such as temperature, rainfall, and ultraviolet radiation. These variables (cold, heat stress, dehydration, thermoregulation, etc.) can impact directly on health status (McGeehin & Mirabelli, 2001; Mercer, 2003; Naughton *et al.*, 2002). Winter is associated with lower levels of ultraviolet radiation, which are strongly associated with low levels of vitamin D (Holick, 1995). Like most animals, humans have various biorhythms (mainly circadian and monthly rather than circannual) (Wehr, 1996). Photoperiod (i.e. the number of hours of light in a 24-hour period) is associated with diurnal fluctuations in various hormones and melatonin (Wehr, 1998). Indirectly, seasonal fluctuations can impact on health status via nutrition (for example, availability of seasonal food products such fruit), energy expenditure (for example, variations in work load across seasons in agrarian societies), and disease exposures (for example, respiratory viruses may be more prevalent in winter; vectors for malaria have seasonal breeding cycles) (McMichael, 2001). In addition to this complex web of environmental changes, human behaviour is modified in a transactional fashion with the environment. For example, in cold seasons, we tend to remain indoors, use internal heating, and wear more clothing. Thus, seasonal changes in weather can result in a complex but intercorrelated matrix of exposures. The task for the researcher is to fractionate out these exposures and generate risk-modifying factors, rather than merely to examine proxy markers of exposures (month of year, temperature, etc.).

We now consider seasonal influences on mood disorders, suicide, and schizophrenia.

Mood disorders

Season of birth influences

In an Australian study undertaken three decades ago (Parker, 1978), evidence was found of increased representation of several congenital abnormalities (i.e. meningomyelocoele and anencephaly) in winter births. To the extent that psychiatric disorders may have a congenital contribution, this could suggest a mechanism whereby some seasonally fluctuating risk factor to central nervous system development (for example, influenza causing maternal hyperthermia) could bring about such general epidemiological findings.

The first issue for consideration here, however, is whether those who develop significant clinical mood disorders show any such season-of-birth association. There have been some positive studies, with Hare (1975), for instance, reporting that winter births were over-represented in those who developed manic-depression (or bipolar disorder). We therefore undertook a study in New South Wales, Australia, examining the season-of-birth patterns of those who were admitted to the state's psychiatric units with a range of conditions (Parker & Neilson, 1976). Females (but not males) diagnosed as having schizophrenia were more likely to be born in winter, and a similar (but less distinct pattern) was evident for those who had received a diagnosis of manic-depressive psychosis. This result suggests a seasonal influence on the likelihood of developing 'psychosis', but issues related to diagnostic assignment need to considered (i.e. some patients with true schizophrenia could have been erroneously diagnosed as having manic-depressive psychosis). One firm negative finding emerged – that those with a diagnosis of 'depressive neurosis' (i.e. essentially having a non-psychotic depressive condition) showed no seasonal predilection of birth season, despite their numbers far exceeding those diagnosed as having a 'biological' mood disorder. As any such season-of-birth effect on the chance of developing a mood disorder has failed to show consistency (in presence) across published studies – and thus is less striking than identified for schizophrenia – it would appear reasonable to conclude that any season-of-birth association with mood disorders remains to be established and therefore there is no requirement to consider possible aetiological determinants of such an association.

Seasonal variation in clinical mood disorders

From the time of Hippocrates, many commentators have observed that the more biological disorders (i.e. mania and melancholia) are more likely to have their onset in spring. Parker and Walter (1982) undertook a study in New South

Wales, Australia, which involved examining data on the month of admission to psychiatric facilities for over 100,000 subjects. When examined against four differing clinical mood diagnoses, we found minimal seasonal variation (i.e. of the order of 3% and not significant for any season) for those with a diagnosis of 'depressive neurosis', despite this being the commonest mood diagnosis category. All three other categories (i.e. bipolar disorder – mania; bipolar disorder – depressed; and 'reactive depressive psychosis) had a peak onset in spring, with the seasonal amplitude being quite considerable (ranging from 6% to 17%). The old 'binary view' for categorizing depression essentially contrasts 'neurotic' and 'endogenous' (or melancholic) types (Kiloh & Garside, 1963); most patients with bipolar disorder tend to have episodes of melancholic or psychotic depression when in the depressed phase. Thus, it would appear that the key biological disorders (both mania and melancholic/psychotic depression) are more likely to have their onset in spring, while there is no such seasonal predilection in the non-melancholic disorders.

This New South Wales study was compatible with northern hemisphere studies in identifying spring as the season of risk for those with mania, but extended such studies in suggesting that episodes of biological depression are also more likely to emerge in spring. Why? When we examined a range of meteorological variables, change in the hours of bright sunshine was judged to be linked most closely with the epidemiological data. Thus, it was hypothesized that it is the rate of increase in luminance (i.e. hours of bright sunshine), rather than the absolute number of hours of bright sunshine, that is important. The rapid rate in late August and early spring would stimulate the pineal gland, and put at risk those who are vulnerable to the onset of a biological mood disorder. The effect of light on the pineal is to modulate the secretion of melatonin, which is known to influence locomotor rhythm. In addition to being a mood disorder, bipolar disorder is a disorder of movement, with individuals essentially overly active during manic phases and showing psychomotor disturbance (most commonly retardation) during depressive episodes. Further, it is thought that when individuals with bipolar disorder travel by air through a number of time zones, their risk of developing a mood episode is increased (Jauhar & Weller, 1982; Young, 1995). Thus, there is some indirect support for the hypothesis that melatonin perturbations may contribute to the spring excess in biological mood disorders.

Seasonal affective disorder (SAD)

SAD, a rather contrived and uninspiring acronym, is held to be a condition whereby there is a pattern of depression occurring in winter, with the episode remitting in the following spring or summer. An Australian study (Boyce & Parker, 1988) supported the northern hemisphere identification of a winter onset. In conjunction with a depressed mood, individuals tend to have both an increased appetite (hyperphagia) and increased sleep (hypersomnia), which are features of 'atypical depression'. The condition is held to affect 1–3% of adults in temperate climates and to be more prevalent in women (Magnusson & Boivin, 2003; Partonen & Lonnqvist, 1998), and to be particularly common among women in their childrearing years (Eagles, 2003). Studies in North America indicate that its prevalence increases as latitude of residence increases (Eagles, 2003), but such a relationship has not been confirmed in European studies. Winter-onset SAD was initially judged to be reflecting abnormal melatonin secretion from the pineal gland, but this hypothesis has not been convincingly supported (Partonen & Lonnqvist, 1998). Those authors suggested that winter-onset SAD may relate more to disturbed serotonergic activity, and that bright-light therapy is the first-line treatment option.

Suicide

A seasonal variation in suicide has long been recognized; Goodwin and Jamison (1990) reviewed more than 60 studies and established a consistent pattern whereby suicides (in reference to the northern hemisphere) show a striking peak in May (spring) and a second, albeit smaller peak in October (autumn). Gender differences have, however, long been described. Thus, in northern hemisphere studies, men have tended to show a single peak in May (spring), while females have tended to show a bimodal pattern with peaks in April/May (spring) and October/November (autumn). The May peak in northern hemisphere studies corresponds with the peak hospitalization rates for mood disorders.

Our southern hemisphere study in New South Wales (Parker & Walter, 1982) also identified differing patterns for males and females. Female suicides showed a biphasic pattern, with peaks in spring (most distinctly in November) and autumn (most distinctly in May), while male suicides failed to show any clear seasonal pattern.

As such seasonality effects have been most clearly demonstrated in regions with distinct seasons, we undertook a study in an equatorial region to determine whether 'seasonality' was the key factor. Singapore lies just 1.5 degrees north of the equator, and with mean monthly temperatures varying minimally over the year (from 26.4 to 28.4 degrees). We therefore undertook a study in Singapore (Parker *et al.*, 2001), which examined suicide rates over a ten-year period (1989–1998). We found no evidence of any patterning in suicidal deaths (for either males or females), thus supporting the hypothesis that there are seasonal influences on suicidal deaths (albeit with suicide being a marker of onset or severity of depressive disorders in general or of the more biological depressive conditions). Our review indicated that 'seasonality' effects appear to be less evident in more recent studies. Aschoff (1981) has previously suggested that as seasonal variation is greatest in the least industrialized countries and declines with industrialization, indirect influences such as artificial lighting may mute 'raw' environmental factors.

If 'seasonality' is influential, how might it be mediated? Preti and Miotto (1998) noted that suicide was associated with higher temperatures and longer daylight hours, so that ambient meteorological variables may be relevant. It strikes us as more likely that, as the seasonality effect is 'in line' with the seasonal pattern in hospitalizations for the biological disorders (e.g. mania, melancholic depression), we are more observing a consequence (i.e. increased chance of suicide) of that general seasonality pattern, for which determinants remain to be identified.

Schizophrenia

One of the most consistently replicated epidemiological features of schizophrenia is the slight excess of births in the late winter and spring. This finding can also be restated as a small decrement in births in the late summer/autumn (Bradbury & Miller, 1985; Torrey *et al.*, 1997). Over the past three decades, scores of articles have addressed this issue. These studies have come from many different sites and have used many different methods. While not all have found an association, the bulk of the studies have confirmed a 5% to 10% excess of births during winter and spring for those who develop schizophrenia. For example, in a study based on Danish registers, Mortensen and colleagues (1998) confirmed a significant but small seasonal excess of schizophrenia births during winter (relative risk = 1.11). However, this risk indicator was associated with a sizeable population-attributable fraction (10.5%). In other words, assuming that the risk-modifying factors associated with season of birth were not confounded by other risk factors, if the entire population was changed to the summer/autumn level of exposure, then the incidence of the disorder might fall by 10.5%. To put this into perspective, the same study reported that while the relative risk of developing schizophrenia was markedly increased if a mother or father had the disorder (7.2 to 9.3 relative risk respectively), the population-attributable fraction associated with having one or both parents ill was only 3.8%. This important public health issue warrants repeating. While the risk factor (or factors) underlying the season-of-birth effect are relatively weak (i.e. small effect size), because a sizeable proportion of the population is exposed to these factors (i.e. half the population are born in winter or spring), these factors can, in fact, be very important from a public health perspective (Rose, 1992).

Is the size of the season-of-birth effect uniform across time and place?

One way to narrow the range of candidate exposures associated with the season of birth effect in schizophrenia is to look for variations in the effect size of the within-year variation. For example, have there been changes over time, both secular and intra-decadal. There have also been some suggestions of a decrease in the magnitude of the effect over time in the northern hemisphere (Eagles *et al.*, 1995). The data from the Finnish site are particularly convincing (Suvisaari *et al.*, 2000), with the reduction in amplitude of seasonal fluctuations in schizophrenia birth rates being linked to the falling incidence of the disorder in the nation (Suvisaari *et al.*, 1999).

It would be most surprising to find that the season-of-birth effect in schizophrenia was uniformly distributed across the globe, especially as the amplitude of seasonal fluctuations in biometeorology are known to vary with factors such as latitude, altitude, and proximity to the coast. Not all sites have four seasons. For example, equatorial sites may have two seasons – wet and dry. Parker and Balza (1977) found a 'winter' excess of schizophrenia births in the coldest three months in an equatorial area. In another study, Parker *et al.* (2000) examined season of birth in Singapore. No significant winter/spring excess was identified. However, subtle differences were found in the patterns of births of those who developed schizophrenia compared to control births – fewer patients were born during March and April.

Latitude also seems to be associated with the size of the season-of-birth effect. Based on a systematic review of studies from the southern hemisphere (Australia, South Africa, Reunion Island), no overall significant winter–spring birth excess was found (McGrath & Welham, 1999). This finding suggested that whatever the risk-modifying factors underlying season of birth, they seemed to be weaker or less frequent in these sites. The nations that contributed to the southern hemisphere review are closer to the equator than most of the study sites in the northern hemisphere. To explore further the role of latitude and season of birth, a systematic review of studies from the northern hemisphere was also completed (Davies *et al.*, 2003). This review extracted data from eight studies based on 126,196 individuals with schizophrenia, drawn from 27 sites. Compared to summer/autumn births, there was a significant winter/spring excess (pooled odds ratio = 1.07; 95% CI 1.05–1.08). When the latitude of the sites was examined, a small but significant positive correlation was found between the winter/spring excess and latitude ($r = 0.27, p < 0.005$).

What is the critical window of exposure?

While the literature provides reasonable evidence linking seasonally-fluctuating environmental factors and the risk of schizophrenia, the critical window during which this exposure operates is unclear. Most commentators assume that the exposure is mainly related to the last trimester and/or the first few weeks of life (Tochigi *et al.*, 2004). However, it is also feasible that narrow windows of exposure prior to conception could be implicated via epigenetic modification (Rakyan *et al.*, 2002). It seems less plausible that exposures during childhood or pre-onset could be tightly linked to season of birth.

More complicated models can also be applied to the season-of-birth effect in schizophrenia. For example, the concept of the 'thrifty phenotype' may be informative here (Wells, 2003). This model proposes that if an organism can make persisting adjustments based on the prenatal environment, then it may be better able to cope with postnatal life. For example, organisms exposed to prenatal famine may be able to adjust their metabolic settings permanently so as to be better equipped for postnatal famine. However, if there is a mismatch between the prenatal and postnatal environments, the organisms may be compromised. This model has been proposed to help understand how intrauterine growth retardation followed by 'catch-up' growth may be associated with adverse outcomes (Wells, 2003).

Going beyond seasons in order to refine the candidate search

Summing schizophrenia birth rates per month across many years, and then combining these months into seasons, may obscure more subtle, between-year fluctuations in schizophrenia birth rates. To overcome this problem, two groups have examined time series data. One study was based on mental health registers in Queensland and in the Netherlands (McGrath *et al.*, 2002). This found a significantly increased risk of schizophrenia in males (but not females) in those born during periods of reduced duration of sunshine. They also found a significantly earlier age of first admissions in both males and females in those born during periods of reduced sunshine duration. A similar study from Scotland did not find any relationship between sunshine duration and risk of schizophrenia (Kendell & Adams, 2002).

Other groups have examined the associations between schizophrenia birth rates on one hand, and various biometeorological variables that fluctuate across seasons. Two groups have looked at rainfall (de Messias *et al.*, 2001; Miller, 1997). In particular, de Messias *et al.* (2001) examined the relationship between rain and schizophrenia births in a tropical region in Brazil, an area with no seasonal variation in temperature but with wet and dry seasons. They found a significant relationship between monthly rainfall and the number of schizophrenia births three months later. In contrast, there was no similar relationship for general population births. They concluded that the relationship to rainfall, rather than winter birth, may be associated with the risk of schizophrenia in tropical regions. Several groups have explored potential correlations between schizophrenia birth rates and temperature (Bark & Krivelevich, 1996; Hare & Moran, 1981; Kendell & Adams, 1991; Kinney *et al.*, 1993; McNeil *et al.*, 1975; Templer *et al.*, 1978). However, the overall results are inconsistent.

In the absence of clues as to the nature of the risk-modifying factor, researchers have explored factors that moderate the seasonal effect. Most large studies have found no association between season of birth and family history (Mortensen *et al.*, 1999; Suvisaari *et al.*, 2004), suggesting that the environmental factor operates equally on those with or without susceptibility genes. Curiously, one Finnish study has provided evidence that parents of individuals with schizophrenia may be more likely to have children (both affected and non-affected) during certain times of the year (the 'procreational habits' hypothesis) (Suvisaari *et al.*, 2001). However, this hypothesis has not attracted much support. The association between urban birth and season of birth remains unclear, with some studies finding an additive association (Machon *et al.*, 1983; O'Callaghan *et al.*, 1992; Verdoux *et al.*, 1997), while others found no association (Mortensen *et al.*, 1999).

Another fruitful direction for research is to refine the endophenotype associated with winter- or summer-born individuals with schizophrenia. As is often stated, schizophrenia is a heterogeneous disorder; thus, those that have a subtype related to seasonality of birth may differ on symptom profile or biological traits. Kinney *et al.* (1999) found that patients without eye-tracking dysfunction (ETD) were more likely to be born in hot or cold months than either those with ETD or the general population. They concluded that because ETD may mark a familial (most likely genetic) risk factor, aetiological factors associated with severe weather near birth may be important sources of non-familial ('sporadic') schizophrenia. Kirkpatrick and colleagues have built a strong case that summer-born individuals with schizophrenia are more likely to have a type of schizophrenia characterized by deficit syndromes (Kirkpatrick *et al.*, 1998, 2002a, 2002b; Messias & Kirkpatrick, 2001; Tek *et al.*, 2001).

What are the risk-modifying factors underlying seasonality and schizophrenia?

Season of birth and schizophrenia is an oft-quoted example of research where the data are stronger than the hypotheses. Over the years, a wide range of candidate exposures have been proposed. In particular, these include meteorological variables, infection, vitamin D, nutrition, toxins, maternal hormones, and sperm quality (McGrath, 1999; Tochigi *et al.*, 2004).

Season-of-birth investigations are extremely crude, ecological studies. Therefore, to make progress in the field, the researcher must propose an underlying risk-modifying factor and then test this hypothesis in a more direct fashion. Case–control studies can explore maternal recall or records to sharpen the focus on whether the mother or infant was actually exposed to the candidate (analytic epidemiology). These methods have been used in studies related to prenatal infections (McGrath & Murray, 2003). However, maternal recall is prone to error, and mothers of cases may have differential recall or attribution of events compared to the mothers of well controls. Thus, researchers strive for biological evidence of exposures (e.g. direct evidence of viral infection, indirect evidence such as antibody titres, nutritional parameters). Because of the lag between prenatal and perinatal exposures and the clinical outcomes (two to three decades), the options for the research community are severely limited.

Prenatal infection remains a lead candidate risk factor underlying season of birth (Brown & Susser, 2002). The epidemiological evidence for these candidates has moved from ecological studies (Mednick *et al.*, 1994; Takei *et al.*, 1995) to analytic case–control studies based on banked sera (Brown *et al.*, 2000; Buka *et al.*, 2001). Specific candidates include prenatal infection with influenza virus, herpex simplex, and rubella.

Another seasonally fluctuating exposure is vitamin D. While long associated with bone health and calcium regulation (Heaney & Weaver, 2003), there is a growing body of literature demonstrating that this seco-steroid promotes cell differentiation and programmed cell death (Darwish & DeLuca, 1993; Zittermann, 2003). The major source of vitamin D derives from the effects of ultraviolet radiation on the skin (Holick, 1995). Therefore, seasonal fluctuations in the strength of ultraviolet radiation can lead to reduced ability to synthesize vitamin D during winter (Webb *et al.*, 1988). Foetal vitamin D requirements increase during pregnancy (related to the increased need for foetal calcium) and maternal vitamin D levels fall during the third trimester, especially if this occurs during winter (MacLennan *et al.*, 1980). Recent animal experiments have demonstrated that low prenatal vitamin D is associated with heavier birth weight and alterations in both brain morphology and neurotrophin levels in the rat pup brain (Eyles *et al.*, 2003). To examine prenatal vitamin D more directly, one study measured maternal 25 hydroxyvitamin D_3 levels in blood sera taken during the third trimester and banked for over four decades (McGrath *et al.*, 2003). However, the results of this study were inconclusive. The vitamin D levels in the mothers whose children developed schizophrenia were lower than those of control mothers, although this difference was not statistically significant.

Because the developing human brain is not open to ready observation, some research groups are translating risk factors derived from epidemiology into animal experiments. While no animal model can replicate the phenotype of schizophrenia, these studies can provide important clues to understanding the mechanism of action for candidate exposures. In particular, they can help decide whether or not a candidate exposure has biological plausibility (i.e. does it impact on brain development, and are there morphological or behavioural features that are related to schizophrenia?). For example, animal models in schizophrenia research have included early lesioning of selected brain areas (Lipska *et al.*, 1992, 1995), prenatal exposure to specific viruses such as influenza (Fatemi *et al.*, 1999, 2000) and Borna virus (Hornig *et al.*, 1999), prenatal hypoxic/ischaemic insults (Mallard *et al.*, 1999), and prenatal hypovitaminosis D (Eyles *et al.*, 2003).

Seasonality of admission in schizophrenia

There is considerable evidence to support a connection between seasonally fluctuating meteorological variables and the onset and recurrence of various types of psychiatric symptomatology (Fossey & Shapiro, 1992). Meteotropism (i.e. biological events linked to meteorological events) has been observed in a number of self-rated characteristics, such as arousal, mood, physiology, and social behaviour (Welham *et al.*, 2000). Several groups have reported seasonal variations in the months of peak first admission for schizophrenia in Ireland (Clarke *et al.*, 1999), England and Wales (Takei *et al.*, 1992), Scotland (Takei & Murray, 1993) and the United Kingdom (Hare & Walter, 1978). The seasonality was more frequently found in females than in males, and the peak time for first admissions occurred during the middle of the year (northern hemisphere summer). A similar summer excess has been found for first and subsequent admissions in studies from Japan (Abe, 1963), Germany (Sperling *et al.*, 1997) and the United States (Strous *et al.*, 2001). However, this pattern does not seem to hold true in the southern hemisphere. One study of symptom onset in first episode patients found a summer excess (Owens & McGorry, 2003), another study found a significant winter excess of first admission (Davies *et al.*, 2000), and a third found no seasonal fluctuations in admissions for schizophrenia (Daniels *et al.*, 2000).

Conclusions

Seasonality in mood disorders, suicide, and schizophrenia can provide researchers with clues to help unravel the aetio-pathogenesis of these disorders. However, the critical task for the researcher is to go beyond 'circular epidemiology' and generate candidate risk-modifying exposures. These candidates need to be examined with respect to biological plausibility, and then re-examined in an analytical fashion. While Hippocrates was right in pointing to seasonality as a first step in understanding disorders, the research community needs to go beyond these studies with more strategic and focused research.

Acknowledgements

JM is supported by the Stanley Medical Research Institute. GP is supported by an NHMRC Program Grant (222308) and preparation of this chapter was assisted by Guy and Eve Sheppard.

References

Abe, K. (1963) 'Seasonal fluctuation of psychiatric admissions'. *Folia Psychiatrica et Neurologica Japonica*, *17*, 101–112.

Aschoff, J. (1981) 'Annual rhythms in man', in Aschoff, J. (ed.), *Handbook of behavioral neurobiology*, Vol. 4 (pp. 475–487). New York: Plenum Press.

Bark, N. and Krivelevich, I. (1996) 'Heatwaves during pregnancy as a risk factor for schizophrenia'. *Schizophrenia Research*, *18*, 105.

Boyce, P. and Parker, G. (1988) 'Seasonal affective disorder in the southern hemisphere'. *American Journal of Psychiatry*, *145*, 96–99.

Bradbury, T. N. and Miller, G. A. (1985) 'Season of birth in schizophrenia: a review of evidence, methodology, and etiology'. *Psychological Bulletin*, *98*, 569–594.

Brown, A. S. and Susser, E. S. (2002) 'In utero infection and adult schizophrenia'. *Mental Retardation and Developmental Disabilities Research Reviews*, *8*, 51–57.

Brown, A. S., Cohen, P., Greenwald, S. and Susser, E. (2000) 'Nonaffective psychosis after prenatal exposure to rubella'. *American Journal of Psychiatry*, *157*, 438–443.

Buka, S. L., Tsuang, M. T., Torrey, E. F., Klebanoff, M. A., Bernstein, D. and Yolken, R. H. (2001) 'Maternal infections and subsequent psychosis among offspring'. *Archives of General Psychiatry*, *58*, 1032–1037.

Clarke, M., Moran, P., Keogh, F., Morris, M., Kinsella, A., Larkin, C., Walsh, D. and O'Callaghan, E. (1999) 'Seasonal influences on admissions for affective disorder and schizophrenia in Ireland: a comparison of first and readmissions'. *European Psychiatry*, *14*, 251–255.

Daniels, B. A., Kirkby, K. C., Mitchell, P., Hay, D. and Mowry, B. (2000) 'Seasonal variation in hospital admission for bipolar disorder, depression and schizophrenia in Tasmania'. *Acta Psychiatrica Scandanavica*, *102*, 38–43.

Darwish, H. and DeLuca, H. F. (1993) 'Vitamin D-regulated gene expression'. *Critical Reviews in Eukaryotic Gene Expression, 3*, 89–116.

Davies, G., Ahmad, F., Chant, D., Welham, J. and McGrath, J. (2000) 'Seasonality of first admissions for schizophrenia in the southern hemisphere'. *Schizophrenia Research, 41*, 457–462.

Davies, G., Welham, J., Chant, D., Torrey, E. F. and McGrath, J. (2003) 'A systematic review and meta-analysis of northern hemisphere season of birth studies in schizophrenia'. *Schizophrenia Bulletin, 29*, 587–593.

Deisenhammer, E. A. (2003). 'Weather and suicide: the present state of knowledge on the association of meteorological factors with suicidal behaviour'. *Acta Psychiatrica Scandinavica, 108*(6), 402–409.

de Messias, E. L., Cordeiro, N. F., Sampaio, J. J., Bartko, J. J. and Kirkpatrick, B. (2001) 'Schizophrenia and season of birth in a tropical region: relationship to rainfall'. *Schizophrenia Research, 48*, 227–234.

Eagles, J. M. (2003) 'Seasonal affective disorder'. *British Journal of Psychiatry, 182*, 174–176.

Eagles, J. M., Hunter, D. and Geddes, J. R. (1995) 'Gender-specific changes since 1900 in the season-of-birth effect in schizophrenia'. *British Journal of Psychiatry, 167*, 469–472.

Eyles, D., Brown, J., Mackay-Sim, A., McGrath, J. and Feron, F. (2003) 'Vitamin D3 and brain development'. *Neuroscience, 118*, 641–653.

Fatemi, S. H., Cuadra, A. E., El Fakahany, E. E., Sidwell, R. W. and Thuras, P. (2000) 'Prenatal viral infection causes alterations in nNOS expression in developing mouse brains'. *Neuroreport, 11*, 1493–1496.

Fatemi, S. H., Emamian, E. S., Kist, D., Sidwell, R. W., Nakajima, K., Akhter, P., Shier, A., Sheikh, S. and Bailey, K. (1999) 'Defective corticogenesis and reduction in Reelin immunoreactivity in cortex and hippocampus of prenatally infected neonatal mice'. *Molecular Psychiatry, 4*, 145–154.

Fossey, E. and Shapiro, C. M. (1992) 'Seasonality in psychiatry – a review'. *Canadian Journal of Psychiatry, 37*, 299–308.

Goodwin, F. K. and Jamison, K. R. (1990) *Manic-depressive illness*. Oxford: Oxford University Press.

Hakko, H., Rasanen, P., Tiihonen, J. and Nieminen, P. (2002) 'Use of statistical techniques in studies of suicide seasonality, 1970 to 1997'. *Suicide and Life Threatening Behaviour, 32*, 191–208.

Hare, E. and Moran, P. (1981) 'A relation between seasonal temperature and the birth rate of schizophrenic patients'. *Acta Psychiatrica Scandinavica, 63*, 396–405.

Hare, E. H. (1975) 'Manic-depressive psychosis and season of birth'. *Acta Psychiatrica Scandinavica, 52*, 69–79.

Hare, E. H. and Walter, S. D. (1978) 'Seasonal variation in admission of psychiatric patients and its relation to seasonal variations in their births'. *Journal of Epidemiology and Community Health, 32*, 47–52.

Heaney, R. P. and Weaver, C. M. (2003) 'Calcium and vitamin D'. *Endocrinology and Metabolism Clinics of North America, 32*, 181–194.

Hippocrates (1992) *Ancient medicine, airs, water, places, epidemics 1–2, oat, precepts, nutriment*, Vol. 1. Cambridge, MA: Harvard University Press.

Holick, M. F. (1995) 'Environmental factors that influence the cutaneous production of vitamin D'. *American Journal of Clinical Nutriton, 61*, 638S–645S.

Hornig, M., Weissenbock, H., Horscroft, N. and Lipkin, W. I. (1999) 'An infection-based model of neurodevelopmental damage'. *Proceedings of the National Academy of Sciences of the United States of America, 96*, 12102–12107.

Jablensky, A. (2003) 'Schizophrenia: the epidemiological horizon', in Hirsch, S. R and Weinberger, D. R. (eds), *Schizophrenia* (pp. 203–231). Oxford: Blackwell Science.

Jauhar, P. and Weller, M. P. (1982) 'Psychiatric morbidity and time zone changes: a study of patients from Heathrow Airport'. *British Journal of Psychiatry, 140,* 231–235.

Kendell, R. and Adams, W. (1991) 'Unexplained fluctuations in the risk for schizophrenia by month and year of birth'. *British Journal of Psychiatry, 158,* 758–763.

Kendell, R. E. and Adams, W. (2002) 'Exposure to sunlight, vitamin D and schizophrenia'. *Schizophrenia Research, 54,* 193–198.

Kiloh, L. G. and Garside, R. F. (1963) 'The independence of neurotic depression and endogenous depression'. *British Journal of Psychiatry, 109,* 451–463.

Kinney, D. K., Waternaux, C. M., Spivak, C. and LeBlanc, A. (1993) 'Schizophrenia risk predicted by meteorologic extremes near birth'. *Schizophrenia Research, 9,* 135.

Kinney, D. K., Levy, D. L., Yurgelun-Todd, D. A., Lajonchere, C. M. and Holzman, P. S. (1999) 'Eye-tracking dysfunction and birth-month weather in schizophrenia'. *Journal of Abnormal Psychology, 108,* 359–362.

Kirkpatrick, B., Herrera, C. S. and Vazquez-Barquero, J. L. (2002a) 'Summer birth and deficit schizophrenia: Cantabria, Spain'. *Journal of Nervous and Mental Disease, 190,* 526–532.

Kirkpatrick, B., Tek, C., Allardyce, J., Morrison, G. and McCreadie, R. G. (2002b) 'Summer birth and deficit schizophrenia in Dumfries and Galloway, southwestern Scotland'. *American Journal of Psychiatry, 159,* 1382–1387.

Kirkpatrick, B., Ram, R., Amador, X. F., Buchanan, R. W., McGlashan, T., Tohen, M. and Bromet, E. (1998) 'Summer birth and the deficit syndrome of schizophrenia'. *American Journal of Psychiatry, 155,* 1221–1226.

Kuller, L. H. (1999) 'Circular epidemiology'. *American Journal of Epidemiology, 150,* 897–903.

Lipska, B. K., Jaskiw, G. E., Chrapusta, S., Karoum, F. and Weinberger, D. R. (1992) 'Ibotenic acid lesion of the ventral hippocampus differentially affects dopamine and its metabolites in the nucleus accumbens and prefrontal cortex in the rat'. *Brain Research, 585,* 1–6.

Lipska, B. K., Swerdlow, N. R., Geyer, M. A., Jaskiw, G. E., Braff, D. L. and Weinberger, D. R. (1995) 'Neonatal excitotoxic hippocampal damage in rats causes post-pubertal changes in prepulse inhibition of startle and its disruption by apomorphine'. *Psychopharmacology (Berl.), 122,* 35–43.

Machon, R. A., Mednick, S. A. and Schulsinger, F. (1983) 'The interaction of seasonality, place of birth, genetic risk and subsequent schizophrenia in a high risk sample'. *British Journal of Psychiatry, 143,* 383–388.

MacLennan, W. J., Hamilton, J. C. and Darmady, J. M. (1980) 'The effects of season and stage of pregnancy on plasma 25-hydroxy-vitamin D concentrations in pregnant women'. *Postgraduate Medical Journal, 56,* 75–79.

Magnusson, A. and Boivin, D. (2003) 'Seasonal affective disorder: an overview.' *Chronobiology International, 20,* 189–207.

Mallard, E. C., Rehn, A., Rees, S., Tolcos, M. and Copolov, D. (1999) 'Ventriculomegaly and reduced hippocampal volume following intrauterine growth-restriction: implications for the aetiology of schizophrenia'. *Schizophrenia Research, 40,* 11–21.

McGeehin, M. A. and Mirabelli, M. (2001) 'The potential impacts of climate variability and change on temperature-related morbidity and mortality in the United States'. *Environmental Health Perspectives, 109,* S185–S189.

McGrath, J. (1999) 'Hypothesis: is low prenatal vitamin D a risk-modifying factor for schizophrenia?' *Schizophrenia Research*, *40*, 173–177.

McGrath, J. J. (2003) 'Invited commentary: gaining traction on the epidemiologic landscape of schizophrenia'. *American Journal of Epidemiology*, *158*, 301–304.

McGrath, J. J. and Welham, J. L. (1999) 'Season of birth and schizophrenia: a systematic review and meta-analysis of data from the southern hemisphere'. *Schizophrenia Research*, *35*, 237–242.

McGrath, J. J. and Murray, R. M. (2003) 'Risk factors for schizophrenia: from conception to birth', in Weinberger, D. R. and Hirsch, S. R. (eds), *Schizophrenia* (pp. 232–250). Oxford: Blackwell.

McGrath, J., Selten, J. P. and Chant, D. (2002) 'Long-term trends in sunshine duration and its association with schizophrenia birth rates and age at first registration-data from Australia and the Netherlands'. *Schizophrenia Research*, *54*, 199–212.

McGrath, J., Eyles, D., Mowry, B., Yolken, R. and Buka, S. (2003) 'Low maternal vitamin D as a risk factor for schizophrenia: a pilot study using banked sera'. *Schizophrenia Research*, *63*, 73–78.

McMichael, A. J. (2001) *Human frontiers, environments and disease*. Cambridge: Cambridge University Press.

McNeil, T., Dalen, P., Dzierzykray-Rogalska, M. and Kaij, L. (1975) 'Birth rates of schizophrenics following relatively warm versus relatively cool summers'. *Archiv für Psychiatrie und Nervenkrankheiten*, *221*, 1–10.

Mednick, S. A., Huttunen, M. O. and Machon, R. A. (1994) 'Prenatal influenza infections and adult schizophrenia'. *Schizophrenia Bulletin*, *20*, 263–267.

Mercer, J. B. (2003) 'Cold – an underrated risk factor for health'. *Environmental Research*, *92*, 8–13.

Messias, E. and Kirkpatrick, B. (2001) 'Summer birth and deficit schizophrenia in the epidemiological catchment area study'. *Journal of Nervous and Mental Disease*, *189*, 608–612.

Miller, C. L. (1997) 'Rates of schizophrenia correlate with mean rainfall in two European countries'. *Schizophrenia Research*, *24*, 254.

Mortensen, P. B., Pedersen, C. B., Westergaard, T., Wohlfahrt, J., Ewald, H., Mors, O., Andersen, P. K. and Melbye, M. (1998) 'Familial and non-familial risk factors for schizophrenia: a population-based study'. *Schizophrenia Research*, *29*, 13–13(1).

Mortensen, P. B., Pedersen, C. B., Westergaard, T., Wohlfahrt, J., Ewald, H., Mors, O., Andersen, P. K. and Melbye, M. (1999) 'Effects of family history and place and season of birth on the risk of schizophrenia'. *New England Journal of Medicine*, *340*, 603–608.

Naughton, M. P., Henderson, A., Mirabelli, M. C., Kaiser, R., Wilhelm, J. L., Kieszak, S. M., Rubin, C. H. and McGeehin, M. A. (2002) 'Heat-related mortality during a 1999 heat wave in Chicago'. *American Journal of Preventive Medicine*, *22*, 221–227.

O'Callaghan, E., Colgan, K., Cotter, D., Larkin, C., Walsh, D. and Waddington, J. L. (1992) 'Evidence for confinement of winter birth excess in schizophrenia to those born in cities'. *Schizophrenia Research*, *6*, 102.

Owens, N. and McGorry, P. D. (2003) 'Seasonality of symptom onset in first-episode schizophrenia'. *Psychological Medicine*, *33*, 163–167.

Parker, G. (1978) 'Schizophrenia and season of birth: further southern hemisphere studies'. *Australian and New Zealand Journal of Psychiatry*, *12*, 65–67.

Parker, G. and Balza, B. (1977) 'Season of birth and schizophrenia – an equatorial study'. *Acta Psychiatrica Scandinavica*, *56*, 143–146.

Parker, G. and Neilson, M. (1976) 'Mental disorder and season of birth – a southern hemisphere study'. *British Journal of Psychiatry, 129*, 355–361.

Parker, G. and Walter, S. D. (1982) 'Seasonal variation in depressive disorders and suicidal deaths in New South Wales'. *British Journal of Psychiatry, 140*, 626–632.

Parker, G., Gao, F. and Machin, D. (2001) 'Seasonality of suicide in Singapore: data from the equator'. *Psychological Medicine, 31*, 549–553.

Parker, G., Mahendran, R., Koh, E. S. and Machin, D. (2000) 'Season of birth in schizophrenia: no latitude at the equator'. *British Journal of Psychiatry, 176*, 68–71.

Partonen, T. and Lonnqvist, J. (1998) 'Seasonal affective disorder'. *Lancet, 352*, 1369–1374.

Preti, A. and Miotto, P. (1998) 'Seasonality in suicides: the influence of suicide method, gender and age on suicide distribution in Italy'. *Psychiatry Research, 81*, 219–231.

Rakyan, V. K., Blewitt, M. E., Druker, R., Preis, J. I. and Whitelaw, E. (2002) 'Metastable epialleles in mammals'. *Trends in Genetics, 18*, 348–351.

Rose, G. (1992) *The strategy of preventive medicine*. Oxford: Oxford University Press.

Sperling, W., Barocka, A., Kalb, R., Suss, S. and Katalinic, A. (1997) 'Influence of season on manifestation of schizophrenic subtypes'. *Psychopathology, 30*, 200–207.

Strous, R. D., Pollack, S., Robinson, D., Sheitman, B. and Lieberman, J. A. (2001) 'Seasonal admission patterns in first episode psychosis, chronic schizophrenia, and non-schizophrenic psychoses'. *Journal of Nervous and Mental Disease, 189*, 642–644.

Suvisaari, J. M., Haukka, J. K. and Lonnqvist, J. K. (2001) 'Season of birth among patients with schizophrenia and their siblings: evidence for the procreational habits hypothesis'. *American Journal of Psychiatry, 158*, 754–757.

Suvisaari, J. M., Haukka, J. K. and Lonnqvist, J. K. (2004) 'No association between season of birth of patients with schizophrenia and risk of schizophrenia among their siblings'. *Schizophrenia Research, 66*, 1–6.

Suvisaari, J. M., Haukka, J. K., Tanskanen, A. J. and Lonnqvist, J. K. (1999) 'Decline in the incidence of schizophrenia in Finnish cohorts born from 1954 to 1965'. *Archives of General Psychiatry, 56*, 733–740.

Suvisaari, J. M., Haukka, J. K., Tanskanen, A. J. and Lonnqvist, J. K. (2000) 'Decreasing seasonal variation of births in schizophrenia'. *Psychological Medicine, 30*, 315–324.

Takei, N. and Murray, R. M. (1993) 'Gender difference of schizophrenia in seasonal admissions in Scotland'. *British Journal of Psychiatry, 162*, 272–273.

Takei, N., Murray, R. M., Sham, P. and O'Callaghan, E. (1995) 'Schizophrenia risk for women from in utero exposure to influenza'. *American Journal of Psychiatry, 152*, 150–151.

Takei, N., O'Callaghan, E., Sham, P., Glover, G., Tamura, A. and Murray, R. (1992) 'Seasonality of admissions in the psychoses: effect of diagnosis, sex, and age at onset'. *British Journal of Psychiatry, 161*, 506–511.

Tek, C., Kirkpatrick, B., Kelly, C. and McCreadie, R. G. (2001) 'Summer birth and deficit schizophrenia in Nithsdale, Scotland'. *Journal of Nervous and Mental Disease, 189*, 613–617.

Templer, D. I, Ruff, C., Halcomb, P. H., Barthlow, V. I. and Ayers, J. L. (1978) 'Month of conception of birth of schizophrenics as related to the temperature'. *Orthomolecular Psychiatry, 7*, 231–235.

Tochigi, M., Okazaki, Y., Kato, N. and Sasaki, T. (2004) 'What causes seasonality of birth in schizophrenia?'. *Neuroscience Research, 48*, 1–11.

Torrey, E. F., Miller, J., Rawlings, R. and Yolken, R. H. (1997) 'Seasonality of births in schizophrenia and bipolar disorder: a review of the literature'. *Schizophrenia Research, 28*, 1–38.

Verdoux, H., Takei, N., Cassou de Saint-Mathurin, R., Murray, R. M. and Bourgeois, M. L. (1997) 'Seasonality of birth in schizophrenia: the effect of regional population density'. *Schizophrenia Research, 23,* 175–180.

Webb, A. R., Kline, L. and Holick, M. F. (1988) 'Influence of season and latitude on the cutaneous synthesis of vitamin D3: exposure to winter sunlight in Boston and Edmonton will not promote vitamin D3 synthesis in human skin'. *Journal of Clinical Endocrinology and Metabolism, 67,* 373–378.

Wehr, T. A. (1996) 'A "clock for all seasons" in the human brain'. *Progress in Brain Research, 111,* 321–342.

Wehr, T. A. (1998) 'Effect of seasonal changes in daylength on human neuroendocrine function'. *Hormone Research, 49,* 118–124.

Welham, J. L., Davies, G., Auliciems, A. and McGrath, J. (2000) 'Climate and geography and the epidemiology of schizophrenia'. *International Journal of Mental Health, 29,* 70–100.

Wells, J. C. K. (2003) 'The thrifty phenotype hypothesis: thrifty offspring or thrifty mother?'. *Journal of Theoretical Biology, 221,* 143–161.

Young, D. M. (1995) 'Psychiatric morbidity in travelers to Honolulu, Hawaii'. *Comprehensive Psychiatry, 36,* 224–228.

Zittermann, A. (2003) 'Vitamin D in preventive medicine: are we ignoring the evidence?'. *British Journal of Nutrition* 89, 552–72.

11 Psychiatric morbidity following disasters

Epidemiology, risk, and protective factors

Alexander C. McFarlane

Disasters, by their nature, are events that are unanticipated and occur when the normal protective mechanisms that contain our environment and ensure the safety of the technology of a society fail. In this way, the normal methods and structures used for civil administration and organization are seriously challenged. Each disaster is unique and poses unusual challenges. Thus, it is not reasonable to make simplistic or proscriptive generalizations about the mental health impact following such events. Rather, these settings are where the adaptation of societies and individuals are tested in many domains. By their nature, disasters impose an intense strain on the resilience and coping resources of those affected. This chapter will outline some of the definitions and concepts that lie behind understanding the impact of disasters on the health and welfare of the affected communities.

The study of disasters sits in the midst of the general body of stress research and, in particular, traumatic stress and post-traumatic stress disorder (PTSD). The field of traumatic stress has developed around victims from three types of events: disasters, war veterans, and criminal victimization. Disasters are unusual because they occur randomly and usually involve large numbers of victims at the same time. They occur infrequently, in contrast with events such as criminal assaults and motor vehicle accidents that occur as a daily occurrence in urban communities. These latter events also generally affect single individuals or small groups, rather than large populations. Thus, the magnitude of disasters are such that there are particular lessons that can be learned by investigating the collective reactions in the victims, as well as the associated communal processes that mitigate or aggravate the effects of these events.

Disasters, inevitably, are events that capture human attention and concern. However, public interest in these events tends to be relatively short-lived and until recently their long-term morbidity was often underestimated. Disaster research has highlighted the often very prolonged adverse consequences of such events. The first systematic research in the field was by the Swiss psychiatrist, Edouard Stierlin (1911). He studied an earthquake that affected Messina in Italy in 1907 and a mining disaster that occurred in 1906. He found that a substantial proportion of the victims developed long-term post-traumatic symptoms. The Messina earthquake was an event of much greater magnitude than has often been studied more recently by disaster researchers, having killed 70,000 people. Stierlin found that 25% of the survivors experienced sleep disturbances and nightmares.

Definition and typology

'Disaster' is a word like 'stress' in that everybody knows its meaning but it is rarely defined. The Oxford English Dictionary (1987) definition of disaster is: 'sudden or great misfortune; calamity; complete failure'. Given this breadth of definition, it is an issue of some complexity as to how disasters are clearly separated from other types of traumatic events (Green, 1996).

In contrast to these general definitions, the early disaster researchers Kinston and Rosser (1974) suggested that the term be used to describe 'massive collective stress', while for Norris (1992), these were events where there were 'violent encounters with nature, technology or human kind'. Arising out of these definitions, various typologies of disaster have been proposed. These focus on differentiation of the type of determinants of the destruction.

While there is a logic to the separation of destructive acts of nature from man-made disasters such as industrial accidents, the differences in terms of the outcomes are not substantial (Norris *et al.*, 2002). There has been some interest in separating the effects of man-made acts where there is the potential for malevolence to play a role, in contrast to natural disasters. However, these differentiations can be somewhat illusory. For example, forest fires or bushfires can be caused by arsonists or by the careless use of machinery. Often, deaths in disasters such transport accidents are due to failures of building design or technology. At times these failures involve frank negligence, the Bhopal chemical disaster being one example. These technological disasters have the capacity to divide communities, particularly where one party is seen to represent a sector of privilege and wealth that is exercised with little concern for the welfare of the broader community.

Disasters cover a range of experiences that are reflected in the typologies; in these distinction is often drawn between natural and technological events. It has been proposed that man-made disasters are more likely to be difficult for individuals to tolerate, whereas natural disasters possibly can be dismissed as acts of God. At the other extreme are events involving active human design, such as assault, torture, and rape. Smith and North (1993) articulated the commonly held opinion that technological and human-made disasters are likely to be more traumatic than natural ones, as they provoke a greater sense of being the deliberate victim of one's fellow human beings. On the other hand, a meta-analysis of the relationship between disasters and trauma-related psychopathology (Rubonis & Bickman, 1991) came to the opposite conclusion – that natural disasters resulted in greater rates of disorder.

A classification that has practical implications is the division of these events according to the intensity and range of their impact (see Table 11.1). The first type of disaster is one where there is a clear demarcation of exposure (e.g.

Table 11.1 Types of disaster

a. Geographically circumscribed
   - Clear margins – fires and explosions
   - Graded destruction – earthquake, storms

b. Travel accidents and terrorism
   - Commuting – impact in local community
   - International – impact on different countries

c. Duration
   - Warning
     - Brief or absent – earthquake or terrorist attack
     - Prolonged – cyclones and floods
   - Impact
     - Brief – explosion or accident
     - Prolonged – fire, flood or hurricane

forest fires). In contrast, earthquakes and storms have a long gradient of exposure in which the exact margins of the disaster are less precise. These disasters pose a risk to all who live and work in the affected communities. The impact, in terms of both destruction and stress for emergency services, will come from within these regions. These disasters are also often anticipated, so that disaster plans and services should be precisely directed towards their occurrence.

In contrast, travel accidents and acts of terror are highly concentrated and will strike a group who happen to be congregated by chance. In these events, very few of the injured or dead may come from the locality of the disaster, for example with an aircraft accident. It is therefore important to separate those events that affect a commuter service, for instance, from those involving an international carrier. The latter may have an international impact, with the bereaved coming from many regions. These distinctions have major implications for how rescues are mounted and the provision of services in the aftermath. One example would be the 2002 Bali bombing, which killed over 200 people. While a significant number of Balinese people were killed, the bombing of a tourist venue meant that people from all around the world were killed or grievously injured.

The impacts of these events may vary greatly, for a number of reasons. First, events that are geographically defined are more likely to have a warning phase and the potential for preparatory defence. On the other hand, the community that is destroyed will also be called upon for rescue and recovery, creating a conflict between the role of victim and that of rescuer for many individuals.

If the aim of a typology is to allow the development of generalizations from research and experience, these distinctions may be of more use than considering the nature of the destructive agent alone.

The nature of disaster and the areas merging with other types of trauma

The definition of disaster involves distinguishing between large-scale accidents and disasters; there is no easy separation and the definition is often determined in the civil domain by government. In smaller communities with fewer emergency relief resources, the threshold for an event to disrupt the capacity to manage and organize an effective response will be lower than in a city like New York after September 11. If a plane crashes on to housing near an airport, with survivors from the plane and buildings destroyed, this may be deemed a disaster. However, the same aircraft crashing in a remote region with no survivors may not be considered more than an accident.

Terrorism and disasters

The boundaries between the effects of war and those of disaster are becoming less easy to define, with the onset of more widespread terrorism that targets civilians. For example, the terrorist attacks in Israel, Palestine, Bali, and on September 11, 2001 could be considered acts of war. Another perspective is that these are man-made disasters that are characterized by extreme malevolence because the victims of these events had no anticipation of their unfolding, in contrast to the combatants in a more typical armed conflict.

In war, when civilians become targets, the boundary with terrorism becomes even more unclear. In many respects terrorism is undeclared warfare, fought by unconventional means and often targeting civilian targets. The resultant damage has the same physical impact as a disaster that leads to death and destruction. What is different is the sense of unpredictable fear and threat that emerges. By its motivation, terrorism also targets the fabric of social cohesion. The lingering distrust and vigilance that result create an environment that has a very different quality from the bringing together of communities that often happens in the face of other disasters. Hence, characteristics of both the event and the recovery environment should be defined when one is attempting to understand the psychological impact of these events.

Disasters, war, and refugees

In major wars, there is often a disaster that follows in the wake of war, although it is not seen as such. In recent history, the destruction of the infrastructure of Kuwait by Iraq and the burning and looting of most of the buildings in East Timor when the Indonesian occupying forces left, following the UN independence referendum, occurred in the setting of military combat. However, the aftermath that the survivors had to endure was very similar to the impact of a major event such as a tsunami. For these communities, the lack of physical safety in the aftermath of the destruction, if combat continues, makes the experience enduring and demoralizing. However, there is much in common with a post-disaster environment and many of the same principles are involved in the planning and mounting of relief efforts.

In considering the impact of disasters, it is important to consider those in developing countries. There has often been the triggering of war by disasters, such as drought and the associated migration of refugees, and these are the least studied. A Red Cross report found that an average of 17,000,000 people living in Third World countries were affected by disasters each year in the period 1967 to 1991, compared with about 700,000 in developed countries (a striking ratio of 166 to 1). Developing communities are particularly at risk in the face of disaster because they are already under strain and with few resources in reserve for times when rescue and protection are required. Their health systems tend to be rudimentary and have little mental health capability.

Furthermore, modern warfare, which is increasingly driven by ethnic cleansing and religious bigotry, has been characterized by major humanitarian disasters. The active eviction of families from regions, thereby creating a mass refugee exodus, is used as a weapon of war. In the setting of population migration, the communities into which they move are also destabilized and sometimes destroyed. As water and other natural resources become scarcer, combined with climate change due to global warming, droughts and other disasters will provoke increasing problems with refugee migration. These modern disasters that come from the impact of war must be studied from multiple dimensions to characterize their full impact and ensure the development of optimal management strategies.

The margins of disaster and background traumas in the affected community

The threshold of exposure needed for an individual to be considered a victim is one of the issues arising in examining the effects of disaster. The determination of this issue is at times a legal one. The recourse to litigation in man-made disasters will generally result in a degree of financial compensation that is not available to the victims of natural events. Contrary to fears about the negative effects of compensation on people's adjustment, it may be that adequate financial relief can provide a buffer against some of the negative effects of these events.

The emergence of a more general interest in PTSD since the publication of DSM-III (American Psychiatric Association, 1987) has led to a dramatic increase in interest in the impact of disasters. In contrast to the earlier belief that these events were outside the range of normal human experience, in the light of systematic examination they have been shown to be relatively common. Norris (1992), in a study of 1,000 adults in southern USA, found that 69% had experienced a traumatic stressor in their lives, including 21% in the past year alone. In that year, 2.4% of households in the southern United States were subjected to disaster or damage, with a lifetime exposure to disasters of 13%.

Kessler *et al.* (1995) found that 60.7% of the male and 51.2% of the female population had experienced an event meeting DSM-IV stressor criteria

(American Psychiatric Association, 1994), in a stratified population sample in the USA. In relation to these events, 18.9% of men and 15.2% of women had been exposed to a natural disaster with the respective rates of lifetime PTSD of 3.7% and 5.4%. Creamer *et al.* (2001), in a stratified sample of 10,641 Australians, found that a similar percentage had a lifetime exposure to traumatic experiences, with 19.9% of men and 12.7% of women reporting that they had experienced a disaster. However, of the 158 cases of PTSD in the past 12 months, in only four was a natural disaster nominated as the stressor.

Such studies demonstrate that while approximately one in six of the population has had a lifetime exposure to a natural disaster, this accounts for a very small component of the post-traumatic morbidity within these communities. Less than 5% nominated their disaster experience when asked to select the most traumatic event in their lives. These figures demonstrate the problem of much of the research, as they are based on the simple question as to whether the individual has or has not been exposed to a natural disaster, with no definition of threshold given. Therefore, comparisons between these population samples and disaster-affected communities are difficult to make. Yet definitions about the level of exposure are critical in attempting to make estimates of risk. Similarly, this uncertainty creates difficulties in making comparisons between different disaster-affected populations.

In the past decade, some important investigations have been conducted into major disasters in non-European cultures. These initiatives are important because they provide a test of how culturally specific to the broader world community are the earlier findings of disasters in Judaeo-Christian cultures. Of particular note are the studies of the recent earthquakes that have affected Kobe (Japan), China, Taiwan, India, and Turkey.

Adverse outcomes

Physical health

Disasters have an impact on various dimensions of adaptation; they pose a major risk of serious injury and death, though the nature of the injuries will be determined by the physical characteristics of the event. Burns are a major consequence of fire, crush injuries occur with earthquakes, and multi-system injuries arise from transport disasters. Frequently the treatment resources of an individual region are overwhelmed and a national approach is required to provide acute treatment. For example, following the Bali terrorist attacks, the severely burned survivors were evacuated to hospitals throughout Australia. The nature of such injuries will also necessitate special rehabilitation programmes.

Disasters also pose a risk of epidemics and malnutrition. Particularly when sewerage systems and water supplies are damaged, a public health emergency must be confronted to prevent a second disaster. Such risks create a secondary sense of threat that further challenges the adaptive capacity of the community. Finally, the stress of the disaster can precipitate exacerbations of endemic chronic diseases. Extreme stress can trigger the onset of acute complications, such as the increase of myocardial infarction in individuals with atherosclerosis following the Athens earthquake (Trichopoulos *et al.*, 1983). In the aftermath, the stress can have other indirect effects including the impact on the rates of motor vehicle accidents and other accidental injury. The impact of disasters on attempted and completed suicide is also important, given the relationship between PTSD, major depressive disorder, and such behaviour. While not examined in a systematic way, the impact of the Port Arthur shootings – where there was the largest number of deaths caused by a single gunman – was followed by a higher than expected number of suicides (Lyn, 1997; Peters & Watson, 1996). This raises the question as to whether events characterized by extremes of gratuitous violence break the normal prohibition to self-harm.

Medically unexplained symptoms

An area of particular interest is the diverse range of physical symptoms in disaster-affected populations. In Holland, the Eindhoven fireworks factory explosion and the El Al jet incident, where two engines fell off a Boeing 747 on take-off from Amsterdam Airport and crashed into a block of flats, have highlighted the fears that can emerge in exposed populations about the hidden health impact of these events. The 747 had depleted uranium as ballast, and there were many fears about its health effects. Similarly, the chemical exposure involved in the firework explosion caused considerable anxiety about potential adverse health effects. There are major risks to the exposed population's health associated with disasters and the optimal response is to monitor the patterns of morbidity that emerge in the aftermath. On occasions, these adverse consequences are not anticipated but can be detected by surveillance programmes (for example, by general practice consultations or population-based health surveys). The difference between health-seeking behaviour and the presentation of disorders that began following the disaster needs to be established. The patterns of causal attribution also should be carefully documented, as attribution of illness to the exposure may not prove to be correct on further exploration (Slottje *et al.*, 2006).

The relationship between unexplained medical symptoms and psychological symptoms is well described in many non-military and disaster populations, as part of the literature about somatization. Katon and Walker (1998) suggested a near-linear relationship between the number of somatic symptoms, particularly medically unexplained, and the number of current and past symptoms of psychological morbidity, especially those of anxiety and depression. Katon *et al.* (1991) suggested that the count of such symptoms may serve as proxy measures of psychological distress, and further raised the possibility (Katon *et al.*, 2001) that this relationship remains even in individuals whose psychological symptoms do not reach the threshold for diagnosis.

A long-standing association has been noted between increased reporting of unexplained physical symptoms and the diagnosis of PTSD (Andreski *et al.*,

1998; McFarlane *et al.*, 1994; Solomon *et al.*, 1987; Zatzick *et al.*, 2003). In a prospective study of 1007 patients in a large health maintenance organization, people with PTSD were more likely to develop somatization symptoms than those without PTSD (OR = 3.7) (Andreski *et al.*, 1998). Hence, further investigation of the determinants of medically unexplained symptoms and their relationship with exposure to trauma and the onset of psychological disorders is likely to be fruitful.

Psychological morbidity

There is now an extensive body of research investigating the patterns of psychological distress following disaster, but it is important that PTSD is not seen as the only disorder that emerges in this setting. The most terrifying and confronting aspects of the experience should be carefully understood and defined, because they form the core of the traumatic memories that play a central role in the emergence of a range of disorders. The main triggers in the emergence and progressive escalation of symptoms in the chronic disorder should be defined in the aftermath of the disaster. Hence, anticipation and description of the triggers are critical to understanding the pattern of reactivity and avoidance that emerges.

The second issue in catastrophic disaster is the interaction between grief and traumatic psychopathology. In normal grief, the individual is able to revisit the memory of the person who died with a sense of longing and pain, but can also search for positive memories. In disasters, however, the traumatic memories intrude to inhibit this normal process, so that the grief may drive the PTSD symptoms. The interaction between the effects of loss and the disorders that emerge following disasters is a phenomenon that varies considerably in those events that lead to the loss of life, while not destroying the people's property and livelihood.

The third issue is the emergence of comorbidities. In the first instance, major depressive disorder (MDD) is common and reflects both the severity of the PTSD and their shared neurobiology. Also, since MDD is more common than PTSD in many populations, PTSD should not be over-emphasized. Both of these are disorders where 'kindling' plays an important role in preventing the normal diminution of distress with time. Kindling is the process by which a seizure or other brain event is initiated and its recurrence thereby made more likely.

One comorbidity of particular interest is alcohol and substance abuse. As the role of these as self-medication for PTSD symptoms is well known, there is an important challenge in minimizing this risk. This comorbidity may further disrupt the community and the intimate relationships of those affected. Hence, these events should be discussed as conveying a general vulnerability to psychiatric abnormality, with PTSD the specific disorder that emerges. We cannot be sure whether other conditions pre-existed the disaster or not. Since there is a substantial prevalence of such morbidity in the general population, the challenge is to investigate whether a disorder was triggered by the disaster, aggravated by the event, or already existed.

Conceptual issues

Defining the disaster experience

Disaster research is part of the social dialectic that is involved in rebuilding a community; it also characterizes the less visible aspects of the damage that these events inflict on communities. Thus there are a series of challenges in conceptualizing the nature of disaster exposure.

To begin with, losses can be in a series of domains, such as property, the death and injury of friends and relatives, the destruction of community resources, and loss of property that is involved in the generation of income and provision of employment. These various dimensions must be estimated, but little work has been done up to now to examine the validity of such methods. For example, in a quantitative sense, how does the death of a spouse rank against the death of a child? The first dilemma that arises is the comparative impact of the loss of property, compared with death and injury to people. Yet in terms of a numerical rating, it is necessary to make these comparisons if scores of disaster exposures are to be estimated. A further dimension of the experience involves the sense of life threat and fear that is experienced by the individual during the height of the emergency.

While these measures may seem to be relevant only to the research community, some understanding of these matters is critical for the comparison of disaster studies. Equally, if information is to be used in making predictions about the likely effects of some recent event, estimates based on the degree of exposure are required. Researchers often underestimate the complexity of characterizing the relevant experience of individuals. Van der Kolk (1996) has argued that one of the primary characteristics of traumatic experiences is that they challenge an individual's capacity to create a narrative of their own experience and to integrate their traumatic experience with other events. Consequentially, their traumatic memories are often not coherent stories, but tend to consist of intense emotions or somato-sensory impressions. These are events that test the capacity of language to capture and characterize experience. As a result, neither researchers nor clinicians may fully embrace the horror and the helplessness embodied in research data and patients' stories. This is a critical issue for the development of adequate methodologies and instruments to describe and characterize disaster experience.

Neuroimaging research (Clark *et al.*, 2003) has demonstrated how there is a disruption of the neural networks involving language in people with PTSD, with a greater degree of activation of a region in the right parietal cortex involved in somatic processing. Hence, there is a neurobiological basis for the difficulty they have in the verbal representation of their experience and its manifestation of somatic distress. Simpson (1988), who survived a horrendous climbing accident in South America, reflected on this difficulty of expression in his biography *Touching the Void*:

> I can add only that however painful readers may think our experiences were, for me this book still falls short of articulating just how dreadful were some of those lonely days. I could not find the words to express the utter desolation of the experience.

Exploration of this descriptive dimension is often lost in the need for scales of exposure that can explore these more subjective dimensions.

The impact of a chronic malevolent environment as against the acute threat

While many disasters are characterized by a sudden and threatening event, such as an earthquake or explosion, others emerge insidiously and the perceived threat progressively magnifies rather than diminishes. In many disasters, the acute threat is contained and there is then a relatively rapid restoration of order and safety. However, in some instances, the post-disaster environment has many ongoing intrinsic threats to the individual and community, especially when there is a risk of epidemics or the income-earning infrastructure has been destroyed. There are also those where the nature of the danger is more insidious and therefore difficult to identify and control. The implications of this prolonged threat are substantial, because they disrupt the development of a sense of safety, while the ongoing triggering of anxiety has the capacity to sensitize the individual's reactivity, rather than quenching the response.

Chemical and radiation threats

The Times Beach contamination disaster and the Chernobyl nuclear explosion are two examples of the pervasive threat that such chemical and radiation events evoke. The first involved contamination due to a housing estate being built on the site of a former toxic chemical waste dump, while in the Chernobyl disaster, a nuclear power reactor exploded. The invisible nature of these chemical and radiation hazards has several implications. Clearly, it is difficult to be immediately aware of exposure, as this occurs invisibly. Second, even when the hazard has been contained, it is hard to reassure the exposed community that it is no longer a risk, especially if there have been initial failures to warn, resulting in mistrust of the information given by the authorities. Also, the harmful consequences of exposures are often slow to manifest, with long latency periods before diseases emerge, such as cancers and degenerative diseases. Genetic damage leading to congenital malformations remains an incipient fear for generations.

Often, as in Bhopal, there is the added dimension of a community being pitted against a large corporation, with the further stress of prolonged litigation and very delayed financial recompense. Public distrust and fear of misinformation erode the sense of safety in the community and maintain the sense of injustice, victimization, and loss. As with all disasters, bringing an end to the sense of threat is critical for recovery.

Defining the end of the disaster

Disasters are not defined by the period of threat from the destructive event. The impact is also influenced by the anticipation and implementation of mitigation and protective strategies, so that many disasters do not emerge as they are prevented. As the threat emerges, there are many actions by communities and individuals that can limit the destruction and protect life and property. Weather forecasts are a major source of information that protects the life of aviators and seafarers, if warnings are heeded.

Equally, defining the end of a disaster should take account of the removal of the malevolent environment and the re-establishment of normal standards of shelter and commerce in a community. The end-stage of disaster represents a gradient of change and readjustment, as the threats to the welfare of the victims progressively diminish. These different phases of disasters need to be understood, as they represent a series of windows where vulnerability and protective factors can differentially come into play.

Epidemiology

Epidemiological research into the impact of disasters has consistently demonstrated increased risks of psychiatric morbidity in the affected populations. In this chapter, the substantial body of information that has been compiled over the past 25 years will not be systematically reviewed, as this has been done elsewhere. Rather, the important general conclusions will be extracted and commented upon. Norris *et al.* (2002) did an extensive review and meta-analysis of the impact of these events, using the available scientific databases. Although it does exclude some relevant studies, this paper is a comprehensive review of the 160 distinct disasters identified. In 2003 a further series of disasters were reported in the literature, particularly a set of sub-populations following September the 11th (e.g. Galea, 2003) and earthquakes (Salcioglu *et al.*, 2003; Yang *et al.*, 2003).

The majority of the published studies examined the impact of natural disasters (88 = 55%), a further 54 (34%) referred to technological disasters, and 18 (11%) documented the impact of massive violence. These events occurred in 29 separate countries, with 57% having occurred in the United States and its territories. A further 29% of the events studied occurred in developed countries, such as Europe, Japan, and Australia. The developing world including Eastern Europe, Asia, and Africa accounted for only 14% of the studies, although recent reports of earthquakes in China and Taiwan have increased this number.

A range of categories of victim populations has been studied. Approximately 70% of the survivors investigated focused on adults (e.g. Donker *et al.*, 2002), with a further 17% examining school-aged children and adolescents (e.g. Laor *et al.*, 2002). Emergency service personnel (e.g. Chang *et al.*, 2003) and family assistance counsellors have been studied in approximately 15% of studies; these are of particular interest because of the risks that they endure during the containment of the disaster. Most of these studies provide a snapshot of the affected population within a six-month window (60%). While there have been some substantial longitudinal studies that have followed populations for as long as 32 years (Aberfan mudslide disaster; Morgan *et al.*, 2003), follow-up in approximately half of the reports was less than one year.

The methods used in the studies have varied considerably. A minority gave structured interviews, whereas others used more easily administered questionnaires. A range of instruments have been used to characterize outcomes, most frequently focusing on PTSD (e.g. Asukai *et al.*, 2002). Patterns of non-specific morbidity have often been studied, using instruments like the General Health Questionnaire. Specific phenomena such as dissociation and demoralization have also been investigated, rather than clusters of symptoms. The most comprehensive studies have used structured diagnostic interviews, such as the Composite International Diagnostic Interview (CIDI), that allow the generation of psychiatric diagnoses (World Health Organization, 1993). PTSD is only one of a number of disorders that emerge in disaster-affected populations. Approximately a quarter of studies have also examined physical health; of particular interest has been the clinical worsening of symptoms and perceived illness burden in disaster-affected communities.

The differential outcomes between disasters are sometimes difficult to determine because of variability in the sampling processes that have been used. Equally, the intensity of exposure experienced has a major impact on the prevalence of disorders identified, which has varied considerably between published studies. Approximately 10% of studies have identified only minimal impact on the population, whereas 40% found significant rates of psychopathology (Norris *et al.*, 2002). An immediate challenge in the aftermath of any future disaster should be to make some estimates of the likely patterns of psychological morbidity, as this is critical to determining the overall health needs of the population affected.

Most literature on harm from disasters has come from the USA, where lower rates of impairment have been identified than in other developed countries (Norris *et al.*, 2002). This may reflect the threshold of severity of the events studied in the USA and the availability of resources to undertake them. On the other hand, the highest rates have been found in developing countries. This may in part be due to the nature of the samples studied, but may also be because these events have greater impact on such communities because of their limited resources to manage the recovery period. Norris *et al.* (2002) identified the Lockerbie (Brooks & McKinlay, 1992) and *Jupiter* cruise ship disasters (Yule *et al.*, 2002) as having the highest rates of impairment. The Lockerbie disaster involved a Pan Am flight blown up by Libyan-sponsored terrorists over the village of Lockerbie in Scotland; 270 people were killed. The *Jupiter* was a cruise ship that sank within four minutes in the Greek waters in 1988 when it was struck by another ship, the *Adige*. There were approximately 400 children aged 11–18 years on board; one child and one teacher were unaccounted for and presumed dead, and two rescuers were crushed to death during the rescue.

Conclusions about the type of disaster that is associated with the highest rates of impairment are influenced significantly by the amount of research that has been done on the different types of events. Hurricane Andrew, which occurred in Florida in 1992, was a particularly devastating natural disaster and is probably the most researched of these events (Ironson *et al.*, 1997; Maes *et al.*, 2001; Norris *et al.*, 2002). As a consequence, the literature tends to suggest that there are few differences between natural and man-made technological disasters.

Prevalence of disorder

The differential outcomes between disasters are sometimes difficult to determine, because of the previously mentioned variability of the sampling processes that have been used. Equally, the intensity of exposure experienced by the population studied has a major impact on the recorded prevalence of disorders.

Post-traumatic stress disorder

The rates of PTSD, major depressive disorders, and substance abuse are very dependent on the sampling used in a study, as well as the severity and nature of the event. Therefore, each new disaster should be considered as a novel event and predictions about the rates of morbidity should depend on which group of victims is being considered, as well as the time that has elapsed following the disaster. Shore *et al.* (1986) examined the impact of the Mt St Helen's volcanic eruption, and compared the exposed population with a control group: lifetime prevalence in the Mt St Helen's group was 3.6%, compared to 2.6% in the control group. In contrast, McFarlane and Papay (1992) studied a representative sample of 469 volunteer fire-fighters exposed to a severe natural disaster in Australia, finding a rate of 16% of PTSD, with half of the sufferers in remission at 42 months. The Buffalo Creek disaster (dam break), which occurred in 1972, is one of the best studied of these events; it found a 59% PTSD lifetime rate among the victims, while 25% still met PTSD criteria some 14 years after the event (Grace *et al.*, 1993), indicating the impact of time on morbidity rates. It appears, therefore, that the prevalence rates of post-traumatic morbidity following disasters vary significantly. Norris (1992) suggested that the rate of current PTSD in disaster-exposed individuals was approximately 6%. One of the highest rates was demonstrated by Goenjian *et al.* (1995), following the Armenian earthquake, where 67% met PTSD criteria 18 months after the earthquake. In a study one to four months after Hurricane Andrew (Ironson *et al.*, 1997), 33% met PTSD criteria, which suggests that even in extreme circumstances the development of disaster-related morbidity is the exception rather than the rule.

However, the gradient is well demonstrated by the study after an earthquake in Yunnan of three villages, of increasing distance from the epicentre (McFarlane & Cao, 1993). The rate of PTSD in the most affected group was 23.4% in a village where most houses were destroyed, compared with 16.2% where only minor damage occurred. Gender also influences prevalence, with 20% of men but 36% of women suffering from PTSD one year after a mass shooting (North *et al.*, 1997). The lasting impact of events such as the Aberfan mining disaster on children was demonstrated by the findings of the 33-year follow-up, where rates of 29% current and 46% lifetime PTSD were found (Morgan *et al.*, 2003). However, in some studies of low-exposure groups, the rates of PTSD are little different from the prevalence in the general population (Norris *et al.*, 2002).

Other disorders

Similar issues influence the rates of other disorders that emerge following disasters. These may emerge as co-morbid conditions with PTSD – in this case, they are likely to reflect complications of PTSD and are an indication of the severity of the underlying traumatic stress response. One review suggested that PTSD occurred four times more frequently in conjunction with co-morbid diagnoses than it did alone, even in close proximity to the event (Smith & North, 1993). Hence, studies of disasters need to consider their capacity to create a range of psychiatric morbidities.

Alcohol usage is often a response to the development of symptoms in disaster-affected populations – particularly among emergency service workers (Norris *et al.*, 2002). In these individuals there is a complex interaction with their prior exposure to trauma. Furthermore, there is an increasing body of evidence that depressive and anxiety disorders may emerge following traumatic events in the absence of PTSD (Green, 1996). For example, the potential role of loss in the onset of depression, as well as that of threat and horror as a determinant of anxiety disorders, has an intuitive rationale (McFarlane & Papay, 1992). While there has been some exploration of the role that different types of disaster experiences play in association with risk factors for the onset of these disorders, this needs further investigation (McFarlane & Papay, 1992). In particular, individuals who have more effective methods of suppressing their traumatic memories may not be immune from the capacity of these events to dysregulate their arousal and affective modulation.

One of the problems in defining the prevalence estimates of these disorders is that while assessments of the prevalence of PTSD are made in disaster victims, the time and resources required to carry in-depth structured diagnostic interviews prohibit the inclusion of other diagnoses in the investigation. Furthermore, though rates of anxiety and depression are reported, these estimates are often derived from continuous scales, making the clinical and diagnostic interpretation of the data difficult. Other studies have found no increased prevalence of these non-PTSD disorders, despite high rates of PTSD (Morgan *et al.*, 2003). A further methodological issue is that defining the onset of disorders such as major depressive disorder and panic disorder is more difficult than PTSD, which can be tied to a specific event by the content of the intrusive memories.

The evidence suggests that depression is the second most common disorder to emerge in the aftermath of disaster (Norris *et al.*, 2002). However, one important issue is how these mood disorders interact with pre-existing morbidity. Bravo *et al.* (1990) studied the impact of a mud slide and flood in Puerto Rico, which killed 800 people. Fortuitously, they had studied this population a year before and were able to re-evaluate 375 of their initial subjects. These people had a significant increase from the pre-disaster level in symptoms of depression and a range of somatic complaints and PTSD, but failed to demonstrate any increase in panic disorder or alcohol abuse. Smith *et al.* (1986) investigated a series of disaster events in St Louis involving exposure to dioxin, floods, and tornadoes. Newly exposed individuals had high levels of new PTSD and depressive symptoms, but the depressive symptoms increased only in those with previous depression.

In contrast, following a high-impact disaster such as the 1988 Armenian earthquake, major depressive disorder was found in 52% of a stratified sample of 1785 individuals. Depression was the only disorder in 177 of these and was particularly associated with exposure and loss (Armenian *et al.*, 2002). The issue that emerges is that the rates of disorders such as depression are both highly variable and affected by the intensity and nature of the disaster. The question of the rates of morbidity of anxiety and depressive disorders that emerge in the aftermath of disasters is an important one for further investigation; it must consider the interaction of these effects with existing morbidity in the community. Equally, the somatic expression of distress in the aftermath of these events has major practical implications for the post-disaster health services (Koopman *et al.*, 1996). The physical presentation of psychiatric disorders also requires better clarification.

Risk factors

One of the consistent findings that has emerged from the systematic investigation of disasters is that post-traumatic psychopathology emerges in a minority. This emphasizes the need to look at other variables that may be contributing to, as well as protecting against, the onset of symptomatic distress. Weisaeth (1996) has argued that the role and effects of exposure in disaster are central risk factors. The meta-analysis of Brewin *et al.* (2000), which examined risk factors for PTSD, confirmed that the nature and intensity of the exposure was the most potent risk factor.

Intensity of exposure

In general, the degree of exposure to a disaster is the critical determinant of who is at risk and of the levels of psychological morbidity (Carlier & Gersons, 1997). The total destruction of a family's home and the loss of all possessions has a profoundly disruptive impact on people's sense of identity and social integration. The consequences of multiple bereavements have long been understood as having a particularly detrimental impact on psychological health, and in disaster settings individuals may indeed suffer such losses. From a descriptive perspective, it is apparent that there is a link between quantitative and qualitative dimensions of trauma and that both contribute to adaptation. Green (1990) has proposed several generic dimensions of traumatic stressors, including: the receipt of intentional harm or injury, exposure to grotesque sights and scenes, witnessing or learning of violence to loved ones, learning of exposure to noxious agents, and causing death or severe harm to another.

Disasters provide an opportunity to examine how these different components act, individually and in combination, to cause psychiatric morbidity. Also, during these large-scale events, the survivor is not alone, which means that there is a need to look at issues such as leadership and dependence on others for one's own rescue. The magnitude of such events often means that in the immediate aftermath, the inadequacy of emergency operations to contain the catastrophe demands that the victim will have to look to a range of innovative solutions in containing the chaos. Furthermore, group processes may play an important component in the longer-term adaptation.

The effects of exposure are exemplified by Weisaeth's study of a factory disaster. A prospective investigation of the acute, sub-acute, and long-term reactions highlighted a number of these issues (Weisaeth, 1989, 1996). He showed that both mortality and injuries were dependent on the distance from the explosion, and that this in turn correlated strongly with the later development of post-traumatic stress disorder. In the high-exposure group, prevalence rates of PTSD were 36% after seven months, 27% after two years, 22% after three years, and 19% after four years. This contrasted with the medium-exposure group, where there was a decrease in the PTSD rate from 17% after seven months to 2% after four years. Thus, the intensity of the stressor accounted for the initial prevalence, and the possible longevity of the symptoms. Recognizing significance of stressor intensity as a prognostic risk factor was an important observation. Weisaeth found that for employees who witnessed the event, even at a close distance, premorbid sensitivity played an important role in the development of symptoms, highlighting the interrelationship between vulnerability factors and exposure.

Several approaches have been used when measuring the severity of exposure. Some investigators have simply counted the number of stressors as an index of the severity of the experience. Predictably, findings then suggest a proportional increase in the number of symptoms as the number of stressors experienced increases. The alternative approach has been to create ordinal measures of exposure based on a series of assumptions about the relative severity and comparative impact of different components of the disaster. Again, this method has shown that higher rates of exposure are good predictors of morbidity. However, once over a certain level where extreme threat and horror are ubiquitous, there appears to be a plateau effect.

It is difficult to make any firm recommendations about what is the optimal approach to estimating exposure, because many of the component experiences in a disaster are not independent. For example, the threat to life and rates of injury tend to be highly correlated. Second, it is difficult to have a standard measure of exposure that can be applied in all disasters, because personal property damage does not necessarily occur in events of mass violence, which tend to be located away from individuals' homes in public settings such as schools and shopping malls.

The interaction between the destruction of a community and exposure to disaster of the individuals who make up the group has seldom been investigated. There is some suggestion that the sense of collective loss has a modest contribution, beyond those of the individual levels of exposure. Pfeiffer and Norris (1989) showed that personal loss and community destruction interacted: the individuals who did worst were those who both came from communities that had a high level of destruction and high levels of personal loss.

The nature of the losses and effects that are documented depends on the nature of the event. How to investigate the need for relocation and financial loss will depend to a significant degree on the extent that people's individual homes or businesses have been destroyed. Almost inevitably, these are events where loss of life occurs, so that bereavement and life threat have been identified as important predictors of psychological symptoms. Similarly, injuries to the individual or family member are significant risks factors. The individual's behaviour during the disaster, such as whether they panicked or dissociated, may increase the risk of symptoms and highlights how the immediate response to the experience can predict longer-term outcomes.

In contrast to the effort put into the development of valid and reliable measures of adverse life events, surprisingly little attention has been given to this issue in the area of traumatic experience, and particularly disasters (McFarlane *et al.*, 1994). There are methodological issues involved in developing measures of disaster exposure in the light of the points already made about the exact losses and exposures that require documentation.

An example of the problems involved in the development of such measures was shown by the study of an earthquake-affected population. They are the only populations to rate stressful items on Holmes and Rahe's (1967) life events scale in a significantly different way from community samples. Surprisingly though, one such population rated the severity of the impact of major losses as significantly less than comparison populations that were unaffected by the disaster (Janney *et al.*, 1977). This suggests that traumatized groups have a different perspective on their experience from populations that have not confronted that particular event. This difference has the potential to create significant errors when investigators are trying to judge the severity of traumatic stresses and to determine what components of disasters are markedly distressing to most people. Furthermore, it suggests that measures of disaster exposure should be scaled on the basis of ratings developed from within communities that have actual knowledge of the experiences.

This is a complex issue both from a clinical and a research perspective. There are many components of disasters that will be influenced by the person's mental state at the time (for example, the experience of panic or dissociation) as well as the person's perception of the risks and capacity to act adaptively. The likelihood of injury and death depends in part on the individual's appraisal of the event and capacity to respond appropriately to it. In examining the role of risk factors, the determinants of such behaviour, and hence the degree of exposure, may be linked in a way that is not routinely considered. For example, a particular personality attribute may be seen as a risk factor for PTSD in a disaster-exposed individual, when the characteristic in question was actually a determinant of the type of exposure. The estimates people make of the duration of their exposure to a disaster can also be influenced by peri-traumatic dissociation (Anderson & Manuel, 1994). This is because the distortion of time is a symptom of that kind of dissociation.

However, there will certainly be objective measures of exposure, such as seeing death and injury or actually being injured. The degree of destruction and loss is also an objective issue. Matters that may be equally important in determining the degree of traumatization include the perceptions that one survived the experience through freak circumstances or was kept safe by chance, and that one had no control over the circumstances. DSM-IV (American Psychiatric Association, 1994) recognized the relative importance of these subjective components in determining the nature of the traumatic experience. Green (1993) has suggested eight generic dimensions of trauma that need to be considered to resolve these issues. Hence, defining the exact nature of disaster and the differences between different individuals' experience is a much more complex question than it would appear on first examination.

Other risk and protective factors

Gender

In general, it appears that women are at greater risk of psychological distress than men, as measured by multiple outcomes, on exposure to these events, except in terms of alcohol abuse, where rates are higher in males (Green, 1996). These findings are similar to data from general population studies (Kessler *et al.*, 1995) that have highlighted the relative vulnerability of women on exposure to traumatic events.

The factors that mediate these differences between men and women are of interest. It appears that when other risk factors exist, such as being a member of an ethnic subculture, the vulnerability of women is magnified. However, perception of the events by men and women is also different in terms of objective characteristics. For example, after the Loma Prieta earthquake, women estimated the duration of the quake as 78 seconds; men believed it lasted 48 seconds (Anderson & Manuel, 1994). Previously, it has been speculated that the greater vulnerability of women may have been due to the strength of their attachments and their nurturing role within communities.

Age

The effects of age on the outcome are contradictory and depend on the samples examined: the effects have been most consistently examined in adults. The conventional wisdom has been that older persons are at greater risk (Kato *et al.*, 1996), as was found in the Newcastle earthquake study in Australia (Carr *et al.*, 1997). However, Norris *et al.* (2002) concluded that 'in every American sample in which middle-aged adults would be differentiated from older adults, the former were almost always more adversely affected'. This might be accounted for by people in middle age carrying many financial burdens and responsibilities for dependants, and so perhaps having least resources in reserve to cope with the impact of unexpected and threatening demands. The conservation of resources model (Hobfoll & Lilly, 1993) is a useful theoretical construct in looking at the interaction between a recent major challenge to the individual's survival and their background attributes that allow them to meet further demands. These authors' view is that life stress needs to be considered in the context of the resources of back-up that the individual already has.

The vulnerability of middle-aged adults is somewhat surprising, as the negative impact on older adults has been presumed to arise because their age makes it more difficult for them to reconstruct their physical losses, physically and financially. The alternative explanation about the resilience of older people is that their repertoire of life experience has acted to 'inoculate' them and so left them with less rigid expectations about the predictability of life.

Socio-economic factors

Socio-economic factors have been difficult to examine in some studies because the affected communities are relatively homogeneous (e.g. McFarlane, 1986). However, the majority of studies suggest that less education and lower income are risk factors for psychosocial morbidity. A social characteristic that interacts with age is marital status. It appears that disasters are one setting where social attachments and the responsibilities that go with those relationships are a risk factor particularly associated with women. Solomon (2002) found that women with excellent spousal support were more at risk than those with less bonded relationships. The psychological state of mothers appears to be particularly important in terms of the psychological outcomes of children. The nature of family interactions is detrimental for the child if there is an increase in overprotection and lack of emotional warmth. The mother's distress and anticipation of danger appear to convey a negative sense to the children that is manifest in their level of observable symptoms and preoccupation with the disaster.

Inter-current adversity

Disasters exist at only one time-point in the continuity of the community; adversity for other reasons will continue to occur. Furthermore, there are often secondary stresses following on from a disaster. These may include legal difficulties over gaining proper compensation, delays in reconstruction, and difficulty in the rehabilitation of physical injuries. It is important to conceptualize the ongoing effects of the direct exposure to the disaster event through its secondary effects, which modify the financial stability and relationships of the individual who has survived the event.

Prior psychological symptoms

The impact of psychological symptoms prior to the disaster has been extensively studied as a predictor of adjustment in the aftermath. Norris *et al.* (2002) concluded that such symptoms are among the best predictors of post-disaster morbidity. However, few studies have addressed the problem that at the time the disaster occurs, a significant minority of the population will be suffering from a psychiatric disorder. Studies such as the US National Comorbidity Study have characterized the pool of symptoms in a community (Kessler *et al.*, 1995). What has not been identified, though, is the impact of the disaster on individuals who were suffering from depression, panic disorder, etc. at the time of the event. It is unclear whether these symptoms are exacerbated or whether they are a risk factor for developing PTSD. Most studies have not been able to separate the effects of existing symptoms from the onset of new symptoms and disorders, and it is the latter which are of fundamental interest. Thus, understanding how individuals account for the symptomatic distress that is described after disasters is an important step in targeting and managing post-disaster psychological morbidity.

Social support

The issue of social support is frequently raised as a critical issue that protects individuals following exposure to these events. One of the difficulties that arises in examining this question is the challenge of separating the reality of social support from the perception of its adequacy. As has been demonstrated elsewhere, the perception of social support is critically determined by an individual's personality, as well as by the adequacy of their social network (Henderson *et al.*, 1981). In other words, social support can be a measure confounded by other vulnerability and protective factors.

In this regard, perceived social support depends on a person's belief about the availability of others to assist, rather than the actual receipt of assistance. Solomon *et al.* (1987) observed that mid-range levels of the availability of support were associated with the most favourable outcomes for women. In contrast, women with a high availability of support did poorly. This study also found that women with excellent spousal support had worse outcomes than those with weaker spouse ties. In contrast, men tended to do better if they had a stronger spouse relationship. This suggests that there are important differences between men and women, in that the strength of attachment for women may be a burden, rather than supportive, at times of extreme stress.

Protective factors

The notion of protective factors is a concept that has particular appeal in relation to prevention and the minimization of morbidity. The problem here is that very little research has been done that has been able to identify positive predictors of psychological outcomes. Most of the protective factors are, in fact, the absence of risk factors, such as a negative psychiatric history or the experience of a positive childhood environment. One area that has attracted a substantial body of investigation though, is coping. The primary hypothesis that attracted interest to this was the suggestion that problem-focused coping would have considerable benefits for long-term adjustment, in contrast to emotion-focused coping. However, Spurrell and McFarlane (1993) found that coping behaviour in both problem- and emotion-focused domains was more frequent in those who developed symptoms following a disaster. In other words, individuals who did not develop symptoms after a disaster reported less coping behaviour than those who did develop symptoms. Such findings highlight the problems of identifying protective factors in the aftermath of traumatic events, where reporting will be contaminated by the presence of symptoms.

Wessely (2003) has reviewed the literature about the prior screening of troops in the Second World War and found that many of the characteristics that were thought to be markers of vulnerability in fact had little predictive ability. This finding indicates that post-disaster morbidity in emergency services cannot be avoided by simply excluding vulnerable individuals. The knowledge base that will accurately predict those who will develop symptoms does not exist, and is likely to remain elusive. In the same regard, protective factors are difficult to identify. Frequently, their effect will only be manifest in conjunction with other variables and may be highly situation-specific. A study of twin pairs in the US services at the time of the Vietnam war found that there was genetic vulnerability to PTSD that was related to personality (True & Lyons, 1999). The roles that individuals chose in the military were predicted partly by their genetically determined temperamental traits, such as novelty-seeking. Individuals with this personality trait were more likely to choose roles that exposed them to high levels of danger in combat. The problem is that such a personality style is likely to characterize those who choose jobs in the emergency services and are exactly suited to the role, since those who tend to be harm-avoidant will choose safer careers. Harm-avoidance is a personality trait that is protective, but cannot be used as a selection criterion for the emergency services. Such paradoxes highlight the complexity of this area of interest.

Vaillant has written extensively on the issue of the psychological health of men, and has studied a cohort of highly capable and relatively risk-factor-free individuals. He recently reviewed the concept of mental health (Vaillant, 2003) and his critique of the field is equally relevant to the area of the study of resilience. He comments that 'To paraphrase Mark Twain's quip about the weather, psychiatry is always talking about mental health but no one ever does anything about it'. Protective factors represent more than the absence of risk factors. One of the problems is that attributes in one setting are not valued in another. For example, punctuality is valued in some cultures, but is seen as a failing in others (Vaillant, 2003). Protective factors are characteristics that may be value-laden. Furthermore, the question also arises as to whom does the benefit accrue from particular characteristics? One example has already been illustrated: we need individuals to join the emergency services and their efforts are protective for society at large, but are a risk to the individuals who volunteer for these roles.

These challenges highlight how the study of resilience is a demanding domain, for 'positive psychology does not rely on wishful thinking, faith, self-deception, fads or hand waving; it tries to adapt what is best in the scientific method to the unique problems that human behaviour presents to those who wish to understand it in all its complexity' (Seligman & Csikszentmihalyi, 2000). Vaillant (2003) crystallized three models of adaptation – normality, positive psychology, and maturity – that provide a context for considering the nature of resilience. Many of the attributes of a well-adjusted life in the circumstances of suburban civility are very different from the skills that would allow an individual to survive optimally some critical life stress. Of the three models, maturity is the one that is most likely to characterize resilience in the face of a disaster. Situations of major loss and threat demand the ability to give up previous certainties and to sense the survival of others as bearing major value, in contrast to the discomforts and suffering of one's immediate situation. This is essential to embodying a sense of hope.

The real challenge is to develop a framework for investigating resilience. There are a series of time windows when such attributes and characteristics can exert their effect. In the pre-disaster period, a willingness to anticipate the risk of predictable disasters can do much to shield an individual and their associates through a variety of mitigative and protective steps. A willingness to prepare for a disaster and practise emergency procedures is a measure of personality that predicts survival in a practical and psychological sense (Weisaeth, 1989). These strategies are about a balance between a realistic appraisal of the future and a capacity for mastery. Such attributes contrast with needless risk-taking on one hand and phobic avoidance of threat on the other. The latter strategy leaves people with a profound sense of fear and threat as well as with no rehearsal of how to manage adversity should it arise. An ability to use life experience to learn, rather than withdraw from future threat, would be likely to protect an individual in the future.

One of the challenges is to consider the interrelationship between many of the known risk factors together with the possibility of there being additive or multiplicative effects. Hence, disadvantage can attract further disadvantage. Hobfoll's conservation of resources model provides a useful theoretical framework to investigate these potential effects (see above). Individuals and communities who have a cushion of material wealth and psychological capacities for adaptation possess a buffer to call upon, in the setting of major losses. They can use this diverse range of attributes to compensate for what they have lost, whereas people subject to a range of social disadvantages will be particularly challenged in the post-disaster environment.

Conclusion

One contribution of disaster research that has largely gone undiscussed has been the relevance of the findings to understanding the more general relationship between psychiatric disorder and life events. A major problem that has plagued researchers endeavouring to investigate the relationship between day-to-day adversity and psychiatric disorder has been the question of cause and effect. Longitudinal studies of life events have demonstrated that these were as likely to have been caused by psychiatric disorder as was the reverse relationship, where the disorder had arisen as a consequence of some adversity.

Disasters, by their very nature, are beyond an individual's control; in other words, they are truly independent life events. Hence, they provide a relatively methodologically sophisticated way of beginning to investigate these causal associations. However, one of the problems that occurs in most disasters is that pre-existing measures of the adjustment of a population do not exist. This is an important issue, because many studies have failed to take account of the existing psychological morbidity that would inevitably exist within disaster-affected communities A critical question is the way in which the existing symptoms within individuals are modified by traumatic experiences, as well as by the nature of the psychopathology that emerges in most people who were otherwise well adjusted at the time of the event. Hence, there is a need to investigate PTSD triggered by traumatic event differentially in those with a predisposition, in contrast to 'true PTSD', which emerges in those who are asymptomatic at the time of the event.

Against this background, epidemiological research into the impact of disasters demonstrates that there are few events that lead to disorder in the majority of people exposed. It is therefore important to conceptualize the various characteristics of both the environment and the individual that may act as relative risk or protective factors. In fact, population studies highlight the variability of the outcome between individuals, though these differences are often lost because of the way in which statistical analysis requires the grouping of outcomes. Particularly in situations of relatively low exposure, vulnerability factors such as premorbid personality and previous psychiatric disorder have an important role to play.

Thus, vulnerability and protective factors are necessary to explain much of the probability of developing PTSD; this and other trauma-related disorders represent the outcome of a complex biopsychosocial matrix of variables, which can operate along a variety of axes. The context in which the event occurs in the individual's life is the base from which the disorder emerges. The nature of the stressor and of the recovery environment involves a series of interactions modifying the ability of the individual to quench their immediate post-traumatic distress. It is in this post-disaster period that the vulnerability factors may play a critical role. In general, it appears that women are more vulnerable and that personality plays an important role, except in situations of extreme exposure. On the other hand, it is important to emphasize that post-traumatic stress disorder emerges in previously healthy individuals whose modest vulnerability would otherwise have little relevance.

References

American Psychiatric Association (1987) *Diagnostic and Statistical Manual III.* Washington, DC: APA.

American Psychiatric Association (1994) *Diagnostic and Statistical Manual IV.* Washington, DC: APA.

Anderson, K. and Manuel, G. (1994) 'Gender differences in reported stress response to the Loma Prieta earthquake'. *Sex Roles*, *30*, 725–733.

Andreski, P., Chilcoat, H. and Breslau, N. (1998) 'Post-traumatic stress disorder and somatization symptoms: a prospective study'. *Psychiatry Research*, *79*, 131–138.

Armenian, H. K., Morikawa, M., Melkonian, A. K., Hovanesian, A., Akiskal, K. and Akiskal, H. S. (2002) 'Risk factors for depression in the survivors of the 1988 earthquake in Armenia'. *Journal of Urban Health*, *79*, 373–382.

Asukai, N., Kato, H., Kawamura, N., Kim, Y., Yamamoto, K., Kishimoto, J., Miyake, Y. and Nishizono-Maher, A. (2002) 'Reliability and validity of the Japanese-language version of the impact of event scale-revised (IES-R-J): four studies of different traumatic events'. *Journal of Nervous and Mental Disorder*, *190*, 175–182.

Bravo, M., Rubio-Stipec, M., Canino, G. J., Woodbury, M. A. and Ribera, J. C. (1990) 'The psychological sequelae of disaster stress prospectively and retrospectively evaluated'. *American Journal of Community Psychology*, *18*, 661–680.

Brewin, C. R., Andrews, B. and Valentine, J. D. (2000) 'Meta-analysis of risk factors for posttraumatic stress disorder in trauma-exposed adults'. *Journal of Consulting and Clinical Psychology*, *68*, 748–766.

Brooks, N. and McKinlay, W. (1992) 'Mental health consequences of the Lockerbie disaster'. *Journal of Traumatic Stress*, *5*, 527–543.

Carlier, I. V. and Gersons, B. P. (1997) 'Stress reactions in disaster victims following the Bijlmermeer plane crash'. *Journal of Traumatic Stress*, *10*, 329–335.

Carr, V. J., Lewin, T. J., Kenardy, J. A., Webster, R. A., Hazell, P. L., Carter, G. L. and Williamson, M. (1997) 'Psychosocial sequelae of the 1989 Newcastle earthquake: III. Role of vulnerability factors in post-disaster morbidity'. *Psychological Medicine*, *27*, 179–190.

Chang, C. M., Lee, L. C., Connor, K. M., Davidson, J. R., Jeffries, K. and Lai, T. J. (2003) 'Posttraumatic distress and coping strategies among rescue workers after an earthquake'. *Journal of Nervous and Mental Disorder*, *191*, 391–398.

Clark, C. R., McFarlane, A. C., Morris, P., Weber, D. L., Sonkkilla, C., Shaw, M., Marcina, J., Tochon-Danguy, H. J. and Egan, G. F. (2003) 'Cerebral function in posttraumatic stress disorder during verbal working memory updating: a positron emission tomography study'. *Biological Psychiatry*, *53*, 474–481.

Creamer, M., Burgess, P. and McFarlane, A. C. (2001) 'Post-traumatic stress disorder: findings from the Australian National Survey of Mental Health and Well-being'. *Psychological Medicine*, *31*, 1237–1247.

Donker, G. A., Yzermans, C. J., Spreeuwenberg, P. and van der Zee, J. (2002) 'Symptom attribution after a plane crash: comparison between self-reported symptoms and GP records'. *British Journal of General Practice*, *52*, 917–922.

Galea, S., Vlahov, D., Resnick, H., Ahern, J., Susser, E., Gold, J., Bucuvalas, M. and Kilpatrick, D. (2003) 'Trends of probable post-traumatic stress disorder in New York City after the September 11 terrorist attacks'. *American Journal of Epidemiology*, *158*, 514–524.

Goenjian, A. K., Pynoos, R. S., Steinberg, A. M., Najarian, L. M., Asarnow, J. R., Karayan, I., Ghurabi, M. and Fairbanks, L. A. (1995) 'Psychiatric comorbidity in children after the 1988 earthquake in Armenia'. *Journal of the American Academy of Child and Adolescent Psychiatry*, *34*, 1174–1184.

Grace, M. C., Green, B. L., Lindy, J. D. and Leonard, A. C. (1993) 'The buffalo creek disaster: a 14-year follow-up', in Wilson, J. P. and Raphael, B. (eds), *International handbook of traumatic stress syndromes* (pp. 441–449). New York: Plenum Press.

Green, B. L. (1990) 'Defining trauma: terminology and generic stressor dimensions'. *Journal of Applied Social Psychology*, *20*, 1632–1642.

Green, B. L. (1993) 'Identifying survivors at risk: trauma and stressors across events', in Wilson, J. P. and Raphael, B. (eds), *International handbook of traumatic stress syndromes* (pp. 135–144). New York: Plenum Press.

Green, B. L. (1996) 'Traumatic stress and disaster: mental health effects and factors influencing adaptation', in Lieh-Mak, F. L. and Nodelsen, C. C. (eds), *International review of psychiatry*. Washington, DC: American Psychiatric Press.

Henderson, A. S., Byrne, D. G. and Duncan-Jones, P. (1981) *Neurosis and the social environment*. Sydney, Australia: Academic Press.

Hobfoll, S. and Lilly, R. (1993) 'Resource conservation as a strategy for community psychology'. *Journal of Community Psychology*, *21*, 128–148.

Holmes, T. H. and Rahe, R. H. (1967) 'The Social Readjustment Rating Scale'. *Journal of Psychosomatic Research*, *11*, 213–218.

Ironson, G., Wynings, C., Schneiderman, N., Baum, A., Rodriguez, M., Greenwood, D., Benight, C., Antoni, M., LaPerriere, A., Huang, H. S., Klimas, N. and Fletcher, M. A. (1997) 'Posttraumatic stress symptoms, intrusive thoughts, loss, and immune function after Hurricane Andrew'. *Psychosomatic Medicine*, *59*, 128–141.

Janney, J. G., Masuda, M. and Holmes, T. H. (1977) 'Impact of a natural catastrophe on life events'. *Journal of Human Stress*, *3*, 22–34.

Kato, H., Asukai, N., Miyake, Y., Minakawa, K. and Nishiyama, A. (1996) 'Post-traumatic symptoms among younger and elderly evacuees in the early stages following the 1995 Hanshin-Awaji earthquake in Japan'. *Acta Psychiatrica Scandinavica*, *93*, 477–481.

Katon, W. J. and Walker, E. A. (1998) 'Medically unexplained symptoms in primary care'. *Journal of Clinical Psychiatry*, *59*, suppl. 20, 15–21.

Katon, W., Sullivan, M. and Walker, E. (2001) 'Medical symptoms without identified pathology: relationship to psychiatric disorders, childhood and adult trauma, and personality traits'. *Annals of Internal Medicine*, *134*, 917–925.

Katon, W., Lin, E., Von Korff, M., Russo, J., Lipscomb, P. and Bush, T. (1991) 'Somatization: a spectrum of severity'. *American Journal of Psychiatry*, *148*, 34–40.

Kessler, R. C., Sonnega, A., Bromet, E., Hughes, M. and Nelson, C. B. (1995) 'Posttraumatic stress disorder in the National Comorbidity Survey'. *Archives of General Psychiatry*, *52*, 1048–1060.

Kinston, W. and Rosser, R. (1974) 'Disaster: effects on mental and physical state'. *Journal of Psychosomatic Research*, *18*, 437–456.

Koopman, C., Classen, C. and Spiegel, D. (1996) 'Dissociative responses in the immediate aftermath of the Oakland/Berkeley firestorm'. *Journal of Traumatic Stress*, *9*, 521–540.

Kraepelin, E. (1899) *Psychiatrie*. Leipzig: Verlag von Johann Abrosius Barth.

Laor, N., Wolmer, L., Kora, M., Yucel, D., Spirman, S. and Yazgan, Y. (2002) 'Post-traumatic, dissociative and grief symptoms in Turkish children exposed to the 1999 earthquakes'. *Journal of Nervous and Mental Disorder, 190*, 824–832.

Maes, M., Mylle, J., Delmeire, L. and Janca, A. (2001) 'Pre- and post-disaster negative life events in relation to the incidence and severity of post-traumatic stress disorder'. *Psychiatry Research, 105*, 1–12.

McFarlane, A. C. (1986) 'Long-term psychiatric morbidity of a natural disaster: the implications for disaster planners and emergency services'. *Medical Journal of Australia, 145*, 561–563.

McFarlane, A. C. and Cao, H. (1993) 'The study of a major disaster in the People's Republic of China, the Yunnan Earthquake', in Raphael, B. and Wilson, J. (eds), *The International handbook of traumatic stress syndromes* (pp. 493–498). New York: Plenum Press.

McFarlane, A. C. and Papay, P. (1992) 'Multiple diagnoses in posttraumatic stress disorder in the victims of a natural disaster'. *Journal of Nervous and Mental Disease, 180*, 498–504.

McFarlane, A. C., Atchison, M., Rafalowicz, E. and Papay, P. (1994) 'Physical symptoms in post-traumatic stress disorder'. *Journal of Psychosomatic Research, 38*, 715–726.

Morgan, L., Scourfield, J., Williams, D., Jasper, A. and Lewis, G. (2003) 'The Aberfan disaster: 33-year follow-up of survivors'. *British Journal of Psychiatry, 182*, 532–536.

Norris, F. H. (1992) 'Epidemiology of trauma: frequency and impact of different potentially traumatic events on different demographic groups'. *Journal of Consulting and Clinical Psychology, 60*, 409–418.

Norris, F. H., Friedman, M. J., Watson, P. J., Byrne, C. M., Diaz, E. and Kaniasty, K. (2002) '60,000 disaster victims speak: Part I. An empirical review of the empirical literature, 1981–2001'. *Psychiatry, 65*, 207–239.

North, C. S., Smith, E. M. and Spitznagel, E. L. (1997) 'One-year follow-up of survivors of a mass shooting'. *American Journal of Psychiatry, 154*, 1696–1702.

Peters, R. and Watson, C. (1996) 'A breakthrough in gun control in Australia after the Port Arthur massacre'. *Injury Prevention, 2*, 253–254.

Pfeiffer, J. and Norris, F. (1989) 'Psychological symptoms in older subjects following natural disasters: nature, timing and duration in course'. *Journal of Gerontological Social Science, 44*, 207–217.

Rubonis, A. V. and Bickman, L. (1991) 'Psychological impairment in the wake of disaster: the disaster–psychopathology relationship'. *Psychological Bulletin, 109*, 384–399.

Salcioglu, E., Basoglu, M. and Livanou, M. (2003) 'Long-term psychological outcome for non-treatment-seeking earthquake survivors in Turkey'. *Journal of Nervous and Mental Disorder, 191*, 154–160.

Seligman, M. E. and Csikszentmihalyi, M. (2000) 'Positive psychology: an introduction'. *American Psychology, 55*, 5–14.

Shore, J. H., Tatum, E. L. and Vollmer, W. M. (1986) 'Psychiatric reactions to disaster: the Mount St. Helens experience'. *American Journal of Psychiatry, 143*, 590–595.

Simpson, J. (1988) *Touching the void*. London: Jonathan Cape.

Slottje, P., Smidt, N., Twisk, J. W., Huizink, A. C., Witteveen, A. B., van Mechelen, W. and Smid, T. (2006) 'Attribution of physical complaints to the air disaster in Amsterdam by exposed rescue workers: an epidemiological study using historic cohorts'. *BMC Public Health, 6*, 142.

Smith, E. M. and North, C. S. (1993) 'Posttraumatic stress disorder in natural disasters and technological accidents', in Wilson, J. P. and Raphael, B. (eds), *International handbook of traumatic stress syndromes* (pp. 405–419). New York: Plenum Press.

Smith, E. M., Robins, L. N. and Pryzbeck, T. R. (1986) *Psychosocial consequences of a disaster*, in Shaw, J. H. (ed.), *Disaster studies, new methods and findings* (pp. 49–76). Washington, DC: American Psychiatric Press.

Solomon, S. D. (2002) 'Gender differences in response to disaster', in Weidner, G., Kopp, S. and Kristenson, M. (eds), *Heart disease: Environment, stress and gender* (pp. 267–274). Amsterdam: IOS Press.

Solomon, Z., Mikulincer, M. and Hobfoll, S. E. (1987) 'Objective versus subjective measurement of stress and social support: combat-related reactions'. *Journal of Consulting and Clinical Psychology, 55*, 577–583.

Spurrell, M. T. and McFarlane, A. C. (1993) 'Post-traumatic stress disorder and coping after a natural disaster'. *Social Psychiatry and Psychiatric Epidemiology, 28*, 194–200.

Stierlin, E. (1911) 'Nervöse und psychische Störungen nach Katastrophen (Nervous and psychic disturbances after catastrophes)'. *Deutsches Medizinische Wochenschrift*, 2028–2035.

Trichopoulos, D., Katsouyanni, K., Zavitsanos, X., Tzonou, A. and Dalla-Vorgia, P. (1983) 'Psychological stress and fatal heart attack: the Athens (1981) earthquake natural experiment'. *Lancet, 1*, 441–444.

True, W. and Lyons, M. (1999) 'Genetic factors for PTSD: a twin study', in Yehuda, R. (ed.), *Risk factors for posttraumatic stress disorder*. Washington, DC: American Psychiatric Association Press.

Vaillant, G. R. (2003) 'Mental health'. *American Journal of Psychiatry, 160*, 1373–1384.

van der Kolk, B. A. (1996) 'Trauma and memory', in van der Kolk, B., McFarlane, A. C. and Weisaeth, L. (eds), *Traumatic stress: The effects of overwhelming experience on mind, body and society* (pp. 279–302). New York: Guilford Press.

Weisaeth, L. (1989) 'The stressors and the post-traumatic stress syndrome after an industrial disaster'. *Acta Psychiatrica Scandinavica Supplementum, 355*, 25–37.

Weisaeth, L. (1996) 'PTSD: the stressor response relationship', in Giller, E. and Weisaeth, L. (eds), *Post traumatic stress disorder: Bailliere's clinical psychiatry, international practice and research*, Vol. 2, (pp. 191–216). London: Balliere Tindall.

Wessely, S. (2003) 'The role of screening in the prevention of psychological disorders arising from major trauma: pros and cons', in Ursano, R. J., Fullerton, C. S. and Norwood, A. E. (eds), *Terrorism and disaster: Individual and community mental health Interventions*. Cambridge: Cambridge University Press.

World Health Organization (1993) *Composite International Diagnostic Interview (CIDI): Interviewer's manual*. Geneva: WHO.

Yang, Y. K., Yeh, T. L., Chen, C. C., Lee, C. K., Lee, I. H., Lee, L. C. and Jeffries, K. J. (2003) 'Psychiatric morbidity and posttraumatic symptoms among earthquake victims in primary care clinics'. *General Hospital Psychiatry, 25*, 253–261.

Yule, W., Bolton, D., Udwin, O., Boyle, S., O' Ryan, D. and Nurrish, J. (2000) 'The long-term psychological effects of a disaster experienced in adolescence: I: The incidence and course of PTSD'. *Journal of Child Psychology and Psychiatry, 41*, 503–511.

Zatzick, D. F., Russo, J. E. and Katon, W. (2003) 'Somatic, posttraumatic stress, and depressive symptoms among injured patients treated in trauma surgery'. *Psychosomatics, 44*, 479–484.

Index

Note: Page numbers in **bold** refer to images, figures, and information contained within tables.

For Product Safety Concerns and Information please contact our EU
representative GPSR@taylorandfrancis.com
Taylor & Francis Verlag GmbH, Kaufingerstraße 24, 80331 München, Germany

www.ingramcontent.com/pod-product-compliance
Ingram Content Group UK Ltd.
Pitfield, Milton Keynes, MK11 3LW, UK
UKHW020020200926
475702UK00014B/1980
* 9 7 8 1 1 3 8 8 8 4 4 6 5 *